Archipelago
Critiques of Contemporary Architecture and Education

A. Richard Williams, FAIA

Archipelago

April, 2009

Exclusive distribution by the University of Illinois Press:
1325 South Oak Street, Champaign, Illinois, 61820-6903

ISBN 978-0-252-07685-5 90000 9 780252 076855

Drawings and photographs by Author except as noted.

Design Development by Kathy Hancox and Michael Kothke

Word processing, Linda Craig
Production Associate, Mary Kay Dinsmore

Printed and bound in the United States

Published by:

Osim**O** press

P.O. Box 210075, Tucson, AZ 85721-0075

For all my students, collaborators and colleagues, near and far, 1937–2009

April, 2015
For Timothy,
with my Compliments.

Dick

Archipelago

Contents

Archipelago

Life is an archipelago of spaces and places, shaped first by nature then by the phenomena of man[1]. Among these, architecture is one of the noblest endeavors earning its eminence over the centuries through its infusion of grace, beauty, dignity and invested meaning in response to human needs, both spiritual and functional. Inseparable with landscape, it is both the face and physical substance of civilization. This timeless regard is reflected in its wider meaning, embracing the design of large scale social, political and economic directions in which the term "architect of ..." is used to identify the originator of any big idea or plan.

It is ironic that this larger meaning is now even more in common use while architecture itself as a cultural value is increasingly under siege. Some of the world's greatest thinkers, as the twentieth century closed, sounded the alarm of cultural exhaustion brought on by the imperatives of rampant materialism[2].

Over a lifetime, paradoxically as my involvement in and love for architecture has grown, I have seen these imperatives gain power and control, at first dimly perceived then loom clearly as we entered the new millennium. This increasing awareness, to the point of anger, has become the spur to dig for cause and effect of architecture's gradual debasement to that of a superficial cosmetic commodity , with exceptions few and far between, in hope that fresh insights for a turnaround in direction might be found.

The central theme for this retrospection and learning process is in bridging between architecture and the broad culture that has or has not sustained it, as seen in oscillation and gathering force on the time line of one's life. At the heart of this theme is the discovery that through intense caring and work the unique ingredients of each design task—and life choices too—gain respect, find expression and unite, as if on their own, through their "existence will,"[3] and that this same principle may be found in sorting out the myriads of influential events, ebbing and flowing, as they try to unify and make sense as a whole-life panorama.

A shadow of doubt lingers. The passing of time and awakening self consciousness carries with it an ever deepening recognition of how infinitely small each of us is in the cosmos. Can or should one more barely audible voice join in the great chorus celebrating art and life? Apart from this hesitation grows the idea of its opposite—the crescendo of learning in company with a host of students, colleagues, clients and friends which becomes over a lifetime a wealth beyond counting, a solid substance, a possession to be shared, an embodiment of philosophy (phylo-sophis, gr., the "love of learning"). I cannot betray this gift and quietly withdraw in silence.

"Do not go gentle into that good night
Rage, rage against the dying of the light"[4]

Not in rage, really. Rather, an emotion of hopeful aggressiveness leads one on to affirm and try to sort out from life experience certain guiding principles for the design of human environment that may then translate afresh as designs for learning.

1   de Chardin, Pierre Theilhard, *The Phenomenon of Man*, New York 1959

2   Solzhenitsyn, Aleksandr, *The Exhaustion of Culture*, Address to the Russian Academy of Science, late September 1997, as reported in DOMENICA, Roman Weekly on Cultural Affairs, Arts and Letters, 19 October 1997, No. 286, p. 21.

3   Martin Buber, Paul Tillich and Louis Kahn have eloquently explained the meaning of "existence will" as the idea that within each animate or inanimate system there is an innate power to shape itself, to express its own being. Buber, Martin, I and Thou, New York, 1970; Tillich, Paul The Courage to Be, New Haven, 1952; Kahn, Louis I, The Work of Louis I. Kahn, San Diego, 1965.

4   Thomas, Dylan, Collected Poems, New York, 1956.

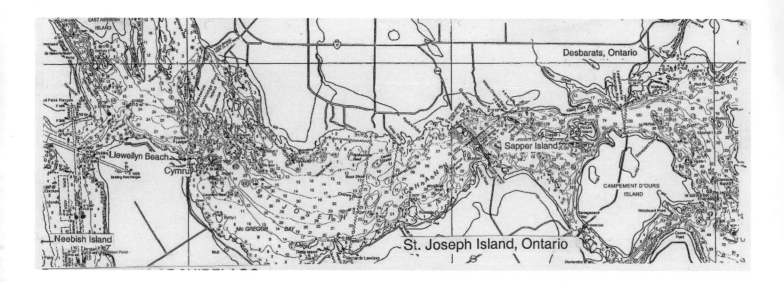

Cymru, Location Map

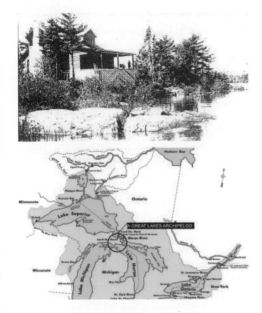

Cymru[5], a summer house now more than one hundred years old, was built by my father and his uncle, an Episcopal priest, later Bishop of Nebraska, on a massive granite outcrop at one end of a crescent sand beach they called Llewellyn, a Welsh ancestral family name. In the last year of Victoria's reign they had staked out a claim for this stretch of shore on St. Joseph Island, Ontario in the St. Mary's archipelago of northern Lake Huron. Framed by a forest of pine, birch, cedar and hemlock, Lewellyn Beach looks across sheltered crystal clear water to a nearby cluster of wooded islands and to the Laurentian hills beyond.

The essence of this summer paradise at the most miniature scale is the point of meeting of water, sand, rock and juniper at Cymru's granite base which became in my childhood, a magnetic, intimate place of attraction. My earliest memory is of this point of meeting: the warmth of summer sun and soft sand, the aroma of pine needles, sap and juniper, the tactile hardness of the rock face rough with lichen, the cries of seagulls, all senses mingling as a singular bliss. Vivid still, this first memory may have inspired a life long yearning in architecture to think of sight, sound, touch, smell and thermal sensitivity as equal and inseparable instruments for design—an orchestration of all the senses forming a setting: the invisible with the visible.

Cymru, of heavy rough sawn timber and boarding, is anchored to its rock base by an

enormous stone fireplace forming a hollow square, an alcove, with bunks on each side, opening to the main living, dining space that in turn has windows and French doors leading to a porch overlooking the water almost directly below, as if on a ship's deck. The unfinished wood surfaces have over the past century weathered a full spectrum from light gray to black, like the bark of nearby trunks and branches of cedar, fir and pine. Inside, the passage of time has deepened the natural tone to a warmer range of sepias to dark brown. To this day, the unpainted wood everywhere is aromatic in the heat of summer sun blending on the interior with the slight smokiness of a blazing fire. Evergreens and other growth embracing the house have matured still more except on the lakeside, intensifying the prominence of the porch and its emergence as an overlook. Time also has clearly reaffirmed the idea of architecture and landscape as one.

Building summer retreats in the upper Great Lakes began in the eighteen eighties along with the extension of railroads and shipping from Toronto, Chicago and Detroit as population and prosperity greatly increased. Mackinac Island in its dramatic location, the link between Lake Michigan and Lake Huron, was the first mecca of newly rich Chicagoans who built enormous "cottages" along the bluffs in the Victorian vogue of elaborate appendages, porches, turrets and gingerbread decoration. By the turn of the century summer migration expanded to other shore side locations, inland lakes and islands in the

Cymru, Llewellyn Beach

Satellite Image of a Great Lakes Archipelago

archipelago that extends up to Lake Superior. Llewellyn Beach on St. Joseph Island was one of these. But the architectural character of dwellings and resorts responding to the new ability to escape from the summer heat and humidity of mid-west prairie and river cities was usually much less pretentious, tending to be informal; geometrically simple and rustic, placed on solid rock formations like Cymru or poised on stone piers or log pilings, in any case with minimal disturbance to the natural landscape. The main desire was to relish a wilderness setting for the freedom of outdoor life as an antidote to the pressures of urbanism.

This was also a time when some of the most progressive minded of the Chicago scene were beginning to support the modern movement of the Prairie School, led by Frank Lloyd Wright. Among these the Pitkin family of Chicago's North Shore employed Wright to design their summer house on Sapper Island, one of many idyllic small islets at Desbarats, Ontario, a few miles east of Llewellyn Beach. The Pitkin house was built in 1900 by the Langstaff brothers from nearby Richard's Landing.[6] These islets soon became a colony of other North Shore families for whom the Langstaffs built houses following the characteristics of Wright's design—an open plan, wide overhangs, porches, decks all of rough-sawn pine and cedar left to weather, like Cymru, but more imaginative in concept and detail. The Langstaffs ingeniously adapted this new design vocabulary in many variations of arrangement and size on steep

rocky, forested sites resulting in a clustering of cottages that remain even now the most harmonic and sensitive to their primeval setting of any similar summer colony in North America.

Perhaps in such magnificent unspoiled places, the power of nature's gift is strong enough to inspire a community like Desbarats to understand more fully the unity of landscape and organic architectural principles as introduced by the Prairie School, not only for each dwelling on its own but in the synergy of following these same design principles throughout the colony. In such a joyful and enthusiastic spirit of recognition and action, "style" covenants or other imposed rules of conformity were hardly thought of or necessary. The only guideline was a shared desire for excellence in the diversity offered by each intervention as it responded to variations of site, such as slope, orientation and respect for neighborhood context. It might be ventured that Desbarats, though vastly different from the flat prairie in its rustic archipelago setting, is a microcosm of Wright's theoretical "Broadacre City," an innovation free of otherwise pervasive European stylistic revivalism such as Neo-Classicism and Victorian imitations then at a peak in North America. Were we then and still now preferring to copy styles from mother countries abroad, rather than rejoicing in our own architectural creativity?

As a mid-continent center of burgeoning growth at the turn of the century, Chicago

was a mirror of contrasting architectural directions. On one side, the innovative new expression of American vitality and inclusive idealism as reflected in the work of Adler/ Sullivan, Holabird and Root, Perkins, Wright, Jensen and others demonstrated a clear breakthrough in the creative integration of technology and aesthetics achieved through the teamwork of engineers, architects, artists, landscape architects, developers and building craftsmen, unprecedented in its freedom from traditional hierarchies of professions and trade discriminations.

This enthusiasm for collaboration in which all players are performing in an atmosphere of high mutual respect, a new American idiom like jazz, opened up dimensions of verticality and drama on the urban scene in the form of skyscrapers that could liberate more open spaces in city centers and new horizontal dimensions of suburban living that so closely interlocked indoor and outdoor space in a society of gardens. The colony at Desbarats, as a summer retreat extension of suburbia uniquely exemplifies this direction. In contrast, as described by A. J. Liebling in "Second City"[7], the vast majority of Chicagoans, elite and bourgeois alike were still eagerly following the Victorian and other revivalist vogues of New York. Victorian and Neo-Gothic mansions on the bluffs of Mackinac Island and other fashionable resorts such as Bay View and Harbor Springs on Lake Michigan still stand as evidence of America's continuing subservience to foreign influence in architectural taste. Sadly, this preference

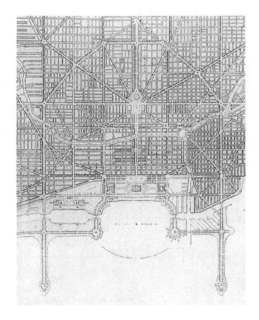

Civic Center, Plan of Chicago, 1911

Chicago is destined to become the center of the modern world if the opportunities in her reach are intelligently realized, and if the the city can receive a sufficient supply of trained and enlightened citizens.
Wacker's Manual

to imitate persists even more today in Disney Worlds, Las Vegas, in gated enclaves as well as in countless square miles of urban sprawl across the country. A conspicuous example of enormous capital resources gone astray is the recent development of Bay Harbor near Petoskey, Michigan on the site of a former limestone quarry on the edge of Lake Michigan. Bay Harbor, an up-scale real estate enterprise of several square miles, presents a curious contrast of excellence in the civil engineering of the harbor and marina, with the mediocrity of unrelieved, fast track arch tectural kitsch employing the gamut of revivalist styles in mansions, condominiums, yacht and golf clubs, shops and other services all cheek to jowl. The missed opportunity to demonstrate what could have been done with that much capital in such a salubrious setting seems unfortunately beyond the comprehension much less the concern of our culture today.

To learn how and why this trend in architecture as a cultural value in America has come to pass, as observed from life in the heartland over most of the past century, has become more and more a personal quest for a clearer understanding if not answers. What can explain the paradox of unprecedented high cultural expectations in the new world, as exemplifi ed by America with all its extraordinary new resources of both substance and multi-ethnicity, with distortions of architecture as the timeless, "mirror of civilization?"

An archipelago is as much described by its waterscape as by its islands. All over the world, in locations like the Polynesian islands of the Pacific, the Stockholm Archipelago or the Cyclades of the Aegean Sea, looking out from shore is loaded with meaning beyond the magnifi cence of a waterfront view. This meaning in mind's eye is a bewildering but enchanting composite of emotions, all the way from the terror of isolation and fear for survival, through the commonplaces of trade and communication to the sublime joy of being out on the water on a fine day. This unique sense of place seems to unify as one the dwellings and settlements on shore with the water craft that serve them, symbolizing interdependence of connection—an inseparable system of water land inhabitation.

This oneness of feeling is most poignant in the smallest of colonies, like Llewellyn and Desbarats. Local craftsmen build both dwellings and boats, learning from limitations of materials and methods and from the imperatives of fi rst having to work at all then having to work best, thereby eking out principles of design that respond to both similar and contrasting needs of dynamic and static structure, their differences having much in common, like endurance and aesthetic satisfaction. A fine Collingwood clinker— built row boat of clear cedar, refined over generations with little change in basic pattern has its counterpart in simple but elegantly crafted cabins of the same cedar, pine and hardwoods.

Every twenty years for over twelve centuries the shrines of Ise in Japan have been rebuilt almost exactly of hanoki cypress with small refinements of proportions and processes of construction such as jointing details and smoothing of surfaces. Along the same time span, on the Setonaikai (Inland Sea), boats and villages, ships and cities slowly evolved a reciprocal elegance of design, both timeless and timely, that subconsciously then knowingly reflected quiet pride of place and cultural identity. The white-washed, rounded edgeness of buildings, steps and streets of Myconos in their harmonics of indigenous sculptural form somehow are in a completely complementary but contrasting relationship to the brightly colored kaiikis drawn up on the beach, as are the many wooden windmills so evocative of their reliance on the Aegean winds.

What has happened that this hard won vernacular design sensitivity, gained over eons of time in so many parts of the world now seems lost in the sophistication and vanities of materialistic "progress?" Even in our own time, what has happened to the honesty and beauty of Shaker design, its legacy unaccredited, ignored and forgotten? Thoreau described in Walden, the essence of timeless design: "There is some of the same fitness in a man's building his own house that there is in a bird's building its own nest. Who knows but if men constructed their dwellings with their own hands and providing food for themselves and families, simply and honestly enough, the poetic faculty would

be universally developed, as birds universally sing when they are so engaged...shall we forever resign the pleasure of construction to the carpenter (read today: to the speculative builder)? What does architecture amount to in the experience of the masses of men?[8]"

Since island dwellers are sailors too, either active or passive, their perceptions and skills are especially sensitive to disciplines of safe passage, to time, distance and orientation, adding nautical flavor to the design and craft of building, no less physical in navigational gear, charts, clocks, flags, in the sounds of motors, horns and chattering rigging and in the smells of salt, oakum, paint and pine tar.

At the broader scale of harbor design, orientation to sun and shelter from wind and storm have been widely understood and respected as planning guidelines. Would that all villages, towns and cities, landlocked or not, had the sensible discipline and charisma of harbor settlements.

As in sea ports and archipelagos, safe harbor is found across the world's diverse expanse of lakes, seas and oceans. In the heartland of North America, a sailor's interpretation of the Great Lakes shorelines and open water reflects the depth of primeval time, ice age after ice age that shapes water bodies, rocky crags, sandy beaches, dunes, forests, marshes and evolving water, land and airborne life: The waterscape also mirrors history over millennia: the migrations of human inhabitation, tentative, fragile, surviving

over centuries then meeting the accelerating pace of foreign discovery, settlement and exploitation, slowly generating along the way timeless lessons in design.

At the gate of the garden
some stand
and look within,
but do not enter.
Others deep inside,
behold its beauty,
but do not penetrate far.
Still others encircle
the garden inhaling
the fragrences
of the flowers,
and having enjoyed
their full beauty,
pass out again
by the same gate.
But there are always
some who enter
and becoming intoxicated
with the splendor of
what they behold
remain for life
to tend the garden.

Abdu'l–Baha

5   Cymru, Welsh for Wales, pronounced: Cumree

6   Richards' Landing, A village on St. Joseph Island, Ontario
    named for the author's great uncle in law, John Richards

7   Liebling, A. J., Second City, series of articles,
    New Yorker magazine late 1950's

8   Krutch, Joseph, W. Thoreau: Walden and Other Writings,
    New York, 1962

Forest Shrine, Ise, Japan
(Photograph: Norman Carver)

The intimacy and closeness of everything around a child—the worlds of family, friends, nature and man-made things obviously have a profound influence on the dreaming and shaping of future life, especially in a summer paradise setting like Llewellyn Beach, in nature's magic zone where land, sky and water meet, the seeds of curiosity, exploration and making things seem most fertile. In the making of things, resources of energies, tools and materials are all direct, simple and exquisitely primitive. The making and using entwine as a single process. Making a bow and arrow is incomplete until using tests it and feeds back on making a better one. The design and making of bird houses and boat models are equally enticing in such a setting because of the immediate opportunity to try them out.

This creation of objects inseparable from their performance was another first lesson in design, evolving in cycles of disappointment in failure and joy in success, foretelling an awareness of what a project wants to be in its own right—its existence will. -evoking an ethic of respect to a kind of intrinsic authority that rises above the pride of the maker. The fascination of making things in this direct hands-on way at Llewellyn Beach and later on Neebish Island foreshadowed more than I could then realize a calling to architecture, coming more sharply in focus in other archipelagos—islands in the prairie and still deeper at a maturing intellectual level—islands in the academic grove and islands of experience in professional life.

16

Islands in the Academic Grove I
Islands in the Prairie
Illinois State Normal University

The seas that bond islands together are like prairie landscapes, embracing farmsteads, villages and cities—islands too with edges as shorelines. If certain of these islands is a university town, another archipelago takes form within. Separate studies and disciplines in the arts, humanities and sciences seek connection and constellation in faith that their collegiality is of highest value in the pursuit of knowledge. Normal, Illinois, a small university community surrounded by rich farmland, was, like Llewellyn Beach, an insular setting for childhood experience and learning—summers north in a "water wonderland," fall, winter and spring in the heart of the prairie. Illinois State Normal University was then a teacher's college, with all its various disciplines directed to teacher training. Attending elementary and high school within the university instead of in a public or parochial school was an advantage beyond our realization as children at the time, that would reveal itself slowly as a special gift—a foreshadow of cultural diversities to come. Although many of our teachers were students themselves "practice teaching," they were under the wing of mentors, some strict, some kind and lenient, all of high skill and dedication. Perhaps most inspiring of all was a sense of being in a family of intriguing complexity: ages, lifestyles, interests, ethnic origins, enthusiasms and expectations, living together in what seemed to be an endless house, almost a small city, full of mysterious, yet to be explored places—exotic laboratories; galleries with dusty exhibits—the sounds and color of music and art

studios—the specialized spaces and gear for athletes, both outdoors and in—all connected by interminable halls, stairs, alcoves and windows that looked in on beguiling activity and out on a campus landscape of giant trees in groves or bordering open greens and gardens. In the richness of this complexity there were no ghettos. Could this unity of diversities pre-figure a kind of utopian urbanism—the city as a university?

In parallel to earliest close to nature memories of Llewellyn Beach are intimate remembrances at home in Illinois—another kind of joy—to draw, to put block letters together to make words and finding meaning as they connected with images—a new kind of adventure as intriguing as exploring the shores and woods of the North. To compose with words, to dramatize, to design settings as in theater came early in life. While my parents were rehearsing for plays in the university auditorium, I was sometimes with them, told to sit quietly in one of the empty orchestra seats. On each side of the proscenium were mural paintings with captions in large letters. On the left was a scene from the Athenian Agora with a quote from Plato that I learned to read and memorize:

Education consists of giving to the body and to the soul all the beauty and all the perfection of which they are capable.

Such a lofty ambition for a fulfilling life could only be vaguely understood in childhood, but somehow it was always there as a promise. Would it take a lifetime for a full awakening,

Archipelago   Advent   **Islands in the Academic Grove I**
Islands in the Prairie
Illinois State Normal University

like the reward of enlightenment in Zen that is only possible through years of discipline and countless hours of meditation?

Daydreaming for a child is surely a path of enchantment, a storing up of images from the Land of Oz and other fairy tales, match-ing and balancing magical new revelations in the real world: airplanes, radio, elec-tric tools, games, toys and replications in miniature of the human cosmos around us. There seems no doubt that the creative urge in architecture or any other constructive art depends so much on storehouses of images and ideas matched by doing and making, both from the world of day dreaming and the disciplines of formal and informal educa-tion. Imagination is surely a skill that can only flourish if the storehouse of images and ideas, always growing, matures in an ever-shifting equilibrium of trial and error, leading to what works best, both functionally and as works of art.

An argument will surely arise whether such early twentieth century imagery from books with glamorous illustrations, news like the discovery of Tutankhamen's tomb as portrayed in rotogravure, comics, popular mechanics magazines, silent movies, and radio, all beheld in an eagerness to make things, could possibly equal the power of today's instant, sophisticated electronic media in stirring imagination to still higher levels of creativity. But a candid look at such a large question will be tempting—to explore archipelagos of experience that extend over

most of the past century. Though this per-spective is mainly of a life in architecture and education, might it serve as a microcosm for observing the wider culture, whether or not it is, as some say, in a state of increasing exhaustion, following a linear, aimless track of fads and fashions, or whether a renewed ethic of making the world ever better is again on the rise?

Map of Oz
Book Illustration, Oz Characters

The Land of Oz is a magic country of strange and alluring towns, cities, witch's castles, truth ponds, lush fields and mysterious forests—the whole kingdom an island surrounded by the Deadly Desert, unreachable from the rest of the world, except for the tornado that carried Dorothy from Kansas, or flying with her magic belt or the Wizard's balloon. Stories from Oz came out about once a year while awareness of the real world around us with its exotic places like Tibet and Timbuktu kept coming into our consciousness in a parallel passing array, no doubt given much added romance by Oz and other tales of imaginary places. Thus, another archipelago of ideas took form blurring the edge between the surreal and real, an ever expanding sea of incredibly diverse islands of enchantment. Could this be a vision of golden ages to come—of human inhabitation in villages and cities, each with its own signature skylines—across illuminated plains, on mountains or floating in lakes and oceans, or even in the sky?

Before the coming of the automobile and rampant commercialism, the edges of prairie communities were defined by slowly growing rings and clusters of houses, with streets simply ending to meet the seemingly limitless agricultural landscape, dotted with farm structures at a distance like ships at sea. Also from a distance out on the prairie the skylines of growing settlements were in low profile of dwelling clusters softened by trees, marked in continuing silhouette by grain elevators, church steeples, the cupolas of court houses at county seats and other institutional building cornice lines. The growing edge meeting the surrounding land and sky was thus a gentle organic process of change that seemed to be instinctively taking care of itself, with little discernible change in building form almost hidden in expanding prairie groves. But now this low key, growing edge has become rapacious with the sprawl of tract housing, industrial blight, inhabited signs, commercial strips and other wasteland disfigurement, more and more identical to the edges of larger metropolitan areas across the world.

Disregarding this ugly reality, what might be alternative visions of future prairie communities that would take advantage of their unique design potential of being entirely man-made artifacts in a largely featureless landscape? Early on, prairie villages developed along man-made trails at points of crossing rivers, later at railroad stops or junctions which from the beginning were fragile marks of man in vast grassland space. How could such clusters of man-made artifacts ever become magnets of high attraction compared to cities like San Francisco, Vancouver, New York and Chicago that drew human inhabitation to magnificent natural harbors or other unique geographic amenities in nature's realm? Can we foresee prairie villages and cities of the future that become, as expressions of human intelligence and art, just as diverse and beautifully magnetic as places to live? Might not the same opportunities exist in hostile deserts, arid lands and steppes once ecological canons and energy use factors are understood and respected? Is it forever a sin to build in fragile landscape and wilderness if we do it most sensitively, to an Omega Point of rightness, becoming human works of art in the global gallery?

Sensitive architecture alone is not the only language and instrument by which this vision may become real. The prairie is not entirely a featureless expanse of grasslands. Subtle gradations of topography allow drainage in networks of brooks and river tributaries, with glacial moraines defining edges of grassland space with groves of hardwoods as dark green to black linear stretches in the distance, irregular and flowing in counterpart to the surveyor's one mile grid overlaid in rectilinear patterns of section line roads, fences and occasional lines of sage, deciduous or evergreen trees. Prairie groves of oaks, beech and maple mature over centuries building inner cathedrals of woodland space, or at edges and in clearings their canopies shelter smaller scale growth of fruit trees and flowering perennials. So the language of landscape becomes an inseparable partner with architecture in the vision of a prairie utopia. As the hill towns of Tuscany around Sienna and their interconnecting vineyard, orchard and grain growing slopes form an endless garden, a precedent set over centuries, might the Great Plains and deserts of the world, including the preservation of fragile wilderness, also become an endless garden?

Most islands of the upper Great Lakes are like the villages and towns of the prairie in their small scale in proportion to their much larger spatial domains. In contrast to islands in the prairies, water edges can only expand with difficulty and great expense with landfill or structures while inward growth usually confronts steep slopes and forest wilderness. For this reason and other restraints such as the influence of Native American sensitivity and respect for nature., all of us as summer visitors, especially as children, were at once sensing our presence, not as permanent settlers but as guests, inspired to learn, to understand the delicacy and beauties of life on the clear waters, along the shorelines and within the primeval forest so close to us.

The narrow edge of shore backed up by the wall of dense woods very naturally prompted the urge to get out on the water for a more complete sense of place, better understood by exploration in rowboats, canoes and launches of connecting waterways and neighboring islands. So watercraft were a key means of feeling and knowing the identity of Llewellyn Beach and other shores by their water edges and spaces while the identity of place of prairie communities unfolded from within, through the special character of their neighborhoods and centers.

Even so, the prairie edge did increasingly become part of our consciousness with hikes out into the countryside on trails or farm roads and then by ritual Sunday rides in self propelled buggies like our Aperson

Jack Rabbit with its top down—to some farm for produce, or to picnic in a grove or just to enjoy the ride, never mind the dust, bumpy roads and sunburn.

In the early part of the century it was customary for families who owned summer houses, to set up residence for the entire summer season; husbands would commute from their work for weekends and vacation periods. My grandmother, who had financed the building of Cymru, followed the same pattern of staying for the whole summer, becoming a dominant presence, holding court in her matronly Victorian manner. At the other end of Llewellyn Beach, her brother the bishop, whom she worshiped, built Elrona on the opposite outcrop, thus completing, along with Cymru, the definition of the beach crescent with a prominent structure at each end. At lower profile, cottages and the chapel gradually filled in the space along the shore between. The bishop was an avid fisherman. In the summer of 1918, on one of his fishing ventures in the islets across from the beach, he suffered a heart attack and died. My grandmother was so desolated that she no longer could stay at Llewellyn and sold Cymru to Bishop Maxon of Tennessee, then bought a cottage at Neebish Island[9]; a few miles away on the American side. This meant that my family moved its summer base to Neebish as well.

Neebish Island was homesteaded in the middle of the nineteenth century by one of the sons of John MacDougal Johnston, a fa-

20

mous fur trader, and the youngest daughter of Wabojeeg, Chief of the Ojibways, setting up his family on the shore opposite St. Joseph Island, Ontario. His grandchildren, Molly, Will and Howard, at the turn of the century, saw the chance to develop cottages and an inn to attract summer visitors at the same time that Llewellyn Beach and the Desbarats colonies began. Molly opened Ononegwud Inn[10] while Howard, by then local Ojibway chief, subdivided shore lots, sold some and built small frame cottages for sale. It was one of these my grandmother bought. My family's first summer there, in 1919 was spent at the Ononegwud Inn until the cottage was ready. By then the inn was run by Jimmy Cummings, who also began a general store, in competition with Johnny Gray who had built a store and a rugged dock on pilings a half mile upstream that could accommodate regularly scheduled vessels that connected Mackinac Island and Sault Ste. Marie. Thus it was possible to come directly from Chicago by passenger ship, usually the North or South American, to Mackinac Island, transfer to the Chippewa and get off at Johnny Gray's dock. The Chippewa was a side-wheeler that could make twenty miles and hour, so the Sault was only one hour away and Mackinac three hours. Her daily trips were big events at Neebish, not only for the excitement at Johnny's dock when she came in at noon from Mackinac and again in late afternoon on her way back, but also for her enormous wake, a thrill to ride over in our small boats or to watch as the waves crashed on shore.

Summers at Neebish were loaded with experiences very different from Llewellyn Beach. The cottage was located just upstream from Johnston Point where the St. Lawrence Seaway shipping channel made an abrupt left turn for up-bound traffic, which by that time was heavy with ore, grain, oil and lumber carriers as well as by many passenger ships[11]. All of these would suddenly appear out of the woods and pass by only two hundred yards offshore. Since this thread of the channel was closest to shore of any point in the Seaway through the archipelago, passengers and crew on the ships were just as elated by this nearness as we were on shore. The captains were generous with their salutes, three longs and two shorts on their horns or whistles. Much later and most generous of all was the captain of the Edmund Fitzgerald, who also was a disk jockey, playing records with jovial interludes of banter over the ship's loud speaker system. The Fitzgerald tragically was lost with all hands in a Lake Superior storm on November 10, 1975, a loss most deeply felt by her Neebish fans.

Summers at Neebish in the twenties were times too that reflected the outer world in other ways than by the passing parade of ships. Prosperity and an increasingly materialism in our culture began to penetrate even the most rustic of settings.

Sleek mahogany speedboats began to appear reflecting the closeness of Detroit as the capital of automotive technology, as well as all varieties of outboard motors for rowboats

or larger models with enough power to make any flat bottomed craft plane at high speed. The waterfront, with the passing of ships and dozens of small boats from near and far, became the main stage by day, and at night gatherings along shore around bonfires, with story telling, charades, and singing, completed the scene. The bright lights and sounds of dance orchestras aboard passing passenger ships added another dimension of allure and a sense of being in touch with a glamorous world. Other sounds might be heard later in the dark of night, of oarlocks and bottles rattling, telling of smuggling in the days of prohibition across from St. Joseph Island, Canada, very close across the calm water.

9   *Neebish*, Ojibway for "boiling tea—rapids."

10 *Ononegwud*, Ojibway for "Happy Place."

11 Passenger vessels in Great Lakes Service 1920-1966
    American Registry:
    North American, South American, Juniata, Tionesta, Octarara, D&C, Eastern States, Western States, Manitoulin, Chippewa
    Canadian Registry:
    Keewadin, Assiniboia, Noronic Hamonic Huronic

Each summer reached its peak in August, building up to the annual celebration of Chief Howard's birthday on the nineteenth. Over the spring and summer he had stacked dry branches and driftwood for a bonfire on the sand cove beach of Ononegwud Inn. The whole shore congregated for pot-luck and performances in costume, climaxed by Howard's call for the bonfire ceremony. He had prepared birch bark torches for the children to follow him in his full regalia as chief, chanting "O holly, O holly, holly," increasing in volume, as we danced around the tee pee shaped bonfire stack, to a final shout "O ho!" when each torch was plunged into the stack. These bonfires were most dramatic, towering and sizzling—passing ships would keep blowing more and more salutes.

Our shore faced northeast, oriented to the North Star, the Big and Little Dipper and most awesome of all, the Aurora Borealis, Chief Howard was our savant of stars, lunar rainbows and story teller around bonfires of Ojibway Legends, interpreting signs of the Great Spirit Kitchi Manitou. Many were stories of ghosts and mysteries long unsolved.

There was something secret, dark and foreboding about the woods. To become lost or to encounter a moose, a bear or some other unknown threat was always an unnerving prospect. Venturing deep in the towering pines, spruce, birch and thickets of balsam became a vaguely sinister foil to the smiling open water as an invitation for exploration.

Howard did much to dispel this uneasiness through his gentle respect for all living things, explaining with great patience the friendly creatures of the forest, especially the smallest animals; chipmunks, beavers, mink and fox. He gave the children Ojibway names from nature that seemed to fit their personality. Mine was "Wagoshens" meaning little fox. Howard was called on, too, to name cottages and boats as was a tradition in the tribes. In 1933 when my family had a housewarming for the newly rebuilt cottage, Howard named it "Wawatay" meaning northern light. He lettered this name at the top of a birch bark scroll and signed his own Ojibway name "Makategibwanasi" for "Blackhawk." The scroll was then signed by all present at the celebration. Like countless other story tellers and name givers of North American tribes, all the way from the Ojibways of Lake Superior to the Yaquis of the Sonoran Desert, Chief Howard quietly radiated an aura of sensitivity and respect for nature's rhythms, balances, intricate variations of species, signs and forces that added up to a special kind of wisdom that seamlessly combined common sense, morality and spirituality. Like Don Juan, the Yaqui sorcerer[12], he was a low key presence without the title of teacher yet he was very much that, especially for the Neebish children, perhaps even more poignantly effective through the casual informality of our random contacts with him. Although hardly perceived then as a formally recognized part of one's total educational experience, these summer interludes away from school, in-

cluding so many other intriguing discoveries in addition to Howard's teaching, now seem priceless treasures of learning. They foretell, for example, the awakening of environmental consciousness of the sixties that gained strength simultaneously along with respect for ethnic minorities, as they have contributed so much to our American culture. This early informal learning in an almost religious atmosphere of love and respect for nature, humbly interpreted in the human dimension, was most fortuitous and canonic for a life in architecture—as a deep and sincere base or foundation, probably made even more enduring because it remained at a subconscious level without pretense.

12 Castenada, Carlos, *The Teachings of Don Juan*, New York, 1972

22

In parallel, another largely unheralded facet of knowledge is travel as learning, not only as a direct spatial experience sharpening one's sense of time, distance, scale and physical characteristics of seascapes and landscapes but also through the relatively painless absorption of history and meanings gained through curiosity and intelligence of what remains invisible but is signified by what is seen.

Traveling back and forth every summer between central Illinois and Llewellyn, then Neebish, unfolded many such physical attributes of the prairie landscape, the metropolis of Chicago, the waterscape of Lake Michigan changing from low shore profiles south to more rugged topography north,, creating islands, promontories and the St. Mary's archipelago of Lake Huron leading up to Sault Ste. Marie, the gateway to Lake Superior. These passages reflected, too, many changes in American culture after World War I, mainly in the sudden impact of the automobile on road systems, wayside services, city traffic and negative pressures on other forms of transportation that offered such a variety of choices of travel through the twenties. A 1922 map of the Chicago region shows rail lines, interurban service by light electric rail, bus lines, ferries to all the towns and cities of lower Lake Michigan, shipping lines to other Great Lakes ports and of course, road networks that existed at that time. This variety of choice gradually narrowed down as the automobile took over, especially evident to the Neebish colony in

the decline of passenger ship access. Out of the sixteen regularly scheduled vessels connecting Great Lakes ports on both the American and Canadian sides, none were left after the first year of the depression, with few exceptions for cruises and combined passenger mail and package freight service in the northern tier of Canadian ports. By 1932 only the local mail boat from the Sault to Sugar and Neebish islands remained to carry a few passengers and cargo.

Learning from summer travel in those post-war years was a kaleidoscope of images, meanings and feelings as vivid, real personal experience: of dusty and sooty train coaches riding the C & A to Chicago; of the sweep of corn fields "knee high by the fourth of July," of prairie town stations with their grain elevators, bins and farm machinery; of the intimidating grandeur of Chicago's Union Station; of the hustle, bustle of skyscraper canyons of the Loop, of Marshall Field's giant clock, Balaban and Katz ultra flamboyant theaters, Louis Sullivan's Carson Pirie Scott department store's graceful and elegant "Chicago windows" and flowing, curvaceous iron filigree; of the grim and deafening "El" (elevated rail system) of the encapsulated world in the Field Museum and the splendors of painting and sculpture at the Art Institute; of the grand facade of Michigan Avenue and Grant Park facing the lake; of the excitement of departure from Navy Pier aboard the North or South American; of the ships as floating resort hotels, of the off limits, fascinating pilot houses and engine rooms

that you might be allowed to peer into; of sumptuous meals on white tablecloths in the dining room; of deck chairs and promenade decks from which the sparkling blue of Lake Michigan seemed without limit; of framed charts of the Great Lakes in the purser's foyer with courses marked, stimulating the urge to be a navigator; of the elation of spotting land and seamarks exactly as they were plotted on the charts–Point Betsie Light, Sleeping Bear Dune, the Manitou and Fox Islands; of the excitement of arrival at Mackinac Island with its white palisades and block houses of the Fort on the bluff and the vast, colonnaded porch of the Grand Hotel heralding at a distance the historic importance and lore of the island; of the smells of horses and fudge and noise of the throngs of visitors; of transfer to the Chippewa, the fast side-wheeler to sail along the shore of Lake Huron to Detour Passage and up the St. Mary's to Johnny Gray's dock at Neebish; of the final trek on foot along the shore or aboard some friend's launch to the cottage.

Alternatively the voyage north from Chicago by ship took us all the way to Sault Ste. Marie. The Sault's history going back almost four hundred years as the main eastern village of the Ojibways, as the first major post of French traders, explorers and Jesuit missionaries all centered at this strategic place where rapids and locks connect the lower lakes to Lake Superior. Although both American and Canadian Saults, in facing each other across the roadstead of the St. Marys, had their own appeal as frontier cities, the image of this crossroads of the lakes is dominated by the presence, close up, of the great ore and grain carriers, multi-masted foreign vessels ("salties") and a mixture of smaller craft, all in such concentration as they wait to lock through up bound to Lake Superior or on their down bound passages.

This capsule of travel experience, tracing a thin line across a piece of Midwest prairie, the Great Lakes and the archipelago where they meet—the center of the fresh water world—is perhaps by the unfolding of its own unique character, a model and powerful incentive for study of other charismatic regions of the world—a generator for increasing curiosity, the prime well spring of learning. Such a myriad of travel impressions may seem too random, too various to have other than general educational value in the usual formal sense. Yet travel, as it involves, for example, learning and using the graphic language of maps and charts, offers a unique educational advantage in understanding the physical and cultural dimensions of the world around us.

Mapping and charting, as a visual, diagrammatic way of describing reality by drawn lines and symbols in scale, is really a picture language recording spatial information of what already exists implying, also, skills in analysis of hierarchal relationships from which decisions based on passive understanding may be made leading to a course of action. The value of this skill is surely obvious to regional and urban planners,

architects, engineers, preservationists, landscape architects, economists and many others involved with beneficial change in the physical environment. Also, the analogy of written and spoken language in its structure of passive, active and subjunctive moods to graphic language is neatly clear. Passive understanding (analysis) is necessary before action takes place (synthesis), especially engaging those who are designers and decision makers to think and draw subjunctively about what might and ought to be in a series of pictographs flowing from the here and now (the before) translated into an idealization of what should be (the desired after).

There can be no doubt that frequent travel with keen observation at any scale of moving in space: in the countryside, over the water, in the air, in the city or at micro-scale in neighborhoods, in buildings and rooms within, is a key exercise or practice mode of linking the graphic language of representation to the spatial realities they signify—a kind of performance in perception that increases in skill through repetition, much as scores in music and choreography in dance as graphic language relate to refining performance by rigorous practice.

Just as composers of music require talent and intensive practice as performing musicians in interpreting the scores of others in order to write great music themselves, or as painters and sculptors must have virtuoso command of reading the cultural scene, their media and processes, so architects and other

environmental designers require practice in perceiving the spatial domain and client needs for new design tasks by close, direct observation recorded in graphic language as a prelude to using the same language in the presentation of design concepts, seeking an enduring point of equilibrium of right choices.

Pondering in retrospect the myriad of happenings in one's early life that somehow focus on one calling or another, I'm sure there are many paths, many fortuitous circumstances that join and point the way. But many paths, like learning from travel as just considered, may not lead to a single occupation but remain as a wealth of diverse perceptions, a treasury of experiences without particular focus, a tapestry of knowledge enriching the human condition, upon which the world of architecture finds its cultural strength perhaps more than that of any other profession. So the advent of a life in architecture may begin with the enrichment of non-focused experience intertwined with the awakening of a highly singular career direction.

More than anything else, the key that unlocks this diverse panorama toward a personal creative yearning is imagination as a verb, carrying well beyond the earlier childish fascination with images as unconnected objects. One can also argue that imagination as a verb inevitably involves talent as well, inseparable from the thirst and curiosity for information and bits and pieces of experience, translating and transforming these to a point of action; a creative act. As with the practice of graphic language, talent requires that countless repetitions follow to tune its power and skill. It pervades dreams, awake or asleep, it rehearses dialogue ahead of speech, it schemes and replays tentative choices in the process of design.

Where does talent come from? Is it inherited, are you born with it or does it by some mysterious process appear out of the blue? Probably all of these origins are involved in one way or another. Whatever its source, talent may be a very broad-based special aptitude of mind from which by chance or design a singular direction identifies itself. I am so lucky to have had parents who were talented in both ways, brilliant over a wide scope of abilities as well as possessing individual skills; my father in scholarship, athletics, coaching and teaching innovation, my mother as an inspiring speaker, community leader, motivator and caring friend to everybody, especially the poor and needy. Although their talents were many faceted, they all seemed to come together or be exemplified by their years in amateur theater, early on in Shakespearian drama at Ravinia Park while they were living at Highland Park on the North Shore of Chicago.

There always was a carry-over at home of those days at Ravinia; quotes, one liners or even longer passages from memory that were triggered by some happening or situation in everyday life. This became kind of a game, to find the right segue from theater that fit even the most commonplace event, transforming it to something more profound in meaning. If you quote from As You Like It, Act II Scene VII "All the world's a stage," what does it mean in real life today? Is it just a romantic metaphor or may it imply that somehow the quality of acting is tied to the quality of life, to think and speak poetically,

to dress in costume most fitting to character, to build our everyday sets and arrange properties with more sensitivity, reminded by Berthold Brecht[13] that "The set needs to spring from the rehearsal of groupings, so in effect it must be a fellow actor?" This was a more literate insight of the inseparableness of performance and setting, an extension of the idea introduced earlier—of the oneness of designing, making and testing bows and arrows, boat models and birdhouses. It was an insight only felt intuitively in its early stages, to grow with more and more consciousness and conviction, to hang on to as our world grew increasingly complex and Balkanized into separate disciplines, trades—even in the arts.

13   Willet, John, Brecht on Theatre, New York, 1964, p 233

In small communities or even in cities the question asked of a child "What do you want to be?" usually sprang from the most prominent or popular walks of life—doctor, lawyer, sailor, flyer. You would likely be called an artist before anyone would suggest some more specific calling like architecture or industrial design. Memory carries me back to school during the Christmas season which was really the most exciting time of the year. Putting up Christmas trees and classroom decorations, making and marking cards, planning special plays and ceremonies all broke up the usual daily routine. There was a joyful air of expectation, we learned old and new carols, sang them in the halls and classrooms and outdoors serenading in the snow. It didn't matter that this was happening in exactly the same way all over America, our school was the center of the world. The top floor hall of Thomas Metcalf School was especially high and wide with a broad band of north light coming in through a clerestory as in an artist's studio. The tree would be set up in the center, decorated and festooned with radiating streamers. The whole school would gather in the late afternoon in the fading winter light to light candles, to sing carols and hear Christmas stories. I felt especially involved being asked to draw the nativity scene on the blackboard in colored chalk and to design the decorative scheme for paper cutouts as class artist. About this time, when I must have been in sixth grade, prompted by the love of drawing and making models I really thought I might become an artist, but was cautioned by my

Auntie Mayme who pointed out "wonderful, but artists starve, think about being an architect." She was our family's link to the sophisticated art world of Chicago, having been a prominent member of the Renaissance Society of the Art Institute. She would send me announcements of exhibitions, prints and clippings from the "brown section" of the Chicago Sunday Tribune, especially those that related to art and architecture. Somehow my own embryo interest was given a special twist because she hated Frank Lloyd Wright, whom I already knew about most favorably through my mother's friend Florence Fifer Borer who had attended the progressive school at Taliesin when she was a child. What was there about modern architecture that generated such love and hate at the same time or was it just Wright's notorious behavior? Also about this time, in "manual training" class (now called "shop") our assignment was to build a birdhouse out of the wonderful clear grain tidewater cypress preferred for woodworking at that period. The instructor had paper patterns of several designs from which we were to choose. I asked if I could do my own design and was given permission to try, having in the back of my mind it would be in the manner of Wright as best I understood it then, not only from what I'd heard described and from photographs but intrigued by my aunt's opposition. I think the birds really loved it because of the extra shelter afforded by its wide roof overhang.

Many years later as a studio critic I began asking exceptionally talented students what inspired them to be an architect. As you might guess, their responses ranged over a very wide spectrum from family legacies in the profession to an urge arising from the hands-on making of things, to a strong sense of social purpose or to the allure of a romantic life as portrayed in the movie "Fountainhead" or some combination of these or other influences. It invariably turned out that their parents were talented in some other field, strongly career motivated, readers, travelers, or supporters of, if not themselves active in community cultural affairs. Once in a while, curiously enough, talent seemed to spring out of rebellion to strong parental opposition, indifference or adversity. Talent as an elusive, intriguing aspect of human nature was to remain an undercurrent of personal interest throughout my life, especially within the creative professions, whether or not they could flourish beneficially to society or be frustrated in our present media saturated, materialist, celebrity and money worshiping culture.

Without being fully aware of it while in high school during the great depression another ethical attitude about architecture began to take root. Though virtually every architect was out of work and it seemed that the future was just as bleak in avoiding starvation as it had been historically for artists, a lingering faith remained that design as a basic form of applied human intelligence was essential for survival in the husbandry of

materials, energy and craftsmanship skills. One couldn't simply go to the store and buy new tools, lumber, paint and the latest gadgets. Somehow the necessity of scrounging whatever left-over materials might be around to "make do" became a discipline that magically changed from quiet pride in meeting a need to a glow of elation that was aesthetically satisfying too. This unexpected dividend has endured to this day—even though goods, services and resources of almost unlimited choice are now abundant for making something new, there remains a lingering preference to work with whatever is at hand that can be adapted and reused. No doubt indulging in this ethic of conservation as a first priority has much deeper roots in the genes and in history way before the depression, yet the fact that it happened then in my most impressionable adolescent years made it more unique and lasting. During the summers at Neebish, one of the ways you could somehow rationalize your guilt of being away on vacation while your friends had to stay at home was by being diligent in saving and reusing material both practically and creatively. It also fit neatly with earlier lessons from nature taught by Chief Howard, Many years later we came to call it the "Neebish syndrome."

From these many promptings, both encouraging and discouraging, the advent of my yearning for architecture survived the depression despite the shadows of doubt cast by some of my parent's closest friends. As long as the timeless value of higher educa-

tion—going to the university—was fortunately still not threatened, why shouldn't it be to study architecture as one of the broadest avenues of learning that embraces the humanities, arts, sciences and technologies? This enthralling prospect, denying misgivings, led the way into another archipelago—the next of many islands in academic groves to come.

From the time of Socrates and Plato the idea of forming a community of scholars so that each could experience the joy of intellectual stimulation led to the discovery that mutual learning among them was enormously advanced as well. More exciting still, it became clear that this mutual enlightenment was infectious in much wider circles of society, a powerful new instrument in forming and sustaining democracy through education.

At first, this excitement was generated anywhere scholars and eager learners might gather, in market places, centers of worship or in secret away from tyrannic rule. Socrates, for example, might appear at random at such places in the city, attracting listeners, colleagues and pupils around him. His followers, notably Plato, sought to bring permanence and order to the substance and method of Socrates' teaching, which meant finding identity of place as well. After Plato returned safely to Athens from Syracuse in 386 B.C., where he had been sold into slavery, his friends used money reimbursed for his ransom, which had been refused by his ransomer, to buy a suburban grove, named Academus for its local god, for Plato to establish his school, thereafter known as the Academy[14]. Technically, the Academy had religious identity, dedicated to worship of the Muses. Indeed, Plato's Academy was called a musieon, honoring the nine Muses as they in turn were known to inspire artists and poets. One would like to imagine that the idea of an academic grove still retains today its ancient sacred identity of place,

combining inseparably the highest aspirations of learning with arts and literature and that education, in its deepest meaning as a cultural value is a sacred quest.

From this enduring inspiration it may be ventured that all levels of education have a noble and even spiritual place in human existence and that higher education as a culmination along with all others, from the simplest beginnings to the most sophisticated, must exist and flourish as learning performances interlocked with and within the most responsive and inspiring of spatial settings. What greater challenge can there be for architecture, landscape and the whole scale spectrum of environmental design to become seamless in their excellence of response and partnership?

Inevitably with growth, cultural development and maturing democracy, academic groves spread more and more beyond the enclaves of monasteries, temple precincts and other privileged enclosures into the wider urban fabric. Oxford and Cambridge became models of town and gown as a unified community – colleges separate as islands but fused in an enclosing townscape.

This maturing process of higher education was mirrored in the new term university – a unity of diversities in the pursuit of knowledge, as defined earlier, now placing more and more emphasis on its nature as an open-ended quest like the expanding universe itself, in which the great achieve-

ment of the Academy as the birthplace and nurturing ground of philosophy is transfigured from within a closed system of privilege to one of unlimited accessibility.

Universities as spatial settings for the performance of learning may be thought of as archipelagos too, in both singular and plural dimensions. A single university campus is ideally composed of many islands of separate studies with evolved networks of connection in time and space, as noted in my initial description of Illinois State Normal University, with all others in the world having the same basic organizational composition and structure, each an archipelago on its own.

In the plural sense the whole living membrane or ecosphere[15] of the Earth is an archipelago too in which each university is an island dedicated to learning that ideally in aggregate continues to advance the collective intelligence of mankind toward what Teilhard de Chardin calls Omega Point.[16] But in the light of this ideal, the reality of university life today, notably in large institutions, seems increasingly at cross purpose to the idea of unity, beset by the Balkanization of disciplines that appear to build higher and higher fences of separation sapping away the essence of mutual learning and collegiality.

To trace this change in what has happened to the university and to architecture as cultural values in a world of rampant mate-

rialism, hedonism, terrorism and a growing absence of moral authority is a central
theme of this retrospection, – looking back
to days of innocence and high expectations
that now seem betrayed. However, as it has
become better understood through history that both academia and architecture,
are of all life's callings most highly reflective mirrors of the culture at large, and that
there have been several cycles of decline and
recovery even over the past seventy years
in my own professional life, hope springs
eternal that the present alarming downward
slope may somehow, someway be reversed,
though the symptoms this time are more
sinister and complex.

Beginning the first cycle of architecture and
academia linked together during the depths
of the depression was hardly a normal
advent into the professional world. The days
of prosperity and youthful enthusiasm of
the twenties suddenly became clouded and
full of contradictions. How could universities and other cultural institutions hold their
own? Would there ever be a chance again
to practice and relish the art of building or
to build anything new at all? If this gloomy
prospect loomed for real for the future what
other study, what other direction of learning
might be more practical for survival? There
seemed no other choice. I was lucky to have
wise coaching reminding me that as long as
the university itself could continue to exist, the study of architecture embraced the
broadest scope of learning and skill development as an all-around education, a synergy

of mathematics, language, history, physics,
art, design, technology, business, philosophy, social and political science. Add to this
the timeless social values of university life,
living intimately and learning to communicate with fellow students in so many walks
of life.

Other awakenings dawned too that would
have arisen even in normal times in the life
of a naïve and shy freshman from a small
town suddenly finding himself immersed in
the meleé of a very large campus like the
University of Illinois. I remember two main
sources of shock. One was the sophistication and maturity of most of my fellow students in architecture who already had a head
start in drawing skills from large Chicago
high schools, including many others who
were experienced out -of-work draftsmen.
The other trauma was life as a lowly pledge
in my fraternity, Psi Upsilon, in the midst
of worldly older "brothers" loaded with big
city and suburban street smarts, dialects
and mannerisms. It took a while for these
intimidations to wear away – now I realize
how fortunate it was to live in two entirely
separate worlds at the same time. In a way
one was a kind of refuge from the other and
yet they were somehow mutually reinforcing
– a microcosm of mixing professional and
social life in the real world to come.

It would be tedious to spell out a detailed
chronology of university life in those days
– so much of it is the same story retold – by
now almost too well known in tales of the

depression years. Rather, it might be more
meaningful to single out a few highlights, as
I have tried to do from childhood memories,
that may interpret certain events, attitudes
and insights that now seem most evocative
in understanding cultural cycles that have so
powerfully influenced the course of architecture and education either as bellweth-
ers or nay sayers of what lies ahead for the
twenty first century.

14 Durant, Will, *The Life of Greece*, New York, 1939
    p 510, 511

15 *Ecosphere*, the membrane of life surrounding the
    Earth (term suggested by Heinz von Foerster)

16 de Chardin, Pierre Thellhard, *The Future of Man*,
    New York, 1959, p 127

Cycles within cycles. Though many of nature's cycles, day and night, winter and summer, transits of the planets, moon and sun are reassuringly regular, most others, such as oscillations in weather from short term cycles of calm and storm to much longer ones like global warming and cooling are largely indeterminate, generating fascinating ambiguities, mysteries and superstitions. For example, the cycling of water levels of the Great Lakes, as much as five feet in Lake Michigan and Huron every twenty or more years, has been known for many centuries by Native Americans, as was told to us by Chief Howard at Neebish. But even the legends of Kitchi Manitou do not offer an explanation. The Army Corps of Engineers has kept records since the Civil War attempting to analyze all the variables; precipitation, run-off, evaporation rates, sunspots and others in order to project annual and longer patterns of change. But like weather forecasting, it was discovered that there remained so many uncertainties in the composite of all forces acting together that accurate prediction is elusive, like the myriad of interactions in the dynamic social, political and economic life of mankind. Sometimes, curiously enough, the cycles of nature and man coincide. During the boom years of the twenties the lake levels were high. As the depression deepened, drought and dust bowl conditions came to the Midwest and the levels went down. Was this more than a coincidence? Another high came with the fifties and post-war economic recovery – the next low, as if in contradiction began

its down turn with the Kennedy Camelot years, the awakening of social and environmental concerns, the Vietnam war, student rebellion all combining simultaneously and rather surprisingly with a high in university life of collegiality and eagerness for pro-active, cutting-edge interdisciplinary research, projects, and out-reach in the public interest.

Then, abruptly, public hostility to Academia mounted along with curfews, riots and unrest related to prolonged frustration with the war in Vietnam, resulting in retreat back behind the walls separating disciplines. Still indulging in my game of cycle watching, this should have been a time of even lower lake levels. Instead, they rose again to peaks pretty much sustained during the Reagan trickle-down years and the prosperity of the nineties, obstinately (and prophetically?) to start down again as we entered the new millennium. Interplaying the level of the lakes to other overlapping cycles in the flow of time is obviously of no large consequence except to tweak one's own daydreaming and in hindsight to posit subjunctively a chain of what ifs, whether this or that might have been done instead, as in architecture the process of making most fortuitous design decisions waxes and wanes.

In contrast to the easy-going elementary and high school years, entering university life, particularly on a very large campus, was a sudden immersion in a highly competitive arena, made much more so as the depression wore on. If any jobs at all were out there, those who had the highest records would have the best chance–an obvious connection of both student and faculty motivation to cycles of economic health or recession. This would be a relationship to monitor as time went by, not only in terms of the direct relation of hard work, talent and initiative in school to future professional opportunity but also in terms of other underlying forces at work such as money, elitism and social privilege as they gradually revealed themselves to be dominant in the selection of architects for most prestigious projects.[17]

This emergent reality seems in direct contradiction to hard-won assurances and expectations in our democracy that all playing fields are level and that opportunity is truly equal for success in any chosen enterprise or personal endeavor. Have there been certain underlying, unacknowledged contradictions like this all along in our culture? Is this kind of self-deception part of a wider national ego that will not tolerate criticism? I leave these larger questions to our most esteemed historians and cultural critics. Still, as architecture and academia mature in partnership as a singularity, a single facet of a composite cultural mirror like that of the giant telescope of Mt. Hopkins,[18] I offer fragments of opinion, a critical view shaped by experience as a mid-continent actor and observer for a long, long time.

Cycles of styles in architecture as in all the arts have been studied and interpreted by generations of scholars and critics disclosing a repeating tendency of rise from a simplistic primitive beginning through refining development to flamboyance, decadence, death and the birth of a new cycle. Although the modern movement in opposition and revolt to the long cycle of nineteenth century revivalism had its start in Europe and America continuing during the late 1800's peak of neo-classicism, many more years passed before the spirit of the movement began to have widespread influence in architectural schools. Illinois, like other American schools was still imitating European pedagogical traditions of which the Ecole des Beaux Arts in Paris was dominant, with its clone, the Beaux Arts Institute of Design in New York serving as the American center of dogma propagation. The BAID was the source of design project programs, competition schedules and final juries for many American schools through the early part of the past century, reaching a zenith in the twenties coinciding with the building boom of those years at the height of revivalism.

It is doubtful that there was any discernible connection between the stock market crash of 1929, the beginning of the depression and the death of revivalism as it had lent itself to the desire of expressing opulence through elaboration of copied architectural styles. Yet it remains an enticing supposition that the hiatus in building during the depression would stimulate a breath of fresh air in architecture when and if recovery took place. Nevertheless, a kind of establishment preference for "tradition" lingered on (as indeed it still does today) so that in the thirties the modern movement was almost at a subversive level in the schools particularly as embodied in the influence of Le Corbusier, the Bauhaus and other European avant guard architects. It seems strangely ironic that the close-to-home innovations of the Prairie and Chicago Schools were not considered as significant or even thought of as a part of this exciting new direction. Another symptom that we were still a colony?

As freshmen we were assigned projects in the classical orders, learning to render them in Chinese ink washes, thereby implicitly affirming that this was the fundamental language of architecture. During the mid thirties project programs were still coming from the BAID in New York at three levels of complexity, from the simplest, Class C and B to Class A the most elaborate, large scale design which set the pace for the two major national competitions, the Paris Prize, administered by the BAID and the Rome Prize of the American Academy in Rome. In these and other design competitions, it was an intriguing time of gambling – would the juries be ready for a fresh, innovative scheme or still expect the "traditional" revivalist solution?

The Ricker Library of Architecture and Art at the University of Illinois, second only to the Avery Library of Columbia, then as now, maintained an extraordinary list of periodicals including vanguard European journals like the Swiss-German publication Bauen und Wohnen and the French L'Architecture D'Aujourdhui. Both of these and others from the Nordic countries became dog-eared by students in their eagerness to keep up with the latest developments in modern design – furniture, industrial design and graphic design as well as architecture. One basic idea was coming through with convincing acceptance – that the modern movement was much deeper than a superficial, visual style, having its inspiration in attempting to meet neglected social and environmental needs as well as to reaffirm the aesthetic rightness of materials, structure, craft skills and intrinsic beauty deriving from all attributes that were both timeless and timely. Little did we imagine then that the public, persuaded by both scholarly and populist critics in their competitive roles of assigning labels, would think more and more of "modern" as another purely visual style – as all others of the revivalist period were known – primarily by their looks alone. In the past, when a great new movement in architecture began, like the Gothic period, wasn't it "modern" in its own time? Was "style" even thought of then as we think of it now in our sophisticated awareness of history's pluralistic panorama of architectural fashions? Isn't there a connection between this awareness and our rather casual arrogance in picking any style that strikes our fancy not only for personal dwellings, businesses and institutions but for community identity as well? Why, for example, must Gaylord, Michigan, in its

flat landscape copy Bavarian chalets that evolved honestly and appropriately in their mountain settings? These and other similar questions will continue to arise as life in both academic and professional archipelagos moves on, prompted by certain key experiences as they now reappear in hindsight. For instance, looking back at the mid-depression years, the mixing of existence in the midst of economic poverty with the excitement of new architectural beginnings now seems a stroke of good fortune, a kind of purging, in the astringency of their occurring at the same time, gathering nostalgia as they were followed by the experience of World War II and its impact on future directions.

17 Williamson, Roxanne, American Architects and the Mechanics of Fame, Austin, 1991

18 Observatory on Mt. Hopkins, Santa Rita Mountains, Arizona multi-faceted mirror

These later thoughts could not possibly have been in the mind of a young freshman preoccupied with personal adjustments to the new world of university life, pondering the unknowns of a career. Reflections of childhood experience recurred, in terms of what métier, what calling made the best fit. Having great difficulty with algebra was one thing that gave pause. Another was the encouragement by the art faculty who taught freehand drawing to architects that I really belonged in the art curriculum. This made me think again of my Aunt Mayme's advice—was she really right that artists starve? I was heavily recruited by La Force Bailey, Louise Woodruffe and Dinty Hogan, all well-known painters, to transfer from architecture to art. No doubt my sense of ineptness in drafting in comparison to my more experienced fellow students contributed to this uncertainty—did I make the right choice? Somehow an inner voice was saying give it another year, picking up authority while a sophomore—mainly because studio projects for the first time opened up design as the central skill to be developed along with a surprising discovery of an aptitude in physics and a fascination with architectural history. Almost overnight, shadows of doubt disappeared—depression or not, architecture took command.

But perplexities of another kind soon loomed up that were at first hard to pin down. As each new design project began in studio, finding a way to get started, seeking a direction was elusive. The freedom to now innovate a concept after a series of exercises in which everybody did the same thing was suddenly more wide open than imagined. Take, for example, the assignment to design a shelter in an arboretum. A host of enticing images would start flashing by. A rustic timber gazebo? A latticed, basket-like enclosure covered with flowering vines? A thin shell concrete mushroom? An arcade around a pool and fountain? Time and again one or another of such schemes would arise with "this is it" enthusiasm only to fade the next day, perhaps through ineptness in translating the alluring image in drawing or modeling—or finding, with time for reflection, that the idea somehow lacked depth or appropriateness for unforeseen reasons. The test of time thus presented itself early on as essential in the development of critical judgment, either externally in the voice of a critic or inwardly in one's own growing capacity and skill in self criticism.

Studio projects, following the BAID's progression in size and complexity as mentioned before (Class C, B, and A) also varied widely in building typologies, program authors always seeming to seek added allure in subject, such as art galleries, foreign embassies, memorials, etc. Duration of project timing ranged from sketch problems of a few hours to five or six weeks, with local juries judging the projects then sending most on to a New York jury for final review and awards. These in turn would be photographed, critiqued and published in frequent BAID bulletins, eagerly awaited by the schools and award winners. Like today's ranking in college sports, a school's prestige depended a lot on success in New York. At the time Illinois, Penn and Yale were leading the pack; published projects setting the pace in presentation techniques and design trends. Eero Saarinen's work at Yale was published often, revealing a high diversity of concept formation, but also a consistent clarity of scale and patterning which was rumored to be an influence from his mother Pipsan's weaving talent at Cranbrook as much as from his father Eliel's architecture. At the Class A level you could choose to do an archaeological study or one in interior design. I elected the latter, a BAID program "A Group of Accessories," influenced by Asian art and design, which, with a lot of luck and help from my critic Elmer Love, won a "First Medal" from the jury in New York. I now wonder whether a sense of success in the simulation media of drawing, rendering and photography like this might have been misleading, delaying the full appreciation of learning architecture as a full scale medium.

As remarked earlier, what a project wants to be in its' own right, only vaguely sensed as a child in the making of things, now began to emerge to a more conscious level. Would this mean that along with each new design opportunity that there must be one intrinsically and inevitably perfect solution, or would the essence of each new set of circumstances allow a variety of equally appropriate resolutions? Although this puzzling question would with time, experience and rising expectations become more daunting and humbling, it would sometimes as well become more and more exhilarating with each new encounter, leading to exciting anticipations of what signs, tell-tales and beckonings would lead the way.

Needless to say, the inviting openness of the modern movement vastly increased the breadth of possible concepts beyond the stereotyped formulas of revivalist styles. Not only was there still the risk of provoking controversy by resisting accepted revivalist fashions but also the challenge of coping with an array of untried innovations, both technological and aesthetic. If the modern movement was truly searching for deeper substance in meeting neglected human and environmental needs, did not this mean that a much more demanding set of architectural criteria must also be addressed?

Of all American schools of architecture in the late nineteenth century, Illinois was most influenced by the Chicago School of architectural practice, which was then becoming internationally known as a center of innovation in its pace-setting, seamless fusion of architecture, engineering, landscape and interior design. This influence was directly reflected in the Illinois curriculum. Under the leadership of Nathan Ricker[19] the school developed a strong program in architectural engineering in parallel with design, channeling the two major European influences of the Ecole des Beaux Arts in Paris and the Bau Akademie in Berlin (engineering and

technology) as they intermeshed in Chicago offices and in turn became a model for the Illinois curriculum. This was exceptional. Up to that time and indeed continuing today, most American architectural schools followed the tradition of training in design, history and theory, with little emphasis on engineering and construction technologies, relying on internship in offices and on specialist consultants to fill this need in practice.

Thus, at Illinois, as you moved into your sophomore and junior years, there was no way around the rigorous disciplines of math, physics and structures interlocked with design, though in the final two years you could choose either architecture (design studio) or architectural engineering as your major emphasis although the degree was the same: Bachelor of Science in Architecture.

In retrospect one can see more clearly that the rigorous combination of design and technology with the new open-endedness and risk-taking of modernism, compounded by the anxiety of the depression years, often led to discouragement and loss of confidence. In contrast, though, the first taste of success, no matter how small or seemingly insignificant, might generate a boost in morale and momentum with each new project. Much later as a mentor and critic in both education and practice, I realized more and more how crucial this first taste of success is in the build-up of motivation and confidence in the mind and heart of the student or young practitioner.

In the face of balancing these unforeseen complications, the battle between doubt and reassurance during the middle years of professional education was bound to contrast with the enthralling, simplistic idea of what architecture is all about when one began as a freshman. From history you could now look back realizing that it was only in the nineteenth century that learning to be an architect changed from a traditional apprenticeship system to one of a formal program in university. Would not the old method of learning slowly at close hand in the thick of the actual building process, have been more straight-forward, a clearer continuation of youthful expectations?

The debate on or about which is the better method still goes on. The common tie in both is that the apprentice or student is the integrator of all the various segments of study and experience. If the student, then, is the integrator of so many separate components, like the blending of so many diverse instruments in an orchestra composing a symphony, is not the underlying skill to be developed in architecture that of orchestration? In the time tested apprenticeship system it seems that this was implicitly understood, and that each aspirant to be a mature architect (from the Greek: archon-tecton-"master builder") would honestly and confidently within himself, be encouraged then by his elders and his society in such a way that either going ahead as an archon "master" leader or stepping aside into some other specialized field of orchestration in the building trades could be done with equal dignity. The singularity of the architect as a leader, designer, orchestrator thus evolved with increasingly clarified identity along with the acculturation and civilizing of society.

In the light of this cultural advance, formal architectural education in the university began by establishing curricula around this time-honored singular identity, surrounding, supporting and enriching it with the various disciplines of scholarship in the arts and sciences hoping to achieve and maintain an ideal balance, a dynamic equilibrium between theory and praxis. In America as in other parts of the world in the nineteenth century, each program usually began with just one teacher, an architect, who encompassed all the subdivisions of architectural skills in design, theory, history, structures and construction technology; thus both the teacher and student were integrators, inherently interlocking the substance and hierarchies of parts and balance among them. But with the rapid growth of universities along with population, architectural schools also multiplied in number and the development of specialist faculties; artists, historians, technologists as well as experienced architects, trusting that the design of the curriculum itself would insure coordination and that the student, even though inexperienced could bear the responsibility of integration.

This reliance on the curriculum design and the students' capacity for synthesis is, of course, the underlying strategy for most

disciplines in higher education, inarguably sound as academic theory. However, a closer look, ranging over more than a hundred years, reveals an unforeseen dilution of the central core of building orchestration skill, as fewer and fewer talented and experienced architects were on faculties. With the best of intentions, top university administrators began insisting on Ph.D. degrees as a minimum academic credential for faculty appointment, thinking this requirement would benefit architectural education in the same way as in other arts and sciences. In history, theory and certain specialist technologies, this policy is clearly enriching, but as schools grew more and more in size as well as sophistication, with many additional specialist options, even in areas of architectural design itself, such as high rise design, housing or historic preservation, one can wonder what has happened to the timeless central core-architecture as a singular discipline. After many years, I would return to Illinois to find this plethora of options, asking: "Where or where is the architecture option?"

Looking back, it's easier now to trace cause and effect in the form and function of curriculum design and faculty composition, along with the enormous growth of universities over the past century in two settings—urban and rural. Illinois and MIT, the first university architectural programs in America, founded in the eighteen seventies, represented these two basic types: MIT in the Boston/Cambridge metropolitan area had direct, close at hand sources of faculty

from professional offices, while Illinois, in its rural location like most other land grant universities, had to recruit faculty who would have little if any opportunity to practice. Add to this recurring cycles of economic prosperity and recession as they affected the ease or difficulty of persuading experienced practitioners to join faculties for long term participation and it may be seen that schools at a distance from metropolitan centers have had to rely mainly on scholars and specialists who were content to make their entire careers in academia. The depression, however, when virtually all practicing architects had no work, might have been a time for schools to bring their faculties back in balance but there were obviously no resources to do this. In fact, huge cuts in salary had to be made and no replacement positions could be filled. Faculties were lucky to keep their jobs and were even forbidden to do any outside work, even small residences.

My father, then head of the commerce department at Illinois State Normal University, suffered two successive salary cuts totaling twenty seven percent as the depression wore on. In those years he came over to Champaign often to participate in an economics seminar. I remember vividly the time he stopped at my fraternity during the bank moratorium in early 1933. He insisted that I take his last five dollar bill.

19   Ricker, Nathan, founder of the School of Architecture
     U. Illinois, Champaign/Urbana, 1872

Fraternity life in the depression was a strange mix of nostalgic dreams, rituals, traditions and privileges of bonding suddenly having to survive in adversity. House bills had to be cut and cut again. Mortgages were pressing in. Rumors of having to close kept recurring—some houses across the campus actually did. The whole idea of fraternities and sororities came under stress as never before, not only as anachronisms born in the age of nineteenth century romanticism, like the Greek revival in architecture, but also in the light of modernity and rising individualism.

As a part of early nineteenth century nostalgia for the Golden Age of Greece and the founding of Greek letter fraternities in America, initiation rites also evolved in emulation. The bliss of membership in the brotherhood required a ritual of passage through harassment, humiliation and endurance, psychological as well as physical. Were sudden summons of pledges to get up out of bed during the night and line up naked some throw back to slaves lined up for inspection and sale in the Athenian market? Or on another, archaic level, a lingering recall of Greek idealization of male beauty? Hazy memories remain of veiled approaches, some not so subtle. Somehow, they could be shrugged off. Now I wonder if each of us as freshmen was in some way a modern kouros[19], rushed in the pledging ritual as much for looks as for pedigree and scholarly promise.

Without doubt, our passage through late adolescence as pledges in those depression years was more innocent and naïve than now. We simply accepted ritual and custom without question, forced to memorize and parrot fraternity history: dates, names, places, numbers, a kind of catechism unexplained. It didn't even occur to us to probe for deeper meaning. Or, if one did, eyebrows would be raised in a kind of amused but intimidating scorn: if you dared ask how did all this regimentation square with ideals of a free democracy, you'd get a vacant stare for an answer. I won't try to make anything out of the fact that these traumatic episodes coincided exactly in time with Hitler's rise to power, but it was a curious coincidence, another ambiguous juxtaposition.

Once having survived the rites of passage through initiation, emerging out of hell into the glow of belonging was a foreshadow of entering all of society as a new citizen, crossing a threshold of acceptance, yet at the same time being made aware of many more challenging crossroads to come. It was also a time despite the depression that one was now free to choose; to coast, to go with the flow of partying, games and carefree existence or to follow the beat of some other drummer[20], a choice not without risk of new forms of hazing. Friendship ("brotherhood") took on new tests: to embrace the blessings of diversity and liberal neutrality or choose sides as if one must, between being one of the boys or becoming a "grind," a slave to the rigors of scholarly discipline. Trying to follow the star of learning from both extremes might have had something to do with my being elected archon (president of the house) in senior year, but those few of us in my class who had tried to keep some sort of balance all along nevertheless became known as the "sisters of suppression." Curiously enough, the no-nonsense overcast of those years was no restraint on traditional high jinks of university life.

Of all fraternal rituals that instill a sense of belonging, singing must be the most inspiring and memorable. Although song was almost always with us every day as a grace note, a kind of blessing before and after evening meals, or along with weekly chapter meetings and less frequent celebrations, memory singles out certain emotional peaks that transcend all the rest. Singing in the open air on a warm spring night was one of these. Competition with other fraternities intensified our own identity still more. Of all these times one is most memorable.

At the end of my sophomore year in June, 1934, I went with my father to attend a reunion of his class at Kenyon College in Ohio. He had first gone to Michigan at Ann Arbor, where he became a member of Phi Delta Theta, then transferred to Kenyon for his remaining three years, living with the Dekes since there was no Phi Delt chapter at Kenyon. So, while he was with his old classmates, I joined with the Psi U's for their reunion celebration. Kenyon was at that time a small denominational (Anglican) lib-

eral arts college of a few hundred students, located in a magnificent hardwood grove on a ridge a few miles from Mount Vernon, the nearest town. Its few buildings in the Neo Gothic style were arranged on each side of a wide central path along the ridge under the trees, like the long nave of a cathedral. At twilight, members of each fraternity took turns locking arms, about six abreast in a number of rows, to march slowly, singing in cadence along the central path to their chapter houses hidden deep in the woods, for meetings and evening revelry. You have to imagine how deeply moving this was to a young nineteen year old, to be a total stranger in the warmth of such a scene yet to feel somehow even more intensely the glow of belonging. Something about the canopy of trees arching overhead and the slight echo from nearby building facades added resonance and volume to the singing, in step to the slow beat of the march.

Much later in life my father, who was also a member of Phi Beta Kappa, the honorary fraternity for scholarship in liberal arts, would speculate that Greek letters inspired by Plato's Academy and the Periclean Age, should be reserved for the singularity of philosophy as the connection of all scholarly and professional disciplines. This would imply that social and residential clubs on campus might find other appropriate names perhaps derived from tribal or other identities—indeed as many of them have—Aztecs, Mohawks, Arcadians and many others. No doubt in the early days of collegiate life, in-

fluenced long before by monastic principles of scholastic guardianship, there was little or blurred distinction between scholarly and living environments—they were one. One can once again ponder what has been lost in collegiality in the enormous spreading fan of modern higher education.

It was also in sophomore year that history of architecture began to give order to the flow of random kaleidoscope images from the past as they had fascinated childhood imagination. At that time in architectural education history had a clear dual purpose—the traditional one of historical study as an essential part of general education now interlocked with architecture as it uniquely reflected the time passage of growth and change in human culture – architecture as the "Mirror of Civilization." The other purpose was more explicit for the realities of practice. Despite the tentative advent of modernism we were still in the age of stylistic revivalism – the skill of direct application of any of these styles was expected as part of one's qualifications for professional life. You could then look forward to specialization in Italian Renaissance, Georgian, Gothic, Tudor, Spanish Colonial, or other exotic styles or become versatile in all of them to suit the whim of the client. It was also a language vocabulary that could become eclectic, to appear again much later as Post-Modernism or as scenography for Las Vegas or other theme parks. The finishing school of revivalist virtuosity was of course the Grand Tour of Europe, with the added prestige of the

Paris or Rome Prize or some other traveling fellowship.

Sir Bannister Fletcher's History of Architecture by the Comparative Method was the Bible, not only of the origins and development of western architectural history but a kind of copy book as well, encyclopedic with precise drawings and photographs. Even though the wave of romanticism was still at a high in the western world, including a fascination with Asian art and architecture, Fletcher's book strangely relegated the architecture of all the rest of the world—Asia, India, Islam, Central and South America to an appendix titled the Non-Historic Styles.

The proportionate emphasis on history in the curriculum at Illinois was then greater than at any other school, influenced by the build-up of the Ricker Library's extraordinary collection and by the administrative leadership of Rexford Newcomb, an eminent architectural historian who became the first dean of the College of Fine and Applied Arts as the architecture department was included in the new college, transferred from the College of Engineering. This dominance of history in the curriculum by its continuation through all three years after the first (most architectural schools were still a nominal four years leading to a B.S. degree) followed the traditional chronology from ancient times, with greatest emphasis on classical, medieval and renaissance periods, less on nineteenth century revivalism and virtually none on the modern movement, vernacu-lar, the near and far East, Central and South America. It seemed odd to us that there was no inclusion in the history courses then of great work in these other parts of the world that had such strong expression of timeless design principles influencing modernism, for example, the Katsura Villa and Zen temples of Japan, the Great Mosque of Cordoba, the Mayan compounds of Central America, the Truli houses of Albero Bello and other inspiring vernacular work. Of course much has changed in this proportional emphasis in the last half of the century, not only in recognition of the redundancy of stylism as a working vocabulary for practice, but also through an awakening that both history and theory have much more to do with underlying design principles that are both timeless and timely.

Gold Mask, Tutankamen (Watercolor)
Cairo Museum, Egypt

Sarcofagus Guardian (Pencil)
Cairo Museum, Egypt

Adding to the prominence of history in the curriculum were the Ricker Prize and Allerton Traveling Scholarships; the former named for Nathan Ricker, founder of the school, was the top prize for a term paper in architectural history in the third year, the latter an award donated by Robert Allerton, given to two students selected by the architectural history faculty at the end of the school year for travel during the summer in New England.

The western world, particularly in mid-America was still infatuated, even in the depression, with the picturesque romanticism of the distant past. My term paper subject, The Treasures of Tutankamen, with its lush illustration potential, was a stimulating subject to me as it had been in childhood. Perhaps because it might have caught the attention of the jury too from their own high interest at the time in archaeology closely tied to the architecture of those ancient historic periods, my paper was chosen for the Ricker Prize. This award was as well a major factor in the selection of the Allerton Scholars.

Robert Allerton, donor of the scholarships, having inherited an enormous fortune, became a connoisseur and art collector for his estate of several thousand acres of fertile farmland in central Illinois not far from the University of Illinois campus at Champaign/Urbana. His son, John Gregg Allerton, had been an architectural student at Illinois in the late twenties, leading to Robert's special interest in the school. It was his feeling that

very few students growing up on the prairie would ever have the enriching experience of visiting and studying historic architecture in the East as well as absorbing its well-established cultural environment. The stipend was four hundred dollars each for the summer, a lavish sum in those days. The only requirement was to follow a rather open itinerary, mostly in the coastal towns and cities of New England visiting and recording sites and significant colonial architecture that would then be written up, illustrated and submitted as a bound final report.

My partner was Tom Danahy, a debonair older student from Albuquerque. Tom had great talent as a designer and delineator, a joyful disposition, most of all an appetite for discovery, which I shared but with far less experience in translating whatever we discovered into how it might fit into the mosaic of life. We soon established a laid-back rapport; the myriad of choices opening up along the path; details of the itinerary, places to stop overnight, where or what or how long to linger anywhere for sketching, photos or making notes were all smooth, light hearted and uncomplicated. Among our first discoveries was that neither of us was really an avid scholar or disciplined recorder of events and places in laborious detail. What seemed to be emerging was simply an on-going curiosity and eagerness to take everything in as it came along, eventually trying to sort out the importance of each new experience in the flow.

Travel was easy in our 1929 Model A Ford coupe, bought for $95 (resold at the end for $65), meandering across Indiana, Ohio, Pennsylvania and New York State over all kinds of roads, mostly local that were just beginning to be linked up in a state or national system. Navigation presented few problems, if maps and signs didn't show the way people were always helpful with directions. Rooms and food were cheap, averaging about $1 a day. Gasoline was only about ten cents a gallon, so we could easily make two or three hundred miles a day for hardly more than a dollar. The itinerary led us through Greek revival towns like Hudson, Ohio, mixed with Neo-Gothic and Victorian exuberance along or near the shore of Lake Erie on into the Finger Lakes district of New York State then past Lake Champlain and Lake George to Montreal and Quebec City.

The route through French Canada was not enthusiastically approved by our advisors, who may have regarded this as an adventuresome deviation from Mr. Allerton's original intention that New England was the central focus area for our architectural and cultural enrichment. But our predecessors of the year before, Dean Hilfinger and Jim Hunter had pioneered this addition to the traditional itinerary and had made a glowing report of its value in understanding the historic panorama of colonial North America that included both French and British influences. Much later this dual presence, particularly as it interacted with Native American culture throughout the St. Lawrence

and Great Lakes waterway system, would turn out to be personally important as an inspiration to more fully appreciate the most positive aspects of blending ethnic cultures in such a salubrious natural setting.

The province of Quebec was for us an entirely new world. It was an awakening that crossing a national border not only included a sudden change in language but also in terms of the many other unforeseen differences across the sensory spectrum—sight, sound, smell and touch all coming together as a kind of cultural shock—a foretaste of future border crossings into distant exotic lands like Nepal, New Guinea or Tunisia.

I had once before visited Montreal and Quebec in 1924 when my family took the whole summer touring Ontario, Quebec and New England in our Hudson Super Six towing a Lippman Camprite trailer at a time when campgrounds were just beginning to accommodate tourists. Even though memories of that trip are still vivid I don't remember feeling the same sense of cultural contrast. When you're ten years old I guess you can take it all in just as you might have imagined it entering another part of the Land of Oz prepared for new surprises. In any case, Tom and I quickly adjusted to this new adventure; by the time we got to Quebec City we were nonchalantly cosmopolitan, feeling comfortable with our primitive French and local customs—enough so on a Saturday night to join the promenade on the bluff below the Chateau Frontenac and to pick up two girls

Tom Danahy, Dick Williams Model A Ford
August 1935

Spiral Stair, Trustees House
Shakertown, Kentucky

who left no doubt they were out to welcome visitors. To our amazement as our banter began in a mix of French and English, when we explained we were architecture students from the University of Illinois, they threw up their hands in disbelief "Non! N'est pas possible! Alors vous connoisez bien Dean et Jimmy!" The coincidence of finding the same two girls as did Dean and Jim the summer before, out of the promenading throng, was hard to believe, yet at the same time a kind of premonition of intriguing small world encounters to come.

The commanding presence of the Chateau Frontenac, one of the great Canadian Pacific hotels, dominated the skyline of Quebec City with its steep roofed tower, like a block-house fortification enormously inflated. Clustered around it on the bluff the steep-roofed houses and other buildings had the same look as French provincial towns with churches or chateaux rising above, radiating an aura of the old country more than the more modern, westernized atmosphere of Montreal. Of all the various architectural details forming a composite urban fabric, the steep roof surfaces meeting the overhanging eaves in an outward curving line was most distinctive, intensified by the contrast of the black of the roofs and the white or light-colored rendering of the walls. Also, the compact, more diminutive scale of open spaces, streets as well as windows, doors, trim and other details lent a most appealing harmony to the overall scene. At that time the edges of the city were clean-cut as they

met the surrounding landscape, not ragged or diffused as we were used to seeing in America and other parts of Canada. Gradually we were beginning to absorb the notion that perceiving villages, towns and cities as single artifacts was as important, if not more so, than moving from one individual historic building to the next, out of context of their setting.

Reluctantly leaving Quebec we headed down through Maine to begin our "official," dutiful trek through New England, basing in New-buryport and Marblehead Massachusetts, as was now becoming traditional for Allerton scholars. These towns were most conveniently and centrally located as hubs for visits to architectural and historical landmarks in this concentrated area of population, some might say the heart of New England, unfolding three hundred years of settlement, growth, change and evolution of America as an independent nation. Our main focus over this time range was to be the study of earliest remaining structures of the seventeenth century, mostly the transplanted vernacular influences from Elizabethan England, on through the more formal Georgian and Federalist periods to nineteenth century revivalism–with little or no emphasis on the architecture of Richardson, Hunt, or other well known firms of the late nineteenth and early twentieth centuries. Thus we were engaged for many weeks in serious architectural sightseeing by day and pleasurable cruising at night, radiating out from our bases in the Model A. On the weekends

the beaches were most magnetic for sun and surf as were the attractions of Boston city life. Often, the diligent days of visiting historical spots and interviewing authorities would turn out to be unexpectedly rewarding in other ways than the normal satisfaction one gets from learning more about the particular examples under study. No doubt the depression had a lot to do with it. The scarcity of tourists seemed to result in more welcoming, informal and warming contacts with patrons, docents and staff at much frequented historic places, private houses of note and museums. We were often taken in, our hosts closing shop for the day to guide us on special tours or just to pass the time indulging in casual talk accompanied by food and drink. There was something about the mid-depression years that led to a relaxed spirit of all being in the same boat –"Let's enjoy what we can."

One such welcoming was most memorable. The owner of the Sparhawk mansion, 1763, in Kittery Point, Maine met us at the door as if we were old friends. After explaining we were architectural pilgrims from the heartland on a quest to acquire culture in the sophisticated East he became even more eager to invite us in, not only to explore the house, but to spend the day as if we were right at home. He and his mother seemed to be just getting by in genteel poverty even though he was editor of Field and Stream magazine and well established as a freelance writer. As we were led around the house, something about its air of benign disrepair because of the depression lent a feeling of the dignity of former days and the depth of time-more than did other mansions lavishly restored and maintained. We enjoyed an entirely impromptu day, pooling our meager funds for lunch and dinner accompanied by delightful dialogue, finally leaving in the twilight of a balmy late June evening; but not without a parting gift from our hosts, which was a square wooden toilet seat rumored to have been used by Washington and La Fayette when they visited the mansion sometime during the Revolutionary War. The gift was embellished with a specially written sonnet by our host honoring the occasion. The seat may still be preserved along with its inscription by the family of "Pop" Lescher, our witty, favorite professor of construction courses, especially plumbing. We presented this treasured antique to him at the annual awards banquet the following spring.

The leisurely weeks in and out of Newbury-port and Marblehead were filled with seeking and finding our destination houses, churches and other edifices of note, sketching, taking photos and otherwise trying to absorb the special significance of each setting. Again, with the best of intentions it became clear that at heart we were not meant to be faithful, enraptured scholars but were more like the vast majority of our fellow Americans, curious but quickly satisfied, perhaps in the earlier stages of increasingly shorter attention spans which were to be so greatly intensified later by media inflation and the accelerating pace of everyday life.

But still the sense of duty was strong. In rereading our final report, dictated to and typed by a charming young secretary supported with funds from some federal program, I'm struck by how bland it is; perhaps revealing a subconscious lack of enthusiasm for having to record methodically all these renowned historic places in a manner something like the dull, repetitious descriptions found in a real estate inventory. What comes through, however, is that we were, without fully realizing it, reacting to and criticizing the design of each work of architecture on scales of quality quite different from the criteria commonly accepted by architectural historians. As designers we seemed to be seeking other standards of measuring architectural quality that were both timely and timeless, less in terms of visual attributions of style, provenance and authorship, more in the evaluation of principles learned in studio: spatial organization to satisfy functional needs, proportion of elements, skill in structural and material appropriateness, harmony with landscape and context, building to ground and building to sky sensitivity and many more subtle qualities of scale and close-up detailing. We found ourselves asking without then considering it so relevant in our report, what great works, whether celebrated monuments or simple vernacular building possess attributes of fine design regardless of time, place, notoriety or established opinion.

From this encompassing point of view, scoring highest, enduring and enriching in value in an ensemble sense over a time span of at least two centuries, were the village greens of New England, like Wiscasset Maine, the all white cascading dwellings tiered up on the granite rock faces of Marblehead harbor, Chestnut Street in Salem with its McIntyre designed facades now framed by giant mature trees, stone and wood weathered barns in the countryside; all linger in memory more poignantly than single venerated buildings. Certainly meriting a place on this list is the restored town of Williamsburg; magnificently proportioned, detailed and crafted Georgian structures composed together with landscape as an inseparable partner—the townscape as a whole ensemble becoming greater than the simple sum of its buildings as single artifacts.

On the way home Shakertown (Pleasant Hill) Kentucky 1830's-40's was enormously appealing in the same way, but at a direct, sparse, unselfconscious level of fine design that resists any style labeling. Like Kenyon College in Ohio and other small campuses, Shakertown's site plan forms a mall of mature hardwoods on the crown of a hill flanked on each side by three story brick dormitory buildings with lower structures for farming, workshops and services placed in subordinate locations aside, or further away from the central space. All are built in fine restrained proportion of overall massing, openings and profiles. Trim in wood is minimal, slim and recessive; finest of all are the graciously simple interiors, staircases, furnishings that in their slimness and functional honesty become vernacular works of art, foreshadowing design principles of the modern movement developing later in the century.

Before setting out on our travels Tom and I were invited out to the Allerton estate for dinner with Robert and John. We were picked up in late afternoon by their chauffeur in an elegant black Rolls Royce limousine for the twenty-mile ride out to the estate, now called Allerton Park. The approach to the grounds was marked by an avenue of evergreens, through a dense woods on the banks of the Sangamon River then between a set of brick pylon gates finally arriving in a gravel forecourt of the Georgian style mansion, built in 1900 from the design of a young British architect friend of Robert's. I can remember still the elegant crunch of the Roll's tires in the gravel.

Since prohibition had been repealed two years before, we enjoyed Martinis (my first) in an enclosed arcade, at ease in comfortable wicker chairs, much as if we were relaxing on some gracious porch in the Kashmir. With many works of art surrounding us from Bali, Thailand and other lands of the Far East, along with exotic indoor planting, it was as if we had been transported by magic carpet far away from the Illinois prairie. During dinner of roast beef and Yorkshire pudding, along with unfamiliar but delicious oriental dishes, Robert and John plied us with gentle questions about our backgrounds and thoughts about architecture, I think as a kind of preface to see how our responses might change

on return from the trip, since it was already an established tradition that we would be invited back in the fall for dinner, when we would present our bound report to remain in the estate's sumptuous library. On our return we were again chauffeured out to the estate in October when the landscape was in full color. Without remembering details of conversation I do recall a sense of greater confidence in organizing our thoughts, a kind of oral summing up of how valuable the whole experience was to us, above and beyond what we had tried to write about in the report. There's no doubt in my mind now, so many years later, that the questions of Robert and John, before and after, asked in such a stimulating setting made a profound impression to dig deeper for inferences and meaning—so to speak like a blade sharpener to always fine tune and communicate intelligently what may be learned from all kinds of experience.

I had a special, continuing contact with Robert and John over the years because Robert was a close friend of Gertrude Aldrich in Bloomington who in turn was one of my mother's best friends. It was always pleasant to have a brief visit with them when years later they would return from their residence in Kauai, Hawaii to Allerton Park for a short stay in May. I still felt the same subtle pressure to find some new insights to relate or edit from whatever recent news or experience might connect our common threads of interest. Once, in January 1964, I was their guest in Kauai just after having

spent some time in the Honolulu Academy of Art, which contains many pieces of Roberts' collection of Eastern art. It also happened that there was also a temporary exhibition of the work of Kionori Kikutake, a Japanese architect who had won the Pan Pacific Prize awarded by the Honolulu chapter of the American Institute of Architects. So I had the challenge of eking out a connection between Pacific Rim architecture and art and what it might mean for the future as the global archipelago grew closer together. The resulting conversation was sprightly even though Robert, in the hospital with bronchitis, had some difficulty in speaking. He died that fall at age ninety-one. I was fortunate to keep in touch with John for many years after that as an informal reporter of news about Allerton scholars I knew.

In long term perspective, I now think that the Allerton travel experience, over and above its beneficial acquisition of knowledge gained from the study on site of historic American architecture, turns out to be even more valuable for future architects in building and sharpening skills in making design decisions informed by timeless principles of excellence that transcend stylistic fashions of the time. From the joy of knowledge gained as passive enrichment, I again affirm that imagination becomes a verb in the action process of making and balancing the myriad of interactive design choices in the creation of architecture.

In spite of ever-changing economic, political and social cycles; depression or prosperity, war or peace, even in doldrums of time, there is a certain same anxiety in the senior year of everyone's university life. The future is suddenly present. As an overlay on the building complexity of both academic and social involvement, the ever-widening scope of learning, the kaleidoscope of subjects expanding yet having to face closure, mixing with the realization that close friendships, too, will soon disperse or end, all combine as a new, very real emotional awakening–a worrisome anxiety yet not without a feeling of exhilaration. The Greeks might call it a KAIMOΣ, a noun, something you can have or be possessed with, a kind of irresistible worry. As the fleet of fishermen leave the harbor of Mikrolimano at dusk for a night at sea, a feeling of KAIMOΣ is in the air – shadows of doubt, fear of storm or bliss of calm, anticipation of the catch , good or bad; a sharp, unchanging sweet/sour dread that is somehow addictive. Zorba had a KAIMOΣ, expressing it as he danced.

Would this rite of passage as a senior repeat again and again in one's career and family life, or would it be treasured in memory and become nostalgic as a unique experience? Whatever the large dimension of the future portended, the immediacy of being twenty one in an exciting if troubled world, added a glowing allure to the path ahead. For one thing, the Allerton travel adventure was a foretaste of ever-widening global consciousness and its magnetism for learning the language of design, combining vocabulary and process-simplistic at first as provoked by childhood curiosity and discovery then maturing more and more through design studio experience in expanding cycles and scales of testing, comparing, trial, error, refinement, evaluation, criticism. The momentum of all this progression built up the lure of comparing local experience, a sense of one's region-its "genius loci"– with the imagined then real exposure to foreign cultures-a balancing scale of the timeless in history with the timely imperatives of today, of shining simple truth and beauty with the fascination of elaboration and complexity.

In the marvelous, open give and take of the studio, almost around the clock, all of this was grist for mixing hands-on work with dialogue; a meta stream of information and involvement riding along with day-in day-out project development and deadlines. The studio as both workshop and marketplace of ideas has long been the heart of an architectural school, its antecedents traceable far back in time—a common central place where projects begin tentatively then take more and more definitive form in a flow or design thinking exchanged, praised or challenged. The very core of this design for learning is exchange between student and critic—propose—dispose, what Donald Schön calls "reflection in action."[20]

What larger dimensions of studio spaces for learning, might now open up ahead?

The quest of exploring the world as an essential part of an architect's preparation for practice and enjoyment of life itself, especially at a time when there was virtually no chance for practical experience, loomed as even more important. How do you go about it? What were other possible alternatives along the way? Graduate school? Military service? What else?

The Grand Tour of Europe, a tradition of privileged young men in Britain, especially those bent toward a career in architecture, had its echo in the colony. The dream of equal opportunity in America meant that travel and study abroad could become real for anyone.

The playing field appeared to be level in the competition for traveling fellowships and prizes open to all who did not have money on their own or some other form or sponsorship. At least so it seemed. But it was also clear that it would take an even greater amount of talent, imagination, determination, hard work and luck than were already a part of the competition for top honors in the academic and professional world, especially during the depression. Even in more prosperous years, awareness of the wider world, its enticements of exotic places, experience and personal enrichment seemed to come all at once into focus during one's senior year along with facing the realities and responsibilities of existence in a world of strangers.

But in parallel with dreaming of magic carpets flying to alluring far away destinations were much more immediate choices. The well-established ideal in normal times was to gain practical experience for a few years then go on to graduate study as preparation for a career in practice, education or both. So the prospect of seeking admission to graduate school seemed the most promising direction. It was another tough arena of competition not only because there were then only a small number of programs concentrated in the East but also because there were so few scholarships, fellowships and other sources of financial aid available. All the schools, Harvard, Yale, Princeton, Massachusetts Institute of Technology (MIT) and Columbia required applications to be made during the winter preceding the next academic year which meant hustling for information and support on top of other senior year pressures. The sense of building confidence in architectural design, seeking prizes and awards, mixed with anxieties, responsibilities and confidence too, as president of my fraternity, Psi Upsilon. Would all of life be like this, so loaded with both problems and opportunities happening all at once? Sorting all this out would not have been possible without the wisdom and encouragement of closest friends, family and mentors. I can't single out one more than others. Together they form a treasury that in time has yielded dividends far beyond anything I could then imagine. Your might say, "Of course, this could be expected, after all, these are timeless values." No doubt about that — all I'm doing now is to celebrate this blessing in life still more in terms of insights that relate to any calling, like architecture, in the thick of working with growth and change in the environment. Closest friends and peers have far more to do with one's learning, choice making and maturing than we usually acknowledge. This atmosphere of mutual learning grows and flourishes in the architecture studio more and more with each passing year.

Earlier on, Professor James Van Derpool, in architectural history had been most helpful to me in pondering the lessons of the Allerton Scholarship on shaping a career direction. He was the perfect embodiment of the gentleman architect/scholar, from Pride's Crossing, Massachusetts, the aristocratic

north shore of Boston. As a graduate of MIT he was especially eager in pointing out the Institute's value as a graduate school that emphasized both technology and design aesthetics as I began sending out applications in winter for the coming academic year to Harvard, Yale, Princeton and MIT It may have been from Prof. Van Derpool's strong support that news came from MIT in April 1936 of my acceptance into the graduate program there with a tuition fellowship and some additional financial aid, reassuring a surge of confidence for the remaining time until graduation and through what might possibly be a final summer at Neebish, should by some chance an upswing out of the depression might produce new job opportunities the following year. Aside from this new sense of direction for the immediate future memories blur of that summer interlude, except for the searing heat and humidity of Central Illinois as it made one appreciate still more the annual retreat to the bliss of Michigan's "water wonderland" once again. But for the last time?

I had received notice of admission to the other schools too but decided that MIT was the best fit to my vision of a future career involved in "hands-on," innovative design technology. Then, early in June another letter came from Yale offering a fellowship. Max Urbahn, a friend who had been at Illinois the year before and was now a graduate student at Yale called too urging me to change even though I had already sent my acceptance to MIT. My parents quickly

pointed out it would be unethical to do this (I'm sure it was frowned on in those days more than now). Naturally, ever since I've wondered how different life might have been if I had gone to Yale instead, but increasingly as time passed I became more and more sure MIT was the right choice.

Life now opened up in new perspective. The chain of summers, for example, now linked together as if there were no breaks between, the long winter months seeming to be another life apart, as if all the summers become one, in which life is speeding by faster than ever, almost surreal; summer romances, dreams and plans for the future made more fragile, transitory, no doubt intensified by the lingering uncertainty of economic recovery and the looming threat of war abroad, although this worry, insulated by the Atlantic, still seemed far away.

20 Schon, Donald, Ford Professor of Planning, MIT study of the architectural studio

Kwan Yin Wood Sculpture (watercolor)
Fne Arts Museum, Boston, Massachusetts

To arrive in Boston on the train from Chicago, sitting up all night, was hardly an inspiring threshold of a new life, especially for a still naïve small town Midwesterner arriving alone in the thick of a congested older city. I had thought that the Allerton adventure, only a little over a year earlier, would have eased the shock of sudden immersion among such a bustle of strangers preoccupied with their own destinations. I soon realized that dipping in and out of the city in our model A Ford the year before was no preparation for way-finding alone on foot, to find a place to stay and begin a kind of scary new life. Somehow going to a Ginger Rogers/Fred Astair movie that first night in the city smoothed everything out, as if one were choreographing a new dance, a new design for learning, not quite so random and left to chance.

Anxiety faded away the next day, reporting in to Maizie Hodge, Dean William Emerson's secretary-the soul of graciousness who knew just how to make one feel at home, get settled and guided through the intricacies of MIT registration. Looking back from today's elaborate academic bureaucracy, entering MIT then seems now to have been beautifully uncluttered, direct and welcoming. The sense of friendly welcome was reinforced still more by Dean and Mrs. Emerson, who invited the nine of us new graduate students to an informal gathering at their home on Brattle street in Cambridge, already well known as the home of Ralph Waldo Emerson, from whom Dean Emerson was a direct

descendant. I soon realized that among the nine of us I was the youngest, bringing back memories of entering Illinois, shy and inexperienced at the age of seventeen. Even now, four years later, notwithstanding added confidence bolstered by my B.S. Arch degree with highest honors and the AIA Medal, the same flash of sudden immersion came back, this time with even more force knowing I was now in one of the nation's top centers or academic and professional challenge.

Of the nine new graduate students, Harris Kemp, Eric Thrift and I were lucky to be invited by our professor, Lawrence Anderson, to sublet his apartment at 459 Beacon Street, since he had just been married and had moved to a town house nearby. The apartment was one large room with kitchenette and bath on the second floor of a typical Back Bay row house, an easy walk to MIT's architectural department, still in the Rogers Building on Boylston Street just off Copley Square. The rest of the Institute had moved across the Charles River into an immense new megastructure, magnificently dignified and grey in its sober, minimal Neo-Classical style. Later on, as we began to pick up an understanding of MIT's highly rigorous academic reputation in science and engineering, often whispered in the phrase "Tech is hell;" the no nonsense grey corridors and grey facades seemed an honest architectural fit.

The Rogers Building, on the other hand, was a rather monumental brown edifice freestanding on its own block, palatial and imposing, concealing a variety of spaces within, accommodating studios, offices and classrooms, which despite the somewhat rigid hierarchy of class years, from first year to graduate studio, still reflected the same informal atmosphere of architectural schools everywhere. Our small class of nine represented universities of Cincinnati, Manitoba, Illinois, Carnegie Tech as well as three from MIT's undergraduate program. Harvard, Yale, Princeton and Columbia all had a similar spread of students coming from other parts of the country as well as a few from abroad. We simply took it for granted that the advantage of this diversity was a characteristic of American graduate schools in contrast to the dominance in Europe of the Ecole des Beaux Arts in Paris.

Ironically, it was the world dominance of the Ecole in the nineteenth century and well into the twentieth that tended to counteract the eagerness of new nations like America to find their own architectural identity. I suppose it always has been arguable which destiny for human civilization is ideal –that of a one–world united culture or a richly variable set of ethnicities, regions, political and spiritual beliefs. Such a concept of polarities has obvious impact on architectural philosophy – one we were just beginning to cope with in the depths of the depression. Our rather provincial notions of this larger significance as we had perceived it at Illinois and other schools now had the great advantage of comparing and arguing a sense of direction, thrown together as we were in

the MIT and Harvard matrix of intellectual concentration; made more astringent by a sense of rivalry to the New York vicinity schools, Yale, Princeton, Columbia, as if they could ever be thought of as rising above their own sibling rivalries. In those days, graduate school contrasted with most undergraduate curricula by concentrating full time in the studio instead of simultaneously dividing time in several other courses. Any additional electives were for minor credit by special arrangement with a chosen professor at either MIT or Harvard. Eager to make up for the gap in the study of architectural history in Asia, I was able to persuade Professor Seaver, an esteemed oriental art historian to coach me in the independent study of Chinese and Japanese architecture, in particular, historic and vernacular examples that embodied structural clarity, use of light and seamlessness with landscape.

At Dean Emerson's initiative and with his financial support we were lucky along with undergraduates to have time with Sam Chamberlain, a fabulous artist and photographer, on Saturday mornings sketching, working with dry point, etching and lithography. Sam's engaging sense of humor possibly emerging from his slight speech impediment, would often lead to his telling hilarious stories of wine tasting at foire gastronomique (gastronomic fairs) in France after World War I in which he had been a combat artist. John Lyon Reed, later a well known San Francisco architect, gave us instruction in the elegance of line drawing, as time on Saturday would permit. So all day every day in the studio was a new experience, a foretaste of future life in practice yet freer for informal dialogue, digressions or individual escape to the library or elsewhere when one's attention span at the desk wore thin.

Studio projects reflected the fascinating threshold of change between lingering Beaux Arts romanticism and the new aesthetic of functional austerity generating in the depression along with an awakening of stricter social and economic relevance. I remember a BAID competition project to design a cabaret on an ocean liner immediately followed by a program to design a market place in a low income Boston neighborhood. Some of the same serious, grey, soft-spoken atmosphere of the main MIT campus across the Charles River in Cambridge persisted in the Rogers building too, notably in the undergraduate studios. Since most of us in the graduate class came from the more exuberant hinterland, this whispering environment was a kind of cultural shock. Our young, much-loved critic Lawrence "Andy" Anderson who had just returned from several years in France after winning the Paris Prize, although coming from Minnesota originally, was himself a perfect exemplar of this quiet, gentle, serious, whispering MIT aura. Even years later when I would occasionally return for a visit with Andy and the school, which had long since moved into new quarters in Cambridge, I would encounter again this un-

changing low key, almost reverent spirit of place, as if somewhere in the precinct dwelt a lord of scholarly science and technology in whose presence you dare not raise your voice.

Some hint of recovery from the depression began to be felt in the winter of 1936-37, though hardly noticeable in private building construction or in a conspicuous rise in employment, although some of the New Deal programs of relief in housing, reforestation and new public infrastructure were more and more visible. We would hear rumors of a few new jobs in architectural offices in Chicago and other western cities but not much evidence of any revival in the East. At least there was a ray of hope that hadn't existed before. If you can find anything good coming out of adversity, a new recognition emerged of how important the architect's role in society had become in finding new solutions to unmet environmental needs made evermore critical with each additional year of economic and cultural deprivation.

It took a while for this recognition to show up in studio design projects, such as non-spectacular, functional, design opportunities in dwelling design, solar orientation, material efficiency, and the design of objects and interior ensembles, strongly influenced by the "humanizing" of modern architecture as it was developing in the Nordic countries. Aalto and Bryggman in Finland, Apslund, Tengbohm and Markellius in Sweden were now becoming known as exemplifying the

new direction beyond the more severe mechanistic character of work by Corbusier followers and the Bauhaus. Humanism was now revealing itself anew as essential in the timeless/timely panorama of designs for learning.

As the new year began, returning from holiday vacations, a sense of excitement grew as the time of entering national competitions approached. It was already clear that getting ahead, especially now that jobs were still scarce, was to win one of the architectural travel/study competitions: the Paris and Rome prizes (national), the Rotch (Boston Area), Plym (Illinois) and a few others. Most of these were organized in two stages: a preliminary, short sketch problem design exercise of a few days. A jury then would select six or eight finalists, for a longer project program of a month or more duration, from which the jury would pick a winner, sometimes an alternate as well. The prize for all of these was for a year or more of travel and study in Europe with some restrictions; the Paris Prize at the Ecole in Paris and the Rome Prize based at the American Academy in Rome. The others were more open for travel, depending on the study objectives of the winner.

In contrast to today, with our students now making oral/graphic presentations open to all, juries in those days were closed, with a following critique. At MIT Dean Emerson presided in reviewing the jury's comments, with projects arranged in the jury's rank order for the first five or six; the remaining number were diplomatically not ranked. The Dean's elegant, gracious critiques were memorable, adding great dignity and worth to each student's work by always pointing out a project's strengths first before criticizing its weaknesses. On one of the first juries, early in the year, I couldn't believe that my project, a neighborhood shopping place ended up number one; Dean Emerson using it to emphasize the importance of landscape in public places. Later, in designing a new city library, most of us had struggled for efficiency in circulation, security and control. The jury placed my roommate, Harris Kemp's project at the top; in his plan, a visitor was led indirectly through a beautiful courtyard to reach the circulation desk, the Dean explaining that efficiency is not always the top priority–that a library is after all a treasury of knowledge, a setting for quiet study and contemplation, in which some enjoyable wandering may be desirable.

With the gradual opening up of jury reviews after World War II, a highly contrasting style of critique developed, particularly in the East, a kind of withering, intimidating attack on the students' projects, in which the sharp-tongued reviewers seemed more interested in verbal duels among themselves and matching wits. In 1963 I was invited by Serge Chermayeff to be on a three day jury at Yale. Naïve and unprepared for this new form of jury dynamics, I think I was more in a state of shock than most of the students who seemed to take it nonchalantly in stride. Later I began to ponder whether this adversarial jury attitude might have its roots in British semantic philosophy; the idea that debate, taking sides, is a stronger, learning stimulus than constructive criticism. Adding to this the attraction of French irony and cleverness, don't you have another example of mother country influence on the colonial elite: the Ivy League, perhaps Yale most of all? I say Yale most of all, because of the university's long-standing intellectual, articulate, witty eminence, particularly in literature from the time of William Lyon Phelps to Harold Bloom and others. A marvel of this aura has been its power to influence all collegiate disciplines including architecture. As a university ideal who could ask for more? Yet I still worry that some Yaleie architects I've known, in Chicago of all places, sometime seem to place cleverness in design above everything else.

Another aspect of closed vs. open juries also looms up: Closed juries, then as now, greatly influence students and practitioners alike to make eye-catching graphic presentations since they weren't there to defend their projects in person. Skillful renderings were in vogue as well as the emphasis on big, dramatic concepts—all of this continuing the powerful influence of the Ecole in Paris and its colony the BAID in New York. Eventually this preoccupation with graphic presentation built up to its condemnation as "paper architecture." Unfairly, I think, because in most cases the quality of underlying design was usually excellent too. For a long time now, the prevalence of open, oral presentations has swung the pendulum the opposite way, engendering the label "talkitecture." Somewhere in between let's hope we find equilibrium in balancing the best of both.

The long winter in Boston/Cambridge was most intensely felt when we had to walk once in a while across the Massachusetts Avenue Bridge against a bitter cold wind to the main MIT campus. Yet the dark and cold days brought us all closer together working in studio and in endless dialogue mostly centered on our awareness of flux in both architectural practice and education. The news that Walter Gropius was coming to Harvard again focused our discussion on foreign influence, this time away from the long-standing dominance of French master critics from the Ecole in Paris. Jacques Carlu had just left MIT a year or so before.

This was not to question the positive aspects of architectural influences and learning from national centers of cultural advance on their colonies when each source of influence was organically healthy and truly modern in its own time. But with the advent of stylistic revivalism in the nineteenth century, cycling and continuing today, one can wonder if this one-way influence is wholesome for new cultures, including colonies, seeking their own identity.

Why had all this happened? The larger question of our continuing addiction to foreign influence is of course the province of cultural critics and historians, but certain traces observable in North American architectural education, even more than in practice, were most evident. Nineteenth century revivalism was influenced in education by those few Americans who had studied at the Ecole in Paris. Then in the early twentieth, a series of French prima donna critics brought the word: Carlu at MIT, Haffner at Harvard, Grapan at Carnegie, Cret at Penn, Arnaud at Minnesota and Labatut at Princeton. Along with the depression, and World War II came the wave of Corbusier disciples, and Bauhaus leaders themselves; Mies van der Rohe, Gropius, Breuer and others like Chermayeff who were eagerly welcomed for leadership in American schools, their influence lasting well into the late century. Later the advent of "talkitecture" paralleled a preference for British heads and deans, almost as much in the U.S. as in Canada, Australia and New Zealand.

While we were still at Illinois, Harris Kemp and I had been in the thick of Scarab fraternity's effort in republishing Louis Sullivan's "Kindergarten Chats," but strangely not much of Sullivan's and Wright's urging for truly American architecture rubbed off in the face of our continued belief that leadership in architectural direction was still coming from

abroad, most recently from Sweden and Finland. Our esteemed head critic at Illinois, Arthur Deam, although most jovially American, especially in stimulating fresh thinking and innovation, reflected the aura of prestige gained by study in Europe. He himself had been a Fellow at the American Academy in Rome some years before. At MII our critic Andy, as winner of the Paris Prize, embodied the same aura gained by study abroad, yet constantly urged us to balance all influences, reinforcing still more how exceptional this particular time was in finding a new, inspiring direction for architecture.

It was in this challenging mood of way-finding that we approached each new design program, especially the annual national competitions, as they were scheduled in late winter. After the Rome Prize preliminary was judged, word came that I would represent MIT in the final competition. The strict rules required that each competitor work "en loge" (alone in a separate studio), without criticism, although fellow students could look in as long as they didn't actually work on your drawings, as was often done on other projects as deadlines came close.

The program subject for this year's Rome Prize was to design a city art museum on a sloping shore overlooking a large lake. The site description seemed identical to the Cleveland Museum of Art on Lake Erie, which I had visited almost two years before on the Allerton trip. The requirements for galleries and other usual museum spaces also ap-

peared to be the same. From this memory, the image of a typical symmetrical neoclassical facade like the Metropolitan in New York and the Art Institute in Chicago loomed up vividly. Would this be what the jury would expect or was now the time to gamble on a fresh idea? As many concept sketches developed, a scheme taking advantage of the slope in a series of terraces down to the lake began to take hold that resulted in a much lower profile of walls and landscape than the usual monumental edifice. This was so tempting to refine and develop but would it be too "modern" for the jury? I guess I was egged on by my fellow students to stay with it as the final presentation on a single sheet of 40" x 60" stretched Whatman's paper took shape. Max Urban and Harry Weese were up visiting from Yale (I never knew if they were spies or not). I.M. Pei and Bill Hartman came in from the fifth year, I.M. insisting on grinding some of his high quality Chinese ink and Bill in loaning me a fine set of ruling pens. Rendering was still most important, building up washes of ink for gradations of light to dark in plan, section and elevation, seeking a strong, pictorial composition.

After some weeks news came that the jury had selected the Yale finalist's presentation as the winner. I heard from Max that the winner's solution, though eclectic in design was praised for its meticulous working out of galleries for special collections. I don't think at the time the Rome Prize jury selected an alternate although I had a congratulatory letter from them urging me to compete as a finalist again the next year. Almost overlapping with the Rome Prize final was the Plym Travelling Fellowship competition open to University of Illinois graduates. Harris Kemp and I were both finalists, also another four week project. The subject was to design a public park on one city block, also on a sloping site. Maybe because I was still infatuated by Asian design, I assumed the site was in San Francisco, therefore an exotic mix of landscape, cascading water, gateways and stone lanterns would be appropriate. Harris chose a more informal Prairie School theme, much like his courtyard scheme for the earlier city library project. The Plym jury awarded him the fellowship and I was named alternate, again invited to try again.

Somehow this news was not discouraging at age twenty two. It seemed such an honor just to have had the chance. The spring by then was at its peak and lots of other exciting things were going on. On May 7, 1937, the airship Hindenburg passed overhead at noon not more than a thousand feet above the Rogers building, its name and Nazi swastika symbols clearly visible, on its way to Lakehurst, New Jersey. That evening I double dated with my sister-in-law's brother Ed Bilby who was in Harvard's Business School and his girl friend Eleanor Steber, a singer, later a Met star finishing her musical studies at the New England Conservatory. Together with a friend of hers we went to dinner then on to a Gilbert & Sullivan production in a theater just off the Boston Common. As we

came up to the theatre, newspaper extras were being shouted out that the Hindenburg had crashed at Lakehurst. This tragedy reminded me of a year or so before when the elegant modern design of the Hindenburg had been featured in the German architecture magazine Moderne Bauformen, a much respected journal that had been publishing leading contemporary work of Gropius, Mies Van Der Rohe, the Dutch De Stihl movement and others., until about 1934 when the heavy censoring hand of Hitler came down requiring that nothing be published but the Nazi version of Neo Classicism. Apparently the editors knew even then and took sly pleasure that the Hindenburg, reflecting the best of modern design, could be published in detail without fear of getting in trouble.

Also in May 1937 the American Institute of Architects national convention was held in Boston at the Sommerset Hotel, not far from the Rogers building. By this time the pressure of project deadlines had tapered off so we were encouraged to attend whatever meetings and events were of high interest, especially those that pointed to opportunities in the immediate future. The most memorable occasion was a dinner at which Walter Gropius was introduced. He had just arrived from Germany to be on Harvard's faculty and spoke in such a heavy accent that it was difficult to get his message. Yet there was no mistake that his tone was optimistic in calling for a new urgency in facing complications arising from the depression through closer collaboration of the design

professions, a theme that he was to foster vigorously in the post war years.

It had been traditional that the Association of Collegiate Schools of Architecture (ACSA) annual convention would take place along with that of the AIA with a close interlocking of themes, events and speakers. Because of Gropius arrival and his willingness to meet informally with ACSA delegates, some of us as students at Harvard and MIT shared in the discussions too. I think then, for the first time, it dawned on me that architectural education could be a most fulfilling career, ideally along with practice, especially as it would have to respond to the exciting new imperatives of change from a century or more of revivalism, and foreign domination. It wasn't until much later that we fully realized how much Gropius' pleas for teamwork coming from a European master, was really a reaffirmation of an American innovation, e.g. the Chicago School, more strongly emphasized than from any of our own well known architects and educators. Thirty one years later, in 1968, the University of Illinois, during its centennial celebration awarded Gropius an honorary doctorate. I had the privilege of being his guide through our "Century for Design" exhibition at the Krannert Museum featuring the work of our Collaborative Design Studio. These were team projects in urban design involving graduate students in architecture, urban planning, landscape architecture and graphic design. Gropius was engrossed and fascinated exclaiming "This is what I always hoped for at Harvard but never succeeded," lingering and questioning students far longer than the scheduled time allowed.

Among the many leading academic and research centers in Boston/Cambridge was MIT's school of naval architecture. It must have been in the back of my head since childhood to somehow get involved in designing and building boats, possibly as a career, or at least as a hobby. So the marvelous intricacy of ship models of many types and sizes along with highly detailed drawings as they were displayed in the halls made an alluring detour whenever I was on an errand to the main MIT campus. It was just too daunting, though, to imagine another few years of study and changing course, but still the enticement remained—would there ever be a way to do both, would the design professions ever evolve to the point where they are more unified instead of increasingly apart and specialized? It occurred to me that yacht design might be a less exhaustive path or study and experience than the full program of marine engineering required for the design of large vessels. But in the midst of the depression this thought was obviously in some other dream world; even the rich were not building yachts. Even if they were, didn't this kind of career now seem irresponsible in the face of newly recognized unmet social needs? Still, the allure of Nat Herreshoff's exquisite, precise drawings of sailboats coupled with the extraordinary craftsmanship of building them that drew on both the best of timeless experience and

timely high technology remained a powerful magnet for future involvement. Isn't there after all an ethical justification for this kind of highly demanding design and orchestration practice as a kind of laboratory that will eventually benefit the quality of life for all?

No doubt this lingering fascination led to my choice of design thesis subject—to design a marina for the upper Great Lakes, to be located in the heart of the St. Mary's River archipelago. MIT's M.Arch degree required the completion of a design thesis off campus after the full academic year ended. There was no deadline but it was expected that in a year or two you could fit it in a work schedule and bring the drawings in for presentation to a jury, to be individually arranged. So all of us in the graduate program began thinking about what subject to choose for the thesis as the end of our time in Boston approached. There was no pressure or requirement to get a subject approved, even though it was in the air that it would best address some current problem or opportunity of community significance. I rationalized that after all small craft in the upper lakes had few harbors of refuge, an unmet need known from my childhood, hearing of loss of life in storms, tales of distress told by our Coast Guard sailors based on Neebish Island. This choice might also have been a scheme to justify finding a site close to the Neebish colony so I could look forward to one more summer working on the thesis in that paradise before the real world's demands closed in.

Departure from MIT, the Boston/Cambridge culture, loaded with fresh memories of intriguing places, events and of new friends who perhaps I'd never see again, was another replay of the mix between nostalgia and new expectations, another of life's cycles, of designs for learning. Little did we realize then that the future would hold such advances in air travel and telecommunications that would change completely our sense of scale that only once in a blue moon could we ever afford to return to more distant places and experiences in our lives. This feeling was eased partially by knowing that my closest friends in the graduate class, Gene Mackey and Harris Kemp would also return to the Midwest; we made vows to get together somehow.

Maybe in some strange way I wanted to exaggerate this sense of distance by interrupting the train trip home at Buffalo to board the D & C stern-wheeler across Lake Erie to Detroit, there to call at the office of Sparkman-Stevens, naval architects to see if there might be a job after all in boat design in the Great Lakes area. I thought perhaps MIT's prestige and the fact that at the end of the graduate year I had been awarded the MIT School Medal, though in architecture, might by chance make the bridge I dreamed about between the two professions. The office was open with only one member of the firm present; in the background, an empty drafting room. I was most cordially received but it was obvious there was no work, so after exchanging some hopeful if wistful prospects for the future, I caught the next train for Chicago and home.

That summer of 1937 remains a blur, clouded by uncertainties of the time, strangely symbolized by dust storms marking the third year of drought in the great plains, prompting the earliest possible retreat from Illinois heat to the "water wonderland" of Neebish. I can't say this was all conducive of diligent work on the thesis, gathering program information by interviews and trying to visit the few prototype marinas that were then few and far between. Still, my father was an eager partner, always curious about waterfronts and from his own experience in boat building, dock building and boating in the islands, was the best source of practical advice I could find. The Coast Guard base at Sault Ste Marie was also most helpful. As I have already described, the Coast Guard manned several lookout stations in the St. Lawrence Seaway, one nearby at Johnston Point on Neebish Island, not more than one hundred yards from our cottage. The guardsman on duty would telephone (the only one on the island) the locks at the Sault of all approaching vessels, giving their name and draft two hours ahead of their arrival at the locks. It was from this lookout station telephone that word came that would change my life for the next few years. This Coast Guard telephone, being the only direct link to the outside world through the switchboard center in the Sault, could sometimes be used by islanders for emergencies and important long distant calls. One day in August Ralph Slocum, our

favorite, veteran Coast Guardsman came out on the bridge of the lookout station with his megaphone (before the coming of electronic loud hailers) calling for me to come over for a message, to return a call from Professor Phil Wilber at Oklahoma A. & M College in Stillwater. I was doubly amazed, how would anyone I didn't know be able to find me at remote Neeebish Island and what possibly could be the connection to a place I knew so little about.

Once I reached Professor Wilber, head of the architectural department at A & M, he told me I had been recommended by Harry Harmon, one of my critics at Illinois, as a candidate for a position on their faculty and, if I was interested, would I please send my resumé. Returning to the cottage I must have revealed my puzzlement and surprise at an opportunity I had never imagined. My father, being an academic himself, I'm sure smiling inwardly, calmly reminded me it was a job after all and wouldn't it be a good situation to finish my thesis, saying go ahead and send your transcript and whatever other resumé materials you have here and see what happens. Perhaps because in the back of my mind I was still imagining a future in practice, days went by without as much eager anticipation as I should have had for what might come from this new unexpected direction. Soon, Ralph called me again for a message, this time it was Professor Wilber's offer of an instructorship at a salary of $1,700 per year. Would I say yes and could I report for work in two weeks? With prompt-

ing from family and friends I agreed, full of mounting curiosity and even elaborate preconceptions of what this new cycle of life and learning might mean.

Passage

Islands in the Academic Grove IV
Oklahoma A & M College
(later known as Oklahoma State University)

Somewhere "across the wide Missouri" I knew lay the state of Oklahoma. Even though as children we were proud of our geographic skills, Oklahoma like Kansas and Nebraska remained a vast featureless stretch of the Great Plains, now the bleak heart of the Dust Bowl. Would there be Indians like the Ojibways I was so fond of at Neebish? Would there still be cowboys riding the range? Would the people be friendly or "show me" frontiersmen, expecting all new-comers to "earn their spurs" all over again, no matter what their advance billing?

These thoughts were much on my mind as I rode the rails again, to St. Louis and on to Tulsa. Waiting several hours in St. Louis, I walked in the station district, then a maze of beer saloons and brothels, bustling even in the open day. It seemed I was walking a new kind of gauntlet—long before Saarinen's arch was built, was this the "Gateway to the West?" As if this wasn't enough I had another shock, to be propositioned in the station's mens' room.

Arriving overnight at Tulsa, I was much relieved to be entering such a clean new city, in spite of dust in the sky. This impression was short lived, though, as I rode the bus two hours to Stillwater. Entering each desolate town on the way, with no sign to tell its name, each one red with dust and debris, dying trees and parched grass no longer green, I kept wondering, is this one Stillwater? This memory was so vivid even fifty years later when I returned for a visit

driving from Tulsa along the same track. In extreme contrast the same countryside and towns were unbelievably verdant, prosperous and welcoming. Fortunately, even back then, Stillwater was not quite so bleak as its neighbors. The bus arrived about noon and I checked in to the Grand Hotel on Main Street, at the rate of $1 a night, until I could find a place to stay. It was only about a five block walk to the campus, so despite the 100° heat, I put on my only suit and tie to report for work. Sidewalks were crowded with students in shirt sleeves all saying "hello." What's going on? Were their smiles and gestures making fun or was I now really entering a new friendly world, so different from the East?

Finally reaching the top floor of Gunder-son Hall, the location of the department of architecture, I was immediately greeted with another big hello and command to take off my coat and tie. All my shadows of doubt suddenly vanished, almost as if I had found my way into a new Land of Oz.

Earlier on, seeing life's flow as an architecture of cycles—short/long, major/minor, now spotlights the thresholds that link them, as their structural joints in time, as their mirror reflecting both ways; the look back a collage of past realities, images, shifting, telescoping and reforming in new hierarchies of meaning, the look ahead mostly obscure but sometimes in sparkling clarity, like dreams. It will be most tempting to keep taking this mirror apart. Between its two faces, are new dimensions of time and space revealed? New insights and wisdom distilled?

Of all the thresholds in everyone's life, the one between cycles of formal education and earning a living in the real world gains importance, nostalgia and deeper meaning as the mirror reflects more and more time over the mid-span of life, especially when this threshold marks a reversal of roles—the student suddenly is the teacher. But this threshold is not so abrupt after all if you think of teaching as never-ending mutual learning, especially when you're starting out at the same age as your students, even younger than some.

Time distance in the mirror also unveils another stroke of luck—beginning an educational career in a very small school of architecture, like a one room country school. Right away I was assigned as a critic to three levels of design studio, two freehand drawing studios and lectures in architectural history. Somehow, as well, our remoteness in the grassland plains, far from urban

sophistication, greatly fostered concentration without distraction on architecture as the love of our life. Social life, too, was a throwback, a deja vu, to childhood and adolescence in a small town, with its social diversity; an across the board spectrum of ages, life styles, rich and poor. My closest friendships seemed quite naturally to form among young and older faculty in many other disciplines, most in music, art, language and literature, and with the students too, friendships grew that were to last a lifetime. A weekend could include formal faculty receptions, a date to a dance with a sorority girl friend, drinking beer with the guys at Dutch Bishop's, a favorite hangout in the south end of town, or attending an Indian pow-wow, that Doel Reed took me to, on the bank of the Cimmaron.

The collage of those times blends and telescopes memories of students winning top awards in BAID projects, Gibby Williams, Tallie Maule, Eason Leonard all scoring high, Gibby later founding the school at the University of Arkansas, the teacher of Fay Jones, Tallie later chief architect of BART in San Francisco, Eason later I.M. Pei's managing partner; of fellow faculty and mentors Ray Means and Jack Lothers, Ray my office mate teaching construction, Jack, a structural genius who designed the trylon and perisphere of the 1939 New York Fair, Rex Cunningham and Don Hamilton, both Carnegie Tech graduates, Rex a smiling, dour, gentle, exquisitely talented fellow studio critic, Don, our strongest Francophile, spurring com-

Egypt, Sketch, 1975
Bill Caudill, FAIA, AIA Gold Medal

petition, Phil Wilber our congenial head also university architect, this office just across the hall; of his associates there Dwight Stevens, Chap Bills and Bill Caudill; Bill, just graduated the year before, becoming my close friend, claiming I was responsible for his going to MIT the next year, later famous as head of CRS in Houston and winner of an AIA Gold Medal; of friends across the campus Dan Huffman, Dick Richards, Yvonne Tait and Gladys Dunkleberger in music, Dick Bailey in French, Doel Reed and Eleanor Buxton in art, Bess Allen in administration, Margaret Maynor in dance, Frances Willison in biology, of many more whose names have slipped away; of our usually impromptu parties at somebody's house or apartment, the most memorable a pot-luck on Pearl Harbor Day, 1941, at Dan Huffman's, building pyramids and passing out one by one as if this was the last hurrah—when we took one of the girls home she pleaded "put a little perfume on my pillow;" of my young landlords, investing in new oil wells and making a killing; of my wonderful first clients Gus and Georgia Bieberdorf, whose house, built of used brick in Prairie Style was published in Architectural Forum; of having been finalist again in the Rome Prize and Plym Competition again without winning; of going up to Winfield Kansas to be former MIT classmate Gene Mackey's best man at his wedding—Gene then on the faculty of Kansas State at Manhattan, later with Joe Murphy, head of his own firm in St. Louis, doing outstanding work for many years; of saving enough money to go to Paris the next summer, 1938, first driving to Montreal, leaving my car with cousins, sailing third class on the Empress of Australia, learning to sneak up to first class for socializing due to the shortage of young men as dancing partners, learning to do the Lambeth Walk, disembarking at Cherbourg, instead of getting on the boat train directly to Paris, finding my way across acres of railroad yards to Cherbourg town, finding the station, assaulted by sudden strange new impressions of a much older culture, strange new scale, strange new sounds and smells, using my limited French to buy a ticket to Mont St. Michel, a destination enshrined in my memory by Henry Adam's book, Mont St. Michel and Chartres, that had come with the AIA Medal at Illinois, of reaching Paris by way of the Loire Valley, of staying at Signor Cassarini's tiny Hotel de la Grille just off the Rue Bonepart in the Left Bank for sixty five cents a night, of six glorious weeks in the city with new friends, one a Canadian architectural student at the Ecole des Beaux Arts whose project I charretted on at the Atlier Debat-Ponson, of ending up crossing the channel to London for a final few days, almost penniless, sailing back to Quebec and Montreal, then to Neebish in August; of return to Stillwater for another year, the world now vibrant with new threats of war that still, despite Hitler's rantings on short wave radio, seemed far away.

Other insights flash back from those pre-World War II days that then seemed isolated events unrelated to the larger picture of learning how "reflection in action" works in validating timeless canons of design. Early on, as a critic, I was accused by one of the older, self assured students of "being un-democratic" spending more time with some students than others. This was a shock, so much so that I asked my office mate Ray Means for help. In his genial Kansas accent he said, "Not to worry, I'll bet you're just responding most to those who've done more work—go back and see if that isn't what's happening." Gaining courage, I went back in the studio, found out quickly that Ray was right, called over my accuser, looked him in the eye and said, "Thanks a lot for calling this to my attention. Look, what's more democratic than working most with those who work the most—get to work!" It was a lesson luckily learned early, verified many times later—lazy students want to be spoon fed, seldom change in later life and if they happen to become practicing architects, are only interested in the easy way, making money, getting by with mediocre or worse work that is somehow sadly tolerated in our culture. Many years later, my accuser did just that—building cheap, fast track shopping malls. Of course, this is an obvious learning lesson. What may not be so obvious is the inverse—that there are no short cuts in achieving excellence, requiring countless hours in discovering what a project wants to be in its own right, a theme with many variations, already introduced as a design principle, always more and more rewarding when it is encountered.

"Reflection in action," the studio experience of propose, dispose, comparing schematic possibilities in the dynamic of student/critic dialogue and action, testing design alternatives on the spot with "bum wad" tracing paper and cardboard models was in those days direct and unencumbered by spin. A scheme looked good or it didn't, based on what was down on paper, not through words alone. It was soon understood that you'd get a "crit" if you really had something to show, just talking about it was a waste of time unless there was some kind of psychological block that needed working out. Little did we anticipate then how the rising fashion of smart talk after World War II would open up new ways to dodge making decisions—we were blissfully naïve and eager, both student and critic, to get right into whatever the project was all about. Drawing was our language, give and take.

By now I was beginning to pick up some hints about what kind of criticism works best, almost by "seat of the pants" intuition, since at that time there was no formal set of courses you could take to learn the art as an academic discipline. It was learn as you go, an apprenticeship of trial and error and observing how your more experienced colleagues handled the process. The first of these hints, later looming up as most important, was to try to understand the student's grasp of the design problem as expressed in sketches, models or more precise drawings in comparison to how you, as critic, from your own experience would interpret the problem, expressed in the same graphic language. This give and take, take and give, at the heart of the critical process seemed from the very beginning to point the way in building critical judgment over the years, in which the critic's talent, growing experience, dedication and patience are all essential. It was also becoming clear that what was simultaneously happening was a building up of ability in self criticism on the part of both student and critic. As so many others already have, I was to learn that all kinds of other skills would develop around this center pole of interaction as well, such as virtuosity in the use of visual and other digital aids.

Extending the thought of how criticism and self criticism works, learning from observing and evaluating the best built examples we know, past and present, local or distant, took on new meaning—a switch from the casual, passive regard of laymen, even of scholars to a level of direct action. What can I now eke out from closer examination that will act as an exemplar to my current project that is not copy cat, not stylistic, but at a deeper level of influence? This amounts to the discovery that mutual learning with your critic in studio is inseparably linked with on-going, self-propelled learning from inspiring work anytime, any where. Indeed, this aspect of learning from emulation is most often a key part of the studio give and take dialogue. "What did you get out of Saarinen's Yale hockey rink design, just published?" In fact, long ago the Ecole in Paris recognized the importance of this form of critical learning in establishing the "Concour d'Emulation," an annual design competition.

Of course the school in Stillwater, at that time, far away from urban centers of architectural excellence old and new, was at a disadvantage, having to rely on slides, magazines and books. Even now, with superb color photography, elegant graphic design and rhetoric, the media still can't take the place of being there. Truly great work, when visited in its reality is always more inspiring than the best efforts to replicate it. Curiously enough, sometimes coffee table books are now so glamorous that actually visiting a site is a let down revealing flaws that have been cropped out or masked by visual and rhetorical spin. Along with observation of how design fashions have come and gone over many, many years, the effect of media inflation and rhetorical hype on architectural education and practice versus direct site visits will continue to provoke increasing concern.

But the benefit of emulation has more modest scope aside from the influence of stars and their work. Referring again to the one room country school analogy, the presence of students at all levels in one studio at A & M had the built-in advantage of learning from talented more-advanced students often at the next drawing table—in contrast to much larger schools that segregated each level in separate studios, even on separate floors. This was about as close as you can get in school to traditional, time tested learning from more experienced peers. Years later, schools discovered the "vertical studio," as if it had never existed before.

Emulation at a more personal level was at work too, each of us beginning to be influenced most by one or more of the exciting, emerging directions in architecture away from imitative revivalism. Perhaps most interesting of all, in retrospect, was the almost subconscious awareness, perhaps even a sense of guilt, that we already had a head start in seeking a new identity, a new direction for American architecture, for example, in the work of Wright and the Prairie School, the Chicago School, the work of Maybeck and the Green brothers out west. How loyal should we be to this quest for an American identity in the face of enticing "international style" propaganda from abroad aided and abetted by Hitchcock and Johnson and the power of eastern media? For myself, the work of Saarinen, Aalto and a few other Nordic architects was most appealing, reflecting a truer understanding of modernism in its effort to get beyond fashionable abstraction into sensitivity to spatial, structural, material, craft and humanistic livability factors that would celebrate excellence in diversity rather than a singular signature style. How could this influence find balance with the best we knew of our own indigenous American work, without copying either one?

In the winter of 1938/39 this emerging focus of interest in the architecture of Northern Europe led to figuring out how to get there soon in the future in spite of the growing threat of war. As if in direct response to this desire, an announcement came from the AIA in Washington of the new Edward Langley Fellowship with a stipend of $1,200 to be awarded to an applicant on the basis of a written proposal for travel and study at home or abroad for the coming academic year. As mentioned earlier, I had competed again as finalist for the Rome Prize and Plym Fellowship without success, so here was a new opportunity, by direct application rather than through another design competition. Even though the chance of winning seemed less encouraging because the competition would probably attract a lot more mature and highly qualified applicants, I decided to try anyway, writing a proposal to study the new work in Sweden and Finland, interviewing architects and clients, concentrating on landscape, interior design, furniture and other crafts as well as architecture as they all work together toward a more humanistic dimension in contemporary design. Little did I hope I could possibly win and had almost forgotten about my submission when several weeks later in April 1939, word came that my proposal had been selected as the winner. Greatly surprised and elated, I was sure that the letters from Professors Deam and Van Derpool at Illinois, Professor Anderson and Dean Emerson at MIT and my boss at Stillwater, Professor Phil Wilber must have had most to do with the award—I wrote to each of them thanking them for their support and promising to try my best to live up to their expectations.

This news meant that planning for the immediate future took on new dimensions of preparation, arranging a leave of absence

100. HOUSE IN STILLWATER, OKLA. A. RICHARD WILLIAMS, DESIGNER

OCTOBER 1939 THE ARCHITECTURAL FORUM 337

Bieberdorf Residence, Stillwater, Oaklahoma, 1939
A. Richard Williams
(Photograph: Gus Bieberdorf)

for the next year, careful budgeting, travel arrangements, most important of all doing homework on projects for study and making whatever contacts abroad would be possible ahead of time. It now loomed up, as well, that I must finish up my MIT design thesis, "A Marina for the Upper Great Lakes," so that I could present it in Cambridge on the way abroad during the summer.

Having to chart this alluring course ahead lent a certain added emotional dash to the remaining weeks in Stillwater, on a personal level with all my friends, as well as with the warm, buoyant studio atmosphere and the work of finishing up outside projects like the Bierberdorf residence. Although end of the semester rituals; juries, celebratory events and random informal gatherings were all now more familiar and warming after completing the second academic year, the coming heat of the summer was bearing down, spurring thoughts of the earliest possible getaway to the coolness of Michigan and finishing up the thesis drawings at Neebish.

The site chosen for the marina project, about a mile downstream at the north end of Lake Munuscong in the Seaway, had been a large sawmill with "slab docks," forming a wide shipwell that could easily be converted to finger piers for small vessels. The Corps of Engineers had dredged the main shipping channel just offshore, depositing the dredged material, mostly limestone bedrock and sand, closer in to shore forming small breakwall islands as a harbor of refuge. The

program for the marina included dockage, fuel and minor repair services and a small inn for fifty guests with expansion plans for growth when the depression ended. Access to the island from the mainland still had to be by water, although plans were already underway for a ferry crossing and road improvements on the island at the nearest point to Sault Ste Marie. The Ononegwud Inn, described earlier, was the prototype but too limited in its water frontage to expand: The "resort" label had not yet been widely used but the facilities for summer visitors, especially for fishing, would be much the same.

Many of our neighbors at Neebish shook their heads doubting that my fairly modest proposal would ever be feasible. I tried to explain that after all it was only a hypothetical thesis and wasn't it OK to dream about future possibilities? Little did we imagine then that fifty years later there would be great demand for a far larger port facility for recreational boating as well as for far better equipped harbors of refuge.

Compared to what students are expected to produce today for their design thesis, I remember how much less we did in those days, in quantity of drawings, maybe four or five 30" x 40" sheets plus a written report, although with no apology for design quality. In retrospect I do wish the design had been less imitative of the "international style" and more responsive to indigenous materials, regional north woods character and craft of detail. To have done the thesis right

after returning from abroad, most especially from Finland, the design would have been far more mature and sensitive to its Great Lakes region. In any case, the presentation at MIT later in the summer went well, but I felt a little restraint on the part of the jury, not in respect to the design, but rather in the choice of subject; as I remarked earlier, everyone else's thesis seemed to be focused on depression related unmet socioeconomic needs.

Early in August 1939, bidding farewell to family and friends at Neebish, I boarded the Canadian Pacific train from Sault St. Marie overnight to Montreal, where once again I was greeted by my cousins, booked passage on the Empress of Britain to Cherbourg and arranged a round trip flight to Boston to present the thesis to the MIT jury. In those days flying on a small twin-engine plane was relatively inexpensive, informal, almost as if it were just a sight seeing adventure. Since there were stops at Montpelier, Vermont and Manchester, New Hampshire, we flew at low altitude over New England's magnificent mountains and lakes to Logan Airport at the edge of Boston Harbor. I have a hazy memory of doing a lot of walking from bus stops to MIT in high humidity heat lugging my suitcase and roll of drawings.

Like the year before, a special boat train made the run from Montreal to Quebec City to board the ship. The six day crossing to Cherbourg was smooth, again full of shipboard partying, promenading and just

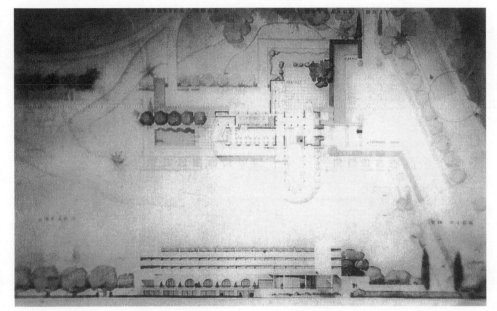

MIT design thesis, "A Marina for the Upper Great Lakes", 1939
A. Richard Williams

luxuriating in a deck chair gazing out to sea. Since most of my new friends aboard were Canadian, I found myself, as an American, in friendly opposition to getting involved in what seemed to be the coming war in Europe. By then Canada, as a loyal part of the Commonwealth was already at the alert while we, as "isolationists," were again reminding ourselves of the Revolutionary War and War of 1812 days of liberation from British domination.

Landing at Cherbourg this time, I took the boat train directly to Paris and familiar haunts on the Left Bank for a week or two including an excursion to the Zurich World's Fair, an exhilarating demonstration of contemporary design—pavilions, exhibits, furnishings, lighting and graphics. Late in the month I left Paris for Stockholm by way of a visit to architect Wilhelm Dudok in Hilversum, Holland, which was memorable not only as an extraordinary expression of welcome on his part but also as an all too rare example of how beneficial an architect's influence can be in the design and building of an entirely new city. Dudok was the first well-known architect I had ever met. Feelings of stage fright and hesitation melted away in response to his warmth and hospitality. He was quick to close in on my mid-American origin and Welsh ancestry as a connection to Frank Lloyd Wright. He pointed out a kind of special obligation we should feel in carrying on the heritage of the Prairie School and Chicago School and was politely insistent that his own work was parallel to Wright's rather than directly influenced. It was clear that he considered their combined efforts to be a most significant direction for the future. This conviction was powerfully reinforced by the reality of Hilversum itself as a new garden city demonstrating so many of the "organic" principles that Wright and Dudok espoused. In fact, I don't know of any architect in modern times who has so profoundly influenced the built form of the city in which he lived and worked. He was firm in his belief that cities should be "finished," establish a strong sense of edge and center, and that growth and change should be in terms of ever improving the quality of its fabric—an idea that of course has had long precedence in Europe. Dudok opened my eyes to a new dimension of architecture as urban design and "contextualism" (long before that term was invented). Most of all, he pointed out the importance of architecture as key in the creation of a truly humane environment. He, and Bakema later, personified the integrity, depth, and professional dimensions of humanism more than any other star architects I have known. Of course this is a quality of many lesser knowns and their clients quietly at work without fanfare.

In 1960, I visited Dudok again, along with my mother, who, as she often did on meeting someone new, established instant rapport; she and Dudok immediately engaged in a dialogue about how important it was to pay special attention to the careful integration of schools in residential neighborhoods in urban

gardens along with recreation, senior housing, libraries and hospitals. Since my mother had been president of the Illinois PTA and on the national board for many years, she was especially sensitive to the importance of enlightened city planning in advancing education as a most important cultural value.

This kind of dream for the future was of course in sharp contrast to the reality of threatening war. As I came out of the station in Cologne Germany, arriving by train from Amsterdam, the station square, a large open paved space was filled by a great circle of uniformed Hitler youth shouting slogans and singing rallying songs, forcing normal traffic to make its way outside the ring. After finding a small hotel, I began to explore the city, walking and riding street cars, the conductor of one looking exactly like Hitler—bar mustache, billed brown military hat, uplifted chin and stern expression. Soon I was seeing other Hitler doubles everywhere along with swastika banners, uniforms of all types in a pervading martial atmosphere. What a change from the carefree panache of France and the more sober serenity and quiet civility of Belgium and Holland! I had no feeling of anxiety, though, since as an American I could assume an attitude of neutrality. However, I was prompted not to linger long in Germany, moving on by way of Hamburg to Copenhagen for a day or two before crossing the straits to Sweden at Elsinor, beholding Hamlet's castle from the ferry. For a host of reasons Stockholm was such a magnet destination that I hardly paid close attention to

the countryside in the glow of late summer; its forests, lakes, fields of yellow mustard and red barns passing by in a magnificent seamless panorama. Suspense built up for the first glimpse of Stockholm's City Hall as it came into view on Lake Mäleren as the train crossed the old town of Skepsbron into the station.

With the help of the Swedish-American Foundation office I found accommodation at the Cosmopolite Pensionat at 15 Nybrogatan in the heart of the city, close to the drama theatre and Strandvägen waterfront. It was the last day of August. The Cosmopolite was a most congenial residential hotel or "pension" for about thirty guests, mostly single young professionals, run by Fru Shunneson, a most attractive, gracious, middle-aged woman who spoke excellent accented English. She had lived for several years in Evanston, Illinois. Since I was born there, we immediately developed a special rapport, like old friends.

Although the Cosmpolite was truly cosmopolitan in its residents from many different parts of Europe and the world, it was typically Swedish, such as in its ritual of beginning the evening at 6 pm with smörgäsbord in the main foyer, followed by dinner in an adjacent room, encouraging guests to get to know each other by changing tables each night. Well before 6 pm we would gather in the foyer around the long smörgäsbord table in casual conversation, listening to news on the radio. Exactly at 6 pm when a musical tone was struck, everybody instantly crowded around the smörgäsbord table to snatch up the choicest morsels like lobster canapés, herring and other delectable hors d'oeuvres that were in short supply amid the usual cold cuts, salads and relishes. You soon got the message to scan the table well ahead and position yourself strategically close to whatever was most desirable and then pounce.

By chance, the first night after the initial stand up smörgäsbord course I was seated at the first table and the first guest to be served, presented with a large dead fish on its side, looking like it had just come, un-cooked, from the sea. What to do? I stared at it in silence, others at the table politely waiting. There was a large spoon alongside which I picked up gingerly and tried to scoop through the side of the fish, everybody at the table smiling and nodding their heads in encouragement. It worked, the fish tenderly responding to the spoon. Smiles all around. Another one of many initiation rites yet to come.

Thanks to Fru Shunneson's introduction, I went with a few new Swedish friends to Skansen, a harborside park, celebrated as the scouting ground for Hollywood stars like Greta Garbo, for a picnic lunch on Sunday, September 2, 1939. The date was memora-ble because over the park's loudspeaker sys-tem came the news that Hitler had invaded Poland. The relaxed mood of picnickers and sunbathers changed suddenly, people gath-ered in worried groups and prepared to go home. What did this mean, not only for tra-ditionally neutral Sweden but also for those of us as foreigners? Was it the beginning of World War II? These were pervasive shadows of doubt all during the month of Septem-ber, intensified as both Britain and France declared war on Germany. After the end of the month and the Nazi invasion of Poland quieted down, there were few outward signs that much would change at least for a while. Still, shadows of concern underlay our thoughts, a vague uncertainty of unknowns. Could America stay out of the war? Dangers in the path of going home? Interruptions in careers and family life? For how long?

Since it looked as if Sweden could remain neutral, Stockholm became a haven for the few Americans on architectural fellowships in other parts of northern Europe. Among them were Jack Faron and "Geeks" Kidder-Smith from Princeton, Bill Hartman from MIT on the Rotch, Vic Gilbertson from Wash-ington U. on the Steadman and Tom Imbs from Illinois on the Plym. It looked as if the war, at least for a while, wouldn't seriously affect our quest for architectural directions: sketching, photography and interviews with leading practitioners such as Marke-lius, Asplund, Östberg, Tengbom and others. When I visited him, Östberg was living in an elegant apartment with a view of his major work, the Stockholm City Hall. The interior of the apartment, though spacious, was dense with memorabilia and furnishings—much of it in the Swedish Romantic National Style, which struck me as Byzantine and Venetian. In fact, I could imagine I was in a palace along a Grand Canal of the North.

Östberg, then in his seventies, radiated as-surance, contentment and amused toler-ance of young Swedish architects who were so eagerly following the influence of the Bauhaus and Le Corbusier. It was clear that he thought these trends would quickly fade and that Sweden would again assert its regional character, a true "architecture of the North," which I took to mean a return to a more severe, heavy masonry fabric, with concentrations of richness in openings, edges, and skylines. He stressed that there should be keener awareness of buildings to ground, to forest, to water edges, and to sky. It was also imperative that "archi-tecture of the North" would emphasize the contrast of seasons: summer living "away from buildings"—with greater concentration on the livability of interior space in winter. I had heard this same idea expressed by other leading architects, interior designers, and craftsmen as a long established Scandina-vian tradition, transcending stylistic change.

Asplund was reserved and somewhat in-scrutable, a quality no doubt intensified by illness. I visited him at his office and studio at the Institute of Technology after studying several of his buildings in Göthenberg and Stockholm. I was perplexed by this work. It seemed strangely arbitrary in spatial com-position and proportion. But I was strongly impressed by the incredible study and care he gave to details: entrances, stairs, handrails, drinking fountains, lighting fixtures, and other fixed furnishings. So what I remember best from our conversation was his discussion of the relation of care in detailing to the dignity of human life and the great respect one should have for the intelligence and emotions of everyone who will benefit from extra sensitivity in design at intimate personal scale.

These autumn days were radiant with color in both the cityscape and in the surrounding archipelago. In spite of the overcast of impending war it was easy to forget this enigmatic threat and to enjoy life as normal while it could last. I was especially lucky to have an introduction from Eleanor Buxton, my artist friend in Stillwater, to Karen Olson, a beautiful eighteen year old student, a younger Ingrid Bergman, who had been at the weaving school at Sätterglentan in the Lake District north of Stockholm the year before, when Eleanor had also been there. Karen lived with her widowed mother and two brothers, Per and Hasse in a modest but elegant apartment in a relatively new district around the famous Engelbrekskyrkan Church on a rise of ground just north of downtown. Karen and Per, her older brother now in uniform of the Swedish army, soon included me in their circle of friends for exploring the city and archipelago, going to small parties, dining and dancing at the Operakelleran and other well known hangouts. This kind of life soon involved my American and other

foreign friends too, which Per and Karen loved—it seemed a fortuitous opportunity to practice their excellent English and relish, if you can ever say that in wartime, the new international atmosphere of Stockholm. It was ironic that the most popular song, "Bel Ami," came from Nazi Germany.

We were trying to fast track learning Swedish too, not easy, and hardly necessary in a country by now almost bi-lingual. Anyway it gave us a stronger sense of connection and respect for Swedish tradition as well as for a closer appreciation for local modern design, particularly in crafts, interior design along with architecture. The mix of social life and more diligent studies as architectural pilgrims oddly came together playing touch football in recreational open space that was a part of the newly famous ten storey dwelling units "point houses" of Järdet, known for their airiness, orientation to the sun, open space landscape between and "model" interior design. We were always besieged by neighborhood youngsters to join in the football, and sometimes invited in for drinks and snacks.

The city of Stockholm was then, more than now I think, a most enjoyable, human scaled, walkable composite of old and new blending together, as Östberg had expressed it, a "city of the north" built on wooded granite islands that demanded every new intervention be carefully inserted in the older fabric, with its water edges and internal parks as well understood and accepted controls. Skylines

too, were most consciously regarded as city signature elements—the churches themselves and their towers on highest ground, the pinnacles of public buildings, and the dominant tower of the City Hall most of all, gave the city its profile in the sky, almost everywhere reflected in the waterscape—"Venice of the North."

No wonder, when after the war, a series of five identical high rises, taller than the "point houses" of Järdet were built in the heart of the old low rise downtown area, there was an outcry, but even in conservative, romantic, Stockholm, materialism and commercial domination was taking hold. The bliss of mixing social and professional life in such an enchanting city was not without its reminders of the threatening conflict nearby, not only from Nazi Germany but also from Soviet Russia, a longtime adversary of Sweden and Finland. Sometime in late September or early October a Soviet Navy vessel appeared in Stockholm harbor on a "friendly" visit, causing consternation among many of the citizens, among them Fru Shunneson of the Cosmopolite, who threw up her hands, exclaiming, "I think it's a Trojan horse!" Another day, when we few Americans were asked to come to our Embassy for a briefing, a large delegation of Polish Americans who had managed to escape Poland showed up demanding that the Embassy get a U. S. Navy battleship to take them home. Another reminder was the daily radio news broadcast just before smorgasbord time. It was a good test of how much Swedish we were picking up, even though there were many willing to translate for us as we all waited for the tone signal to attack the smorgasbord.

About that time, word got around that I would be celebrating my twenty fifth birthday on September twenty third and the Cosmpolite threw a party, asking Bill Hartman, Ben Irvin, Tom Imbs, Vic Gilbertson, and I, to invite our Swedish friends too. It was a special evening buffet well lubricated by aquavit and beer. Next morning I hardly felt in shape to face the next quarter century.

Bill Hartman and Ben Irvin had already been to Finland and Russia earlier in the month, briefing us on travel to Finland where I hoped to go soon before winter set in. Tom Imbs wanted to go too, so we went to the Finnish Embassy for visas but were turned down because of new threats of a possible Russian invasion. Only some journalists and certain key business people were allowed visas by then. Tom, who had been a graduate student at Yale the year before and had met Alvar Aalto when he came over as a visiting professor thought that we should call him in Helsinki for help. (Long distance calls then were cheap, about ten cents U.S.) Given added courage by aquavit we easily reached Aalto after dinner to see if he could intervene for our visas. It was easy to tell he too was feeling no pain, saying he would try, but we were sure he was in no shape to remember our call, so we almost forgot about it.

Meanwhile, several of us planned a weekend

trip up to the weaving school at Sätterglentan, which welcomed visitors overnight, sharing space with a dozen or so girl students. On the way five or six of us stopped at Gämla Uppsala (Old Uppsala) near the university city of Uppsala, an historic village that specialized in meade, a beer made with honey that you drank from oxhorns lined with silver. While having a sandwich lunch around a long table, the horn of meade was passed around—you were supposed to hear the sound of the sea as you drank. Needless to say the rest of the short train trip on to Insjön and Sätterglentan was blissful, adding gaiety to our welcome by the weavers. It turned out to be an Ingmar Bergman movie, playing "orientation" in the woods, and dancing in the studio. I thought I was coming down with a cold and the genial head of school gave me a shot of cognac. Soon everybody else was coughing and more medicinal cognac flowed. About then the telephone rang, a call from the Finnish Embassy in Stockholm, saying our visas were ready anytime we came in. I don't know how they traced us, it must have been that the Cosmopolite knew where we were, Tom and I must have left our names and address along with our visa applications. Anyway, this was a sign for another celebration, toasting Aalto; it must have been his intervention, after all, that did it.

A few days later we took the ferry to Helsinki staying at the Hotel Torni in the heart of downtown (then very affordable, unlike now). Thus began a most rewarding two-

day visit with the Aaltos, beginning with lunch in their newly completed restaurant atop the Savoy Hotel. Imagine two sturdy, very friendly people in their forties who seemed more like rugged outdoorsmen than white collar aesthetes. Their hospitality, warmth, and joy in both work and play set a tone that I now recognize as characteristically Finnish. What I remember best in discussion of their work and possible future trends centered on the design of the new Villa Mairea for the Gullichsen family. They were joking and self-deprecating in describing the process. "We had the budget and could use all the tricks." It became very clear as we saw more of their work at Sunila, Paimio, and a few days later when we were guests at the Villa Mairea itself, that making fun of themselves and their fondness for high-jinks was a cover for their love of people and the exuberance of working with the full palette of design: architecture, lighting, materials, furnishings, and all other details of the setting as a single work of art. This idea of ensemble harmony and orchestration skill to the level of art was just as evident in the worker housing at Sunila as it was in the Villa Mairea. I was excited to see such fulfillment of the same principle Asplund had introduced. Human dignity, identity, and well-being deserve, indeed require, that the designer strive to make every setting for life a work of art. The Aaltos seemed more successful than any architects I had known so far in responding to this principle.

Tom and I spent about ten days in and around Helsinki guided by an itinerary suggested by the Aaltos of their own work, including that of Saarinen, older traditional structures as well as new schools, housing and churches, all of which were outstanding in the skillful handling of limited materials; wood, masonry, copper, ceramics and fabrics. I would follow up this study of more recent works as years went by with visits back to Finland in 1954,1983 and 1998.

The most rewarding of all our stops on this first trip in early November 1939, was indeed our visit to the Villa Mairea, near the village of Noormarkku on the west coast, on our way back to Stockholm by way of the ferry from Turku, the principal western port. We were welcomed at the villa by Harry and Maire Gullichsen, the owners, who had been called by the Aaltos that we were coming. It was ten in the morning—we thought we would be lucky to be given a brief tour and would then head down to Turku by noon. Instead, they insisted we stay the whole day and evening to help celebrate Harry's birthday. He was already in uniform as a reserve officer and there was a feeling in the air that this might be the last chance for revelry before the expected invasion. In fact, news had just come that Passakivy and Tanner, the two Finnish diplomats, were returning from Moscow after failing to negotiate any agreement. Tom and I tried to insist that this was no time for us to stay, but no, they insisted we were, as Americans, a part of their family, symbolically representing our

country in their time of stress. A close tie to Finland had been established ever since we were generous with loans during World War I and so welcoming to Finnish immigrants long before and since. They took quiet pride too, I think, although it was not mentioned, that Finland was the only European country that had repaid its war debts to the U.S.

The visit started out with morning tea and Scotch in front of a blazing fire in the living/gallery area looking out to a snow covered courtyard with a pool and sauna on the opposite side. Beyond an open tread wood staircase leading to the upper floor bedrooms, the dining room, kitchen and service wing formed another side of the courtyard. A library in the main living space was partitioned off with hollow, moveable screens for storage and changing displays of modern painting. The use of delicately scaled wood in grilles and furniture, fabric and floor to ceiling glass played against solid stuccoed masonry framing indoor, outdoor transparency. Narrow, round structural columns picked up the rhythm of the closely spaced slender pine tree trunks in the woods outside. All of this, of course, is by now so well known in publications that further description seems hardly necessary, except to say that the reality of being there when the villa was in its first year made us realize what a masterpiece of modern architecture it was and still is. No doubt our luck to be present the whole day—for lunch, horseback riding through the woods to the old Alström mansion (Maire's family) having a sauna

Villa Mairea, Noormarkku, Finland
Alvar Aalto
(Photograph: Henry Plummer)

and family birthday dinner there for Harry until a very late hour, all lent an extra glow of enchantment to the whole experience—a very rare privilege in anyone's life. I didn't know until I visited the villa many years later in 1954, that we were the first Americans to inscribe our names in the villa's guest book.

Our last call in Finland was with Erik Bryggman in his office in Turku. He took us on a personal tour of his work. This included the Sampo Insurance Office Building and his now-famous Resurrection Chapel. The directness, simplicity, and quiet elegance of the chapel immediately placed it at the peak of any modern place of worship I had seen anywhere. It was easy to understand the source of this quality in meeting Bryggman. He was shy, slightly gangling in movement, gentle, smiling, and humble, reflecting like Asplund and the Aaltos, a sincerity, respect, and love for people. This kind of quiet integrity was clearly evident in his office, which I remember as somewhat rambling and cluttered, but expressing through the abundance of partial study models at large scale and drawing fragments from rough to fine, a strong sense of purpose that they were means in the creation of the full scale building—and in no way ends in themselves. It was in Bryggman's office and in visiting his magnificent chapel, which I did again in 1954 and 1998, that I felt most strongly the contribution Finland has made to world architecture: that a limited vocabulary of materials and economic means can be an asset rather than a liability in the making of

fine buildings. Handcraft skills and sensitivity in the assembly of limited materials and means had matured among the people for centuries. Architects emerged from apprenticeship in such a culture as versatile designers; skillful, and sensitive over a wide range of crafts in a highly design-oriented society, rather than as separate, synthetically trained, label-identified professionals. This also explains why public response to good design in Finland is so knowing and widespread. It also supports the general use of juried competitions in the selection of architects for new projects.

When Tom and I returned from Finland in mid-November, our embassy in Stockholm called us and advised that we'd better plan to leave Europe soon and that the best way would be to go south into Italy to arrange passage from the Mediterranean rather than sail back through the U-boat infested North Sea. This was a sudden but not unexpected early end to my stay in Sweden and Finland, having planned to complete the Langley Fellowship there the following Spring. So there were many tearful farewells with Karen and her family and also with new friends at the Cosmopolite and elsewhere in Stockholm.

The Embassy had also advised traveling one at a time through Germany and to rendezvous at our consulate in Venice. Arriving by rail at night in blacked-out Berlin was an abrupt awakening that the war was real. The sidewalks were crowded with pedestrians wearing phosphorescent buttons

that danced, tracing an arc around Stettinerbahnhofplatz. Opening almost any door near the station led to a bar with rooms where one could stay. While in Berlin for a few days, I mustered up enough courage to call at the Nazis' architectural office in Adolph Hitler Platz, Charlottenburg. The German cultural affairs office in Stockholm, when I was getting a transit visa and ration coupons, had made a pointed suggestion that I should have the word firsthand about architectural directions of the Third Reich, so when I actually arrived at the office, I had the uneasy feeling of being expected as if by command. At the rounded end of a flatiron shaped building (still standing), the entrance lobby presented an elaborate display of huge scale models of tribunals, the new Air Ministry and Reichschancellry, the 1936 Olympic Games, all decked with banners, swastikas and other Nazi symbols. Despite this sinister impression, I was cordially shown around and taken in to meet the young head of the office who must have been Albert Speer. But in all the blur of introductions, I can't really be sure. I felt intimidated to ask the same kind of questions about housing and the future urban fabric that I asked in Sweden and Finland. The rest of the train trip south through Nuremberg was uneventful yet a constant reminder of war status—uniforms everywhere, black-outs and by day, a dark pervasive grayness under cloudy skies and rain. Crossing the Brenner Pass into the mountain sun of Italy truly felt like an escape.

Over a few days Tom, Bill, Vic and I checked in at our Venice consulate. By then arrangements had been made for us to stay at the still open American Academy in Rome while making travel plans to return home. On the way to Rome we explored Venice totally empty of other tourists. Thanks to our consulate, we were guests at historic villas outside the city, palaces along the Grand Canal as well as visiting the usual museums and churches. Then on to Palladio's work in Vicenza, to Milano and to Florence, then as now a special mecca for expatriate Anglo-Americans as well as for young architectural pilgrims like us, its ageless character blending art, literature and history—the center of both renaissance and contemporary Italian culture that would irresistibly beckon, returning many more times in the future.

I remember so well the last leg from Florence to Rome, stopping at Orvieto, acquiring a large bottle of Orvieto Bianco that vanished toast after toast at each kilometer mark on the way to Roma Termini. Horse and buggy taxis were waiting. We chose one to deliver us, feeling especially joyful, up the Janiculum Hill to the American Academy.

In spite of our salubrious condition, Director Chester Aldrich and his sister Amey welcomed us warmly. Even as "refugees" we were immediately made to feel a part of the Academy family. The fact that projects and studies of fellows and others still in residence were mostly on hold intensified our bonding and feeling of collegiality.

The aura of the Academy as a Roman Valhalla for study abroad had been magnified in my imagination ever since I was a finalist in the design competition for the Rome prize in architecture two years earlier while a graduate student at MIT and again in Stillwater. But I was totally unprepared for the vast scale of the McKim, Mead and White building that seemed even more awesome in volume with so few residents. Although the ambiguity of the war in suspension loomed over us, daily life was almost normal. There were no real problems of communication, getting around the city, food supply or other peacetime conveniences. We went to exhibitions, receptions at other academies, museums, monuments, the new EUR under construction for a planned World's Fair in 1942, a papal audience with Pope Pius XII, and the opera to hear Benjamini Gigli sing in Il Travatore. The most noticeable effect of impending war was the increasing length of lines everywhere—at permit offices, travel agencies, banks, post offices and at embassies for visas. My desired port of departure was Lisbon by way of North Africa or southern France through Spain. But France had closed down its Italian boarder so it was necessary to get transit visas for Tunisia, Algeria and Morocco from the French Embassy in the Palazzo Farnese. After waiting hours at a side door and giving up, Chester Aldrich gave me a note to William Phillips, our ambassador, who in turn wrote a letter of introduction to Francois Poncet, the French ambassador. This time I went in the main door of the Palazzo Farnese and within

ten minutes had my visas, being escorted by Poncet himself to the same office where I had waited so long in vain.

Another vignette of those days revealed the difference of dictatorship in Germany and Italy. Hitler was unmistakably the specter of awe, fear and power, realized even more in the years since then. On the other hand, Mussolini, for most Italians, was a light-hearted clown who "made the trains run on time and drained the Pontine Marshes." This mixed irreverence was first evident at the Pensione Annalena in Florence where we stayed a few days on the way to Rome. Gianpiero Russoni, the son of the owner, made a show with ironic humor of dressing up as a Blackshirt while "Aunt Jean" Poirier, an ancient American resident, would smilingly scoff in hearty hoarse voice and gesture imitating Il Duce. In Rome we sometimes found ourselves in a massive gathering in the Piazza Venezia when Mussolini came out on a balcony for a rallying speech. You could spot sidelong glances and smiles as the crowd would exaggerate their shouts, cheers and salutes.

As the shorter and darker days of winter came on, our feeling of being temporary unexpected guests melted away. The kindness and hospitality of Amey and Chester Aldrich plus that of the remaining fellows and residents erased any sense of status and at the same time quietly instilled an even deeper understanding of the Academy's value as a catalyst for art and scholarship—a powerful presence felt without show, more poignant under the cloud of war.

This feeling of camaraderie, almost of a last hurrah, lent an added glow to the traditional Christmas Party in masquerade. Somewhere in the attic a miscellany of costumes was found that led to an anything goes mix. I found a Tibetan robe that combined with Finnish snow shoe boots with upturned toes I had bought for $2 somewhere in the country outside Helsinki. Chester Aldrich dressed up as a sultan. Stuart Mertz, fellow in landscape architecture, found an Oriental garb something like mine. Most of all I remember several beautiful girls from other academies and Roman families all in toga-like dresses and coronets. We had done a mural on newsprint paper of stick figures in progressive states of inebriation as a backdrop for the bar on the south wall of the salone where the tapestry now hangs. Much later I found photo prints of this scene which were later sent to the Academy's New York archives. Soon after the party, Rome was paralyzed by a snow storm greater than any in memory. Far from being ominous, the whole city turned out to celebrate—sleds and skis appeared on the Janiculum, guided by snowmen.

Bill Hartman and I finally left Rome about mid-January 1940 for Naples and Palermo, parting company there. Bill headed for Greece to join Ben Irvin and they made their way back home through the Mideast, India and the Pacific. I boarded an Alitalia tri-mo-tor plane for Tunis (fare $7 U.S. dollars—lire were not accepted), then by train, bus and occasional car rides across Tunisia, Algeria, Morocco, Tangiers, southern Spain and Portugal, sailing to New York from Lisbon on the Italian liner Saturnia. The crossing was smooth and uneventful despite the winter season and lurking presence of submarines. I couldn't even spend my remaining lire on board (the amount I had intended for the plane fare from Palermo). So when leaving the ship in New York, I tipped the cabin steward with these lire who in disgust threw them down on the deck. When he thought I was out of sight, I looked back and saw him scooping them up again. Entering the Arab world at Tunis after the flight from Palermo was another cultural shock of new sounds, smells and exotic Kasbah life, very unlike in sensory experience from entering France at Cherbourg for the first time in 1938, but the same in terms of sudden unexpected impressions of an entirely different world. The French had wisely kept their own quarters apart from native Arab and Berber settlements all across North Africa, in major cities like Tunis, Algiers, Fez and Casablanca, so that when you would enter the gates of the native communities, into the souks, dwelling and mosque precincts, it was like stepping back it time into an unbelievably intimate, colorful world now suddenly real in experience, only dimly foreshadowed in picture books and movies. Experiencing this vibrant scene alone had added impact, in a strange way a similar haunting feeling one has exploring alone in a ruined city like Carthage.

Carthage just outside Tunis near the airport was then a seemingly ignored deserted, desolated landscape by the sea, a few sheep grazing here and there. Some ruins were mound like, fragments of walls forming rooms without roofs almost like beach cabanas of some ancient time. Rounding one of these corners I inadvertently surprised a couple copulating, as if a dead city were coming to life again.

All along the path back home were reminders of coming war even though tension between the Rome-Berlin axis and France, Britain and Russia still had not reached a breakout of violence. You heard terms like "phony war," "Hitler's bluffing" or from our side of the Atlantic "Here they go again, let's be sure to stay out of it this time." In Fez Morocco I had met Jack and Pat Heavey, who were ending a long vacation trip in Europe, driving their small Quatre Cheveaux Renault, after a three year tour of duty at a copper mine in Peru where Jack had been resident physician.. They offered to squeeze me in the Renault for the rest of their way through Morocco, by way of Casablanca, Rabat, Tetuan, Tangier and on to southern Spain, Ceuta, Gibraltar, Malaga and Granada where we parted company as they headed back to France while I traveled by bus to Seville and Lisbon to catch the Saturnia for the U.S.

Tangier had long been a winter retreat for British retirees. We stayed in a hotel there that had a great long porch overlooking the city and the ocean. After dinner we joined the many retirees in their rocking chairs on the porch, all talking about impending war. I'll never forget their know-it-all sly smiles and nodding heads saying, "wait and see, we'll get you in—as soon as England appears to be really in trouble, we'll get you in, get you in!," like a stuck groove on a record. We then had to conceal how furious we were—it was as if we were still an obedient colony, which in their minds we obviously were. It's with nostalgia now I realize how honestly

isolationist we were at that time and continued to be with conviction until the attack on Pearl Harbor a year and a half later.

Another reminder came on entry into New York Harbor aboard the Saturnia. The boat bringing the harbor pilot also brought a bunch of reporters on board whom, like paparazzi swarmed all around us peppering us with questions. Several spotted me wearing my alpine hat which was fashionably loaded on the left side with souvenir buttons, among them a Nazi swastika which I'd forgotten about. Somebody said "You'd better take that damn thing off before anyone sees it on shore." I assured him I was no Nazi sympathizer, much surprised at how much war anxiety had built up since I'd been away for only six months. Frustration with the premature ending to what was to be a whole year abroad soon melted away in the elation of being back home, out of danger, to have a brief visit with my parents who I guess were more worried than I was, then on to Stillwater in early March 1940 to get back to work.

The U boats were beginning to sink ships almost indiscriminately in the Atlantic and pressure mounted to build up convoy escort by transferring old U.S. Navy destroyers to the British flag. Short wave radio brought us much closer to the conflict through BBC broadcasts every evening at 6 PM with the sound of Big Ben's bells and a heavy voice saying "London calling—the news," followed by five minutes of reporting the latest

incidents of bombing and other war related events, building up more and more over the summer and fall of 1940 as the Nazi Luftwaffe increased its saturation bombing of London, soon to be know as "the Battle of Britain." Sometimes there was a lull. One night as Big Ben chimed, the voice came on as usual, "London calling—the news—there is no news tonight." Can you imagine any American newscast beings so direct, missing the chance to fill in with some sort of spin? In spite of the daily reminders of the war, either by radio or in the press, we managed almost as if in denial to carry on with much the same routine of university life. If anything, as each new tragic episode in the news from abroad added up in appalling dimensions, our feeling of response became a paradoxical mix of concerned sympathy yet even stronger isolationism the further away you lived from the East Coast.

It was strange, too, that even in the face of the war abroad the depression seemed to be ending. Construction, agriculture and manufacturing were all picking up. The prospect for our graduates to get a job now looked encouraging for the first time if somehow we could say out of the war. It was that summer in 1940 when I went back to my hometown, Bloomington/Normal, Illinois that I had my first job in an architectural office, Lundeen & Hilfinger, working on the design of new and remodeled residences, institutional and commercial projects. This would turn out to be a most rewarding relationship after the war too, lucky to continue gaining experience in both practice and academia. I can't help contrasting this period of time with today. Everybody was more patient then, both fellow workers in the office and clients. On the job sites every move was more careful, deliberate, in a mood of low keyed enjoyment that at last we were getting back to work, still with worry that recovery might be cut off again, either by war or another sudden downturn in the economy. Nobody could foresee how the rush to build in the years after the war would more and more escalate in scale, speed, anonymity of workers on the job. In the days before the war you knew most of them then by their first names.

In the office I began for the first time to understand and fully respect the experience needed in construction detailing, in integrating structural and mechanical systems, even though all this had its start in designing and building the Bieberdorf residence in Stillwater. Larger projects were much more intricate and demanding, involving codes, standards of practice, most of all the intense discipline of costs and construction management. Since I was kept busy with schematic design and presentation drawings both before and immediately after the war I began to feel uneasy and inadequate in not "earning my spurs" in working drawings and knowing "how to put a building together." Even then in small offices and much more so in large ones "designers" tended to be separated from working (construction) drawings, engineering and job supervision. You felt

not only a sense of guilt in not gaining a full spectrum of experience but often dismay that so many changes had been made in the built design—proportion, material, detail refinement due to "practical" considerations, all because you hadn't followed through with enough information beyond the preliminary design concept.

Without thinking of them as "working drawings" I gradually tried to fill this gap on my own by simultaneously doing freehand details on tracing paper of wall sections, material relationships, interior perspectives and many notations to try to avoid surprises as the whole drawing package reached its final form. It still took quite a number of years to make up for what I still imagined was my inadequacy in all-around experience.

That summer of 1940 was also a foreshadow of future years of working straight through without much of a vacation. But August at Neebish was high season there, so I begged off work for a few weeks before returning to Stillwater for the fall semester to drive up north in my 1936 Ford convertible to join my parents and summer friends who likewise had the feeling that this might be the last time we could gather around bonfires, indulge in water sports and celebrate Chief Howard's birthday as in all our childhood years.

Since we were only a half mile across the water from Canada there began to be an increasing awareness of tightened security.

While shopping one day in the Sault and seeing my grandparents, one of our Canadian cousins, Daisy Foster was also visiting, exclaiming "we got your destroyers!" She was also full of news of other relatives in lower Ontario being called up for service. However, on our side of the border everything still seemed unchanged except for news from abroad on the battery radios that almost everybody had by then.

On returning in September my parents and I had our last breakfast together, since we were driving separately, at the Homestead in St. Ignace (it had always been a custom to get an early head start on the road before breakfast), They would go down the Wisconsin side of Lake Michigan and I the Michigan side. Amazingly there in the restaurant was Ben Irvin, one of my friends from Stockholm days and Ben Baldwin who were both headed for Glen Lake to visit Harry Weese and his family, where they had several cottages. I had already met Harry while I was working on the Rome Prize at MIT so when the two Bens insisted that I follow them to Glen Lake, about two hours south, saying there was plenty of room at the Weeses, I decided to tag along.

Here again was another stroke of luck, not only to visit Harry but as it turned out to meet several Cranbrook Academy of Art people who were also guests there. It was indeed like a small summer camp seminar of artists, friends of Harry, who was also at Cranbrook after finishing his degree at Yale and MIT. They all urged me to side track to Cranbrook on the way home, since the academic year was just beginning and the Saarinens would be there, as well as other notable faculty and new students. When I arrived in Bloomfield Hills, just north of Detroit, I was welcomed as if I too was a fellow student, indeed almost as if I was a potential recruit in their new spirit of collaboration among artists and architects; an atmosphere already familiar to me after being in Sweden and Finland the year before.

I had a brief talk with Eliel in his city planning studio then visited the buildings on the Cranbrook campus that he had designed which together with their integration with landscape and sculpture by Carl Milles demonstrated a level of harmony of human scale, materials and freedom from the affected stylism (e.g. Gothic, Georgian, Neo Classicism, etc.) of so many American campuses. Most of the rest of my time was spent with his son Eero, meeting other faculty and students, observing how much they were inspired by each other's efforts as they came together, in a quest for low key, unpretentious excellence, fresh yet in contrast to then current flashy, "look at me" trends in modern art.

Both at this time and eighteen years later, when I took a group of graduate students for a visit to Eero's studio, I was impressed by the same atmosphere and sense of direction. The quest for excellence was insatiable but maintained in a spirit of quiet enjoyment,

mutual respect, and friendliness—reminding me of the Aaltos and Bryggman. Eero's version was an even greater intensity of study of alternative schemes in the search for a satisfying solution. We were amazed at the diversity of projects going on simultaneously—the TWA Terminal as a sculptural approach, John Deere as a Miesian, almost Japanese essay in weathering steel; Concordia Seminary, Fort Wayne, as a kind of romantic village; and others equally diverse. What communicated most was that they were all recognizably Saarinen through the excellence of all phases of the design process from initial concept to definitive detail. This characteristic of excellence in diversity that we were observing in models and drawings is of course now most vividly evident in the body of Saarinen's completed work. Though originating in Finland in the capacity of highly talented people to work together so compatibly, as I had noted in 1939, we took it as very American too; and that the idea of excellence in diversity was then, and it seems to me still is, the most profound and meaningful direction for architecture, with or without stylistic labels.

By slow degrees the threshold to war ratcheted up in our lives. It became a matter of when not if we would be involved, especially for those of us who were in the prime of youth and good health. Each new project, either in studio or in outside practice carried with it a degree of uncertainty whether it would be cut off or change shape for whatever reasons as a consequence of war esca-

lation, coming closer and closer as sinkings in the Atlantic increased just off our shores and disruptions of the global economy built up. This stretch out of suspense continued all through the fall, winter and summer of 1940-41. I think I understand now, many years later, that the zest of moving forward the spur of creativity in any profession, depends so much on being able to look ahead to the future, free of worries either on a personal level or because of a general malaise in society.

This did not mean that in this doldrum of time the quality of work or enthusiasm for learning was entirely depressed. I realize now even more that the greatest reward for teaching (a glorious process of mutual rather than a one way street learning) is seeing inspired improvement in your students' work as time goes by, despite adversity. It would be now almost four years since 1937-38, when students I then knew as freshmen were now showing so much talent and maturity. It was a tremendous thrill the first time and has never lost its high of elation since then. On a parallel track in practice it compares to the high one feels as an architect, say twenty years after one of your projects has been in use, your clients express how much they have valued your work over time, even more than when the project was brand new. I like to think that in both cases, whether with students or clients, that it takes many years for all the particles of thought, all the minutia of exchanged ideas and design decisions that have been invested to reveal themselves, adding up in new perspective and appreciation, like compounded interest on financial investments made long ago.

News kept coming in of new escalations in the war; in the Mediterranean, North Africa, the Balkans and Russia as Hitler's invasions fanned out in all directions. In Europe, Sweden and Switzerland alone had managed to remain neutral, avoiding occupation by the Nazis. All this, including disastrous shipping losses in the Atlantic, prompted President Roosevelt and Congress to initiate the draft and other defensive measures short of declaring war. All of us in line to be drafted had to register with our local draft board, filling out forms of vital statistic information leading to a physical examination, draftability classification and a lottery number for being called up. The form also required that you declare whether you were a "conscientious objector" or not. Since I was very much an isolationist I filled in this blank that I was opposed to our getting in the war, knowing full well that conscientious objectors would either be sent to prison, to labor camps or otherwise deprived of their freedom. But I still didn't worry about this very much since it seemed we might by diplomacy or for whatever reason be able to stay out of the conflict.

All shadows of doubt vanished suddenly, of course, as news came on the radio of the Japanese attack on Pearl Harbor. Even though December 7, 1941 was on a Sunday I was with the students working in the studio as the usual radio background music was abruptly interrupted, everybody disbelieving at first that this news could be true. Then as reality began to sink in, our whole familiar world of learning architecture together came apart. The look of bewilderment was like a shroud. You could tell; even if it seemed we were all in the same boat, everyone's thoughts turned to puzzle out what it all meant to each of us personally. Now it was clear that we could no longer kid ourselves that our lives could go on as free as before. I remember that an air of disbelief and shock still remained until Congress declared war not only on Japan but Germany as well. We tried to carry on as before—what else could you do until the machinery of war worked its way down, changing each of our lives?

Within a week or two Phil Wlber, our head, called me into his office, looking concerned but sympathetic, saying "The governor's sleuths have discovered that on the draft questionnaire you are a conscientious objector, is that really true?" I said "yes, but now that we've been attacked at Pearl Harbor, I feel very differently about it, but maybe it's too late to change my statement." Phil didn't think so, suggesting I go the to draft board to see if they would permit me to withdraw my CO declaration, which they did. I still had a hollow feeling that there must be something yet unexplained about tying our enemy status with Japan to our involvement in Europe's war.

Writing about this time in our lives over sixty years later, so many details of entering the war and its personal consequences remain vivid in memory while everything else in civilian life that was still going on in parallel is much less clear and blurred in the face of immediate personal concerns of unwelcome change, even of survival. Because I had been since childhood an avid student of history, I realized that America had been at war, beginning with the Revolution, for almost each generation of thirty years more or less, since then. Having been born as World War I started, I began to have a premonition, first in the early thirties, in the ROTC at Illinois, that my generation would be ripe for the next one. Sure enough the time had come.

Facts and rumors mixed as to what options you might have before your number came up. Unless you had some physical disability, there seemed no choice other than in the military. Joining the Navy loomed up as closest to my love of boats, either on ship or on shore with the CB's (Construction Battalions). At that time the Navy would not accept architects for the CB's, only engineers, so I signed up for the V-7 program to become a line officer (a "90-day wonder"), beginning as an apprentice seaman for 30 days, then 60 days as a midshipman, then commissioned as an ensign for further special training and orders for duty aboard ship as either a deck or engineering line officer.

All this came to a head in June 1942, so I could finish up the academic year at Stillwa-ter, knowing that goodbyes this time were really final—no way to know what destiny might bring when and if the war ended. All my older friends tried to be reassuring, Phil Wilber and President Bennett made it especially clear that the university would welcome me back. Leaving for duty for the first 30 days training at Notre Dame was not exactly a hardship, to be in a familiar academic setting even though regimentation was heavy—in all white sailor uniforms we marched endlessly on the campus almost as if the Navy hadn't yet figured out what else to do with us. Since it was summer, weekend liberty meant we could get to Chicago in little more than an hour for sailing out of one of the yacht clubs, crashing parties in the evening. Somehow the word and introductions had gotten around from native Chicagoans. Tough duty! Harry Weese was in my class so I got to know him better as we moved on to New York for our 60 day period of training aboard the old battleship Illinois, permanently tied up in the Hudson River mud opposite Columbia University. Before we left Notre Dame, Harry returned from a weekend at home full of excitement that at a party he had met Serge Chermayeff of recent fame in England who had just arrived to take over as head of the Illinois Institute of Design. Little did I imagine then that I would become a friend of Serge and his family when he took refuge on weekends soon after the war from the turmoil of IID administration to visit our mutual friends Laura and Ludie Zirner who were as I was, new on the faculty at Illinois, Urbana/Champaign.

By the time we were headed on a special train to New York the Navy had more time to organize its V-7 intensive study program for the next 60 days, including a lot more marching. We were crammed with courses in navigation, seamanship, ordinance and communication. Again it was really no hardship to be right in the city for liberty, especially to get a chance for an appetizing meal away from the awful undercooked turkey and other heavy, greasy food of the ships galley, or to be invited for the weekend as house guests in upscale suburbs out of town. I also had a most pleasant reunion with Carol Stanley, one of my Oklahoma girlfriends who was visiting in New York, and a reunion with Ed Bilby and Eleanor Steber from MIT days who were now married. Eleanor had just won the celebrated Metropolitan Opera auditions and was a rising mezzo soprano, notably in Mozart roles. One weekend I went ashore with Harry to meet his fiancée Kitty Baldwin, from Montgomery Alabama, who it turned out was Ben Baldwin's sister. I had met Ben as mentioned earlier when he and Ben Irvin, my Stockholm friend, ran into each other at St. Ignace, and had gone on to the Weeses at Glen Lake in September 1940.

Strangely, the war seemed farther away in New York, maybe simply because the city was then and is today so overwhelming, even intimidating to those of us from the uncrowded hinterland. Except for more uniforms on the streets and the constant presence of war news, the allure of museums, theatre and other metropolitan night life was hardly diminished—summer tourists from all over the country were still crowding in the city as if nothing had changed. What a difference from blacked-out Berlin when I had passed through in late 1939 and from what everybody knew from film of war-torn London!

By this time the Navy was already mass producing vessels of all types, finding there would be a massive shortage of engineering officers for duty on board as launchings increased exponentially. Long before the computer there must have been some way to scan college transcripts to find anybody who had taken physics, for a fast track course in marine engineering. It turned out that no matter what duty we might have requested, all of us at the end of the alphabet, from R to Z, ended up at Penn State for another 60 days before being assigned to pre-commissioning as engineering officers on new ships with diesel engines.

Penn State in State College Pennsylvania had long been known for its strong program in mechanical engineering notably in diesel engine theory and marine propulsion. So the Navy was able to set up a short comprehensive course for prospective engineering officers that included concentrated theory and laboratory instruction. We were most comfortably quartered at the Nittany Lion Inn, a gracious colonial style hotel at the edge of the campus that had been built mainly for alumni and other university visitors as well as for the general public. But our contingent of about fifty trainees just about took over the full capacity of the inn. My roommate was Dick Wilkins and adjacent rooms were occupied with other W's, among them Chuck Walker, who along with Dick and myself were to be assigned to new YMS minesweepers being built in Seattle. Our paths would cross many times in the future—on duty in the Pacific and after the war.

The experience at Penn State was again much like the university life I was used to as a student at Illinois and MIT. I soon got to know some of the architecture faculty especially Ken and Dorothy Heidrich who had been at Stillwater before I arrived there in 1937. They in turn introduced me to others on the faculty and to their neighbors, Prof. Sweitzer and his wife who had come over from Germany a few years before and had built their house in striking Bauhaus style on College Avenue near the Heidrichs, just a few blocks from the Nittany Lion Inn. Prof. Sweitzer, who had studied with Otto Diesel, was our instructor in diesel engine theory, made thermodynamics (we called it "thermogodamics") seem easy. He believed in frequent quizzes, often requiring drawings to illustrate principles. I happened to score 100 on the first test, also on the next and the next. Knowing I had made numerical mistakes, I hesitatingly brought this to his attention. He smiled and blinked through his heavy horn-rimmed glasses, saying "Yah zo—zee , but you're an architect, you can visualize it and draw it—zat's what really counts!" Never before had I had such a forgiving reaction from an engineer.

So the magnificent, colorful fall days in the surrounding, mostly wooded landscape of State College passed by, ending as winter approached. After a short leave at home in Illinois and in Stillwater, I went on by rail through the Rockies, arriving in Seattle in a snow storm to report for duty at a shipyard in Ballard, on the north side of the city, along the waterway that connects Lake Union and Puget Sound. Here was another familiar archipelago setting like the Upper Great Lakes yet with an added sense of the ocean nearby, a complex mix of working vessels of all sizes for fishing, ocean cargo, ferries, Navy warships, docks and other seaport facilities with their distinct sounds, smells as well as visual impressions.

YMS 336, under construction at the Seattle Shipbuilding and Drydock Company in Ballard, was one of many hundred wood-hulled, identical minesweepers being built at various yards on both coasts as well as on the Great Lakes, 136 feet long with a 24 foot beam, from plans by Henry B. Nevin, a famous naval architect known for his elegant designs of yachts as well as commercial vessels. The yard in Ballard had long been experienced in building "tuna clippers" of about the same size as the YMS series. Here again was a familiar scene, since most of the workers were of Scandinavian descent demonstrating the same great craftsmanship skills that I had admired in Sweden and Finland. I was assigned a desk in a kind of storage/file room off the main office, full of rolls of blueprints, ship models and catalogues, with only a vague idea of what my duty might be in relating to the building process. It was soon very clear that I was hopelessly lost and inexperienced in really understanding the complexities of this new assignment—guessing that I was probably just meant to be a symbolic presence in Navy uniform among the builders who after all had the ultimate responsibility and know how to get the job done.

Getting together often with Dick Wilkins and Chuck Walker at other nearby yards building YMS's, we soon realized our main task was to observe each step in the process, most importantly as preparation for operating the vessels once they were in commission. Navy supervision was in the hands of seasoned professionals at district headquarters. Among those of us who had been at Penn State I was the only architect and soon realized that my earlier feeling of being miscast in some other seemingly unrelated field for the duration of the war was not only narrow and selfish but missed the bigger idea that I could be learning a lot more about the design and integration of complex systems of construction materials, structural and mechanical engineering with exacting human ergonomic and performance demands all interlocking as it must in naval architecture.

This revelation, like a light bulb turning on in a comic strip, lent a new zest in studying Nevin's drawings with awe and admiration as I had examined Nat Herreshoff's meticulous sailing yacht drawings as they were exhibited at MIT. The elegant lines of the hull , deck plans, details of keel, ribs and planking, their fittings, profiles and cross sections at modular stations from stem to stern, intricate cabin and pilot house carpentry drawings like those for custom furniture, the precise layouts of engines, propeller shafts, rudder and steering mechanisms, fuel lines, water lines, electrical distribution lines forming meticulous color-coded patterns, gunnery and minesweeping gear placement and details, mast and rigging details, were all organized in sections related to special skill trades and contracting categories involved in the entire assembly process. Since the YMS 336 was nearing completion of the hull when I arrived, it helped to study these hull drawings first, then other details as each phase in the sequence of systems was coordinated, often simultaneously. At the yard each of the experienced shipwrights working in turn was patient and took real pride in explaining what was going on.

The power of precise drawings took on new depths of importance as a key to accuracy in the fit of so many three dimensional relationships of parts, much more exactingly than required for normal building practice up to that time. If you examine the anatomy of spaces for ducts, pipes and wires in usual architectural drawings, such as dropped ceilings, vertical shafts and other utility spaces, you'll find a lot of unused space that could not be tolerated in ship design, where human occupancy as well as for machinery and other equipment requires much more rigor in fitting together small spaces, solids and voids; for engine rooms, staterooms, passageways, storerooms, chartrooms, radio shacks and many other special functions. Maximum efficiency, stability and safety all demanded minimum headroom and sideroom as much on pleasure craft , passenger ships and cargo vessels as on naval craft.

This kind of most exacting design discipline might at first seem tediously unrewarding, like working out the hidden working parts and connection in cars, airplanes or any other kind of moving vehicle. On the other hand this design challenge can result in works of art, thereby enormously gratifying whether visible or invisible. Although the power of drawing at this level of intricacy is the initial driving force of design thinking, the reality of assembling everything together still relies inevitably on the craft of the maker, who may in turn encounter other levels of possible refinement. Since some, perhaps even most of these subsets of design may be exposed, either for accessibility, weight saving or clarity of purpose, the beauty of each detailed assembly becomes a seamless component of the total orchestration design. One can note particularly the skill of electricians, plumbers and others in organizing wiring, pipes, controls, dials, panels in exquisite patterns that would really not be functionally necessary, unless you could be persuaded that aesthetic function is just as important. In fact, in pilot houses, engine rooms and other critical control spaces, visual and acoustical aesthetics become inseparable from operational efficiency and safety. A twilight zone always seems to remain in which subjective notions of art willfully added (decoration) are in harmony or not with art emerging from the intrinsic beauty of function.

How true it is that a small coincidence of time, place and circumstance can set the course of one's life for years to come. Just as a call from Phil Wilber on the Coast Guard telephone at Neebish Island began my career in architectural education at Oklahoma State, so an unknown crossing of papers in the Navy Department might set one's wartime duty in the Pacific theatre rather than the Atlantic. Little did we know at first what part of the vast Pacific Rim would be our ultimate destination, or what the course might be to reach it. Maybe the Navy didn't know either—but at least it was clear that "shake down" and training in Puget Sound and the San Juan islands would be our initial operational area, then on down the coast somewhere for departure, probably for Hawaii as a way station to fleet action on the front. This secrecy and mystery of eventual assignment naturally became a hot-bed for rumor—between the two extremes of safe home port duty and front line combat— would it be another toss of the coin?

But still there was time for enjoying life as much as one could in the Puget Sound area, liberty in Seattle, or in the mountains. A weekend in Victoria, BC, staying at the Empress Hotel was a glimpse back in British Empire time, dining and dancing on Saturday night as if in some Edwardian setting of colorful military uniforms, ladies in long sweeping dresses, lighting by elaborate chandeliers, all to the music of Strauss waltzes. On Sunday afternoon there was tea dancing to the Billy Tickle Trio. Almost thirty years

later I was back, in 1971; sure enough, the Bill Tickle Trio was still playing; there were no uniforms but nothing else had changed.

As always in life, new revelations turn up that you had never imagined. I had thought that as an American, whether as an officer or enlisted man, we were all members of the same team, respecting and relying on each other as equals, and that difference in rank was a necessity because of war discipline and chain of command, not of social class. It had turned out that well before Pearl Harbor military recruiting had succeeded in attracting volunteers mostly from the south of the country, who soon rose in all the services as senior officers when the draft brought in millions at lower rank. So by the time in 1943 when so many new Navy vessels came in service, many of the captains were from the South. It didn't appear to the rest of us as junior officers from other parts of the country that this would present any problem until it became apparent to the crew that they were not used to being treated like anonymous serfs (I hesitate to say slaves) when it came to arbitrarily heavy discipline for minor mistakes or absence of a pat on the back for a job well done. Long before we were in any danger zone, either in storm or enemy fire, I worried what this Captain Bligh, Mister Roberts syndrome, might mean in terms of morale for the crew and for those of us in the middle, trying to ease tension both ways. I think everybody gradually realized that this tension was not really a matter of individual personalities but a larger cultural

American Samoa (Pencil on Cameo Paper), 1943
A. Richard Williams

YMS 336 in Puget Sound, Washington (Pencil on Cameo Paper), 1943

American Samoa (Pencil on Cameo Paper), 1943

difference that none of us, North or South, had realized could still exist. But for a time it was an added concern on top of all the other anxieties of war.

"Shake down" training cruises out of Port Townsend to Discovery Bay, Friday Harbor in the San Juan islands became an idyllic daily routine, checking speed, station keeping, streaming minesweeping gear, maneuvering, anchoring, docking, signaling and many other exercises. Like the Upper Great Lakes, navigating in the San Juan archipelago was exacting in setting courses, recognizing land and seamarks, avoiding underwater hazards but at the same time relishing the aroma of salty air mixed with the scent of tanbark, in the brilliance of late spring sun on sparkling water, forming a carpet of channels, bays and straits, interlocking heavily wooded islands close up and far into the distance.

You might think of finally going to sea and to war as the beginning of another much longer cruise, perhaps this time never to return, on a course out to the open ocean through the Straits of Juan de Fuca then south down the coast about three miles off shore, without a break, all the way to San Diego, passing the Golden Gate Bridge leading into San Francisco Bay, having to ignore siren songs enticing us in, passing Big Sur, the Santa Barbara Islands, Los Angeles, San Pedro, Santa Catalina to starboard and Point Loma to port, making harbor after three days of easy beam- sea sailing, typical of summer days along the Pacific shore.

San Diego was in many ways a replay of
Seattle, a concentration of maritime hustle
and bustle, but much more dominated by
the Navy from smallest craft to aircraft
carriers, battleships and all types of service
vessels crowding the harbor and major bases
on shore. Signs were everywhere of massive preparation for the fleet's departure to
zones of action on all sea frontiers; generating activity of checking supplies, gear and all
other forms of readiness. Liberty time had
the character of a last fling, last goodbyes to
old and new friends on shore. By chance I
had found one of my closest Neebish friends,
Molly Ryan, just married to Chester Bender,
a Coast Guard officer who had been on a tour
of duty at the Sault. Chet was also a flyer,
now assigned to the western sea frontier,
later to become an Admiral and top com-
mander of the Coast Guard in Washington
after the Vietnam War. When Chet retired,
he and Molly lived in the San Francisco Bay
area where I had the luck of reunions with
them while on occasional invitations in the
seventies and eighties as a visiting critic at
Cal Poly, Berkeley and the San Francisco
Center for Architecture and Urban Studies.

Every few days convoys would form, usually
departing for Pearl Harbor then reforming
under new orders for various other the-
atres in the central or southwestern Pacific.
Along with other small craft, tankers and
miscellaneous other slower vessels we set
out in September 1943 for a rough ten days
crossing to Hawaii, there to wait for further
orders. For unexplained reasons I caught

USS Pokomoke, Seaplane Tender En Route American Samoa (Pencil on Cameo Paper), 1943

American Samoa Approach (Pencil on Cameo Paper), 1943

pneumonia and had to remain in the Pearl Harbor hospital for several weeks, while the 336 went on to join some unknown fleet. While recovering I inadvertently became a kind of tourist, comfortably quartered on the base but with days spent at the Royal Hawaiian Hotel, taken over by the Navy as an R&R (rest and recreation) center. I soon realized that along with many other service personnel—I had entered a kind of limbo, waiting for doctors to give the Ok for return to active duty, then more waiting for orders to report back to the 336 somewhere out there in the Pacific. Meanwhile, I was lucky to be invited often by the Eindhoven family to their house above Waikaki. Mrs. Eindhoven was a "Gray Lady" visiting the hospital at Pearl Harbor, an angel bringing books, radio, flowers and other thoughtful amenities to patients, most of all graciously spending unhurried time just to visit. It turned out that she and her husband, who was an admiralty lawyer, had come from Holland twenty years before. I think we became special friends because they too were fans of Dudok and his work in Hilversum. I had run into Chuck Walker from Penn State and Seattle days who was on another YMS based at Pearl Harbor. So Chuck and I were, so to speak, "adopted" by the Eindhovens while in Hawaii, keeping in contact ever since. I saw them several times later during and after the war while waiting between flights to and from Okinawa and Japan. The last time was in the spring of 1946, when I found they had sold their house—I'll always remember it as the essence of quiet tropical luxury, in

its mountain garden setting, truly Hawaiian without imported stylistic gingerbread—and had moved to the Moana Hotel on Waikaki Beach waiting for a ship to California to join their son and daughter and their families. I was shocked that they too, like many others had "island fever," impatient to leave, thinking that they, more than most other islanders I had met, expressed the true Hawaiian spirit of belonging there. But it was obvious that "island fever" had been greatly intensified by being civilian "prisoners," not allowed to travel to the mainland for the duration of the war, and now having to wait again an unknown time for passage off the islands.

Looking back, while waiting for orders to rejoin my ship by whatever transport might be available, I had the same shadows of doubt feeling. Time after time I would go to Admiral Nimitz' CINCPAC headquarters for information with no results. It looked as if even the top command didn't know the whereabouts of YMS 336; they in turn referred me to the central Fleet Post Office who only knew the initial destination port in the Samoan archipelago. So I was given open orders to board a seaplane tender bound for Samoa and check the fleet P.O. there for the next forwarding port. I began to have the weird feeling that I was becoming a Navy nomad, as it turned out later many others were "lost," some, no doubt, playing this game as long as they could.

Thus began a series of hitch hiking links first from Samoa on a C47 aircraft (later known

as the work horse DC-3) to Espiritu Santu, south of the now famous Solomon Islands, then on to Noumea in French New Caledonia, where I again had rather lush quarters near the Hotel de Pacifique, that had the "longest bar in the world," in an extremely long narrow room with the bar on one side and a seemingly endless row of slot machines on the other. While in Noumea I at long last discovered a trace of the 336, in the Seventh Fleet based n Brisbane, Australia. So I got a six hour ride on a PBS flying boat almost straight west to Brisbane, landing on the river there only to find the 336 had moved on north to New Guinea, probably to Milne Bay, a long harbor on the southeast tip of the island. So after another C47 ride to Milne Bay I was hot on the trail, finally getting back on board at Lae further up the coast just in time for landing craft action across to New Britain in the Admiralty archipelago. All this island hopping search had taken more than two months until December 1943, now summer in the southern hemisphere.

Soon the world would know of General Douglas MacArthur's strategy of skip-stop, island hopping up the New Guinea Coast, leaving Japanese bases behind, cut off from their lines of supply and reinforcement. Little known, though, was the relatively small scale of each of these invasions, until Operation Musketeer II, the massive assault on the Philippines. Now that Japanese air power was no longer a threat, except for solitary raids at dusk, each of these minor moves up the islands was mostly unopposed. Each fleet was usually a miscellany of landing craft and their escort, made up of YMS's, sub chasers and a few larger US and Australian destroyers with General MacArthur and his staff aboard, coming ashore in a landing craft. Since there were no mines, our duty on the YMS was usually as "point vessel" near the beach to guide the LST's, LSM's to their designated shore marked on the operation plan layout.

Since there were so many of these skip-stops each one fades in memory, except at Hollandia, a magnificent harbor where the main, long landing beach had a swamp behind it, unspotted by aerial surveys. So the formidable loads of supplies including ammunition that were landed could not be moved further inshore right away, piling up in stacks. At twilight, a single Japanese plane came in low, dropped a bomb and the whole beach began to blow up, fortunately with few casualties. We watched from out in the harbor as this gigantic fireworks display continued all night. Next day we checked out an inner bay, found a hastily deserted enemy base, with breakfast still on the table and large stores of food and other supplies including cases of Asahi beer, many of which were "liberated" for further consumption (against Navy regulations).

But regulations of this kind by now were casually regarded. When everything quieted down at Hollandia, now becoming a major base, vessels anchored in the harbor for many days waiting for the next move up the

coast. We were among two or three YMS's rafted—one anchored and the others tied up alongside along with several PT's, the high speed torpedo boats made famous by John Kennedy's exploits earlier in the Solomon islands. During these languid waiting periods military formalities relaxed still more—distinction of rank tended to disappear as clothes (or absence thereof) adapted to the tropical heat. Friendships became closer among all the crew, evidenced by more and more imaginative nick names, following a fad that either made light of your identity at work (I was known as "Prof."), or, influenced by the Australians, you might become known by the opposite of some personal characteristic. If you were a redhead, your name would be "blue;" if you were skinny it would be "fatso." We also picked up Australian slang that had derived from the native islanders' use of double syllables like bora bora, pongo pongo, etc. If you were pleased by something, you'd say "good good" or "hear hear" or more simply "goodo." To this day I'll still hear myself saying one or the other of these.

One of the YMS skippers was Bob Topping of the wealthy New York and Newport, Rhode Island family, and a friend of George Vanderbilt, captain of one of the PT's. The flying bridge of Topping's YMS became the happy hour gathering point each evening fueled by liberated Asahi beer or by canned grapefruit juice spiked by an unlimited supply of Australian gin that Topping had smuggled aboard from Cairns, Australia. It was then

I figured out that influential social position could be a factor in Navy duty' assignment, George Vanderbilt, John Kennedy and several of their socialite friends all became skippers of glamorous PT's. More recently, thinking of John Kerry's fast boat duty during the Vietnam War, maybe the same mechanism of influence was still at work. Whatever. During this congenial interlude in Hollandia, Topping asked me to design a hunting lodge to be built after the war, which I worked on, using our chart room table. Later in the war when I was in Washington and Topping was back in New York, I went up for a visit, staying at the Algonquian Hotel, meeting Topping at "21" to talk some more about the project but nothing ever came of it. I guess his post war marriages to Hollywood stars must have had impact on what form of hunting lodge he was interested in.

The Bats of Yorkies Knob

Another interval breaking the leap frog advance up the coast of New Guinea was a brief tour of patrol duty behind the Great Barrier Reef based at Cairns, Australia. At that time Cairns was a commercial port town serving the outback, now quiet and laid back because of the lingering threats to shipping. But by this time our coastal patrols had become entirely routine and uneventful, taking on a languid, relaxed aspect, a feeling intensified by flatness of the sea and the hazy tropical air. All this made returning to port and anticipation of happy hour the peak of the day. The Aussies had converted a small seedy beach resort named Yorkie's Knob into an R & R club for service personnel about five miles from town. To get there you had to catch a van or commandeer a jeep, cross a river in dense woods. This all would fade in memory except for the sudden, out of this world plunge into the woods in eerie crimson twilight through a dense cloud of enormous bats, the only sound the beat of their wings. It was at once an awesome threshold into a kind of threatening underworld and yet it seemed the bats were escorting us through to the glorious beach of Yorkie's Knob beyond as if it were some kind of paradise under their protection.

Navy routine at the front included making reports of action summing up whatever this experience might mean in changing tactics, procedures or modification of ship design and gear. As executive officer it was my duty to make and keep track of these reports. So without thinking it was anything unusual I was used to making drawings along with written descriptions to illustrate a miscellany of battle operations carried out or work to be done by fleet tenders or at bases. These were largely suggestions from the crew for improvement of ship functions, such as placement of guns, sweeping gear, loading balance, visibility and many other details of possible change evoked in the thick of action that otherwise had not been discovered earlier from initial design and testing. For me using drawings to record recommendations was a natural part of the reporting process, hardly expecting any feedback. I was greatly surprised, just after we made our invasion of Moratai and while watching at close hand MacArthur wading ashore from a grounded LCM, to receive dispatch orders to report to Admiral Barbey's operations staff. Based at Milne Bay and soon after at Manus in the Admiralty islands this seventh fleet command was in high gear to fine tune operation plan "Musketeer II" for invasion of Leyete and Linguyan in the Philippines as well as to make repairs, upgrade gear and otherwise make the fleet ready to go. It took some time before I found out (from fleet engineer officer "Grumpy " Carlson), that my drawings had triggered this new duty which included fleet layout planning and time tables for the

invasion as well as directing preparation of smaller craft, many special training exercises, repair and supply. All of this meant an almost around the clock, frantic two weeks of trying to get things done, very much like a "charette," the last days and hours of finishing an architectural project. Just before the fleet left Manus, I had new orders back to the Bureau of Ships in Washington, no doubt again prompted by the drawings which had been forwarded there, as well as by the fact that I had by then fifteen months of overseas duty and was due for return to the US.

The long twenty day voyage back to the States was aboard a huge tanker headed through the Panama Canal to Aruba, for a new load of diesel fuel; I would then disembark at Panama and catch a seaplane to Miami and wait for further transit orders. Life aboard the tanker, following a course straight east along the equator was blissfully calm and uneventful. As the only passenger, I had spacious quarters in the ship's hospital just below the pilot house and sumptuous meals with the crew aft in the stern. Though our course led through hundreds of uninhabited islands on each side shown on the charts, all of them were out of sight just over the horizon; nor did we see any other ships or aircraft.

This idyllic passage day after day with nothing to do but eat like a gourmet, sleep or daydream, was a Zen like time of pondering afterthoughts of archipelago life, nature's glories of tropical flora and fauna, seeing

the sea floor of coral, sand, or rock through diamond clear water up to almost a hundred feet deep, passing giant manta rays, sharks, dolphins, and thousands of smaller colorful fish alone or in schools moving as one; of vistas so vast that all interventions of man—of native villages or of modern toys of war; ships, bases, aircraft—seemed infinitely small; of time flashing back in a random stream of consciousness trying to sort out some larger dimension of understanding.

Although this was all food for exhilarating thought, one of the few blessings that long periods of idleness during war can bring, one could not shut out the darker side. Visions of wartime jungle life ashore would crowd in; foot soldiers on both sides dying, wounded, or barely existing in the miserable heat, humidity, mud and tangle of tropical rainforest so dense that no ray of sun could reach the ground. After every brief foray on shore for whatever reason we would return to our relatively safe, clean life aboard ship feeling lucky but with an accumulating sense of anguish and frustration that these disparities are the inevitable consequences of war. More depressing yet, it would be a reminder that even in peacetime, the same extremes of poverty, disease and enervating quality of life, in contrast to comfort and wealth, continue to exist around the world. On reflection, now many, many years later, this polarization of the human condition appears to be intensifying more and more. Is it a new unacknowledged, undeclared kind of war at global scale, symptomized by terrorism, rampant disease, deprivation and environmental decay on the one hand and well-gated extravagant luxury on the other? It is a reminder, too, once again, of how architecture is a true mirror of cultural change, if we compare today's lavish, showy, shallow glitter of privilege alongside the cheap monotony and squalor of poverty, to yesterday's more harmonious quality of civic architecture in balance with honest, even exquisite vernacular building in so many parts of the world.

Fast forward to the end of the war; from waiting at Dinner Key and Miami Beach for new orders , then after thirty day leave at home in Illinois, on to the small craft division of the Bureau of Ships; to endless meetings, to lunch breaks, unchanging to this day as scenes for bureaucratic gossip of politics, advancement in rank or pay, speculation of all kinds; to celebrating VE and VJ days in the summer of 1945; to sharing with my room mates who had been part of the Manhattan project to build the atomic bomb, our mixed emotions of success and horror of Hiroshima and Nagasaki; to being part of the celebratory swarm to the White House when Japan surrendered; to being suddenly ordered to fly to Okinawa and Japan via Hawaii as part of Admiral Struble's command aboard the "Panamint" to clear the Inland Sea of our own mines; to being held as a "military necessity" just after my eligibility for discharge was reached, then to be asked by the admiral to design the Fifth Fleet's Christmas cards; to make a cruise aboard the

"Panamint" checking Japanese harbors at Yokohama, Nagoya, Kobe Osaka, all the way to Shanghai and back to Sasebo; to finally have orders to fly back to Washington by way of Hawaii again; to have a flight delay at Oakland allowing time to visit Berkeley and to be recruited as a possible faculty member there once I was out of uniform; and finally to have another month or so at the Bureau of Ships before celebrating freedom and return to civilian life.

This was a time of extraordinary exuberance—after fifteen years of depression and war—to get down to work again on a huge backlog of unmet needs to build houses, schools, churches and all other kinds of civilian structures that had been delayed for so long. It never dawned on me that I would ever return to academic life, though Oklahoma State was calling me back and Berkeley seemed too far away in the face of immediate opportunity for working again with Ed Lundeen and Dean Hilfinger in Bloomington, living with my parents and enjoying once again social life with old school friends.

The Navy's "terminal leave" lasted through the spring of 1946 so there was still a feeling of transition in the air, almost as if new orders back to active duty might again appear out of the blue. While still in Washington and at Norfolk meeting with senior Navy personnel about advanced design of minesweeping systems there was a definite undercurrent that conflict with Soviet Russia might be imminent, foreshadowing the Cold

War. I remember my sense of shock that at this high level of command there was such urgency of bringing the Pacific Fleet home to be ready for possible trouble in Europe. The "hawk" mentality was already flourishing. By summer though, this sense of uncertainty faded away as more and more momentum built up in the swing and excitement of new projects getting underway.

For the first time in my experience the full breadth of learning in practice unfolded. Being interviewed by school boards, church and other building committees was new in feeling the pulse of the time and how to find rapport with committee members not only to get the commission but to find sympathetic allies as the give and take of design decision making took place. Up to now we had been used to a tandem sequence of one project at a time in academia and in practice too during the depression. Learning how to manage time and energy flow, to match overlapping schedules of work simultaneously involved new skills that of course had long been a part of practice in normal times. Even though there was plenty of new work, competition was stiff, especially for new schools. Each firm would have its turn and time slot for interviews with school boards, usually in a room with the door open. You could sometimes overhear your competitors make their sales pitch. As I remember, these presentations were remarkably the same, all reflecting the new spirit of recovery, opportunity for a fresh start, but still stressing the "practical" qualifications of the firm, keeping costs down and playing up as much as possible the few examples built just before or during the late years of the depression that might establish the firm's reputation as specialists in school design. In addition to this formula we learned to seek eyeball contact with whoever on the committee, in addition to special interest in schools, was concerned with larger community matters. In those days there always seemed to

be people of this sensitivity, dedication and interest, highly respected by their peers, whom you could count on to back you up in matters of aesthetics and design refinements that we thought were especially important in children's lives, just as much as in their home environment. Then if your interview succeeded these few would be your stalwart supporters through the entire design and construction process as well as most valuable referees for other new projects.

We began to take it for granted that this level of client intelligence, rapport and respect for architecture's value in the community would go on unchanging in the future. But no, it was not to be, a tale to be told later when the whole dimension of American culture was changed by the war in Vietnam. Most architectural offices that were well established before the depression managed to survive somehow up to and during World War II, so they had an advantage as the post war boom began. A few, like Skidmore, Owings and Merrill got their start in the mid-thirties along with others doing work for the 1933/34 Chicago World's Fair. George Fred Keck and his brother Bill, with their experimental house of the future for the Fair, became well known for their recognition of solar and other environmental design factors, gaining a head start for post war practice. Hugh Stubbins in the East, Neutra and Schindler in Southern California, among others, were first and primarily known as residential architects, foreshadowing the immediate post war years when it looked

as if everyone, not just the rich and famous, could have an architect designed house. It was becoming clear even to the wider public that modern design, as it incorporated uncompromised inside-outside spatial relationships, maximum space and energy efficiency, clarity of structural and material possibilities, made great sense to millions of new young clients who were free of stylistic prejudice. But this fresh new opportunity in residential design soon turned out to be unrealistic as conservative banking, real estate and developer interests saw more and more profit in catering to the majority of people who still wanted Colonial, Spanish, Tudor or whatever style to "keep up with the Joneses." Within just a few years these forces gradually squeezed out tailored, architect designed houses for lower and modest income families by marking up architects plans out for bids as much as twenty five or more percent and mortgage bankers required higher and higher down payments for construction.

In the first half of the twentieth century almost all offices of whatever size in large cities or small developed practices across the entire spectrum of building types; houses, schools, churches, institutions and commercial work. In small cities like Bloomington, Decatur, Peoria and Champaign/Urbana offices were usually only a few people up to maybe as much as twenty or so, taking pride in their versatility to respond to all types of community design needs even some pro bono projects, expressing their strong sense of identity with their city and its surrounding countryside. Even though it had been clear for years that you couldn't make money doing houses, it was still understood to be a part of one's community responsibility. Indeed it was an essential way for a young firm to get started, profitable or not. This was especially true in Southern California, as this part of the country emerged after the war as pace-setter for new growth and change in America.

Arts and Architecture magazine based in Los Angeles under John Entenza's editorship set a refreshing new direction in sponsoring the Case Study House series for a number of years, publishing houses, mostly small in size, designed by talented architects like Neutra, Soriano, Elwood, Koenig, Eero Saarinen, Charles and Ray Eames and others lesser known, all of progressive, contemporary design that in turn had major impact on owners and builders who would then engage young architects to maintain the same high standard of residential architecture. This exciting new movement intensified the older precedent of getting a start and becoming known in the profession and to the public by doing houses well, thereby gaining a reputation leading to an expanding variety of commissions. In fact, some architectural schools like USC, when I visited there in 1950, based their whole design studio progression from first year up to senior year almost entirely on designing houses, the idea being to concentrate on improving quality without increasing size and complexity

of each project. This directly reflected the tradition of doing houses if you're just starting out, which was flourishing even more at that time but has gradually diminished to a tiny minority today. No doubt this is another consequence of big box merchandising of almost everything in the economy. Like the fate of the mom and pop general store, the small neighborhood architectural office may soon be a thing of the past.

After several of these innovative post war years had passed one would hope to find clusters of dwellings, even neighborhoods of consistent design excellence—we might call them archipelagos of a new direction in architecture—that in turn would build momentum toward even more widespread public acceptance.

But this was wishful thinking. With very few exceptions in America like parts of Pacific Palisades and Carmel California, in the San Francisco Bay area and the Pacific Northwest, Reston, Virginia and in Florida (all of these tending to be regarded as too upscale to be within reach of modest income people) the influence of excellent contemporary design had to rely on single houses of exceptional merit, isolated or within subdivisions made up of a miscellany of standard copycat revival styles that only accentuated the public's idea that modern architecture was just another visual fashion, lacking understanding that this new direction embodied fundamental design principles, of optimal spatial organization, orientation, energy use,

structural and material integrity, many of which are invisible.

In spite of the development of prototypes in prefabrication like Lustron and Wright's Usonian house proposal, these promising innovations did not catch on in the face of the public's lingering preference for "safe" familiar images of times past, and within this nostalgia being unable to distinguish levels of design quality. Large scale developers and even smaller speculative builders could then and still do exploit this inability of the public to make fully informed decisions in purchasing their dwellings, perhaps the most important of all their lifetime investments. One can also wonder why leaders in charge of public education, from elementary through high school still have not recognized training in design appreciation as a critical quality of life factor, as an integral part of instilling wisdom in making major economic choices of highest aesthetic as well as substantive value. One could even suspect that this omission might in some way be a vestige of historic tendencies of the elite to deliberately withhold in-depth education from the masses.

Strange and ironic too, even in those promising early post war years, was the attitude of so many of the public to be stingy in voting on bond issues for community development; infrastructure, schools, libraries and other institutions to accommodate growth as well as in maintaining the urban fabric. Time after time these bond issues would be turned down, especially for new schools, even after being cut down to a bare minimum. A case in point was the Oakland School in Bloomington, Illinois. When finally we as architects got the go ahead, the design was carefully integrated in its wooded site, built of native Joliet stone and redwood including a generous lobby/gathering space with a fireplace; with classrooms in a contemporary open plan using lots of glass and wide overhangs. The overall feeling was of a welcoming residential character—a relaxing retreat in the woods. The children and teachers loved it. Even so, letters appeared in the local paper complaining of "frills, how could the school board allow such a lavish expenditure of taxpayer's money?" Ed Lundeen, senior partner in the firm wrote back, affirming that the school was well within its meager budget asking "what did the complainers mean in begrudging their own children of a beautiful learning environment just because it appears to cost more when it really did not?" Later on we encountered the same parsimony in designing a parochial school—the priest insisted on bleak concrete block proclaiming that virtue in children could only be gained in a stark highly disciplined abstemious setting. I have wondered long since whether this mentality of meagerness as virtue would ever be capable of understanding sensitive minimalism in design, whenever the underlying forces within a project would point in this direction.

This tendency of the public to be indifferent and unresponsive to good design may seem to contradict my earlier observation that at least some of the members of building committees could be counted on to support excellence in institutional building. But it became evident as time moved on into the sixties and seventies that this strong influence on the architectural quality of community projects began to diminish, giving way to the dominance of pragmatic, bottom line decision making that had taken over in the rise of commercial and tract residential building. Up to this point both architects and clients had been willing to spend many more hours in the quest for excellence in the thorough study and refinement of each project. But with the build up of materialist imperatives it became more and more difficult to overcome these pressures. Since projects came increasingly under tighter and tighter budgets and fees more competitive and beaten down it was clear that much extra time had to be volunteered if high design quality could be achieved. Testimony is abundant that the finest work cannot be done without relentless effort even for those most talented and experienced—there is no short cut except for those who adopt a formula or "signature style" that allows new program requirements to be plugged in on a repetitive fast track but denies the canon that each project deserves its own special attention and recognition of its own intrinsic authority—again its "existence will"—always requiring extra depth of study and search for optimal solutions. In the face of the added patience and dedication needed to reach for this ideal, since the fee is not usually a

variable, it's easy to see how tempting it is for some to spend the least amount of time on a project that they can get away with in a market place that is more and more tolerant of mediocrity. This siege on architecture as a cultural value for most of society has been and continues to be a tale to be told yet again and again as certain episodes of experience will continue to reflect it—a grim prospect for the future but not without rays of hope along the way.

It must have been some premonition of this destiny confronting the archipelago of islands in practice that made me think once again of returning to the academic grove, not as a retreat but as a calling that might combine the pursuit of learning in the university seamlessly with practice—one simultaneously reinforcing the other—a possibility now after the war that had been verboten during the depression. When Professor Provine, head of the department of architecture at the University of Illinois, my alma mater, called me in the summer of 1946 offering me a job on the faculty there, my first question was whether or not the taboo forbidding practice during the depression was still in effect. He said indeed it was not, so with the encouragement of the office in Bloomington only fifty miles from Champaign/Urbana, I rejoiced in this new opportunity for the immediate future to be deeply involved in the thick of both theory and practice.

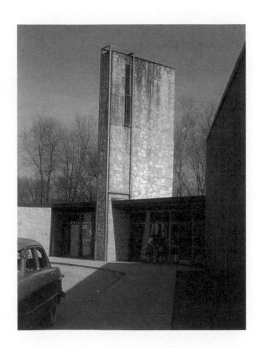

Oakland Elementary School Entrance, Bloomington, Illinois, 1948
Lundeen + Hilfinger Architects,
A. Richard Williams, Architect for Design

The same refreshing spirit pervading the post war revival in building could be felt in the academic world; perhaps even more so, since there was such a concentration of GIs eager to catch up on their education that had been cut off by the war. It was soon evident that they set a pace for the usual eighteen year old entering freshmen through their added maturity and motivation. This was an inspiration for the faculty as well. I still considered myself a student too, even with my earlier experience at Oklahoma State, this feeling was ratcheted up by the awareness of a higher level of competition that comes with the much greater size and complexity of the setting—almost like coming from the provinces to perform on the New York stage. Again, many of the students were my own age—it helped to be a veteran also, so I shared even more the excitement of learning among my peers, no doubt intensified since most of the faculty who had been my professors and critics in the thirties were still at their familiar posts in design, history, structures, art and construction technology. In contrast to the "vertical studio" experience at OSU—several levels of design studio, freehand drawing and history all at the same time, I was now assigned to third year design alone, along with Bill Scheick, Elmer Love and Gran Keith all of whom were my valued critics when I was a student. So I felt very lucky again to be an "apprentice"—somewhere in between learning from them and from my own students.

Cycles of time in youth, measured in spans of four or more years in elementary, high school, university, apprenticeship and World War II now reached a plateau stretching out into a future that looked forward for the first time since the twenties to a return to peacetime life as far as one could see ahead. Building a career as a personal preoccupation was somehow less important in the surge and shared optimism of postwar recovery, than later when self promotion would become so prominent, the "me generation" of the seventies. In a curious way peacetime recovery was a replay of accelerated mobilization during the war; those who already had even a small amount of experience advanced rapidly in rank and responsibility. This happened in the academic world as it did in all walks of life. Before the first year at Illinois passed I was recruited by the University of Minnesota, offered a salary of $5,000 (my Illinois Salary was $3,000) and rank of associate professor, having been recommended by Andy Anderson, my professor at MIT. In those days we were still naïve in playing the game of self-promotion in the academic marketplace. Indeed, later on when this kind of practice became more and more common, for those of us brought up in the depression it still seemed a less than honorable strategy. So at the time of this offer I simply reported it to Dean Newcomb saying that I really saw a great future at Illinois and would be reluctant to leave, especially since I was already fortunate to have a start in practice in nearby Bloomington. The very next day the Dean called me in to say that the university

would match the offer. I wasn't even aware that this meant tenure as well. No elaborate preparation of credentials, no tenure track protocols, no "publish or perish" anxieties, it was all done directly and simply without fanfare. Many years later I was on the university's promotion and tenure committee with all its bureaucratic complexity developed by then, realizing how lucky I was to be part of that returning GI generation, riding the wave of unquestioning trust, acceptance and fast-forward action.

The late forties also brought an enormously enriching influx of European refugee artists and scholars to American universities including Illinois, many of whom became close friends of mine partly by chance, partly by design on my part as an unsophisticated heartlander in order to satisfy a reawakening of intellectual curiosity that had first been aroused at Oklahoma State before the war, having then been blessed by close friendships across so many disciplines in the arts and sciences. It had been a quality of collegiality that had normally existed on small campuses, but that now in a very large university required a lot of initiative—it was so easy, really without thinking much about it, to be caught up within one's own academic ghetto. This time though, it began to dawn on me that there was a fascinating difference—my new ex-European friends became collectively a kind of Jewish mother, subtly but no less pointedly letting me know I needed to keep abreast with the cutting edge of thought across the whole front of

cultural advance—in art, music, literature, philosophy and scientific research, as well in American pop culture which was new and exciting to them. This meant not only keeping sharp on current affairs but knowing and pondering the background depth of any of these topical events. Along with this new stimulation I was getting the message that it was up to me to translate new insights so gained to my own calling. I began to get more and more excited. More than anything else in the university archipelago, this critical awareness across disciplines had most to do with advance in architecture beyond but still demanding relentless practical, technical ability and experience as a base, particularly in the investment of ever deeper meaning and signification in responding to the human condition and environmental ethic. I could now see more clearly how strongly this concept reinforced the idea in architecture of excellence in diversity over any quest for a signature style, and would now enter the pantheon of timeless, timely canons as a most central theme, to be returned to time and again as designs for learning enrich each other and form new hierarchies of direction. It had seemed that gaining experience, maturing ability in managing technical orchestration, human relations, establishing a respectful body of work and client contacts was what counted most on the road to success in architecture, at least as perceived by the public. So investing deeper intellectual, aesthetic and humanistic meaning in each new project beyond experienced "know how" had to become more and more a personal quest with faith that the extra effort involved was worth it in the long run, whether fully understood or not. Also the notion of talent as a mysterious gift began to shift to a fuller realization that it means little without inspired, intense and continual cultivation. Practice, practice, practice seamlessly on all fronts practical, intellectual and emotional. Who could ask for more—to be in the thick of professional life on the outside and to be stimulated by the best brains in the university on the inside?

Best brains in the university of course included many others in addition to my European refugee friends, stimulating and leading anew to all the knowledge one had access to in books, journals, recorded in whatever form long before. Rereading Shakespeare, Montaigne, Socrates, Plato along with new reading of recent authors like A. J. Liebling, Lewis Mumford and the New Yorker's great critics of books, theatre, art and politics all tended to focus most on existential philosophy, especially Martin Buber and Paul Tillich as they illuminated "the in-between realm;" the mutuality of forces taking form themselves in the zone between the egos of opposing participants; finding the "existence will" in each new course of action, as described earlier. I was so excited by this reading and its implications in architecture that I invited my faculty colleagues one evening to share my enthusiasm, thinking that these new insights had particular relevance for us in architecture; that we should be free of imported stylistic influence and could find

a new interpretation of Prairie School and Chicago School openness to innovation and collaboration; free of discipleship. Sad to say, these ideas went over like the proverbial lead balloon. Already it was becoming clear that Illinois, like so many American schools was on the bandwagon of current fashion emanating from Europe, the East and new California stars. A few students would come from other states and later on from Australia and New Zealand thinking that Illinois was still the center of Prairie and Chicago School inspiration only to be disillusioned, even given a hard time if they still clung to their expectations that they had come to the historic heartland of new American vision.

These new experiences all tended to remind one that perhaps there has always been a conflict between idealism and reality—idealism being to keep seeking new depths of excellence in diversity or to face the reality of going with the flow of fashion. Now the conflict was up front, both colleagues on the architecture faculty and students, though eager and hard working wanted to follow the latest design clichés sanctioned by the glamour press. The general idea was that whoever now wore the crown, LeCorbusier, Mies, Rudolph or Kahn or more recently Gehry, Koolhass or Piano, this was the star to follow. Or, among the young "hot shot" designers, they too could become stars, leading the way with a signature style. Seeking excellence in diversity, as epitomized for example by the work of Eero Saarinen, never reached the full understanding and appreci-

ation it merited, perhaps because it seemed too eclectic (a sin) or, at a more unacknowledged level, too much work.

All this seemed ironic, recognizing the exceptional appetite of the postwar GI students for hard work, reinforced still more by an influx of eager third year students transferring from the new two year program at Navy Pier in Chicago. Most of these were from ethnic neighborhoods in the city, from Chinatown, the Polish north side, the African American south side, Hispanic and Italian neighborhoods on the west side, few of whom before the war would have had a chance for higher education. Together with the GIs, the school had perhaps never experienced such eagerness to learn, such relish for hard work, similar to the depression but not so intensely competitive, now more directed to each individual's sincere desire for self improvement. How could this extraordinary energy be pointed toward the broad scope of knowledge, cultural enrichment and diversity offered by the university as well as to the rigor of developing design and technical skills that were so immediately imperative and marketable? Since this was a difficult sell I began to think more and more I was living in an ivory tower of my own, seemingly in contradiction to the straightforward, pragmatic, materialistic values of American culture.

Again referring to my European refugee friends, a little story may illuminate the nature of old and new cultures. Once at a party at Ludie and Laura Zirners' house or it might have been at Heinz and Mai Von Foersters', the conversation turned to lamenting about Urbana/Champaign provincialism, lackadaisical public service or whatever. I began to feel a bit uneasy as the only native born American present and found myself thinking out loud "Yes, but why are we here?" Sudden silence, then wry smiles all around. Another time after that when the drift of conversation again became critical of the local scene, someone turned to me saying as if on cue, "Dick, time to speak up!" Of course it was implicitly clear all along that what we truly desired was the best of both our cultures old and new.

Building that ivory tower in reality now loomed up as a test as evidence of practicing what I was preaching. I guess it had always been in the back of my mind to build a house as soon as time, place and money could be saved to get a start. The depression ethic of pay as you go rather than borrow was still ingrained as well as the desire to be personally involved, "hands on" in the building process, going way back to childhood, designing and making bird houses and boats, later on inspired by Thoreau, whom I quoted earlier "There is some of the same fitness in a man's building his own house as there is in a bird's building its own nest..." As the threat of war had built up in the late thirties, any thought of building in Stillwater had to be dismissed although the desire was already strong then, especially as my confidence grew from designing the Bieberdorf residence.

As soon as it became clear that the future looked good at Illinois rather than trying to move on anywhere else any time soon, building a house was irresistible, but where to find a site? Somewhere on the west side of Champaign seemed the most logical area since this was the closest to the office in Bloomington, fifty miles away. I was excited to find a wooded lot on west University Avenue, a stroke of luck that combined the idea of a prairie grove and the allure of an address that directly bespoke an academic connection. The lot was owned by a farmer, who I knew would understand my offer of $100 less than the asking price of $2,000 because of the cost of removing trees. The offer was accepted—I never admitted that I intended to save as many trees as possible, which no farmer would do except to form a wind break on the northwest side of the farmhouse at some distance away.

Designing a house is like trying to record details in a dream, details that are so vividly precise in the dream but fade into a blur when you wake up. These images become even more confusing when you add all the other tantalizing illusions from all other dreaming awake or asleep. Eventually favorites will sort themselves out but when the time comes to decide on what to do now that the commitment has been made, what's the first step? Which of the many alluring directions will lead the way?

Memory flashes back to those first days in design studio when instead of copying some

Williams Studio/Residence Courtyard, Champaign, Illinois, 1958 (Photography: Ralph Line)

Symbols:
Archetypal settings and service symbols are stereotyped from conventional notation sources. They will appear in most illustrations to follow.

96

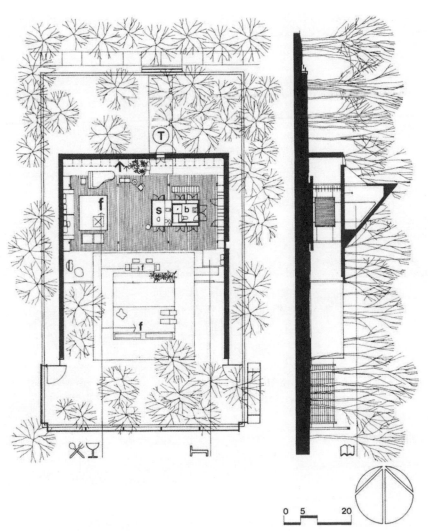

Williams Studio/Residence: Plan and Section

0 5   20

routine drawing exercise you're suddenly on your own. No client needs and desires to respond to, other than your own, no set rules to conform to except codes, site limitations and strict budget constraints. But these limitations still permitted many options of spatial organization, structural system and vocabulary of materials. I now faced the fact that professing allegiance to what a project wants to be on its own, suppressing ego, was much more daunting than following the latest hero, following personal taste or what was most fashionable. "Excellence in diversity," my new motto embodying the broadest criteria of state of the art quality was now front and center; no place to hide. It began to feel like a trap that I had set for myself without even realizing it. Still, excitement mounted and scheme after scheme came to the surface, one at a time, each one glowing for a while, then fading away the next day, just as I had experienced time after time before, first in school and now in practice. It didn't take long, though, to smoke out the governing realities that began to lead the way.

The house had to be small for pay as you go and yet as big as possible in space—a one room house-like a cottage up north? Why not, after all, the site was wooded like Nee-bish Island and would take advantage of the added sense of privacy, open up the south side with glass to a walled courtyard, gaining shade from trees in the summer and welcoming sun coming in at a low angle in the winter when the leaves were down. (Later

this would be called "passive solar design").
Along with the idea of opening up as much
space as possible came the notion of tying
outdoors and indoors together seamlessly,
with slimming down glass settings wall to
wall and carrying the same materials inside
and out. As these details became set and
cost estimates began to add up it was clear
that the whole plan had to be worked out in
two stages—whatever would be built first,
a single large room, would be structured so
that its north, south and east walls could be
moved out to maximum allowable setback
lines. The desire for maximum living and
studio space as one meant that bathroom
(head), kitchen (galley) and closets all had
to be compact as on a ship, located at the
east side, later to become an island as space
was expanded all around this core element.
It also became evident that if the scale of
all fittings and furnishings could be kept as
slim and simple as possible, the entire space
would appear larger. Somehow as all these
design decisions fell into place I began to
realize that usual style considerations had
slipped into the background, the process
itself was taking charge. The choice of different earth color materials; natural wood
finishes, dark exposed structural columns
like the tree trunks outside, Chicago common brick walls of autumn leaf color covered
with ivy all tended to emerge on their own,
as a kind of camouflage in its prairie grove
setting. When the house as fully expanded
ten years later and was published in Progressive Architecture, the editors titled their
written description "A Space not an Object."

Williams Studio/Residence: Interior
(Photography: Ralph Line)

Indeed, except in the winter when the trees were bare, the house was almost invisible, nothing but a thick ivy covered wall with a single vertical slot for the deeply recessed front door, its east/west corners obscured by trees and ivy foliage. My neighbor, Bill Werstler, a florist, called it "a walled garden for living." There's no doubt that this recessive character avoided the usual stylistic labels given to other dwellings along the street. Perhaps this is why it never seemed to be controversial as was often the case when a highly contemporary design would appear in an older or new "traditional" style neighborhood.

When Fran Myers, the feature editor of the News Gazette, came to do a story on the house, she kept asking me to name a style. Especially in regard to the interior, with its low furniture, teak floor, Zen like gravel garden, absence of pictures on the walls, she asked "Isn't it Japanese?" I tried to explain my intention to avoid any stylistic influence, desiring to let it determine its own character. Then it occurred to me to make a corny remark that if it had to have a label, why not call it "antidotal," in opposition to the poison of copy cat styles or in terms of its restful understated feeling, as an antidote to our noisy, cluttered urban life.

Returning to the academic studio as well as to a new sense of direction in practice, this almost compulsive need to assign labels could be seen as an obstacle to an honest, healthy advance for architecture in respond-ing to both societal and environmental needs as they now grew apace with accelerated economic recovery and population migra-tion. For architectural students as well as for all others in higher education, for both clients and colleagues in practice and for the public at large, a paradox of understand-ing architecture as a cultural value now had reached a new critical level of concern. The scholarship of architectural history had long established standards for measur-ing excellence by studying and identifying noble works from the past as they inform the present and future. But this gift of critical judgment, ironically limited by its provenance from art history in its preoc-cupation with outward visual characteristics with labels then applied, tended to pay less attention to invisible qualities of substance intrinsic in architecture such as functional and spatial organization, context, ethical questions and integration of structural and other hidden systems of energy manage-ment and sustainability. Ironically, the classification of architecture, along with painting and sculpture as art has limited its appreciation as a broader cultural value by being judged primarily as single artifacts in formal visual terms. Although scholars and experienced professionals have long tried to bring this discrepancy to the attention of the public, architectural criticism in the popu-lar press is still relegated to journalist art critics or real estate commentators. These journalists often joust with each other with smart writing about superficial appearances, most often applauding extravagant show piece work celebrating the latest trend as in modern art. No wonder certain celebrity architects and those aspiring to celebrity strain to gain attention by doing outrageous architecture based on eye appeal above everything else.

Even though this regard of architecture as mainly cosmetic has been building up steadily in most recent years, its symptoms were already beginning to show up in the fifties, years that some critics likened to "roaring twenties," making it all the more difficult to convince eager students of the shallowness of media hype, particularly in view of the fact that criteria of architectural excellence have as never before become broader and deeper due to the ever increasing availability of information. Thus, the accumulation of knowledge, recorded experience, research results and retrieval technology through publication systems, libraries and the internet offer the potential for evermore stringent critical judgment. Along with all other frontiers in science and technology the search for canonicity in architecture has become more rigorous involving the interface of timeless and timely components of quality measurement which are never permanently fixed but in dynamic equilibrium—always building in intellectual accountability and wisdom. In this view the build up of facile oscillation from fashionable style to style is revealed as fast track change for the sake of change, egged on by media-enhanced, ever-shorter attention spans, rather than steady qualitative advance.

This state of affairs reflects back on our tendency in the immediate post war years to take for granted or not fully appreciate the best work being done at the time, assuming that of course you're always going to be moving ahead, and that, as Wright and other heroes had been quoted when asked many years before which of their projects did they think was their best, their response was— "the next one." This more positive look in spite of superficial media hype and stylistic clichés would lead into the sixties, a time now recognized much more now than then as the twentieth century's finest hour.

In so many ways the flow of time in everyone's life is like a river, a mainstream with many tributaries, each tributary having a mainstream of its own. Just as in the early days as a university student the two streams of study and social life were most often clearly separate, each one expanding, changing course on its own. So later in life when work in two different settings with practice in architecture in a city fifty miles away from teaching in the university, two different streams of social life were also flowing and changing in each place. I suppose this was somewhat unusual compared to the majority of our fellow citizens, but for me it hardly seemed exceptional, in fact it was a continuation of earlier experience, winters in the prairie, summers in the islands up north—a dual existence that much later on, winter in Arizona and summer in Michigan became such a mutually enriching pattern of life.

Social life in Normal/Bloomington combined the reward of keeping close to my parents, who in their maturity of wisdom and love were each so active in community affairs, as were my brother, sister-in-law and their lively and growing family who were always stimulating in fresh new directions. Friendships grew as well in the circle of my own contemporaries, Dean and Avis Hilfinger, Ted and Dorothy Fagerburg, Frances Elfstrand, Bill and Alice Bach, Pearl Hitch, Yvonne Tait, Helen and Bud Ritchie, Frank and Gladys Mittlebusher, Gene and Maurine Asbury, Wade and Jeanine Abels, all of whom, like my closest friends in Champaign/Urbana were in different professions, businesses and had other interests. In retrospect, memories of so many years make a collage of recitals, parties, picnics, dances at the Country Club, high jinks in masquerade, volunteering in political campaigns and community drives, entertaining visiting concert artists and other cultural involvement with the two local universities, Illinois Weslyan and Illinois State.

Just as my parents had been many years before, as liberal, compassionate democrats became expert diplomats in the midst of their rock-ribbed republican friends so I, too, learned from them how to avoid controversial political discussions when I was among my own generation. Something about the history of Bloomington as the county seat of McLean County, one of the most fertile farming areas in America, engendered ultra-conservative republicanism yet tolerated and even took pride in a tiny minority of hometown liberals like Adlai Stevenson.

My mother, who had been president of the Illinois PTA and was very well known as a speaker across the state, was a friend of Adlai's and campaigned for him when he was governor and when he ran for president against Eisenhower in 1952. I would sometimes drive her to speaking engagements and was always amazed that her liberalism in no way diminished her esteem in the minds and hearts of her audiences who were in large majority conservative farming people and tradesmen. My father, who by now had retired as head of the school of commerce at Illinois State but continued as a tax consultant for local businesses, also enjoyed high respect and close friendships with his largely republican clients. Politics didn't seem to be nearly as prominent in those post war years as now, possibly because the exuberance and pace of recovery from war and depression swept away most feelings of partisanship.

I learned too, at that time and ever since, that you can't assume there's a correlation between liberal thinking and contemporary architecture. I had prepared a design for the new Unitarian church in Bloomington to replace its decaying older building in the downtown area. Encouraged by the building committee, the design was a simple, rectangular, chapel sized space made up of exposed steel tube structure with stained glass infill, a contemporary recall of Ste. Chappelle in Paris. The church members were very enthusiastic about it but when Adlai Stevenson, also a member of the church, was in town and was shown the model, he threw up his hands in shock exclaiming "How can you do this glass box?" Some years later in 1961/62 when John Kennedy, a liberal democrat, too, was president, Life Magazine published photos and description of his and Jackie's new house in Virginia—a large, sprawling Cape Cod style mansion in juxtaposition to arch conservative Senator Barry Goldwater's new modern Frank Lloyd Wright style house in Phoenix, Arizona.

Social life in Champaign/Urbana was bound to be influenced by the dominance of the University of Illinois which had reached a size of at least 40,000 students and faculty, its campus located between the two cities, with its south edge spreading out in the country-side accommodating athletic facilities and experimental agriculture. Such great size meant that each college, school or other academic institutes and research units tended to be mainly self-contained including its internal social structure. But of course many of us had other networks of friends, too. I've already mentioned my good fortune in having become close to our exceptionally bright new faculty both European and American across the board of disciplines; art, music, physics, mathematics, theatre, literature, language, classics and many others. Add to this one's immediate neighbors, especially Bill and Esther Werstler and Harold and Hap Colbert whom I've known and treasured for almost sixty years.

So just within the Champaign/Urbana community alone these three tributaries of friendship kept flowing and enriching; faculty and students in architecture, a constellation of brilliant people across the university spectrum and closest of all my neighbors. As cycles of university life passed in both the mainstream and tributaries, year after year, decade after decade, certain highlights of learning and living will take form, sometimes foreseen sometimes happening unexpectedly as from the land of Serendip. Highest priority in telling these tales will

be to express my depth of gratitude to this host of friends as each in turn by name, or in clusters like a jazz combo, who have added so much wealth to each new cycle of experience, shifting, sorting and then enduring in life's archipelago.

By the time one approaches the midspan of a career, crossing new thresholds of experience in both architectural practice and education, an awareness grows of how much the search for a center focus and the quest of finding the spirit of one's time and place depends on clues of direction, gateways of entry through a membrane surrounding a nucleus of meaning and purpose. From practice it's increasingly clear that each new project tends to generate a central spatial idea or concept that requires the accumulation of previous experience in understanding peripheral forces as guides toward the center. It doesn't seem to matter whether the project is a school, a house of worship, a museum, a hospital, a store or most embryonic of all, a house. There is always a potential singularity of essence to be found, then clarified and reinforced by all supporting detail design decisions around it—use of light, structure, material, energy, landscape, furnishings and many more. Maybe all this takes twenty or more years before practice, practice and practice some more builds confidence and maturity for the crest of a career that may be sustained and keep on growing for a long, long time. It is at this point of approaching maturity in one's career, I truly believe, that a new dawn breaks in more fully realizing the importance of stepping up continuing education in the liberal arts and sciences at new levels of enrichment around the central core of architecture—that had only vaguely begun to be understood, as discussed earlier on, inspired by the dynamic intellectual pace set by colleagues across the university, as well as by new inspiration of all sorts from work, travel and independent study as they all built up momentum.

This idea of seeing one's calling at the center core and focus of learning in an expanding sphere of experience and knowledge is at once a timely state of the art MRI set of cross sections as well as a telescope back to origins in history, illuminating the timeless values of simplicity, directness and truth in design as gained over the ages. To illustrate this thought, I would like to return to the house as the embryo of all other typologies of sheltering human activities as they have evolved over time. Referring to Joseph Rykwert's Adam's House in Paradise, the notion of the primitive hut may be seen as the point of origin of all subsequent building types, each house in time becoming the setting of whatever special skills the occupants might develop, as warrior protectors, as teachers, as healers, as chiefs, as priests, as farmers, as craftsmen, all generic occupational origins forming different edges and centers, in nomadic life, or in villages, towns and cities of ever developing ethnicities and civilizations. As Lewis Mumford has described in The City in History, the anatomy of towns and cities consistently reveals two identities within—the citadel, the fortified house of the ruler and the temple, the house of God. Each of these in turn, like the primitive hut or individual house has its center focus or hearth, protected by its enclosing edge which over time became increasingly complex, as did the center space in response to evolving ritual. In theatrical terms, this enduring edge-center relationship is that of a front-stage action setting served by backstage support space, fine tuned with thresholds between, these also of two basic types—points of entry highly visible, celebrated and ceremonial and exits, discreet and behind the scenes but still highly functional spaces in service to front stage action. In this hierarchy of relationships we seem to have a generic spatial pattern that is pervasive through the ages, therefore of fundamental value to designers as needs are analyzed then brought to a new synthesis. Once this core insight is understood and accepted it is perhaps the most persuasive argument for continuing relentless yet exhilarating study of both software and hardware precedents throughout history in enriching the design process, in distilling the best we know from this panorama of central theme and edge variations as they relate to each new design task. From Shakespeare's metaphor in As You Like It "all the world's a stage" to Aldo Van Eyck's more recent insight "The house is a city and the city is a house," the search for essence of invested meaning in design is not only stimulated by understanding the timeless reciprocity of edges and centers in life but by poetic inspiration as well.

The reciprocity of key elements as ingredients in the design process, like the interlocking of edges and centers discussed above, may be illustrated in other ways, resulting also from maturing experience and knowledge in mid career. These, too, as they fuse together find new dimensions of depth and expression. I am now referring to the reciprocity of analogy and metaphor as they become grace notes in design. Similarities of function carrying across from one art to another or from science to a technical problem solution have their roots in the use of analogy as a rational design tool. More subtle but no less important as a design tool is the use of metaphor in understanding the nature of a thing or process from its poetic and emotional side, analogy sources tending to be organic from nature while metaphoric sources are largely from art and literature.

Organic sources of analogy include the physical sciences and life sciences in respect to observations that can be made of functional behavior that suggest solutions for new problems, for example, Robert Le Ricolais' models of three dimensional light weight structural systems as they were inspired by the geometric triangulation of ocean radiolarian. Later on this became known as the "synectic method," a problem solving technique that relies on conceptualization and design decision making inspired by innumerable functioning mechanisms in nature. Another kind of analogy that is closer to the normal processes of design is the wide range of historic man-made prototypes

that may suggest solutions to totally new problems, analogous in either form or function to primitive structural forms such as pottery shells, basketry, fabric membranes, utensils, etc. for all kinds of architectural and engineering forms. In a similar way prototype functional concepts of controlling the flow of air and fluids in veins, tubes and channels have contributed enormously as analogies for complex circulation problems of environmental conditioning, material and people movement. Surely it is this kind of low tech knowledge that is spurred by nature related curiosity as well as from direct "hands on" experience that becomes most creative in the search for direct and simple solutions.

The understanding and appreciation of metaphor in enriching the design process is of course less direct than analogy, since it is distinctly a poetic device that intensifies meaning through finding curious and appealing contrasts of images "the moon is a ghostly galleon riding on cloudy seas." Its contribution to the stream of design thinking is both intellectual and emotional, not so directly related to the physical nature of an object or system to be designed, but to intensify both its real and symbolic meaning, taking the chance that this investment of intention and meaning at this level of literacy may not be as fully perceived as by direct analogy. But one has to have faith that this poetic dimension of design skill development adds to the qualitative refinement of beauty and integrity of all growth and change in

architecture as well as in all other forms of the built environment. Indeed it is a direct inference of Plato's definition quoted earlier: "Education consists of giving to the body and to the soul all the beauty and all the perfection of which they are capable."

All these thoughts were building up during the postwar years in both teaching and practice. By now, a long time later, it's hard to be sure which realm of learning contributed the most to their overall orchestration in the quest for excellence in architecture. The above quotation from Plato would suggest that the design of settings for education offers the most direct opportunity to trace how practical architectonic skills combine with aesthetic, poetic dimensions in the design process.

Bloomington High School Gymnasium, Bloomington, Illinois, 1955
(AISC National Honor Award, 1956)
Lundeen + Hilfinger Architects
A. Richard Williams, Architect for Design
Gene Asbury, Associate for Design Development

Perhaps at other times in history after a return to peace and recovery from economic depression there was a surge in building new schools, but the magnitude of the post World War II building boom far exceeded any earlier time. We first responded to the beginning of the "baby boomer" generation by building new elementary schools, then as this generation moved into their teens, high schools, colleges and universities, the latter reaching its peak in the sixties, a time, as observed earlier, of a parallel awakening of civil rights and environmental consciousness. I think that this progression from the relative simplicity of primary school design to the increasingly complex spatial organization of advanced education, of evermore specialized disciplines, was an especially direct, fortuitous path of gaining experience. Designs for architectural learning coincided so neatly and sequentially with designs for learning itself. All along this path the challenge of solving rational problems of space, structure and materials included the harmonics of light, color, acoustics, tactile and thermal design decisions on a parallel track intrinsically inseparable and desirable for all educational environments. Needless to say, this goal of seamlessness, including landscape and beneficial urban context should be the same for all types of building, but it seemed such a clear-cut and singular ideal for designing settings for learning. The sequence of moving from simple to complex, each step along the way becoming a process of rehearsal, action, critique, recycling time and time again is surely one of the most basic of all principles of learning and building skill through experience. Time and time again, the full palette of design decisions including enclosure, equipment and properties as in theatrical set design, would be orchestrated as a singularity that most responded to the particular educational intention. What was pinned up on the walls, artifacts brought in, the ambience of changing lighting and acoustics all became part of the whole, giving new complexity to the idea of form following function.

It was also most fortunate that this postwar time became an opportunity for the design of new places of worship. Perhaps even more than for schools, the skill of orchestrating the full spectrum of sensory harmonics, within a singular architectural space became more inspirational and important, now potentially liberated from the restraints of revivalist Gothic, Georgian, Classical or other imported styles. I say potentially liberated, but in reality it was much more difficult to persuade congregations that this was a new direction they might want to follow, much more so than for new schools.

Fortunately a few new churches like Eliel Saarninen's First Christian Church in Columbus, Indiana set a pace for excellence in contemporary design, close enough to Central Illinois for visiting and highly persuasive for emulation to any congregation in our region that was considering building a new church, as many were. Among these the First Methodist Church, a large parish in Bloomington, had already acquired a prominent site on Washington Street on the east edge of downtown. I was lucky to be given the opportunity to develop the design for a new church on this site and soon discovered that the building committee included several members who, as I have remarked earlier, were most eager and eloquent in expressing their desire for a fresh new start that would not only respond to a well studied program of their own needs but aspire to enhancing the stature of the community as well.

The inspiration of the Saarinen church in Columbus was centered most on elegantly proportioned form and space—a simple rectangle with natural lighting of the sanctuary concentrated on one side, the north, with the nave lighted with tall windows on the south side, oriented to an open court defined at back by an educational wing and by a tower at the front tied to the west entry façade. The palette of materials on the exterior included Indiana limestone for the front with sand colored brick elsewhere and on the interior smooth plaster and natural finished vertical wood strips and paneling. Perhaps because there seemed to be a strong similar regionality of both Bloomington and Columbus and an almost identical size of congregation, the design of the new Methodist Church in Bloomington took shape almost as a twin, with of course some differences in ancillary spaces and architectural detail, for example the entry façade opened up in full light glass instead of a solid limestone front facade as in Columbus, and the tall nave windows included some colored glass. It was the first time in my experience that the importance of balancing light and acoustical qualities had become so positive and critical as atmospheric design decisions along with the choice of solid materials forming the spatial and structural enclosure system. This became a most valuable rehearsal for projects that soon followed, St. Matthews Episcopal Church in Bloomington and the First Presbyterian Church in Urbana, both smaller in size but with the same desired importance of lighting and acoustics. Both of

First Presbyterian Church, Urbana, Illinois , 1966
Lundeen + Hilfinger Architects
A. Richard Williams, Architect for Design
Wade Abels, Associate for Design Development

First Methodist Church Interior Renovation, Champaign, Illinois , 1968
Lundeen + Hilfinger Architects
A. Richard Williams, Architect for Design
Gene Asbury, Associate for Design Development

Chapelle Notre Dame du Haut de Ronchamp, France, 1954
Le Corbusier, Architect
Communion Rail Area: Example of Multisensory Ambience

these parishes were already well known for their choirs and the eloquence and diction of their pastors. Also, their building committees were eager to explore architectural qualities that would be restrained and compatible with their residential settings, both sites already graced with mature hardwoods, allowing generous set backs from the streets and space in back for educational and social facilities.

Although there was no explicit reference in detail to Elizabethan character, the design of St. Matthews developed with a similar vocabulary of low stone walls and relatively steep gabled wood roof structure, gluelam rafters and plank ceiling exposed on the inside with dark slate roofing outside. The roof overhang on each side with stained glass continuous strips just below allows reflected light from the ground to come in on top of the stone side walls. The First Presbyterian Church design in Urbana evolved in the same way, but with greater overhang on each side, on the entry façade even more, achieved by the use of hip roof form allowing a vertical opening for light where the hip met the gable ridge. In both churches the sanctuary wall was more highly lighted, St. Matthews covered with gilded fabric and the Urbana church by back lighted stained glass. The Emil Frei Studio in St. Louis did the stained glass for both. The resulting architectural character of each of these new churches, although of restrained contemporary feeling, seemed no great departure from the past, relying on low key natural materi-

als, subdued lighting and a familiar aromatic atmosphere arising from wood resins, wax finishes and candles. Likewise, the dark pitched roof forms and grove settings were already familiar everywhere past and present, another timeless quality of architecture and landscape as one.

If there was anything particularly unique or of special emphasis in design and not limited only to houses of worship, it was in attempting to refine the sonic environment stimulated by the choirs and spoken voices as mentioned above. A year before, while on a trip back to Scandinavia, I had been given a tour of the new Royal Broadcasting Studios in Copenhagen. Most impressive of all these spaces was a special studio of recital hall size for small musical ensembles, both vocal and instrumental. The entry into this studio from the public circulation as well as from backstage space was through air lock vestibules. As we entered the inner studio space, it was as if we were entering a building within a building, or, expressed another way, as if we were entering the interior of a giant violincello, I was struck by the absence of sound or, if you will, by the sound of silence experienced as never before. The feeling of the whole room as an instrument was amplified by the use of mahogany or spruce stained and waxed the same color and finish as a Stradivarius violin for all surfaces, no doubt intended to add resonance to the sound quality. Ever since this experience I have been convinced that all-wood interiors offer the finest acoustic ambience. Indeed for the Urbana church, we used a tongue and grooved oiled redwood flush surface for the entire ceiling, coming down to the low eaves and the narrow horizontal strip of glass along the top of the low stone side walls. Ever since the church was built in the early sixties visitors have come especially to enjoy the acoustical atmosphere. At the twenty year anniversary celebration, many of those who had been and still were leaders in the church, the minister, Rev. George Easley, the elders and building committee, its chairman Rolly Zimmer, referred to the quality of sound more than any of the other design features in expressing their pleasure and appreciation over this span of time. Earlier on I had re-marked that there is probably no other more rewarding feeling for an architect than this expression of gratitude by clients and users for one's design effort after many years have passed since a projects completion. I believe that this appreciation is a result of a complex mix of reactions—to a satisfying functional design first of all, entwined with response to more subtle multi-sensory atmospheric qualities like sound, aroma, tactile and thermal senses combining along with vision to create an enduring, shared experience. It flashes back again to my first memory of multi-sensory enjoyment as a three year old child at Llewellyn Beach, and its timeless importance in my calling to architecture.

Over the years experience in the design of churches began to take on broader sig-nificance across the whole spectrum of architectural design, first spreading to other faiths—Judaism, Buddhism, Muslim, Hindu, Shinto and Zen then to considering what common qualities exist in the creation of spiritual space that would add grace to all forms of built environment. In hindsight this greater quest began for me without fully realizing it in first joining the Liturgical Arts Society, a Catholic organization dedicated to the advancement of contemporary church art and architecture, then later to mem-bership in the Interfaith Forum for Art and Architecture, IFRAA and Art, Religion and Contemporary Culture, ARC. All of this par-ticipation gradually worked toward a more encompassing understanding of spiritual space as its perception extended more and more toward a fusion of sensitive design of man made settings for all walks of life and in appreciation of spirituality in nature as well. As time and experience move into the present and look to the future this quest for the ingredients of spiritual space will join with and become an inseparable part of the search for canonicity in architecture, landscape architecture and all other design disciplines in which the human mind may affect the quality of life. Is this too tall an order? Couldn't it be another challenge like Daniel Burnham's famous quote "Make no little plans that fail to stir men's minds?"

As the academic world adjusted to peace-time after the trauma of depression and war it took a few years of responding to the new influx of numbers by simply extending time tested curricula before momentum could build up for a fresh look to the future as it would influence change. At Illinois Professor Loring Provine,. head of the School of Archi-tecture, retired in the late forties urging that the faculty search for a new director who would carry on the strengths of the school in history, architectural engineering as well as design yet be open to new directions opening up in practice. Dean Rexford New-comb, who, as mentioned earlier, was a well recognized architectural historian, would stay on for several more years. He was most influential in bringing Professor Turpin Bannister, also an historian as the new head of architecture. Professor Bannister's high reputation as a scholar was built on his spe-cial study of the history of American archi-tectural practice, especially in the twentieth century. From this background he seemed a most appropriate choice for Illinois as one of the two oldest schools in the country, along with MIT. About the time he was on board in 1948 as head, he was given a grant from the AIA to do a definitive study of The Architect at Mid Century. It was his view along with that of the faculty that the curriculum at Illinois needed to be updated, and studied on a parallel track to benefit most from this coincidence in timing.

In 1950 the curriculum committee of which I was chairman suggested that it would be a good idea to seek the opinion of lead-ing practitioners across the country as to a new proportion of content and emphasis in the curriculum, particularly in design studio projects and their integration with all other course requirements including electives. Professor Bannister proposed that this might best be done by inviting a list of leaders in the profession to a conference in Urbana to address such an agenda leading to a new curriculum for the five year B. Arch degree. But the budget required for such a confer-ence turned out to be much too high, so Bob Smith, Driver Lindsay and I as members of the committee proposed that we visit each of these leaders in their own offices in Chica-go, New York, San Francisco and Los Angeles following the same agenda, but at a fraction of the cost of the conference proposal. Once this idea was approved we coordinated sev-eral trips over a few months time with other meetings, juries and conferences in each of the above cities. Bob visited Perkins and Will and Skidmore Owings & Merrill in Chicago, I met with Harrison and Abromovitz in New York while on a BAID jury and during the winter of 1950–51 Driver and I spent a week in L.A. and San Francisco meeting in L.A. with Neutra, Bob Alexander, Craig Elwood, Welton Becket, John Entenza, Art Gallion and several others, then went up to San Francisco to interview Gardner Daly, John Lyon Reed and Bill Wurster. In every case we were graciously welcomed and were able to spend much more time with each of our hosts than expected. It became increasingly clear that this was a far more effective way to explore ideas in depth with each of these leaders on their own turf than it would have been in a conference where ego dynamics and debate might have clouded getting at the essence of issues that would lead to new priorities and methods in revising the curriculum. In those days the consensus was that there needed to be a much more seamless relation between design and technology best achieved through giving more time to smaller scale projects and in stressing the importance of refining cycles of construction detailing and integration of mechanical systems, landscape and furnishings. I have already discussed Southern California's rediscovery of developing skills and a reputation in designing houses as a path to earning commissions for larger work—the influence of Art & Architecture Magazine's Case Study House Series and the concentration on house projects all through the curriculum at USC under the deanship of Art Gallion. The Chicago and New York architects argued for the same redirection toward building orchestration skill in small projects even though these firms were best known for their larger scale work in office buildings, high rise dwellings, schools and other institutions.

The result of these interviews distilled into a new curriculum proposal titled Design for Practice that maintained the same sequence of studio progression from the first to fifth year, but recomposed each of the studios for the upper three years on the atelier model, calling them "vertical studios" each of which would include students from each

of the upper three years. In addition it was proposed that project programs be chosen to make sure that each of the familiar building typologies would be experienced such as residential, educational, spiritual, etc., but at the most simple, direct level, avoiding complexity until basic command of conceptual and orchestration skills were understood and demonstrated. Although the faculty voted to adopt these changes and they were put into action the next year with great enthusiasm by younger faculty and students, the "old guard" resisted the idea, apparently because they were used to the traditional hierarchy of critics, the most senior faculty in the advanced studios in which the students too were all at the advanced level. So quietly over the next summer the vertical studio arrangement was changed back without a vote of the faculty. To this day I'm convinced that the real reason for the switch back was laziness—the vertical studio requiring more work, patience and rigor in criticism. About this time and perhaps even earlier I began to have a clearer idea of how academic bureaucracies become self-serving and phlegmatic. It was more and more disillusioning to wake up to this reality—yet at the same time to be inspired with more determination than ever to invest time with the students regardless of the raised eyebrows of my older colleagues. This wake up too, added new depth of appreciation of my bright friends across the university and to new arrivals from abroad—a new dimension to the inspiration of collegiality I already have expressed.

**Serge Chermayeff, Gabriel Guvrekian,
Robert Le Ricolais**

Among my closest ex European friends were Ludie and Laura Zirner. Both from Vienna, Ludie had had a promising career in opera and Laura in graphic design. Before Pearl Harbor they had migrated to the U.S., Laura eventually to Chicago to the Institute of Design, while Serge Chermayeff was president of the Institute. Ludie was drafted in the U.S. Army late in the war which soon ended allowing him to be recruited to the music faculty at Illinois. There turned out to be some difficulty in transferring credits, to the equivalent of an American degree, so he broke some kind of record in acquiring over one hundred hours of credit by passing proficiency exams, to be then appointed to the School of Music faculty and placed in charge of the opera workshop. Laura continued at IID in Chicago by commuting once a week from Urbana but soon became engaged assisting Ludie in the opera workshop in costume and set design. I was lucky to meet them early in the fall of 1946 at a Fine Arts College reception and we immediately became friends as if we had known each other for years. Even this early after the war had ended Chermayeff was having administrative problems at the IID and would come down to Urbana as a refugee on weekends to stay with the Zirners, bringing his wife Barbara and their two young sons Ivan and Peter. It soon became clear that Serge, already well known internationally as a talented architect, had a haughty aristocratic temperament. Coming from a privileged family in the Ukraine, migrating to England for school and with an early start there as a vanguard

modernist, he came to Chicago about 1942 and was immediately recruited as head at the IID, only a few years following the arrival of Gropius at Harvard and Mies Van Der Rohe at the Illinois Institute of Technology, IIT, both as heads of architecture programs, continuing the wave of importing European stars for top leadership positions in American universities. Far more than the others, Serge was a true prima donna, uncompromising, authoritarian—the archetype of a maestro, not understanding that this demeanor may work in a studio but not as an administrator in an American academic setting. Hence the trouble at IID in Chicago and the need to seek refuge in Urbana. I guess in much the same way that I was adopted by Ludie, Laura, Heinz and Mai Von Foerster and my other ex- European friends, I became some kind of steady, mild, cheerful, responsive, non controversial, typical Midwestern native American friend to Barbara and Serge, for many years to come after they left Chicago for Harvard, then later at Yale and at Wellfleet, Cape Cod. Sometime in the late fifties when they were back visiting in Urbana, Serge presented me with one of his paintings inscribed "for Richard, fine and applied." (I guess this was a play on the name of the College of Fine and Applied Arts at Illinois, which included architecture, art, music, dance, drama, planning and landscape architecture.)

Soon after Turpin Bannister came to Illinois as head, he succeeded in bringing Gabriel Guvrekian to the faculty. Gabriel had come from a prominent family in Armenia, studied architecture in Vienna and began working in Paris in the early twenties where he formed a close tie with Le Corbusier and Robert Mallet Stevens resulting in their initiating the new organization Congress Internationale des Architectes Modernes, CIAM, soon becoming known around the world as the cutting edge of modern architectural philosophy, fostering a singular rather stark interpretation of modernism, bare boned, usually black and white, glassy openness played against rather scaleless horizontal and vertical planes, soon to be labeled by Henry Russell Hitchcock and Philip Johnson as "International Style."

Gabriel, through his own work became known for his contribution to this trend in the design of gardens. He and his wife Ninette had no children and soon after arriving in Urbana became a much loved couple in our multi-ethnic social circle. Gabriel himself was an exacting but gentle critic. Once the students got used to his rather uncompromising European style of leading a project in an unswerving direction, they learned to respect and value his sincerity and contribution to their own positive absorption of different points of view.

I got to know and treasure my friendship with Gabriel and Ninette almost as if they were one person. They would return to Paris and the Riviera every summer and when I was there too, I enjoyed their company so much seeing and experiencing their Paris in ways I would never have been able to do

otherwise—certain small restaurants like Mere Michelle's, off-beat street life, visiting some of the early work as well as new city edge growth that Gabriel knew about through old friends.

There will be other memorable episodes to relate as this tale unfolds, one that my serve as an introduction to Robert Le Ricolais, the great French structural theorist I have already mentioned. Gabriel knew Robert from the old days in Paris, so soon after Gabriel came to Illinois, he suggested to Turpin Bannister that Robert might be persuaded to be a visiting professor in the architectural engineering division of the school. This division, under the leadership of Newlin Morgan was particularly strong in the mathematical analysis of structures rather than the empirical, having developed over many years in this direction from the days of Nathan Ricker and the influence of the Berlin Bau Akademie and the school of architecture's location in the College of Engineering.

So when Le Ricolais arrived for a semester as a visiting professor in the early fifties, his relation as an empiricist to the formula, calculating method of Newlin and the rest of the architectural engineering faculty was not easy, in fact Robert was regarded as a lightweight, almost as a flake by this part of our faculty, which only endeared him more to the rest of us who were open to an imaginative approach to structural design. Robert, too, was, like Gabriel, a highly stimulating thinker, a most engaging conversationalist

on all fronts of theoretical speculation. More than anyone else I've ever known, Robert was most eloquent in his gestures, which were a most perfect simulation of his ideas of tetrahedral and other three dimensional structures—arms, fingers, even facial expressions forming trusses, lace like bracings, bridges and towers.

Gabriel, Ninette and I boarded a TWA Constellation flight from O'Hare airport, Chicago overnight to Paris. They also were looking after Maurice, the twelve year old son of friends in Urbana who was to meet his grandparents at the Aerogare in Paris. Gabriel and Ninette also brought along Oulie, their pet Pekinese— the airline then permitted pets in the cabin as long as they were kept in their portable containers. The seating arrangement was then in pairs facing each other on each side of the central aisle, Gabriel and Ninette and another couple on one side with Oulie, Maurice and I facing forward on the other side with a beautiful young girl and a man in his late thirties, who looked like Salvador Dali, sitting opposite to us. As night came on over the Atlantic, Maurice put aside his MAD magazine and went to sleep when the lights were turned down, as we all tried to do. Before long there was a stir, apparently Oulie had slipped out of his box and was exploring the cabin and almost at the same time the girl opposite was being disturbed by the Salvador Dali character. I managed to get a light on and give him a stern look threatening to call the cabin attendant. Oulie was found and returned to his box and all was quiet again for the rest of the flight. At the Aerogare Maurice was greeted by his grandparents, Gabriel and Ninette left for her sister's apartment and we made plans to meet again in a few days. The girl waved goodbye, little did we imagine that we would ever meet again as we did a month later in Delos, Greece—that will be another story.

Later that afternoon, after I had caught a few hours more sleep at Signor Cassarini's Hotel de la Grille on the Rue Bonaparte on the Left Bank I went for a stroll in the late afternoon on the Boulevard Ste. Germaine, and was amazed to run into Robert Le Ricolais who was striding along in his usual jolly, brisk manner. After embracing and expressing our surprise, Robert insisted I come along with him for dinner at his house which I thought must be nearby. But no, we strode on and on along the sycamore lined quays of the Seine which were then in full bloom triggering an almost unending series of sneezing. As we crossed the Ile de la Cite and Notre Dame Robert kept chatting and gesturing and I kept sneezing. Finally we crossed the Place des Voges, reaching his top floor apartment in the Marais district. I was already exhausted when we had climbed the stairs and met Robert's charming wife who was busy preparing dinner for a number of friends who were soon to arrive. Meanwhile Robert showed me his office and laboratory which was loaded wall to wall and floor to ceiling with models of all imaginable kinds of three-dimensional fragile looking structures which in the dim light seemed to be alive. I worried about stumbling or spilling my aperitif. Soon other guests were arriving, maybe ten or twelve in all. It was as if I had stepped back fifty or more years in time—to the Edwardian age of gentlemen in high stiff collars, wearing monocles and their ladies in fluffy coiffeurs and costumes. As delicious course after course was served and the lively conversation bubbled, I was often lost, my French was continuing to fall further and further behind. I found I could almost get back on track by asking a new question about something recent in the news or about modern art or politics but finally resigned to simply enjoying this highly unusual experience, a kind of blurry bliss, a mix of marvelous food, wine and good company. Finally about midnight the party ended, bidding goodbye to Robert, his wife and friends, somehow finding my way back to my hotel, running an obstacle course at that time of the night of prostitutes soliciting at almost every street corner. I can't believe to this day that so much could happen in little more than thirty hours, June 1 & 2 1959. That summer was full of other events that became more memorable than I could then imagine and would replay again years later.

I suppose that it's the very nature of seeing one's life in retrospect that the chronology of events and interpreting them blur in a kaleidoscope of flash backs mixed with images and memories of much more recent experience. The choice of what to relate from this kaleidoscope eventually seems to depend on sorting out what was simply fascinating as isolated experience or what may now reveal itself clearly as contributing to the flow of learning. This choice making was perhaps going on intuitively from the beginning of my chronicle but by now I see it more purposefully as a structure and discipline upon which to search for and hopefully find new depths of significance for architecture in the future. For example the happenstance and

luck of being born in the heartland of North America with almost as much connection to Canada as to the United States and later on to Hispanic America carries with it a growing sense of confidence rather than intimidation in speaking up in a world of criticism still dominated by European, east and west coast elitism. This awakening is at once one of thanks not only to be a heartlander, by nature open to influences and by diverse friendships from all over the world but also as a consequence of learning thereby, almost as if one is a referee, what an advantage it offers to rise above adversarial, authoritarian, elitist dogma now magnified more and

more by media inflation.

Stating once again the goal of finding excellence in diversity I realize I may have been neglecting the tribute that is so much deserved by students and colleagues in this flow of time and learning from cycles in the academic grove, in practice and in the wider world. In many ways it is tribute just as much earned by so many whose names have faded into the past as it is to those who have remained as closest friends. Together they form a fabulous family of all ages yet all still young in heart and mind. I have already tried to recall times places and events earlier in life as this family was forming, in childhood, in school in Illinois, summers at Neebish, at the University of Illinois, MIT, Oklahoma State, in Europe, in World War II and now in the professional world. From now on it will be my hope to connect each of these treasured friendships as they developed to the special insights about design that they have inspired.

Early on in Champaign/Urbana just after the war I became especially close to Fred Salogga and Jack Baker, also returning veterans and new to the faculty. Fred, who already had office experience in Decatur Illinois and was also an officer in the Navy, was the epitome of integrity and all-around professional ability, especially in thoroughness of orchestration of construction processes leading to highest quality of results—endurance, both material and aesthetic. Fred's personal integrity was uniquely manifest in his work, both as an architect and as an

educator more than anyone else I have ever known. His influence on me and many, many others in demonstrating by example the importance of sustained patience and devotion to every task down to the finest detail has been unmatched through his long life. Facets of this experience will unfold as I relate this tale of events ahead, particularly as Fred and I would travel many times to Mexico and Europe, would serve in the American Institute of Architects and would collaborate on projects.

Jack, who had been in the Army in Italy, returning to finish his degree in 1946, is a native of Champaign and has all his life set an unequalled example of excellence of contribution to his community. Rather than become an academic or professional nomad as so many of us have, Jack has been an exemplar of talent and steadfastness in one's home town over a lifetime. I think of him as a reincarnation of Palladio in Vicenza and as with a very few other historic figures whose identity with their city has been so lasting and unique. Jack's life contribution has been even more exceptional in its breadth of cultural participation and benefit, in outstanding skill as an architectural educator at Illinois, as design architect of exemplary residences, churches and other projects in Champaign/Urbana and other communities, as life long mainstay of the Krannert Center for Performing Arts, particularly in dance and as a benefactor and consultant in civic improvement. As with Fred, Jack and I have learned so much together from collabora-

Nelson Residence, Urbana, Illinois, 1979
(AIA Illinois Honor Award)
Jack Baker, FAIA, Architect, Illinois Medal 2007

tion, travel and putting our minds on new tracks of design thinking. This theme too will surface again as I recall my friendships over the years with Bill Caudill, Fay Jones, Charles Moore, Cesar Pelli and Joe Esherick, all AIA Gold Medalists.

Along with Fred and Jack my closest friend-ships included Harold Young and Bill Eng both of whom were advanced students in the late forties, Harold then joining the faculty, Bill going on to Penn then to the Saarinen office before returning to Illinois about 1960. Har-old and Bill both shared the same talent and design sensitivity, Bill in form making, scale and proportion through relentless study, restudy, especially with models, Harold in much the same way, tending to focus most on refinement of material relationships and interior design. For many years up through the sixties. Fred, Jack, Harold and I fine tuned a lot of our design thinking during vacations in Mexico, mostly in Acapulco but in many other places too, Oaxaca, Yucatan, and Puerto Vallarta. This thinking of course was mostly light hearted and casual, what else would you expect in such salubrious settings lubricated by Margaritas and Dos Equis? Yet on the more serious side I think we firmed up convictions of how important it is in any project to strive for "genius loci," spirit or character of place, again the harmony of the total setting, true to its cultural heritage interlocked with the grace of its natural setting, in this case the blending of pre-Columbian cultural influences on their art and architecture and to the majesty of their

setting. What can you learn about scale from the temple ruins of Tulum in Yucatan, from their dramatic location on a bluff overlooking the sea or from the terraces of Monte Alban and their spatial sensitivity to the surrounding mountains? What can you learn about the use of strong color in its balance with natural material surfaces in basketry, pottery, sculpture and other man made artifacts? Also, it was evident that we as Anglo-Americans had overlooked or not been sensitive to the positive influences of Spanish colonial policy and Jesuit missionary effort on new town planning in its organizing principles of establishing a plaza as a com-munity center with its multi-purpose func-tions of market place, social and religious gathering, mothered over by a church and citadel both as real and symbolic presences. Though evolved over the ages, as Mumford has reminded us, these spatial relation-ships as a guiding hierarchy of town design was knowingly exercised by the colonizers, an historic fact in architectural history like learning from the vernacular that curiously enough, we were not exposed to in our three years of history courses at Illinois.

In those years too I continued to value my close ties with students as I had done before the war at Oklahoma State. There still was not much separation in our ages intensify-ing still more our sense of learning together, not that this feeling ever stopped but rather changed as it naturally would later as you become a kind of uncle or father figure and now as an "ancient mariner." All along,

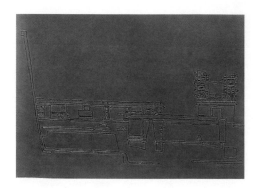

Uxmal, Yucatan (Ink on Paper), 1969
A. Richard Williams

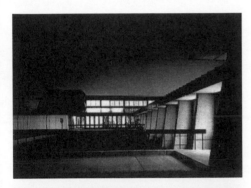

Small Animal Clinic, University of Illinois, Champaign, Illinois, 1965
Ray Oversat, FAIA, Architect with Perkins + Will, Chicago

Goodyear Technical Center Plaza Fountain, Akron, OH
Theodore E. Kurtz, FAIA Architect

though, the common denominator is as a friend and hopefully a mentor, though I think that label often works both ways.

Naturally you tend to remember most of those with whom you have been able to keep in touch near or far away. For no particular reason I tend to group these fond friends past and present in threes, as I did with Serge Chermayeff, Gabriel Guvrekian and Robert Le Ricolais, or earlier in Oklahoma State days before the war, Tallie Maule, Gibby Williams and Eason Leanard.

Now I am recalling Jim Scheeler, Chuck Gathers and Annie Halpin. They were all students in the late forties. Jim, whose thirst for knowledge, experience and capacity of applying talent know no limit, worked first for the firm in Bloomington then won a Fullbright in England then with SOM in Chicago, later a partner with Ambrose Richardson, along with John Severns, in their Champaign architectural office doing the new College of Law and other buildings on the Illinois campus, then to Washington, D.C. to join the leadership of AIA for many years, being awarded the Kemper for distinguished service to the profession. He is now a key coordinator of the international movement for reciprocity in the registering and licensing of architects.

Chuck, very talented as a designer, worked for Eero Saarinen for several years at the time of the TWA terminal at Kennedy airport in New York, then had a successful office in

Denver for many years. Both Jim and Chuck had worked for me at different times on the Stein and Proctor residences in Bloomington in 1952.

Annie, one of our first women students directed her talent to cosmopolitan experience in San Francisco and Rome reaching her career peak in New York as a leading resource for organizing construction information at Dodge Corporation and becoming one of the few women to be made fellow in AIA up to that point in time. Our reunions were always exuberant wherever and whenever they occurred in all the above cities and at AIA conventions and special meetings across the country. Annie was among the vanguard of women leaders in architecture foreshadowing the talent women in great numbers are now bringing to the profession around the world.

Recognition was now increasing of the importance of strong graduate programs in schools of architecture in stimulating motivation and setting the pace for undergraduates. Up to the mid 20th century mark in North America graduate study had been concentrated in eastern Ivy League schools, Harvard, Yale, Cornell, Columbia, Pennsylvania and Princeton. But after the war, with enormous growth of enrollment across the country, both demand and desirability of a higher level of advanced study prompted the initiation of new graduate programs, especially in the largest schools in the Midwest and west coast.

Illinois initiated its new program in the late forties when Professor Bannister brought Ambrose Richardson in as director. Ambrose ("Am") was a design team leader at SOM in Chicago, of great talent, imagination, buoyancy and persuasive personality. He immediately attracted some of our brightest new graduates, Jim Scheeler, Harold Young and John Replinger and a new influx of students from other schools across the country and abroad.

Among the latter were several from Egypt, who were somewhat older, having been unable to go abroad during the war as they had before in peacetime, mostly to Europe. After the war ended the schools in Europe had not recovered sufficiently and were far from ready to accept new students including their own. Our ambassador in Cairo, Jefferson Caffrey, taking note of this backlog of mature students, numbering in the hundreds by then, announced that the U. S. would be delighted to grant visas to those whose credentials would meet the standards for admission to American universities.

By the fall of 1947, more than two hundred were accepted across the country in a variety of disciplines including architecture. Among these, Yussef ("Joe") Shafik and Moustafa ("Moose") Ibrahim were most exceptionally gifted, already with some professional experience and command of English and were able to adjust quickly to the work ethic and design talent of our own students, becoming valued members of the graduate class. After the graduate program had a few months start, its impact on the undergraduates was dramatic. Am developed project programs much like those of SOM and other leading Chicago offices, and would frequently take the students to these offices for project reviews and discussions, all of which had an immediate effect on the pace and quality of design project development, in drawings, notably in models and in oral presentations. Even though the graduate class was located in temporary army barrack buildings away from the main architecture building, undergraduates would come over in numbers soaking up what was going on, especially for project reviews and exhibits of work.

This influence of professionalism soon permeated the whole school, building on the rigor and appetite for collaboration already well established at Illinois. It took several years more for a similar wave of influence to build up through the wave of new building on the campus and its close at hand impact on student reaction both positive and negative. Again I would like to refer the reader back to my earlier discussion of the influence of emulation as a key force in designs for learning.

Somehow university budgets began to grow despite the fact that there never seemed to be enough support for new programs and new facility development. However, we began for the first time to be able to invite visiting lecturers and critics for jury reviews. Illinois was like most other schools in trying to attract big names for lectures, invariably from the east coast. It was as if the whole reputation of a school depended on who could build up an annual lecture series of the most current stars and advertise this list with glamorous posters for pin up in all the schools. This tradition has grown enormously with media inflation and by now if all these posters over the last fifty years could be collected and exhibited it would reflect not only the parade of stars but the array of both architectural and graphic design clichés as a portrait of our American cultural tendency for all serious pursuits like education to rely more and more on their entertainment value.

Webster defines the meaning of a cliché as a "trite expression or idea." Whether the application is to architectural or graphic design, or in any other form of creative endeavor, the implication seems to accent the difference between superficial trendy fashion and solid, enduring qualities in advancing the quality of life. In the last hundred or more years of modern architecture the parade of design clichés has now revealed a vast array of imagery from flamboyant "bump and grind" sculptural form to stark minimalism, from structural exhibitionism to opaque shapelessness, from brutalism in concrete to delicate filigree in wood or metal, from scale abstraction to "post modern," "decorated shed" appliqué of classical or other historic style details out of scale and their original context. The common denominator of all these superficial aberrations is their short life and to some extent their tendency to recur again scores of years later as did the architecture as sculpture influence of Erich Mendelsohn then turn up again in the work of Frank Gehry. I think the main thing we learn from observing this panorama is that the shallowness of each of these short lived visual clichés illuminates and reinforces our appreciation and understanding of the much broader, deeper, timeless/timely canons of modern architecture. It may not be an ideal of educational methodology to find virtue in negatives as they inform the positives, or that you have to learn by mistakes, but it does seem, ironically, to be an intrinsic element of learning from experience. On the more positive side a stronger appreciation

of a region's uniqueness of character, proud of its maturing free of imported stylistic influences, should be more able to resist the allure of superficial fashion.

For example, what is Chicago about Chicago? Is there a "there" there? How important is it for any human settlement anywhere to develop and relish its own "genius loci," its unique spirit of place? This question loomed up more and more for those of us so close to Chicago, the mid-continent urban center of North America, as time allowed us to recover from depression and war, building momentum into the nineteen fifties. How do we now see the significance of our heritage from the early days of the Prairie and Chicago schools of architecture, both in practice and education? In what way do we now direct this new momentum—to revive the heritage as another replay of stylistic revivalism like Neo Classicism or Neo-Gothic or to turn over a new leaf in carrying on the same spirit of place, a fresh interpretation? I have already commented on the growing power of the media and elitist influence from elsewhere in alluring our students and colleagues away from our Chicago heritage, not only in architecture but in art and literature as well inferring that Chicago should perceive itself as "Second City" despite the creativity of native talent like Carl Sandburg, Frank Lloyd Wright, Studs Terkel, Saul Bellow and its more anonymous vigor in cultural innovation.

Nevertheless, something was happening in Chicago carrying on this vigor, also appearing in Minneapolis/St. Paul and in the metropolitan Detroit area. The new work of SOM, Perkins and Will, C. F. Murphy, Mies Van der Rohe at large scale in office and institutional building, Harry Weese bridging between residential and larger scale work, the Keck brothers, Paul Schweiker and others breaking new ground in dwelling design, all setting a new pace of excellence in the orchestration of structural, material and environmental innovation that at least in substance if not in exact visual recall, picked up the Chicago school heritage. Add to this the excellence in diversity influence of the Saarinens in Cranbrook and Ralph Rapson along with others carrying this tradition from Cranbrook to Minneapolis/St. Paul and you have the emergence of an even broader Midwest influence on its regional architectural offices and schools like Illinois, Michigan, Notre Dame, IIT and Minnesota. It's interesting now to see the integrity, strength and endurance of this underlying set of regional influences even though on the surface it would appear that celebrity starchitects elsewhere were enjoying priority status in establishing new directions.

This blooming of energy, talent and professional assurance in the fifties was embodied in many of our own leading Illinois students like Jim Scheeler and Ray Oversat working in Chicago offices, Jim with SOM, Ray with Perkins and Will. Through Jim at SOM I was lucky to get to know Walter Netsch and Ralph Youngren and to renew my old friendship with Bill Hartman from our time at

MIT, in Sweden and Italy in '39/40. Through Ray and others I soon became close friends of Larry Perkins and Phil Will. By then I was also able to renew contact with Harry Weese when he was just staring out with a small practice, sharing space with his wife Kitty Baldwin and her partner in their cutting-edge contemporary furnishings store, Baldwin/Kingery, on the near north side. I happened to be visiting there one day when the store had its first delivery of Eames chairs from Herman Miller. I was lucky to persuade Kitty to sell me two of these chairs to take back to Champaign, which I'm sure were the first to arrive there. Because of frequent visits to Chicago and close ties to friends in the thick of new work there as well as my own involvement in practice and education down state, this was a most exciting time of life, free, really for the first time, of depression worries, war anxiety, narcissism, political partisanship and spin, on the crest of new prosperity that now seemed without limit.

Even though I had been greatly saddened by the illness and death of my father of heart disease in 1952, I rejoiced that my mother would be able to rise from her grief, renew and increase her own vitality in contributing even more to both local and statewide community affairs. I was heartened too by the friendship of Dean and Avis Hilfinger and other Bloomington friends—through working at that time on new school and church projects as well as Elizabeth Stein's house. Elizabeth was especially sensitive and ap-

preciative of contemporary design, since she herself was a gifted artist and taught art at Bloomington high school. She was a strong ally when a few years later I was busy designing the new high school. As well as with the office in Bloomington, Jim Scheeler worked with me on Elizabeth's house, as did Hideo Sasaki for landscape architecture. Jim was also working on other projects in the office, then won the Plym Fellowship and a Fulbright for study in England; after that he went on to SOM in Chicago and later with Am Richardson in Champaign as I have already related. Also at that time in Am's graduate class was Cesar Pelli from Argentina, whom I got to know well. I persuaded him to work with me during the summer of 1953 in the Bloomington office on the design of the new rural electric cooperative building on the edge of the city. I remember how both Ed Lundeen and Dean Hilfinger as heads of the firm raised their eyebrows when Cesar asked for $3 an hour.

Atrium, New Building for the College of Business
University of Illinois, 2008
Cesar and Raphael Pelli, Architects
(Photo: Henry Plummer, 2009)

This is break time. Our forefathers in academia long ago recognized the need for cycles of rest and renewal in pursuit of advancing both intellectual and professional inspiration. The sabbatical year was invented. Every seventh year, like every seventh day of the week for short term restoration, seemed, probably on the basis of trial/error experience, the best time measure for reflection and renewal for those of us whose callings year in and year out reflect our trusteeship in advancing the cause of learning. At first it would seem odd that in the heat of prosperity and forward momentum one would want to take time off for an abrupt change of setting and to seek a new perspective. If you believe as I do that what you're trying to learn all through life is cumulative and knows no particular ideal time spot in the flow of professional involvement to grasp for new insights—it must be intuition rather than the result of pragmatic reasoning that leads one to choose the time for a new cycle. In 1954, celebrating my fortieth year might have been the reason after all to go on sabbatical.

The tempo of the fifties saw an awakening to how new growth and change of our towns and cities needed to look more closely at larger issues of urban planning and design that were being negatively affected by the helter-skelter postwar building boom that was responding to highly localized pressures in both the private and public sector. Each family, each business, each school, church and civic committee was so eager to catch up on its needs, that how all this made sense coming together as a whole was not given much thought. It may have been partially due to Europe's recovery and the magnetism of tourism that opened America's eyes to the fact that something was missing in the quality of community life at home, like the sidewalk cafes, markets and festivals in squares and piazzas of Europe, the alluring majestical sense of city centers in London, Paris, Rome, Madrid and the charm of even small villages that reflected the depth of invested meaning and civic pride over centuries, for both rich and poor. For the first time in history we began to hear the term "urban design" as an expression of this new consciousness even though human settlements have been designed, evolving anonymously or otherwise by centralized intelligence for thousands of years. It was all at once a question whether this new recognition of the city as a singular artifact like a building could be beneficially designable in a free enterprise culture like ours. It was natural for idealists, especially in academia to think it could , yet fully aware of the lingering pioneer mentality of *"don't tell me what to do with my land and my property."*

It was also a time, along with material prosperity, that our attention was directed more and more to good design at smaller scale; of furnishings, tools, clothing and industrial products, the car, of course, as an American icon leading the pack in design awareness. But sadly it now appears in retrospect to have been a missed opportunity for a major shift in public education to develop design sensitivity programs that could have had great impact on the public as well as private quality of life. Still, it seemed then to be a break through of direction for architects and other design professionals to broaden one's perception and skill across the whole scale spectrum of design–micro to macro. So, in thinking about a focus for sabbatical travel and study, this new inspirational direction took hold, singling out Italy as a destination where the elegant new modern design of small objects, graphics and at larger scale architecture, was seamless in its relationship to the older enduring charm of hill towns, their silhouettes and piazzas all the way up the scale to Rome, the Eternal City, for lessons in urban design. This excitement to look through a much wider angle lens was a refreshing opposite to the ever more intimidating pressure of universities to equate advanced study with narrow specialization and minutia, inferring without saying it that the big picture was reserved for the intellectual elite, sometime later if you could make it. Somehow those of us in the fine and applied arts enjoyed greater freedom—with a smile from above, I might add—we were not to be thought of as subject to the usual rules of scholarly rationalization and discipline.

So a plan for the spring semester of 1954 took shape, first to fly to London for a few days in the dead of winter then on to Egypt, Palestine and Greece for a month before arriving in Rome as base for the rest of the time until mid summer. Jim and Jean

Scheeler met me at Heathrow airport early in February, in their small Renault 4 Cv that turned out to be the only source of heat in London, so it seemed. The Hill's hotel in Kensington was a typical B &B of three town houses of different floor heights awkwardly joined together, without central heat, at a modest daily rate of a little more than two pounds. In each room was a small gas heater that would light up for about half an hour on deposit of a shilling coin, which had no effect at all on the frigidity of the air. Waking up the first morning, the wash stand pitcher of water was covered with a thin film of ice. In the dining room for breakfast everybody was in their overcoats, their visible breath blending with the steam vapor rising from bowls of oatmeal. London, at that time in 1954, appeared to have changed little since my first visit sixteen years earlier in 1938 except for pockets of bomb damage still not cleared and rebuilt. I was still struck by the strange coexistence and extent of so much poverty in the midst of the pomp and circumstance of royal affluence and the pride of history and empire expressed by Westminster, Buckingham Palace, Trafalgar Square, the Tower of London and other celebrated sties.

I soon boarded one of the new turbojets for a flight to Rome and on to Egypt where I was sure to thaw out. An impressive elderly lady seated next to me on the plane seemed quite agitated and anxious as there was some delay in taking off. I tried to reassure her, asking if this might be her first flight.

She immediately brightened up exclaiming "Gracious no, I flew with Bleriot across the channel in "08!" Introducing herself as Lady Richardson, on the way with her maid to Cyprus for a mid-winter holiday, she said that her agitation was due to her impatience with the ineptitude of the pilot, crew or flight controllers causing the delay—flaring up again as the pilot first tried to land on a taxiway at Rome airport instead of the main runway. Needless to say, I too, was less than at ease.

I stopped just long enough in Rome to check in at the American Academy to make arrangements for my longer stay on returning from Egypt, the Middle East and Greece several weeks later. Landing in Cairo was truly a fulfillment of a childhood dream. I was met at the airport by "Moose" Ibrahim one of our postwar Illini graduate students who took me into the heart of the city to spend the first night on a Nile passenger ship now a hotel—then to Gresham House, a pensione run by an Italian family, located very close to the Cairo Museum, for a stay of about two weeks. "Moose" had organized a series of visits to not only landmarks like the pyramids of Giza, mosques and other historic sites but also to several leading architectural offices and to his own government office, where he was one of the leaders in planning the new Tahreer project, an enormous desert reclamation settlement on the western side of the lower Nile toward Alexandria.

One of the first agenda items in Cairo was

to get a special pass from the Ministry of Culture for free admission to museums, monuments and archaeological sites. As an architect, professor and member of the Archaeological Institute of America, this was a courtesy offered by the Egyptian government and turned out to be most valuable not only for access to sites not open to the public but as it afforded a high status of respect one was not used to at home, as I shall presently explain as I explored sites in and around Luxor.

The Cairo Museum was so loaded with the panorama of history—sculpture, painting and all types of artifacts that after spending three days there all day I realized I had only just begun to appreciate the extent of the collection, especially of the many rooms given to contents of Tutankhamen's tomb, all of which had been so enchanting in childhood at the time it had been discovered and later when I had won the Ricker Prize in architectural history at Illinois on this subject. Despite the dim light and cavernous museum spaces, the gold of these objects seemed luminous from within as I shall describe again while visiting the interior of the tomb itself in the Valley of the Kings. The collection in Cairo was of course an added spur to fly to Luxor, in addition to a sense of satiation and escape from the crowded, teeming city, in spite of all its fascination.

It seems odd now fifty years later to reflect back on those days in Luxor, staying with a handful of others at the Winter Palace Hotel,

and being virtually the only tourist exploring Karnak, the Temple of Luxor and across the river at Dier el Bahri and its many sites, compared to 1991 when I returned for a few days finding these sites so crowded with hundreds of visitors and the Nile itself in traffic jams of cruise ships. Back then I had rented a bicycle for a few cents a day, took it across the river on a small felucca vessel, also for a few cents, to pedal around several miles through sugar cane fields to get to Hatcheptsut's temple, and to the base of the cliff upon which were the tombs in the Valley of the Kings. It was a very hot day in February to be pedaling several miles along a dusty road. Though I was not particularly thirsty, some smiling peasants gathering sugar cane in carts stopped me, offering sticks of cane to quench my thirst. After reaching the base of the cliff I left the bike with an attendant at Cook's rest house, totally empty of other tourists and climbed up the cliff on a well marked path. At the top there was only one other person in view, a lonely looking uniformed guard, who, after looking at my pass, bowed and saluted, exclaiming "Mohandes, Mohandes," which roughly translated means "your honor" or "your grace." The guard then led me through many tombs for two or more hours, in each one gesturing elaborately and vocalizing in the resonating acoustics of the long passages and chambers. Of course I remember best our entry to Tutankhamen's tomb, small compared to the others, but amazingly fresh in its painted wall surfaces as if they had just been done yesterday instead of over three thousand

years ago. Of course, the chambers were empty, their contents in the Cairo Museum, but the mummy was still there in one of its several coffins. This memory of freshness of delineation and color is still so vivid that when TV coverage of the recent traveling exhibition of Tutankhamen treasures was so extensively telecast with meticulous photography, I could not help noticing how much the tomb wall painting had deteriorated since I had seen it in person fifty years before, even though the tomb had been closed to the public most of the time since then.

By far the most impressive of all structures on the west bank of the Nile is Queen Hatcheptsut's mortuary temple. Over three thousand years one can still sense the creative imagination of the architect in understanding that the traditional spatial sequence in temple design on a usually flat site of entry pylon, then a courtyard, another slightly smaller pylon, another courtyard and pylon opening into a final sanctuary courtyard would be dwarfed against a cliff background. So the same spatial sequence leading into a sanctuary was achieved by employing a series of colonnaded terraces stepping up with ramps, instead of pylons and courts, leading into a rock-cut sanctuary in the cliff itself. Somehow this imaginative shift in concept collapsed the time gap between then and now, another instance of the timelessness of design thinking, an impression powerful enough to make me feel I had been there in another life; I was to feel the same intense déjà-vu sensation years later when visiting the Villa Pisani "La Rocca" near Vicenza, by Scamozzi, a pupil of Palladio.

While exploring Hatcheptsut's temple alone with a guard as I had the Valley of the Kings on the cliff above, I ran into another solitary tourist, Herbert Cerener, from Osnabruck, Germany, a traveling salesman of a large power cable company. Herbert, a most genial, outgoing person as most salesmen are, had been a Luftwaffe pilot in World War II. The fact that we had been enemies then made absolutely no difference in our friendship for a few more days of sightseeing, then several years later when I happened to be in Osnabruck to pick up delivery of two Karmann Ghias in 1957 and 1962.

Also, while still in Luxor I had the advantage of contact with Chicago House, the long time headquarters of the University of Chicago's archaeological excavations in the area, already well established and known for its meticulous documentation of temple ruins, especially of wall inscriptions of the Temple of Luxor. I so enjoyed visits with archaeologists there over afternoon tea, by then a well-established tradition. When I was in Luxor again in 1991, thirty seven years later I was again invited for tea. Nothing at all seemed to have changed, the same low key congeniality, the same cavern like interior, the walls lined with the same files and shelves, the same sense of quiet meeting of Middle East and West cultures, all reassuring that the quest for knowledge based on learning from the past is enduring in the face of today's fast-paced conflicting events and political impasses.

Returning to Cairo by air following the Nile and its alternating flood plains and rock-eroded wadis and embankments, I began to see natural pyramid-like forms, both smooth and stepped, surely a primary influence on the man-made pyramids as they began to appear as we approached Cairo. I had much the same impression in Mexico of nature's powerful impact on the temple builders of Tulum, Teotewakan and Chichen Itza. Realizing that this striking yearning of man to imitate nature had not been presented as a source of influence of any importance in history of architecture, I began to wonder if I was letting my own imagination run wild naively and superficially. Still it was one of those moments you can enjoy, smiling inwardly.

One of the offices "Moose" took me to in Cairo was that of Yussef "Joe" Shafik, who had also been a graduate student at Illinois, and his partner Sami Hassid on Kasr-El-Nil one of the main streets in the downtown area. They had already established a highly respected practice that would flourish in years to come. While I was in Luxor "Joe" had returned to Cairo from the States so we celebrated a reunion at a well know café in Heliopolis, one of Cairo's thriving edge cities. Unknown to us while we were there, nearby in Heliopolis a coup led by General Naguib took over the government from the corrupt regime of King Farouk. Without admitting it, my architect friends who were part of the new leading, young, energetic, intellectual, professional class, many of whom had been graduate students, like "Moose" and "Joe" in the U.S., were possibly indirectly involved in the takeover. When news came to the café there were cheers and toasts adding to the celebration of "Joe's" return. It turned out that "Joe" and his partner Sami had made an agreement that when "Joe" returned back to their Cairo office, Sami would then go to the U.S. for advanced study. In fact he had already applied to Harvard but had not yet heard of his acceptance. By that time Serge Chermayeff had moved to Harvard from Chicago so I wrote to Serge from Cairo strongly supporting Sami's application, finally hearing from both Sami and Serge after I had returned home that Sami would indeed be admitted to Harvard to work on a Ph.D. Before leaving Cairo I was entertained several times by Sami and his delightful wife Juliette. Little did we anticipate then that our paths would cross again, but after Sami finished his degree and drove with his family across country, they stopped in Champaign for a visit on the way to his new position on the Berkeley faculty. It would be such a pleasure again to see them there over the years when I would be in San Francisco or Berkeley for meetings. Just how it worked out that Sami never did return to Cairo to resume his partnership with "Joe" remained a mystery. "Joe" himself went on to be one of the most successful and highly recognized architects in Egypt, eventually serving for many years as Dean of the architectural school of Cairo University. Thirty seven years later, in 1991 when I returned to Egypt I was saddened to learn that both "Moose" and "Joe" had passed away. But "Joe's" widow and family were most gracious in showing me much of his work as well as guiding me on special visits in old Cairo and to a farm for Arabian horses they owned very close to the pyramids at Giza. I was also entertained by another of our later graduate students at Illinois, Adib Wahbah and his wife Marianne, in their town house in Garden City, at a concert at Giza and at several fascinating cafés in Zamalek, an island in the heart of Cairo. We have kept in close touch ever since.

I felt on leaving Cairo then in 1954 and again in 1991 a special sense of family and friendship that is indeed rare, it also strikes me in retrospect that the warmth of the U.S./Egypt relationship then, no doubt enhanced by our ambassador's initiative in promoting postwar graduate study in the U.S. for so many young Egyptian leaders and later by our government's veto of England and France's attempt to take over from Egypt the Suez Canal as "protection" during the conflict with Israel, is now in such contrast to our recent fragile relations with the whole Arab world.

Even back in 1954 it was difficult for an American to visit both Israel and any of the Arab countries on the same travel itinerary. You could get a visa for one but not the other for the same trip. Before leaving the U.S., I had to prove I was not Jewish to get

a visa for Egypt. Likewise it was impossible then to fly direct to Jerusalem over Israeli territory, the plane from Cairo had to fly east past Aquaba, then turn north, land at Aman, Jordan, before going on to Jerusalem. In Jerusalem I was welcome to stay for a few days at the American School for Oriental Studies, a small enclave of biblical scholars and archaeologists, since I was a member of the Archaeological Institute of America, as well as the other AIA, the American Institute of Architects. In light moments I would sometimes sign my name as AIA[2].

Among the dozen or more residents and scholars at the School was Frank Cross, a biblical archaeologist who had just discovered the Dead Sea Scrolls and was now deeply engaged in their analysis at the Jerusalem Museum. Though only a visitor for a week or so, I was immediately made to feel as if I had been an intimate colleague for a much longer time, engaged in ongoing site investigations and discussions as to their significance. One memorable excursion was to Jericho, where a long-term archaeological excavation was in progress under the direction of British archaeologist Kathleen Kenyon. It was Lord Kenyon, who had founded Kenyon College, in Gambier, Ohio, my father's alma mater. Many years later in the sixties, while I was president of the Central Illinois chapter of the Archaeological Institute of America, I was host for a reception at my house in Champaign in her honor after her lecture on Jericho at the university. It was a much larger audience than we had

expected because the lecture had been announced in local churches. Professor Revilo Oliver of the Classics department introduced her, and instead of just members only, he invited the whole audience to a reception afterward at my house. This suddenly was a test of the houses' capacity and the miracle of loaves and fishes. More than two hundred came—all ages, ethnicities and religious beliefs. In those days it was still a ritual that shoes would be removed at the entry before stepping up on the teak floor. This time the mound of shoes was almost two feet high—how would everyone find their own pair on leaving? But amazingly it was no problem. Miss Kenyon enjoyed it all immensely, writing a note later saying it had been one of her most memorable visits.

Two most vivid recollections of our visit to Jericho in 1954 remain. One is of Miss Kenyon's conviction that the lowest level of the excavation revealed through its radio-carbon dating to be ca. 7000 B.C., surely one of the very first of permanent human settlements in towns. The other memory is of the endless line of Palestinian women coming from their refugee camp a mile away to gather water from the ancient Jericho well, filling their ceramic containers and carrying them back to camp balanced exquisitely on their heads.

Jerusalem itself at the time of my visit seemed still to be timeless in its unchanging character as a peaceful meeting place of East and West, the Wailing Wall, the golden Dome of the Rock, the Garden of Gethsemane, the ancient town wall gates and the almost total uniformity of warm colored building stone; except for some evidence of weathering over the ages, still blending harmonically with newly quarried blocks wherever new building or restoration was going on.

My stops in Beirut and Istanbul on the way to Athens were so brief that only fleeting memories remain. Beirut's dazzling blue Mediterranean where the center city met the sea even then seemed more modern and Western; hotels, beach resorts, multi-storey office buildings and crowded streets closely resembled other Mediterranean water front cities all the way to Spain. But Istanbul was again an exotic return to the Islamic world with its densely packed markets, souks and filigree buildings surrounding Hagia Sophia and the Blue Mosque; the sounds and smells a recall of Cairo. In contrast, a brand new high-rise Hilton Hotel designed by SOM was under construction on high ground overlooking the teeming Bosphorus River and east to Asian Turkey, foreshadowing the enormous modern expansion of the city later in the century. In the midst of all this intriguing atmosphere of the Middle East I was still impatient to get to Athens, having imagined since childhood that Greece, like Egypt, Rome and Italy were dream destinations long before the rest of Europe and other alluring parts of the world.

Another connection to the Archaeological Institute was the American School of Classic

Studies in Athens; so after arriving there I was referred by their director to the Pakis Pension an annex nearby along the east base of the Acropolis. I found myself again in a congenial mix of scholars, classics students and archaeologists. Among these I met Homer Thompson who was then in charge of excavations in the Agora and the restoration of the Stoa of Attilos. Also in the Agora, Allison Franz was restoring a small 13th century Byzantine chapel. She right away assumed that as an architect I would be able to help interpret foundations of the ruined façade of the chapel in order to decide among several possible alternatives what the original façade might have been. I had to admit I was not an architectural historian or specialist, any suggestion on my part would be guesswork. Five years later in 1959 I saw that the restoration had been completed, I'm sure based on some other in-depth source of expertise.

Even ten years after World War II Greece was still struggling to recover from German occupation and civil strife. However, crisp new building was underway in the city center, new hotels, office buildings and shops, all in contemporary mode but still extensively employing the same Panathenaic marble used to build the Parthenon and other ancient structures. As through Europe, the dollar was strong in Greece, dining in the best cafés and restaurants was amazingly inexpensive; most enjoyable was the Corfu restaurant, specializing in "artichokes a la polita" and other local dishes I had never found in Greek restaurants in the

U.S. Also highly affordable were sight-seeing tours to historic sites, Corinth, Delphi, Sounion, Epidauros, even far north past Mt. Olympus to Kalimbaka and Meteora, where the monasteries on rock pinnacles are only accessible by basket-like gondolas hauled up by ropes on windlasses. Local air fares were also cheap. I flew to Corfu for about $10 to spend a few days communing with Ulysses before catching a ferry on to Brindisi, then by rail to Rome.

Bass Garden , American Academy in Rome

Principessa Rospigliosi, secretary of the Academy, found a splendid room for me with a friend of hers, Mrs. Lang-Scuder, for three months at 8 Via Nicola Fabrizi. It was on the top floor overlooking the city to the south-east. I would start each sunny day looking out across the street to the roof deck of an Irish convent, observing young novitiates all in white hanging out laundry as if in a ballet. At the Academy I was welcome to dine, as well as use the library and other amenities as if I were living there. But I soon realized hierarchies existed that I had not experienced before.

Director Laurence and Isabel Roberts went out of their way to dispel this atmosphere, but it was something you sensed. It seemed to be a combination of withdrawal into inner sanctums of individual artists doing their own thing with a pretense of collegiality that had a hollow ring—not doubt a symptom of the postwar rejection of tradition in the art world now so well documented by historians and critics. The architects too were affected by this tone, feeling uneasy in rationalizing their presence in Rome. On the other hand, fellows and residents in classical studies, archaeology and other scholarly subjects were genuinely congenial, totally involved and enthusiastic in their pursuits, and great company as I had found in Luxor, Jerusalem and Athens. They were truly a cross section from all parts of the country in contrast to the architects, painters, musicians and sculptors who were almost all from the Ivy League or New York. I was beginning to

understand the unchanging nature of elitist patronage in architecture centered in New York in much the same way the city is the center of power in the financial world. As a still naïve prairie and Great Lakes native, this worried me a great deal. Many years later after learning how the game is played, I wondered if opportunity in architecture has ever been a level playing field in America compared to the Nordic countries, for example, where architect selection is made by design competition for most if not all public projects.

What had happened? Along with recovery and prosperity after the war, old privileges, networks and pedigrees were re-established and intensified. Self promotion and crony mechanisms took advantage of old and new PR techniques centered in New York. Award programs, exhibitions, glossy magazines and coffee table books glorified a succession of manufactured stars. The honor and recognition of truly excellent work and eminence achieved earlier in the century could now be artificially generated. Couple this with what Harold Rosenberg called "the tradition of the new" in modern art carried over into the architectural world marking the beginning of ever faster cycles of visual clichés, eroding respect for the full spectrum of criteria of excellence learned from history. The skin now counted most in the race for frame in both art and architecture. No wonder the atmosphere of the Academy was deeply affected. Its very existence as a symbol of honoring Rome's centrality in western culture was placed in direct contradiction. It was a time of withdrawal into closed studios—the antithesis of shared enthusiasm in collaboration. In contrast, the center of collaborative spirit in America had shifted to Cranbrook Academy in Bloomfield Hills, Michigan, under the influence of the Saarinens, sculptor Carl Milles and other artists, designers and craftsmen who were working and celebrating their mutual respect in setting new standards of excellence in diversity, an updating of the same American version of innovative collaboration that characterized the Chicago and Prairie Schools at the turn of the century. This spirit somehow could not penetrate the Eastwind—now stronger than ever from Europe and New York.

The retreat into closely guarded secrecy and introspection among the Academy's art community did not, however, dampen the unchanging excitement of spirited conversation and the serendipity of unplanned events and encounters. At that time Rome radio was sponsoring a symposium of modern music. I got to know Ben Weber, a composer whose talent was supported by skill as a musical draftsman of scores. One of his sonatas for strings in three movements was performed. Virgil Thompson was also briefly in residence. The center of the musical congress was in the Foro Italico, newly refurbished, a vestige of Fascist modernism like EUR.

Apart from the hectic pace of change and celebrity inflation in the transatlantic art world, anything Italian came into vogue. A rediscovery of hill towns like Urbino, vernacular architecture like Sperlonga and Alberobello, a new recognition of the piazza as an urban design icon, the emergence of Italian industrial and interior design as world leader exemplified by the Triennale in Milano, all drew us away from the Academy on different kinds of missions than the grand tours of tradition. Pilgrimages to Ivrea, a prime example of enlightened company town patronage by Olivetti, projects by Franco Albini, Gio Ponti and Ludovico Quaroni opened up new insights and directions in modern design, particularly in the elegant detailing of traditional materials along with new technologies. Journals like Domus and Casabella were in ascendance in spreading these new concepts around the world.

When finally in May work came out of hiding for the annual exhibition, everyone went into a state of shock and embarrassment, though politely suppressed, at the meagerness and reluctance to show anything at all as if it were an invasion of privacy. It was even more embarrassing in comparison to the dash, excitement, and diversity of work at the French Academy and even the more conservative British School. Was this the same American Academy that had for so many years been the pace-setter at these annual exhibitions?

From this longer span of time in contrast to my brief visit in '39/40 I began to understand and appreciate much more fully how the Academy in bringing together such a diversity of scholarship and the fine arts is such a powerful counter force to modern trends in higher education of isolated specialization. I saw in this strength of collegiality in high concentration a paradigm or synergetic model that fit my ideal in architecture as an ever-richer orchestration of technology, art, scholarship and humanism—again a unity of what each project wants to be ideally in the hands of talented, enlightened team players.

Now in retrospect, forty years later, this ideal has gained so much in clarity and conviction that instead of continuing my chronicle on the usual chronological time line I will skip-stop ahead in pondering the story of the Academy as I have experienced it as a visiting architect for the years already described, 1939–40 and 1954 and from then on in 1964, 1975, 1985, 1991, 1995, 1996, 1997, 1998, 1999, 2002.

The paradigm takes on deeper meaning when one considers that since its founding as an American school of architecture in Rome, it embraced not only the idea of collaboration in the fine arts but soon developed a close association with archaeology and classical studies as well, rather than as a singular discipline on its own.

In the academic grove of higher education, this was a breakthrough recognition of architecture's centrality in human society as "mother of the arts," "the mirror of civilization." Whether or not this breadth of concept was fully appreciated or intended by the founders, the very idea of it remains a fascinating idealization. The historical reality is that the Academy's identity became that of *"the foremost overseas center for independent study and research in the fine arts and humanities,"* in which no single discipline occupies the centrum. This surely is a noble identity, but as a Chicago architectural chauvinist, I can't help feeling a sense of architecture's time-honored centrality as a keystone of cultural values and expression of new world vision.

In the full light of study given by historians to the Academy's achievements and destiny, my own insights are tangential, a perspective maturing over more than a half century—a point of view from America's heartland which is no doubt at some variance from the critical reflection the Academy has had of itself. It suggests that the French aphorism "plus ca. change, plus c'est la meme chose" (the more things change, the more they stay the same) may be a convenient way to describe the life of the Academy over the years, pondering one's view of what has been versus what might have been instead. At least it's a framework to sum up impressions that have filtered through the screen of time. They come in focus as I look back: synergies, serendipities, contradictions and disillusions, at first random then sorting out in a kind of order in or out of balance with the classical European model of an architectural school in Rome as envisioned by McKim, Burnham and

other founders when they met at the site of the World's Columbian Exposition in Chicago in 1893.

What has changed and what has stayed the same is of course a subjective perception—in the eye, mind and heart of the beholder, unfolding in a chronology of one's own experience. From this chronology I hope at the end to sift inferences of direction.

I don't think anyone has yet fully explained the change that took place in the early sixties—an awakening of concern about civil rights occurring simultaneously with a new environmental consciousness. But it was a sea change at the Academy. A new wave of collaborative spirit returned—a new openness—not in terms of team projects but in a direction of individual work that invited sharing visions and criticism.

I was invited by director Dick Kimball to spend the spring of '64 at the Academy, largely at the suggestion of Jim Hunter, then national president of the American Institute of Architects, in response to an effort of Dick's to have more participation in the fine arts from others parts of the country beyond the East coast.

The two fellows in architecture, Milo Thompson and Tom Larson, were both from Minnesota, with further benediction from Harvard. Both were into large scale urban design projects that reflected an awakened concern for the architect's role in multiple-client interrelationships, and in new visions of urban growth and change. Tom was also involved in Spero Daltas' office downtown working on new growth projects for clients in the Middle East and Africa.

The spirit of interchange, give and take, was radiant again. I rejoiced to be involved, with others, as a critic across disciplines much as we were in the thick of collaborative projects in Illinois at that time. It had become clear that motivation for collaboration was inspired far more to do projects that addressed unmet social and environmental needs than by motherhood virtue alone.

The spring of '64 was memorable, too, as the schema (agenda) of Vatican II was being formulated, involving the effort of bright young Jesuit scholar/theologians who would occasionally come to the Academy to visit Fr. John O'Malley, S.J., a fellow in religious art history. Since I had become a friend of John's, I would often be present as a bystander in some of these informal sessions.

Although way above my head in theological terms, it became obvious that so many of the proposed new or revised liturgical concepts would have direct impact on church design, both for remodeling and new construction. It was an inspirational time in painting, sculpture, archaeology and classical studies as well.

Edgar Ewing, a well known visiting painter from Los Angeles, had become intrigued by the dome of St. Pietro, dissecting and exploring its geometry as a series in oil and in small bronzes cast through the lost wax process. Since I had a car I could take him to a foundry near S. Giovanni in Laterno that had been continuously active for many generations.

Ed Bacon arrived from Philadelphia for a week or so to work on his book Design of Cities. Again I had the delightful task of

chauffeur as Ed filled in gaps of photo and sketch illustrations which already were blocked out in a mock-up of the book. Each page was already composed with captions and text laid out in blank lines. I asked Ed if I could see drafts of the texts intended to fit into these blocked-out spaces. He said, "Oh, I'll write that later."

Helen North, also by then a good friend, would often ride along and from her amazing knowledge and sensitivity to things Roman, help keep us in balance when we would be exuberantly imagining the urban design of the city in each of its many alternating eras of flourishing growth or decay.

Of course I now wish I had been more diligent in committing to memory or to have taken better notes of dialogues with Frank Brown on trips to Cosa or listening more attentively to others like Gisela Richter as she would discuss with glee some new insights about Greek sculpture she had uncovered.

Another unchanging quality of the Academy atmosphere is the sedate, quiet, soft spoken aura of the salone, almost intimidating to new arrivals. Of course with exceptions, as I remember one night when I had two young lady friends from Belgrade, Gee Gee Robinson and Yelitsa as guests for dinner. Yelitsa was a talented singer and pianist who had noticed the grand piano in the salone, sat down after dinner to play and sing some lively tunes, with great humor and bravura. Everybody gathered around and caught the

spirit. Gisela and her sister were jumping with joy exclaiming, "We haven't had as much excitement around here in a long time!"

Director Dick Kimball had become excited about hill towns as we all had, which led to many picnic gitas up to nearby villages which remain nameless in memory except for Subiaco and Palestrina. These excursions blend in a delightful blur, mixed with villa visitations like Bomarzo becoming blissful in the glow of Frascati or other local wines. So passed an enthralling time now even richer in memory.

These were years when in the late fall I was a guest critic at the Notre Dame Architecture program at Via Monterone 76 downtown. So impressions of the Academy then are not as distinct. But from the memory of a few visits, it seemed the atmosphere was more like the fifties, but at a more subdued level with hierarchies firmly in place, with retreat of the various disciplines into even deeper isolation—a retrenchment from the interdisciplinary exuberance of the sixties that was typical of university campuses at home as the Vietnam war hung on and finally ended. This was less true in 1985 with a return to more openness that I suppose came along with the affluence of a "trickle down economy." I guess I felt more positive about this brief time because my old friends Fay Jones FAAR 81 and his wife Gus were in residence as were Ron Gourley FAIA and Phyllis. Ron, Phyllis and I drove up to Orvieto celebrating All Saints Day by attending mass at both the Duomo and a small church, greeted there by the children's choir singing "When the Saints come Marching In" (of course in Italian).

Bargello (Ink and Wash on Paper), Florence, Italy, 2000
Paolo Sica

The nineties began a series of almost annual October visits to Rome. It became an ideal transitional interlude between the coming cold of northern Michigan and the still unrelenting heat of Tucson in September. Also, rapport with the Notre Dame program under the directorship of John Stamper and his wife, Erika, beckoned.

Off and on during the sixties and seventies, I had visited Paolo Sica, his wife, Grazia Gobbi, and their family and friends in Florence. Paolo was one of my finest graduate students at Illinois who on return to Florence became an eminent architect, professor, author and leader of the team Arco Progetti, now widely known for their remarkably progressive studies of the Florence region. Sadly, Paolo died in 1988 of liver cancer. A grateful city turned out a year later for a convegno in his honor at the Salone dei Cnquecento in the Palazzo Vecchio on October 11, 1989. I was honored to be one of six speakers at this full-house memorial service—it was a most moving and memorable experience that now gives even deeper meaning to my annual brief visits in October to Grazia, her family and friends.

This was also a time of renewing my long-time contact with the Academy, made especially welcoming by director Joe Connors and Francoise and by the presence again of Fay and Gus Jones.

I think I felt even more at home because both Joe and Fay were as close as you can get to understanding the Americanness of the Prairie School of architecture and its still largely unrecognized contribution to our culture.

This feeling was extended still more when Bill Lacy, former AAR president, arrived for a short stay with his friend, pianist Judy Carmichael. I knew Bill from his early days at Oklahoma State and later when he was head of the new school of architecture at the University of Tennessee. Judy played a resounding concert of stride piano at the Villa Aurelia, another reminder of a conspicuously mid-American idiom: jazz.

There may have been other times than the ones I know, as in 1964, that this spirit at the Academy flourished for a while but somehow I feel they were rare. This openness was in contrast to the still prominent influence in architecture of European Noli Plan formalism, of figure/ground, rationalist concepts and doctrine of the then stars like the Kriers, Aldo Rossi and others whose influence held sway in current thinking in some Ivy League schools. Tom Schumacher, AAR resident in architecture 91-92, had been a student of Colin Rowe at Cornell. I was on a jury with Tom at the Syracuse program in Florence while on my annual visit there. The project was a study of segments of the city in the figure/ground manner at a highly abstract level of discussion. I felt somewhat awkward asking direct questions like, "What do the people think and how does it fit their needs?"

By the nineties at least fifteen American architectural schools had established overseas programs in Rome. About five years ago a Roman architectural journal featured an entire issue on these programs and each described its own rationale for its presence in the city.

It was interesting to compare the wide variety of their attempts to find relevance, many quite eloquent, with the Academy's original manifesto over a hundred years ago. Some came close but still missed the most telling arguments of all, resorting to elaborate defensive justifications almost as if each was in peril that its program might be withdrawn. Statements of those like Notre Dame and Cornell that have come closest to the Classical and Renaissance tradition are more sure-footed and most like the Academy original; that is Rome as the everlasting source model for future practice in the classic revival styles.

That this may be an anachronism today could be a blessing in disguise, if its ambiguity provokes a new understanding of canonicity. A clue to this possible direction emerges in jury reviews of projects in which criticism rises above stylistic debate in emphasizing both timeless and timely design principles. In my summary of inferences I'll try to address this opportunity.

The time of the Academy's closing for renovation in 92-93 was also a time for reflections, soul searching and reaffirmation of purpose intensified by the coincidence of its centennial anniversary and its documentation so magnificently compiled and presented. It was also a time of personal reminiscences stimulated still more by the prospect of the new millennium.

I like to think that the splendid job of restoration is also a restoration of the soul of the idea as well as the soul of the building. It should not diminish the dignity of this thought by commenting on how vastly improved is the cucina and other creature comforts and delights.

The Florentine Villa (Book), 2007
Grazia Gobbi Sica

The Octobers of 95, 96, 97 and 98 have flown by. Memories fuse together through repetition. In order not to wear out my welcome at the Academy, I would stay at the Villa Bassi, a former convent, nearby on the Via G. Carini, dining frequently at the Academy and using the library. Caroline Bruzellius, the new director, would keep me informed of special events such as the dedication of the Walter Cain studio. I was eager not to miss the brief presentations in early October by the new fellows of their projects and study interests, often a basis for informal later dialogue. In 1996 Fay and Gus Jones were back so we could renew our long friendship. Malcolm Bell, Mellon Professor in charge of classical studies, and I had a common tie of interest in the excavations at Morgantina in Sicily, since I had had close contact with the site work there when the University of Illinois, under the direction of Hugh Allen, had taken it over from Princeton when Erik Sjoquist retired. Hugh had been Sjoquist's assistant. Then at the time Hugh left Illinois, the University of Virginia carried on under the direction of Mac Bell. The history of Morgantina as a Greek colonial new town had fascinated me at the time our collaborative design studio was working on a hypothetical edge city design proposal for new growth near Chicago. Ann Perkins, our esteemed classical scholar, suggested that we name the new city Temenoplis (temenos, meaning platform temple in Greek/Sumerian and polis meaning people place: city). This led to a comparative study of urban design principles in my book The Urban Stage of these two new towns, Morgantina and Temenopolis, 2500 years apart in time: what had changed and what had stayed the same?

Visits to the Notre Dame program went on as before. The adoption of classical tradition as the school's direction somehow did not seem so anachronistic in Rome since the students were assigned projects on sites that had strict context problems. As I remarked earlier, our critiques most often turned to underlying principles of concept formation—spatial organization, circulation, hierarchies and directional cueing, scale and harmonic material relationships rather than dwell on stylistic appropriateness. Still, I would sometimes speculate out loud what Carlo Scarpa, Giancarlo de Carlo or Massimo Carmassi, all sensitive, contextual, modern architects might have done in a similar situation, but this was not an option encouraged for the students.

As much as I could observe them, projects and studies of fellows in architecture at the Academy were hard to pin down. Some seemed tentative, casual, even lightweight, almost as if asking for a clear definition were an invasion of privacy, giving the impression that the opportunity of a fellowship was a form of vacation or break that was long deserved—as sabbatical leaves from universities are sometimes regarded. Several were embarking in new directions of painting or other visual arts, certainly a worthy form of refreshing artistic sensitivity, notably Daniel Castor's exquisite studies of Bramante's

Tempieto (1998). One missed the more rigorous speculative kind of project study, including collaboration, that had characterized the spirit of the architectural presence at the Academy at memorable times in the past. One could also see this period of indecisiveness as a symptom of the wider ennui, sophistication and fast tracking in our recent culture. Over the passing half century, attention spans have become increasingly short.

Sixty years have passed with accelerating speed. In a strange way memories of past peaks of experience are more vivid than those of recent days. Perhaps this is simply because gaps of time between have allowed more reflection. But life in the present is no less rich in its immediacy of impressions, a penniless wealth of new friendships and density of exchanged ideas.

So now sixty days have just passed, reaffirming in microcosm highlights of all those sixty years. It's all too soon to make any attempt at fitting my recent thoughts into a longer view except to comment on a few fragments—serendipities that flash by like glimpses in one's handheld video camera: Lester Little's timeless/timely/candid look at the millennium, Lisa Moore's fantastic rapport with the Steinway playing Martin Bresnick's and Carolyn Yarnell's compositions, Al Guttenberg's warm and sly view of Rome's urban planning problems—the legal doing battle with the illegal, Charles Baroody's open studio and joyful work, Blake Yarnell's drawings of his new/old city that he so proudly and constantly works on and explains, the scene, sound and costumes of the Halloween party, and of course many more informal encounters, dialogue vignettes—the essence of what the Academy is all about. It was the musical ambience especially that inspired my own offering of "Antiphonies in Architecture."

Bramante's Tempieto
wireframe

Bramente's Tempieto (Wireframe)
Daniel Castor FAAR 1998

SIXTY YEARS IN
PERSPECTIVE
◆
THE AMERICAN
ACADEMY IN
ROME

SESSANTISIMO
LX
ANNIVERSARIO

I
ADVENT
II
PASSAGE
III
EPILOGUE

A. RICHARD WILLIAMS FAIA
VAAR 39, 54, 64, 91, 99

ROME
1999

Montage inspired by Midway Gardens, Chicago, 1914
and the Bass Garden of the American Academy in Rome.

Following three weeks with the IFRAA seminar in late September '02, visiting recent outstanding examples of contemporary architecture in Portugal and Spain, mainly work by Calitrava, Siza and Gehry, I took the train from Madrid up through Southern France, then down to Rome, arriving at the Academy on the 10th of October for a stay until the 22nd of November. On the way I had a delightful rendezvous with Bob and Terri Heatley formerly from Stillwater, at their house in a village east of Avignon. Michael and Gloria Plautz were also there, following their annual fall sketch break leading Illinois students from the overseas program based in Versailles. An all too brief, four star Michielin reunion of my fabulous family!

Arriving in Rome, I was given the top floor apartment in the Villino, a part of the Villa Aurelia, across the street from the Academy's main building. The Villino is on one of the highest points of the Janiculum Hill, affording spectacular views of the city and the Alban hills to the east. The roster of fellows, residents and visitors seemed even more diverse than in earlier years. I enjoyed especially the new fellows Rachel Allen and Andy Zago in architecture, Joel Katz and Paul Seck in landscape architecture, resident David Soren and his wife Noelle, in archaeology, (David, a colleague on the faculty at Arizona) and Joyce Pomeroy Schwartz from New York, also a visitor who is one of the nation's leading authorities on public art. We became especially close on a two day visit north to Orvieto and other centers of

Etruscan excavations and museums, where David has been instrumental as a leading archaeologist. Resident artist Vija Celmins and her sister had an apartment just below mine in the Villino and Hiroshi Takayama from Tokyo was just across on a terrace. We often got together for happy hour then out on the town for dinner at Focolare or one of the other neighborhood restaurants. Unfortunately I was unable to visit Grazia in Florence this time because she was in Milano to be with daughter Anna who was ill at the time. So the days sped by—Tait Johnson, one of my closest young friends, a graduate of both OSU in Stillwater and Arizona, son of Allen and Irene Johnson (Allen had been one of my administrative assistants when he was a graduate student at Illinois in the mid-sixties) came over for a week to stay with me in the Villino and help with my lecture presentation at the Academy in mid November. I continued to keep working on ARCHIPELAGO, whenever there was a gap between such an abundance of both formal and informal evens—Director Lester Little was most helpful in reacting to shifting points of emphasis in the text and choice of subtitles. Toward the end of this visit I began to wonder, at age 88, that in all prudence it might be the last—that surely all the wonderful times over a span of sixty three years was long enough as a full bank of memories to sort out and rejoice in as a rich singularity of experience, without add-ons or anticlimaxes.

Returning to my primary focus and question of how the Academy through its history and mission has influenced the state of American architecture today and into the future, I would like to summarize my thoughts following the view of what has appeared to have changed and what has stayed the same, as proposed at the beginning of this retrospection. By now I have confidence that these insights have become more objective, gaining so much from long reflection, but most of all from dialogue with friends, colleagues and students, old and young, who have shared a part or almost all my own experience. Many ideas have already emerged as they have ebbed and flowed as a consequence of the foregoing time passage. So now I have the task of forming a hierarchy, a distillation, a set of design choices that through repetition and emphasis should venture into the subjunctive mood. Given all the best we know, what might become a new golden age for American architecture in service and celebration of our society?

Certainly unchanging is the idea of presence in Rome, the Eternal City, as the western world's center or creative study and work—now revealing still deeper and timeless dimensions of canonicity in architecture, art and landscape that transcend neo-classicism and other stylistic limitations.

Unchanging as well is the continuing presence at the Academy of scholarship in the study of Roman and European culture—from pre-classic time until today—in juxtaposition to creative thought and work in the fine arts. This remains an enormous blessing despite its Balkanization into so many fragments of time and subject. But wouldn't this presence be much richer if its synergies could be distilled in time perspective, perhaps by a new Pirandello, vividly and poetically illuminating canonic principles as prelude to creative work? Planners, architects, landscape architects, industrial designers and engineers are all subjunctive thinkers in the thick of transfiguring the then, here and now into what should or might be. Their creativity is more than ever in need of eloquent interpretive scholarship and cultural stewardship in the face of our era's rampant materialism that now thwarts the subjunctive process.

At the risk of offering a few thoughts that may seem radical, naïve or both, I would like to suggest images of alternative beginnings and future visions yet in full applause of the finest accomplishments of the Academy in the fullness of its time.

Imagine if at that first meeting in Chicago, Burnham had brought in Adler, Sullivan, Holabird, Perkins, Jensen and even the young Wright and others of the Chicago School. What if the excitement of the new already flourishing spirit of collaboration including engineers, artists of invisible systems, as well as painters, sculptors, architects and landscape architects had become the heart of a manifesto for the proposed school in Rome instead of the classical revival regimen that was adopted? Would not this innovative

Roman Grandeur
(Photograph: Elmo Baca, FAAR 2000)

Memorial to the Swiss Guards, Porto San Spirito, Vatican City
(pencil and watercolor) Johannes M.P. Knoops, FAAR 2000

and inspiring new expression of mid-American vitality and inclusive idealism, surprisingly well understood and supported by the new multi-ethnic society have brought a breath of fresh air as a truly American presence in Rome in contrast to the then current European dogmas of architectural education?

Historians of the Academy have somehow missed seeing the significance of eastern money and elitist taste in influencing the architectural ideology of those first years and since. The Chicago School's architectural and engineering innovations had little influence on the design of the 1893 Chicago World's Columbian Exposition, except for Louis Sullivan's Transportation Building. McKim, along with financial backing mainly from New York, insisted on European neoclasicism as the overall architectural theme. Likewise it was this continuing taste preference of J. P. Morgan and other eastern millionaires who funded the Academy's initial and continuing existence. Thanks, indeed for that, but at what cost in direction?

It is ironic that Post Modernism, an American movement characterized by borrowing European stylistic fragments applied as ornament, often whimsically, has had more influence than indigenous American developments like the Prairie School, San Francisco Bay area and the Pacific Northwest. The fact that important leaders of Post Modernism—Robert Venturi, Michael Graves and Charles Moore—were Academy fellows

and residents suggests an interesting connection of time, place, restless intellectual drift and the persistence of elitist taste-making. More recently another iteration of esoteric influence has arrived in the form of deconstructivist philosophy, e.g., the writing of Jacques Derrida translated architecturally into bumps, grinds, skews and structural irrationalities by American vanguardists. One fears as well that the latest worthy American idea of "sustainability" will be misunderstood and have its day as just another visual cliché!

One can't help imagining how different the ethos and image of the Academy might have been on its glorious Janiculum site if its built environment had been distinctly American, like the Midway Concert Gardens in Chicago built in 1914 the same year the McKim, Mead and White building for the Academy was substantially completed. At Midway Gardens, architecture, engineering, painting, sculpture, landscape, acoustics and lighting became a total orchestration—pavilions, terraces and landscape interwoven around a central garden. Instead of a monolithic villa image one can visualize a flow of spaces erasing old hierarchies of status in the arts, scholarship and social standings: collaborative and individual studios mixed with study rooms, work shops, living/dining arrangements all gathering around a magnificent library and exhibition area taking best advantage of light, view and inviting aspect to the Rome community. In harmony with its Roman setting, in particular its proximity

to the Aurelian wall, heavy, ground-hugging, supporting materials like brick, concrete and travertine for retaining and screen walls, paving, terraces and stairs could be composed in antiphonal relation to delicately supported structures; enclosures, roofs and trellises. Orchestrated with this wandering spatial structure would be canopies of Roman pines, cypress, citrus, fig, flowering trees and aromatic hedges in much the same way as now. Once can think of this vision as an antithesis to the singularity of a monumental palace; a set of spaces rather than an object. Thus its sympathy to the Roman scene would be that of airy structures in a park, non-controversial like the glass enclosed cafés, metro kiosks and pavilions in Paris' boulevard spatial system, pavilions in New York's Central Park, or like the almost invisible structures surrounding a Zen Garden in Japan.

Pondering these images should in no way be taken as a denial or oppositional critique of the McKim, Mead and White building as a splendid setting in its own way for the ambience of the Academy as it has matured and flourished for the past 90 years. I offer these alternative visions entirely as an example and plea for subjunctive thinking as a more conscious and celebrated expression of our American presence in Rome—a presence that works both ways—what can Rome learn from us, even though the weight and ratio of cultural time is 2000+ to 200+ or 10 to 1?

From the foregoing thoughts one may dis-

cern, in addition to synergies and serendipities, certain contradictions and disillusions.
They appear to have evolved with more clarity in hindsight awakening in consciousness
along the path. For example, I don't think
any of us earlier in the century questioned
the "American" part of the name, accepting this necessary distinction from "French"
or "British." It represented de facto our
national identity, but did it really? Is the
name a contradiction, a true representation of American democratic culture and
opportunity in view of its long existence as
an elitist eastern establishment? This is a
complex, long recognized question. I'll only
suggest one aspect from my personal experience in architectural education that mirrors
the larger issue. Over the last sixty years
it's been my good fortune to know many
brilliant students and practitioners in the
Midwest and West who would measure up to
the highest standards of an Academy fellowship. As long as selection was made through
a staged design competition, as it was up
to the end of World War II, they had a fair
chance. After the war, selection by design
competition was dropped. It became clear
after a time that applications of highly qualified candidates without the benediction and
sponsorship of certain Eastern schools, offices and individuals had little or no chance.
Word quickly got around so it was difficult
to persuade bright candidates even to apply.
Meanwhile, other national design competitions carried on like the Lloyd Warren (Paris)
prize, the Van Allen and the LeBrun, resulting
in a geographic balance of winners. Director

Dick Kimball and other directors since have
tried to correct this situation without much
success. The imbalance still persists. One
observes much the same tendency continuing in other fine arts as well while most other
disciplines at the Academy seem to be much
more representative of the whole country,
reflecting the spread and growth of major
universities and professional/cultural urban
centers across the continent.

While this contradiction remains serious, it at least is capable of solution by the
Academy itself. I'm more worried about a
larger disillusion, also intensifying over the
years, which the Academy reflects but is as
much a victim as is our American culture
as a whole. I've already touched on it—the
strange combination of continued absorption
of sophisticated European cycling fashions,
as if we were still a colony, mixed with our
own bottom line, fast track, media inflation,
celebrity worship values. The big question
merges, what can our steadfast institutions, universities, foundations and overseas
centers like the American Academy in Rome
do about it?

Though the outward image of the Academy
seems remarkably the same since its founding, I would observe two most apparent
changes over the past sixty two years. One
is the ever-widening scope of disciplines and
individual scholars and their great diversity
of projects and studies. The other is that at
long last there is a fine balance of women
in leadership, and as residents, fellows and

staff. It is definitely no longer a gentlemen's
club in Rome. But shadows of doubt may
still persist that there is much change in
elitist hierarchical structure. While some
may worry that the greater diversity of
individuals and their interests may dilute
the Academy's original mission as a fine arts
study center, particularly in architecture,
I think this is an enriching complexity if at
the same time both leadership and highly
talented participants are inspired to achieve
a new summit of collegiality, mutual respect,
harmony and astringent dissonance like the
best of jazz combos—highly talented individual artists doing their own thing in turn,
yet in a joyfully agreed beat and idiomatic
combined signature, a very American thing,
mirroring our democratic character that now
finds itself in a position of world leadership.

On return from Egypt and Greece in 1954, I had acquired a Volkswagen Beetle for getting around Rome, and up through northern Italy to Switzerland, Germany, Denmark, Sweden and Finland renewing 1939 friendships and visiting favorite haunts before ending the sabbatical in August, returning from Paris on Air France back to Chicago, Neebish and Champaign in time for the new academic year.

This nomadic passage was another collage of memories; of enjoying relatively empty roads, parking anywhere; of meeting my old friend Fred Salogga from Decatur, Illinois at Zurich airport who had come over for several weeks to visit new work in Switzerland, the pace setter for new schools and churches; at the suggestion of Alfred Roth, interviewing Henri von de Veldt then in his nineties at his home in Zug, his daughter serving as interpreter; asking what he though of Zurich's new airport, remembering his response gesturing sweepingly, "Pas de unité," meaning no unity of composition of its many elements of concourses, hangars and circulation systems, speculating on the future of modern architecture as learning from the French Beaux Arts mastery of compositional skills combined with the meticulous architectonics of Swiss/German detailing; then after a loop back into Italy driving to Vienna through Linz, enjoying an organist playing Bach in the St. Florian monastery's great Baroque chapel—an amazing interlocking of music and architecture, your eye could dance following the fugues as they cas-

caded across the sculptural fusion of arches, moldings and rippling surfaces whether solid material or painted; of relishing the exuberance of Vienna, restored again after the war to its former glory as a capital of music, street and café life; of saying goodbye to Fred at Vienna airport; of driving to Graz through the Russian occupation zone to visit the rector of Austria's finest architectural school—finding we had much in common in fostering the vertical studio concept; back in Vienna to have one more fling in the wine gardens of Grinsing, then on to Munich up the Autobahn to Denmark, exploring the city for the first time by car, paying homage again to Tivoli gardens, Oscar Davidsen's restaurant, visiting the latest showings of Danish furnishings at Den Permanente; on up to Hamlet's castle at Elsinor, crossing over to Sweden and up the main highway, seeing red barns, yellow mustard fields, glimpses of inland lakes, passing through garden cities like Linköping (to be visited later in 1962) arriving in Stockholm across the old center island Skeppsbron as before feeling as if I were coming home again; being greeted by Fru Shunneson at the Cosmopolite—it hardly seemed that fifteen years had passed—that the central core of the city had not changed; of revisiting the Olson family all now flourishing, Per having changed his last name to Odebrand, Karen married to Thold Lange now living with their young family near Borås, the textile capital of Sweden near the western port city of Gothenberg; of reunion with Jim and Jean Scheeler finishing up their Plym fellowship in Stockholm; of driving to Oslo to

meet Dick Nevara, another talented former student on the next year's Plym; of driving with Dick back through the mountains to the Swedish lake district around Mora; crossing to Finland to revisit the Villa Mairea and more recent work by Aalto; finally driving back to Paris, bidding goodbye to Dick, selling the car, boarding the Air France flight to Chicago and home.

How may I now see this sabbatical collage of so many images all the way from Tutankamen's tomb in the Valley of the Kings to having a sauna again at the Villa Mairea—of life spanning over three thousand years or longer still if I include the 7000 B.C. first settlement of Jericho? Perhaps more than anything else it now seems clearer than ever before that travel as learning is always expanding as a treasure in one's life, a spreading fan of stage sets and the play of performances, past and present, linked inseparably with our fabulous human family wherever we once lived and now live today.

It may be trite to remark that the process of accumulating wealth of sabbatical time, space and fresh insights is like recharging a battery, but it is an especially apt analogy for all of us who are trying to build our imagination for design in both practice and academic life. The studio is again the prime crucible of action in design learning—criticism sharper than ever, inspiration more up-front and critical judgment more solidly based. So the mid-fifties combined maturity gained by now from almost ten postwar years of honing architectural experience enriched with new intellectual and emotional zest. Symbols of this spirit now appeared across the design spectrum not only in architecture but in graphic and industrial design, landscape, furniture, electronics, sporting gear, in other words all the properties equipping our life settings, most of all the car as an American icon. On a more personal level I could feel this maturing from recent influences like the Milano Trianale in product design, Olivetti, the journals Domus, Casabella, Bauen + Wohnen, Swedish and Finnish periodicals and at home the emerging eminence of designers Charles and Ray Eames, George Nelson, Knoll, Herman Miller and other manufacturers bringing excellent contemporary design not only to architects and other design professionals but to the wider public.

My good friend and colleague Jack Baker's brother-in-law was the Ford dealer in our area, offering to order two 1956 Thunderbird sports cars for us at family discount prices,

so Jack and I were driving our own icons, matching this symbol along with building collections of contemporary furnishings— chairs and tables by Eames, Wegner, Breuer, Mies, Aalto and others, Arabia pottery, Marimekko fabrics, Akari lighting plus many of our own designed objects. All of this build-up of an orchestrated environment in fresh design was not only personally satisfying but turned out to be an enormously reinforcing adjunct to studio criticism—along with our other architectural work, an example of "practice what you preach," another instrument of emulation as a key force in design education.

As awareness of the widening design spectrum from micro to macro built up, especially in terms of fine tuning the harmonics of all elements working together, the more my quest for models was directed to older cultures world-wide where this sensitivity had already existed for a long time in both high civilizations and vernacular settings. From this spreading fan my favorites had by now centered on Egypt, Italy, Finland, Tibet and Japan, knowing full well how subjective such a set of choices might be. Still, I think this perception had arisen largely from my mid-American openness to influences from such diverse, romantic, intriguing, picturesque parts of the world, from the distant past to today's cutting edge in comprehensive design, rather than from unilaterally opinionated, elitist sources, as I have remarked earlier. For example, later in the seventies, a central region conference of the Association

Thorncrown Chapel, Eureka Springs, Arkansas, 1981
Fay Jones, FAIA, Architect

of Collegiate Schools of Architecture, ACSA, on the subject "The influence of publication media on architectural education" was held in Eureka Springs, Arkansas. I quote from a guest editorial I wrote reporting on the conference in 'Inland Architect' at the time:

"As a Great Lakes sailor, I have long been used to prevailing winds from the West. As an architect and educator, I have braced all my life, to prevailing winds of another kind, always from the East. From Europe to North America, from our Atlantic coast to all other parts of the colony, comes the Word and the Way in steady drafts, occasional gales, and rare periods of calm.

In times of architectural health, one is not so concerned with this one-way direction of influence, as long as the quality of published work is high. But in times (today) of economic, social, and cultural malaise, one observes that cynicism, camp, narcissism, and superficiality reign in elite circles and are propagated in every more prurient modes from the same old sources (some in new scholarly dress). Media inflation now brings torrents of trivia to every nook and cranny of the land.

The effect of this journalistic pollution is bad enough on practicing architects of integrity who, depressed by it, shrug it off and keep trying to do good work. But its impact on architectural education is poisonous and devastating.

This sad state generated the theme of the conference. While its organizers are to be commended for choosing such a timely subject, they can be questioned for having exposed us to new drafts of Eastwind without giving equal time to educators at the front line, or enough time for discussion. It was like finally realizing the need for an Environ-mental Protection Agency and then appointing a committee of major polluters to form policy.

With few exceptions—the brief recognition of the Prairie School, the Bay Area style, and the excellence of Eliel and Eero Saarinen - establishment journals, books, film, TV, lecture-circuit missionaries, all emanating from the East - continue to bring the message to us heartland natives. The papers that were presented illuminated some old as well as current problems of architectural journalism, cronyism, star-making, superficial criticism, cover-and centerfolditis, bi-coastal dominance, sibling rivalry, etc.), but several big issues were not even addressed: for example, how to encourage and strengthen regional Journals, how to increase literacy in the schools, how to identify, critique, and study local work of high quality that never enjoys the benediction of national publicity. These are certainly age-old, difficult questions deserving sustained attention by ACSA on both a regional and national level.

The saving grace of the conference after all the sound and fury of rhetoric, was a visit at twilight to Fay Jones' Thorncrown Chapel, a work of architecture so fine, so eloquent in its own language, that the words and pretensions of the day faded away as seafoam sinks into sand. The chapel is fast gaining fame around the world, as it well deserves. What other fine works of architecture that lie outside the publishing establishment will go unnoticed, and never each the halls of learning?"

Inland Architect Nov/Dec 1981

The "baby boomers" were by now moving through high school on to college and campuses across the nation were having to expand on a large scale for the first time since the twenties. Also, responding to new pressures of growth in sciences, engineering and business at a faster pace than in liberal arts, architects had to broaden their expertise in new technologies on both spatial planning and construction as well as face new imperatives of tight budgets and sped up time schedules. As we began trying to meet these new realities, our attention was directed more and more to innovating new combinations of "off the shelf" materials and systems beyond the traditional tailored wall bearing masonry, millwork and other older methods of building fabric assembly and integrating mechanical systems. Without fully realizing its implications for the future, we were pioneering the "curtain wall" and other sub-assembly systems, beginning with the design of the Gibson City High School, then in college and university buildings, developing three dimensional modularity in structural framing, window and door assemblies, floor and wall panels, surfacing and other finishing details that heretofore had been largely a custom labor-intensive process.

For example we "discovered," long available from nearby steel mills, tubing in both round and rectangular sections in a great variety of sizes. To us, this abundant inexpensive material was especially "ours" since we were in America's heartland of iron ore mining, smelting and steel fabrication. It was by now

our "stick" material like dimensional lumber of all sizes and shapes had been and still is in so many parts of the world. Together with new capabilities of welding, steel tubing had great diversity all the way from major beam and column structural frames to space frames and sub-assemblies of smaller scale elements like window mullions, railings, grilles and trellises. Earlier on I described our design of the proposed Unitarian Church in Bloomington using this mono-material system along with glass infill and how, stimulating Adlai Stevenson's negative reaction, it may have been ahead of its time even for liberal thinkers. However, we did succeed in gaining approval for this approach for several new campus buildings across the state, most extensively at Eastern Illinois University at Charleston for the student union, fine arts and science buildings.

The big advantage of this steel tube system was not only its economy in avoiding the complexity of so many other material and labor sub-contracts but also in the aesthetic satisfaction of interlocking principal skeletal structural elements with minor systems across the scale spectrum resulting in a feeling of lightness, transparency and reflectivity to the landscape in contrast to the traditional heavy, opaqueness of building mass typical of campuses in the past. Of course at that time energy was cheap and no one worried much about that as a restraining influence. Paint technology had also advanced so that long term maintenance was not the major factor it had been, almost coinciding in time

Student Union, Eastern Illinois University, Charleston, Illinois , 1958
Lundeen + Hilfinger Architects
A. Richard Williams, Architect for Design
(Photograph: Gene Asbury)

with the development of weathering steel alloys as exemplified by Saarinen's design for John Deere headquarters in Moline. This mono-material compositional harmony of major to minor elements had the same timeless quality of the all wood shrines of Ise in Japan, vernacular lattice-like building methods all the way to the Prairie School, the work of Fay Jones, the Green brothers in California and others in the Pacific Northwest.

I think this new awareness of materiality and solid/void scale harmonics in architecture pointed to and intensified our desire to be more involved with the whole palette of design decisions in furnishings, graphics and other stage set properties equipping each setting. At the other end of the scale this widening scope of design orchestration coincided in the late fifties with a growing concern for larger context relationships of urban and regional design, and organic seamlessness with landscape. Reminded again that as heartland Americans it was our nature to be zestful team players as in jazz; we should embark on a new renaissance of collaboration to make this dream of design seamlessness come true, but what could we do about this in our Balkanized, increasingly segregated university organization? For those of us active in practice, experiencing a well adapted and respectful appreciation of collaboration, it was more and more exasperating in academia to encounter resistance in trying to generate team projects in the fine and applied arts. In contrast to the emerging appetite for coordination in the biological and physical sciences, agriculture and business extension and research, a long tradition in land grant universities, most artists, architects and designers were still placing highest priority on his or her own signature work, free of having to relate to a given context through cooperative discipline.

Pondering this question I reflected back to my 1954 sabbatical, trying to understand and appreciate more fully the essence of Italian sensitivity in design across the scale spectrum of landscape, urban design, architecture, interior and object design, thinking that learning the language itself, at least as much as I was able, would open up new connective insights through reading and conversation. So in the spring of 1957, I decided to take the whole summer off staying in Florence, the acknowledged center of purest Italian, returning to the Casa Analena pensione as a base with occasional side trips in Tuscany and again to Rome. The Russoni family was still in charge and I worked out a deal with Signora Russoini's father Signor Calastro, a retired sculptor, for lessons. This arrangement was most informal, mainly to drive Signor Calastro around to visit monasteries nearby so he could visit old friends he knew while working on new or old sculptural installations or maintenance. These visits to the Certosa, to Vinci, to Volterra and to other more isolated villages were a kind of ritual, maybe with no more than three or flour monks all at least in their seventies, gathering in their salone with bread, wine and cheese. I think because I was an eager, attentive guest, they were especially cordial and meticulous in their diction, speaking slowly, using an exquisite limited vocabulary. Their suggestions for reading ranged from Dante, Leopardi to modern writers like Moravia. Fortunately I had a bit of a head start as an "auditor" in Italian classes at Illinois with Angelina "Peter" Pietrangeli, a marvelous teacher. Not that I ever became fluent but this combination of contacts from the literary elegance of Signor Calastro and his friends in pure Tuscan dialect to the TV quiz show every Thursday night at a local bar "Lascia o Radoppia" ("Double or Nothing") in vernacular Italian, I began to have a feel for the language that lent a special glow of closer connection to Italian culture and design that I had not experienced before—a catalytic link. This would continue to be a most rewarding feeling for years to come, a sense of belonging quite apart from my long time span as a visitor to the American Academy in Rome where you didn't hear much Italian.

For this summer in Florence I reasoned that I should order a Karmann Ghia car, designed by famed Italian designer Ghia, to be delivered in Osnabruck Germany then to drive down to Florence. Herbert Cerener from Osnabruck, whom I had met in Luxor three years before and his wife Renata gave me a great welcome and send off for this new pilgrimage. In 1962 I was to be greeted again by Herbert and Renata when I picked up another Karmann Ghia, this time all black inside and out. All black cars were not standard. When I had placed the order with the dealer in Champaign several months ahead, I was told that the standard interior was grey and that a special order for black could not be accepted. Worrying that it might be too much to ask, I wrote to Herbert to see if he might know anyone at the Karmann factory to ask if there might be a chance after all for this special order. A few weeks later the dealer in Champaign called in surprise to say he had had a telex message from Osnabruck that indeed I could have the black interior (for a small extra charge). So on delivery of the new car at the factory, Herbert and I were met by the reception staff in white uniforms as in a hospital surgery, suppressing their smiles, unable to resist asking "are you a priest?" "No." "An undertaker?" I shook my head again, "No, I'm an architect." "Ah, zo!" I guess this was not a surprise either, we were already moving into a period of sophisticated black and white minimalism. In any case when we drove into the Cereners' elegant white gravel courtyard, Renata greeted us exclaiming "So förrnehm!" ("so noble!"). I ended up that summer taking the car aboard the sleek black hulled Leonardo Da Vinci from Naples to New York, along with a black leather Gucci suitcase and a black leather covered Arne Jacobsen chrome legged studio chair I had bought on sale at Den Permanente in Copenhagen.

The salubrious summer days of 1957 in Florence are memorable most of all for the feeling of timelessness. If you are sur-

rounded by such an accumulation of cultural richness going back hundreds of years yet vibrant up to the present day in art, music, architecture, landscape and language, you soak it all up more and more as each facet of new experience builds up. Certain of these stand out and epitomize the rest; like the music festival "Maggio Musicale," a series of concerts held in various piazzas or other open public spaces or gardens like the Boboli, interlocking history, architecture, landscape, urban stages in the life of the city. It became increasingly clear that enjoyment of performance and setting linked together was ever more exhilarating depending on how much you were learning in parallel from all cultural sources past and present, and as I had hoped, greatly enriched by knowing a bit more of the language.

Life at the Analena was low key, quietly convivial, with the family and guests, some old friends from home. Jack Baker and Harold Young arrived for a few days to explore hill towns nearby. I was a guest several times at the Villa Caponi in Arcetri on the hills just south of the city, rented for the summer by Elizabeth "Buffie" and Ernest Ives, – "Buffie" was Adlai Stevenson's sister from Bloomington and a good friend of my mother's. At one of these gatherings quite a number of young Americans of college age were present along with young Italians, all of privileged social status. The Americans had just returned from several days of manual labor helping fix a road in Calabria, a needy district in southern Italy, full of pride and elation for

their work. The Italians shook their heads in disbelief smiling and frowning, not able to understand why this volunteer work made any sense at all—why should anybody possibly want to do this, as if it were some kind of a betrayal, stooping below the dignity of the aristocratic class. It was so strange to see this cultural gap show up among young people who otherwise were so much alike in looks, mannerisms and sophistication of modernism in the world around them. I had already found the same contrast between American architectural practice as a melting pot of ethnicities and the long standing European model separating the elite identity of "architects" from draftsmen and technicians as "artisans." This gap was first evident to me when I visited the design studios of Olivetti in Ivrea; the draftsmen, both technicians and designers called "geometra" were clearly understood to be apart from the architects, who in my view all seemed to come from upper class families. As I have suggested earlier this kind of class distinction has long existed at home too but to a far less acknowledged extent.

Sometime in July word came that I would be in charge of the graduate program at Illinois when I returned in the fall, taking over from Am Richardson who had resigned to give full time to practice. This news coming in the morning mail coincided with a day in Fiesole, the glorious hill town just north of the city, inspiring me to linger there the whole afternoon on a bluff overlooking Florence, at that distance a gold/red mirage, pondering how a new collage of ideas might be arranged for the graduate program that would build on the momentum of both professionalism and intellectual curiosity already established by Am and the increasing numbers of highly talented and mature students coming from all across the country and from abroad. What a salubrious place to dream about future destiny!

Ideas cascaded one on top of another, mainly in trying to imagine bridges between art and science, theory and practice, individuality and teamwork, intellect and emotion, low tech and high tech, truth and bullshit. Is this really a time for closure of all these pairs of learning or am I kidding myself that our culture is ready for this kind of synergy? After all isn't this desire for closer ties in higher education more and more missing today? There was still just the hint of this awakening in the late fifties, foreshadowing its flourishing a few years later. Why not try to get a head start? I began to think in more specific terms. Counting on the news of an even more highly qualified group of entering students, most of whom already had a year

or more office experience after their bachelor's degree, why not start with a short two week shakedown design project, the results revealing a correlation right away between portfolios of work and advanced billing through transcripts and supporting letters as well as serving as a guide for counseling and tailoring each individual's educational goals? The time seemed ripe for another crack at team projects, too. Couldn't we do both, foster individual direction and maturity as well as skill in collaboration? Couldn't we also, relying on the abundance of talent, encourage, side by side, highly theoretical projects juxtaposed to highly realistic ones? There didn't seem to be anything radical in this strategy—it appeared workable given the strength of the existing program accepting timeless/timely new reinforcement that was emerging not only from my own eagerness for greater diversity in the quest for excellence, building in crescendo here in Italy and at home as well; but perhaps most of all from the exciting new "seit geist" ("time ghost") of the time that I have tried to describe earlier—a new world for design.

Returning to the Analena from Fiesole on an emotional high, I wrote a letter summing up these hopes addressed to Alan Laing, chairman of the school and to all the new students asking for their reactions to be discussed as soon as I got back in late August. Meanwhile I had an assignment from Walter Creese, our eminent historian, to help fill out the slide library collection by photographing Palladian villas around Vicenza. On the

drive up to the Veneto area I passed through the Po valley observing the harmonious uniformity of all red brick and tile towns and farmsteads, suddenly deciding I should photograph the vernacular architecture of barns and dwellings as well as the villas. This would be a search for good design across the spectrum of building types toward a better understanding of the "genius loci" of northeast Italy from the fertile clay based river plain to the foothills of the Alps and their mix of clay products and stone. The "Rosa Verona" stone of Verona was somehow rosier in balance to the red brick of the plains.

Driving from Bologna to Ferrara I began to play a game of spotting the best brick columned barn. All were two storied square plans, four two foot square columns on each side with an inner square of four, the ground floor open on all sides for farm equipment and animals, the upper floor for hay, each upper bay filled with vertical strips of weathered wood set slightly apart for ventilation, the slight overhanging roof a low-pitched pyramid covered with tile, a little more varied in tones of red than the more uniform red brick columns. The game became one of trying to notice those of particularly sensitive refinement of proportions and craftsmanship, or any other evidence of the builder's awareness of these characteristics. Before long though I found a model example, saw a farmer at work nearby and drove in to ask if I could photograph his barn. It was another test of my Italian. I was welcomed heartily with a big smile and after being assured it was okay to photograph, I asked if he thought his barn was the best in proportion and craftsmanship around and if not where could I find a better one in the neighborhood? Although he was an uneducated tenant farmer, I quickly understood he was completely at home with my question and we discussed these aesthetic qualities as if we were in an art museum pondering subtle differences in painting or sculpture. While enjoying a glass of wine, I remarked how fine his crop of corn ("granolo") looked. He responded, "Ah, si, é Funkś Super G hybrid da America!" I couldn't believe it—telling him that this hybrid was developed by the Funk

family from my home town Bloomington, Illinois. I ended up leaving the farm loaded down with fresh fruit and cries from his family "Torna ancora! Ci vediamo fra poco!" ("Come back, we'll see you soon").

I had much the same experience visiting villas in the Veneto. The Ente Provinciale da Turismo in Vicenza was most helpful in arranging these visits—except for a few, like Palladio's Villa Capra that were open to tourists, others that Professor Creese wanted me to photograph were not open to the public, requiring special arrangements. I enjoyed three days doing loop drives out of Vicenza, always being welcomed by a caretaker, offered vino rosso da casa, then shown around with broad smiles and gestures (I could sense it was a change from their usually boring, solitary existence), always seeming to value the frescoes more than the architecture and landscape design. The exception was the Villa Pisani "La Rocca" at Lonigo by Vincenzo Scamozzi, a pupil of Palladio, built in 1585. The Countessa Pisani, about 75, happened to be in residence. She had had an English governess and spoke English, though archaic, it was better than my Italian. She delighted in showing me how she was finally putting in bathrooms after almost four hundred years, and offering me lunch, this time with vino blanco. It was here I was struck again with a feeling of "déjà vu"—I've been here before! It happened as we were in an upper circular gallery around the central dome looking across the base of the dome through elegantly proportioned elliptical

windows. I thought I had a fleeting glimpse of another face that looked like me in a renaissance cap and beard, as if in a mirror! Had I been an architect then, perhaps even Scamozzi himself?

With this kind of spooky feeling the wheels of the Karmann Ghia seemed to float above the highway to Genova where I shipped the car to New York, to be picked up there two weeks later as I made my way to Lisbon to fly back home aboard a TWA constellation. Along the way I was amazed to sail from Genoa to Cannes, second class, aboard a luxurious liner all day for about $8, then from Cannes to Marselles by rail in time for the weekend promenade along the Cannabiere boulevard, a Mediterranean custom for thousands of years. On to Barcelona to stroll the Ramblas, visit the barrios, pay homage to Gaudi and fly on to Madrid, the Gran Via, Escorial, the Plaza Mayor and the famous underground café of the toreadors "Las Cuevas" to enjoy sangria with some young Australians I had met. My revisit to Lisbon brought back memories of escaping Europe in 1940 aboard the Saturnia. This time I woke up to Lisbon's unique mosaic sidewalks as they tie the city together like the warp and weave of a giant, beautifully patterned carpet.

San Francisco Center for Architecture and Urban Studies

A REFLEXION OF ARCHITECTURE AND URBAN DESIGN
A. Richard Williams

The Urban Stage (Book)
A. Richard Williams
(Cover Illustration: Mark Romack)

One of the things you learn as each new threshold in life is crossed is that in so many ways you have to "earn your spurs" all over again. Even though reputations do build up, proof still remains to be demonstrated of one's capability to handle each new responsibility. Directing a graduate program in architecture is a special challenge, because the new students often are more like peers and colleagues than were inexperienced undergraduates. In practice too, each new project brings with it a host of new conditions, new clients and new collaborators presenting much the same challenge of proving to them and to yourself that the new experience will measure up to the quality of your work so far and ideally advance it still more.

This challenge in both academic and professional life, though distinctly separate activities, often fused together, mainly through contacts across disciplines in the university and in offices in Chicago and other parts of the Midwest, as well as through my own continuing activity as design architect with the firm in Bloomington. But as suggested earlier, I think we all sensed that together we were on the threshold of a new age of collegiality and collaboration, so the inspiration and new ideas I had had on the bluffs of Fiesole began to take hold—the new students were truly excited to do both their own individual design projects and research as well plunge into team projects, collaborating with students in landscape architecture and urban planning. Out of the blue in late 1957 came a plea from Don Logan, planning direc-

tor of Joliet, Illinois asking our students to take on a downtown redevelopment project for that city. This was not really surprising since Illinois as a land grant university was already well known in communities around the state for its outreach in business and agriculture extension services, but this was the first time any such request had come to us in the design professions. We indeed had the abundance of talented and eager students in the three schools in order to form a team of eight, first to gather information then develop sketch studies leading to a final model and drawings of a proposal for presentation to the city at a large gathering of civic officials, service clubs and interested citizens. This project met with such success that we soon had many more requests from cities around the state, in and around Chicago and from Columbus and Indianapolis, Indiana, leading to a series of downtown and other redevelopment studies spanning the next ten years. We made it clear from the start that each of these collaborative projects was not a substitute for professional service, as from established architectural and planning offices but an educational exercise for both the students and each local community. As it turned out, many of the projects stimulated subsequent development by professional firms, as in Columbus, Indiana, two yeas of student projects led to the master plan of the downtown by SOM in Chicago, a follow through plan, that was actually carried out. In addition to Joliet, from 1958 to 1965, other similar collaborative projects included urban design studies for Decatur, Bloomington,

Springfield, Jacksonville, Humbolt Park, Chicago, and for Columbus and Indianapolis in Indiana.

In each case the requesting community would fund expenses for travel, photography, drawing, and model materials and publication of monographs. Soon, as publication of these projects in both local and national media built up and became a powerful attraction for many more highly qualified graduate students, we were also able to organize team projects of a more hypothetical nature, such as new towns around Chicago, on a parallel track with the realistic ones of existing cities, thereby gaining a great advantage of learning through comparative, side by side studies in critique sessions. The theoretical projects were funded mainly by the Graham Foundation in Chicago and occasionally by other foundations.

Through experimentation to find the most workable sequences of steps in carrying out each project, usually two in each academic year, a program of requirements, maps and other special information would be acquired during the spring and summer ahead of the next academic year, usually by collaboration of the faculty. Then as the new semester began, each student of a team of six to ten would prepare his or her concept of an overall scheme to be reviewed by faculty and representatives from the community involved, leading to a consensus for a basic concept. The author of the chosen scheme then became leader of the team for further

refinement, each team member choosing some special phase of study such as spatial organization, movement systems, open space, preservation and new growth proposals. All of this would result in a set of diagrams and drawings recording the before and after progression of studies, also in three dimensional model form, to be presented orally with slides by the team, along with a summary documentation, usually as a portfolio of reproductions that could be subsequently published in a variety of formats. Perhaps one of the most remarkable aspects of this experience for the students was their opportunity for direct personal contact with leaders of whatever community was under study; mayors, city managers, planning commissioners, bankers, local design professionals and of course politicians—in both formal and informal working sessions.

In respect to the more visionary, hypothetical projects like the lakefront development of Chicago, radial corridor studies, new edge city and new free-standing town proposals, the students' contacts often included both community leaders as above and vanguard thinkers in the university from other disciplines such as in theatre, theoretical physics, cybernetics, critical writing, political and social science as well as the fine and applied arts. Several of these Chicago based projects, funded by the Graham Foundation, were presented and on exhibition at the Foundation, attracting an even wider audience of future oriented civic leaders and journalist critics, eventually leading to

Drawing for The Urban Stage
Lebbeus Woods

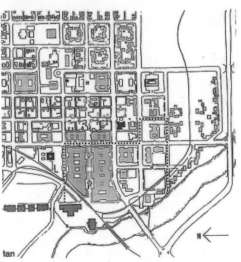

Columbus Indiana, Downtown Redevelopment Study,
As published in Architectural Forum, December 1963, Drawing by Louis Narcissi

Students: Lon Frye, Ivan Glover, Tom Hartley, David Kahl, Tom Katsuyoshi, Louis Ng, Adib Wahby, Larry Cannon, Derwood Schrotberger, Critics: Stow Chapman, A. Richard Williams

director John Entenza's hint that the series of projects might be put together in a book. I took the hint, to apply for a grant from the Foundation to accomplish this, which, along with other insights and design experience resulted in the publication of The Urban Stage—A Reflection of Architecture and Urban Design.

The wealth of student talent and wide scope of projects, building up year after year through the sixties, was something we took in stride as it reflected and was inspired by the wider cultural shift to more and more concern about civil rights and an awakened environmental conscience, coinciding for whatever reasons yet to be fully probed by cultural historians. As I tried to trace earlier, using Italy, the Nordic countries and our own Prairie and Chicago School innovations as models for good design across the scale spectrum—from table ware to cities and the countryside as a garden—all of a sudden we as a nation were beginning to get the message that collaboration was much more than a theoretical motherhood value—the unmet needs of society and the environment were now clearly up front as motivation to use our talents in other than self-serving ways yet with no sacrifice at all to our own individuality and creativity as a part of a team, like the Beatles or the Modern Jazz Quartet. These were years of high expectations and fulfillment more than we knew at the time—now in retrospect glowing as a kind of Golden Age long gone, killed by the Vietnam War.

Still, as the reference to jazz implies, I honor all my students and colleagues with whom I had closest contact from 1937 to the present, especially those I worked with in the sixties.

Their zest in working together on collaborative projects and communicating their enthusiasm in wider community circles around them was infectious. At the same time, this inspirational zest was just as strong in fine tuning their own work on both short and longer design projects. This comprehensive breadth and depth of curiosity, talent and initiative for involvement in micro to macro scale projects had, in my experience, never existed before with the same intensity. What is even more interesting is that it was shared by almost all of our graduate students wherever they came from, across America or from abroad; Bal Baswant from India, Chalerm Soocharit and Witchit Charenbak from Thailand, Tsuto Kimura from Japan, Brian Binning and Graham Brawn from Australia, Bill Alington, Ivan Glover from New Zealand, Tom Katsuyoshi from Hawaii, Guido Francescato from Argentina, Anna Cannavou from Athens, Adib Wahba from Cairo, Paolo Sica from Florence, Gary Hack from Canada, Ken Featherstone, Tony Goddard and David Saile from England, Alan Forrester and Bill Grenoch from Scotland and others whose participation was part time, in seminars or from some other area of concentration. The list of students from across America is so long it's hard to name them all. Perhaps the best way to remember them is by their participation in whichever of the collaborative teams they were involved and by certain of the most outstanding individual projects.

All through this period my colleagues on the faculty who were most active in the Collaborative Design Studio included Bob Katz from urban planning and architecture, Norm Day and Gerry Exline in architecture, Don Molnar in landscape architecture, plus other notable contributors on certain projects, especially Jack Baker in architecture, Louis Wetmore and Lac Blair in planning. From time to time colleagues from other parts of the university would be guests for critiques especially during the university's centennial in 1968; Heinz Von Foerster from cybernetics, Dan Alpert and David Pines from physics, and others. Also during the centennial we had many visitors from elsewhere, Serge Chermayeff from Yale, Chris Alexander and Charles Moore from Berkeley, Walter Gropius from Harvard, Aldo Van Eyck from Amsterdam, John Entenza from the Graham Foundation, Walter Netsch and Ralph Youngren from SOM Larry Perkins, Phil Will and Ray Ovresat from Perkins and Will, Jack Train from SM&D and Carter Manny from C. F. Murphy, all from Chicago.

Many of the above Chicago firms were hosts for seminars in their offices for our graduate students, critiquing student projects based on one or more similar ones done by the offices. Bill Hartman at SOM, Larry Perkins of Perkins and Will and Harry Weese in his own office were particularly helpful in arranging these exchanges.

Shadow Box, 3D Montage of Nine Architectural Projects, 1984
Chicago Women in Architecture: Progress and Evolution 1974–1984
Bruno Ast, Gunduz Dagdelen

Residence, College Park, MD, 1990
Guido Francescato (Prof. of Architecture, U. of Maryland), Architect

Nichiren Mission Temple, Honolulu , HI, 2002
Tom Katsuyoshi (M. Arch, U. of Illinois, 1964), Architect

Perhaps describing a few of the individual projects will give a clearer idea of how the program was building up; especially as they may mirror attitudes and appetites for learning at the time. The initial "shake down" two week project for new students, as I had imagined it originally in Fiesole, had some surprising results in addition to working out as I had hoped as a guide for counseling. One of the programs called for the design of a small conference center like a small motel in the woods of Allerton Park, an estate given to the university by Robert Allerton, as described earlier. The idea was to see how the students would adapt their designs to such a dense prairie grove setting, particularly how access, parking and service areas would be sensitively integrated. The response was rewarding in prompting low key, almost hidden residential quarters and social spaces in vocabularies of natural materials, showing restraint from show piece "look at me" architectural expression. Bill Alington, from Wellington New Zealand, influenced strongly by Mies van der Rohe, did a sensitive job of fitting seemingly transparent structures discreetly among the trees, with a large clearing in the approach for parking with the major meeting and dining area facing the parked cars. When asked if maybe he should have tried to hide the cars in the woods, Bill was surprised saying, "I think the colors of the cars are beautiful together, like a mosaic!"

Another time I gave a program to design a "High Rise Apartment House of 24 Units" with no more than two apartments per floor, on a site at the edge of hardwoods on the bank of the Sangamon River at Mohamet, Illinois, a village a few miles away from Champaign, surrounded by rich agricultural land. At least half of the 12 to 14 students objected to the idea of a high-rise in a small town. I said, "Okay let's go look at the site and see if you may want to change your mind." So we went out to Mohamet to look around observing the lushness of the trees along the river, then I asked "What else do you see?" "Oh, yes, that big grain elevator by the railroad." Then we had a lively debate, questioning why it was perfectly acceptable for grain to be in a tower 200 feet high but not for people?

For another starter project I used the same site, this time for single houses along the edge of the trees, where it met the corn fields, asking for living spaces that would offer distant views at tree top level, well above the maturing crops. Many imaginative solutions resulted, the one by Bruno Ast was most memorable. His scheme involved using a slip-formed round standard concrete silo system 12 feet in diameter about 40 feet high, enclosing vertical circulation, utility and storage space supporting a large circular platform, roofed with a Bucky Fuller geodesic dome enclosing the main living space in the tree tops, the open side offering a sweeping view of the countryside. The series of dwellings along this meandering prairie grove edge looked as if giant mushrooms had chosen to grow there.

Among the projects allowing more time for definitive design development was a program to design a small recital hall addition to Smith Music Hall on the campus, at a time, about 1959/60, when the university was accelerating its building expansion program. Although it was understood that this was only a demonstration exercise, not intended as a substitute for a real project by an architectural firm, the exceptional talent and maturity of the 12 graduate students, led to a result of such a high level of professional quality that the music faculty arranged a special exhibition of the projects in the gallery of the student union. Probably what excited everybody most about the exhibition was the set of 12 large scale models that could be peered into, revealing interiors that seemed like stringed instruments in their delicate fragility. It was really the first time that student projects had been carried to such a high level of refinement and rigorous detailing well beyond the usual preliminary schematic two dimensional diagrammatic presentations. This recital hall project, more than any other up to this point in the school set a pace of design refinement and professionalism, a powerful influence for emulation, not only for individual masters design thesis projects but for undergraduate studios as well.

It was with a feeling of elation that the summer of 1959 approached, almost like a celebration, to get away again to Europe. I have already reminisced about the 1959 flight to Paris with the Guvrekians, Oulie and Maurice,

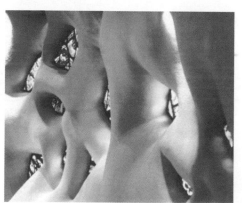

84 St. Katharine's Way, London, UK, 1986
RIBA North East Thames Architectural Society (NETAS) Award
Goddard Manton Architects
Tony Goddard, Architect

Unitarian Church, Deerfield, IL, 1985
Ron Dirsmith (B. Arch, U. of Illinois, Rome Prize, 1957–58), Architect

154

the events of the night over the ocean and the serendipity of running into Robert Le Ricolais on the boulevard Ste. Germaine in the late afternoon, the dinner party at their house in the Marais until midnight all in one exhausting but delightful day.

The following weeks were more relaxed, wandering through the south of France, again to Florence, the lake country, reunions with Gabriel and Ninette in Rome along with other younger friends from Illinois, Ron Dirsmith, fellow at the American Academy, then on to Greece with Chuck Gordon, another of my great students, to explore Corfu, Olympia, Delphi, Athens and the Aegean on a five day cruise aboard the "Angelica," earlier the "Princess Anne" formerly in service out of Vancouver, a small passenger vessel carrying only about 40 on the cruise, like the ones I was so familiar with as a child on the Great Lakes. The fare was only sixty U. S. dollars, the cruise embarking from Piraeus in late afternoon on a Sunday, to Crete, Rhoades, Myconos, Patmos returning on Friday.

The captain, Nick Paridis, asked Chuck and I to sit at his table, along with Bruno Leon an architect who had been on the Illinois faculty and a friend of his, a fortyish American woman with her Greek lover and her teen age daughter, and a tall blond young woman who operated a beauty parlor in Brooklyn. I guess it was just a coincidence that all of us, except the Greek lover were Americans at Captain Nick's table; he was a most congenial host. It turned out that he had been

a captain of an American built YMS mine-sweeper in the Greek navy, exactly the same type of vessel on which I had been executive officer in World War II in the Pacific, so we had a few extra ouzo liqueurs toasting our experience. Also on board were four American journalists who had just attended a conference in Athens, all jovial, witty conversationalists. It was beautiful clear weather in July, the seas calm, encouraging us to lounge between islands on the top deck around a small pool. Every day the blond from Brooklyn would appear in a skin colored bathing suit and comb her long hair reclining in a languorous position that inspired the journalists to whisper her name as "Lady Godiva." While at Myconos we took smaller boats to explore Delos. Another tourist group mostly Greek-Americans was there, out of whose midst rushed the same beautiful girl who had been disturbed by the Salvador Dali character on the overnight flight to Paris, to embrace me with exuberance as her rescuer. I proudly introduced her to my companions as Helen of Troy. Chuck and I found our way up to Salonica, then to Skopja by rail, by air to Dobrovnik and Zagreb, finally crossing to Venice by hydrofoil. We parted there gong home by different routes in August.

I still remember this summer as almost sinfully the most carefree of all times away, not exactly irresponsible but a welcome change from academic and professional rationalization. Maybe any such feeling of guilt can be erased by thinking of it as needed R & R,

or seeing it as another "travel as learning" episode, this time pointing to each future adventure though seemingly random, as adding to a repository like a bank for selective future withdrawals of ideas that might be appropriate to new design tasks.

As we entered the sixties I doubt that anyone's crystal ball foresaw that this decade would turn out to be so much more extraordinary than any others in the twentieth century. The flow of post-war prosperity had appeared seamless in its forward momentum, each year linking to the next with much the same optimism and expectations of an ever brighter future. But gradually, then suddenly, we woke up to the fact that a higher private standard of living for most of America seemed more and more hollow without a corresponding rise in well-being for all of our society. Of course it can't be said that this awakening conscience was universally shared; selfish special interests persisted in their indifference, but were more and more exposed as hypocritical and blindsided as growing social injustice and racism could no longer be denied as it had been for so long. In parallel, this build up of social conscience began to include concern about waste and depredation of the natural environment as well, bringing out of dormancy a new ethic of inhabitation and consumption of the earth's finite land and energy resources.

In both architectural education and practice the power of this wide spreading consciousness was at work inspiring both individual ambition and eagerness to collaborate in finding solutions far beyond anything we had experienced before. We got the message in spite of our still cloudy view of it; that as environmental designers we were destined to be in the thick of building the fabric, the

setting for a new Golden Age, if it ever were to exist, naïve as this inspiration may now be seen. There was a certain sense of enchantment about this threshold in time—the circumstance of a young president, John Kennedy, coming into leadership on the upswell of great expectations of what America could now become—a new vision of Camelot. Little did we ever imagine then that this glowing, utopian image of a new reality to be enjoyed by our entire society would later be side tracked into Disney Worlds, into make believe cities like Las Vegas, into even larger surround sound movie palaces, into countless new giant stadiums, into TV extravaganzas at home, even into war as entertainment—all abrogating and absolving political leadership from the trust and responsibility of bringing the American Dream truly into all our lives. Are we now, in the new millennium, replaying Rome before its fall?

Nevertheless, the spirit of a new renaissance caught us up in its spell. In many ways the university was the epitome of settings, the bellwether intellectual, emotional, dynamic place to foreshadow what an enlightened future could be like everywhere else. You began to hear such expressions as "the city is a university—the university is a city." We were reminded again of the timeless quotation, "some are born great, some achieve greatness, some have greatness thrust upon them." It seemed that all of these were inherent in the university's destiny. For the moment at least we were swept up in this enthusiasm, hoping that at long last, realistic

or not, we could lead the way in making new images of the future that had some chance of pointing the way out of rampant materialism and mediocrity in the sprawling built environment.

Other bright colleagues could write the script but it was up to us as architects, landscape architects, planners, engineers and all other artists and designers to make the new images and to challenge our most eloquent economists, social and political scientists, poets and media experts to communicate these visions near and far.

Rather than try to ponder the entire, broad panorama of optimism, inspiration and momentum on the threshold of a "great society" and "war on poverty," I feel more confident in recalling the smaller part of it I know best—of the design professions as they came closer together on a common mission, focusing especially on architectural practice and education reaching out in bringing our shared enthusiasm to all levels of our communities.

Perhaps one facet of this sharing may exemplify the larger dimension of this moment in time. It had been traditional for many, many years for annual conventions of the American Institute of Architects, (AIA) and the Association of Collegiate Schools of Architecture, (ACSA) to meet together, usually in late May or early June, with overlapping themes, schedules of events and socializing, especially during the first major welcoming party given by the host AIA chapter. What a stimulating experience it had been for me earlier on in May 1937, while still in graduate school at MIT, to be in the midst of this AIA/ACSA joint spirit in greeting Gropius to America and feeling, as we came out of the depression, a new collegial sense of mission that bonded practice and theory seamlessly. Of course at that time we were only a handful of wide-eyed enthusiasts, ACSA members numbering only in the twenties and AIA delegates in the few hundreds compared to far greater numbers in the post-war years, building up with prosperity, more and more segregation into special interests and less and less outward concern for our common cause.

So it may seem a contradiction to try to reconcile this expanding specialization and inward preoccupation during the fifties with the sudden reawakening of a social and environmental ethic at the end of the decade. Somehow, as in May 1937 in Boston, and then again at the joint meeting in 1960 of AIA/ACSA in San Francisco and Berkeley, the same spark was ignited, but with a difference. The difference was, I believe, that by this time we were "feeling our oats," as maturing young Americans achieving individual recognition, even stardom through a well publicized body of fresh new work, springing free of foreign influence and discipleship. So what if most of these new names like Elwood, Eames, Koenig, Harris, Alexander, Wurster and DeMars were West Coast with a Hollywood feel of celebrity?

Still, this new Americanness included others across the country; Rudolph, Jones, Saarinen and most of all Louis Kahn. I think it's worth noting, too, that almost all of these became well known through excellence in the design of houses and other small scale structures, a fulfillment of high expectations set by the Case Study House Series in Southern California just after the war. It's also true that most of these architects of rising fame were fully or partly engaged in architectural education too, so in retrospect it's hard to separate exciting presentations, dialogues and social encounters, whether they were AIA or ACSA—it was another jazz combo of work, ideas and energy free at last, of European hierarchies. Night life in San Francisco, too, almost as if by design, was symbolically memorable. Two chance encounters, one at a bistro featuring Thelonius Monk at the piano, another at a bar with everybody singing songs we all knew.

Across the bay in Berkeley, two other almost impromptu meetings set the tone, one a party at Bill Wurster's and Catherine Bauer's house where many of the already well knowns like Lou Kahn, east and west, were mixing along with new risers like Charles Moore, Bill Turnbull, Don Lyndon, Joe Esherick and all the rest of us basking in a new aura of shared inspiration—we couldn't wait to get back to work in our offices and academic studios—there seemed no difference at all whether you were a practitioner or educator, the realm of learning between reached a new high. The realm between was

in truth our students—a foreshadow of "a love-in there," later made famous as a part of San Francisco's charisma.

We gathered with our students from all parts of the nation in the courtyard of Berkeley's rambling old School of Architecture at high noon, tightly crowded around Mies Van der Rohe, the students' guest of honor. From the morning exuberance of debate about which of the alluring directions and stars in modern architecture might lead the way, the student chairman asked us all to quiet down, then addressing Mies, asked: "Mies, where do we go from here?" Mies, puffing solemnly on his cigar, finally looked up saying: "We stay here, do good job."

Alas, as the sixties ended, our hopes that we were on the brink of a new Golden Age were dashed in the anguishing throes of riots and other disruptions on campuses and elsewhere in protest to the war in Vietnam.

It now seems ironic that AIA/ACSA rapport, as it portended a new renaissance for the sixties and beyond, began to slip away, while, so it seemed, the crescendo of doing something about unmet socio/environmental needs had built up with such urgency. In retrospect one can now see that along with prosperity an upswing took place in practice to equate success more and more with bigness and other earmarks of material reward, typical of burgeoning priorities of profit above everything else in the world of business. This trend, despite the continued nod to design through Honor Award programs and other forms of recognition of all around excellence, like the AIA Gold Medal could be directly interpreted in the changing agendas of AIA conventions as they became dominated by PR, liability and other pragmatic issues of competition and growth. By the eighties this shift in orientation was almost total. I remember one AIA national convention theme in the seventies, "Value Architecture" (when I was president of the Illinois Council AIA), that I completely misinterpreted, thinking that the theme was a signal for all of us in the profession to improve ourselves, to increase our own value to society. Instead it turned out that the emphasis was on marketing, in making the public more aware of the value of what we already do, without inference that it meant any internal obligation of qualitative improvement–we're already A, OK! This trend in practice, with AIA its mirror, eventually became a source of disillusionment among educators.

And many practitioners became increasingly disillusioned with the schools as well because "they're not training students adequately for the new realities of putting a building together." Change could be observed in the agendas of ACSA meetings too as tenure track imperatives greatly multiplied the numbers and specialization of papers presented, allowing less and less time to address emerging high priority issues arising directly or indirectly from external cultural changes as remarked earlier but intensifying still more as we entered the new millennium.

Aleksandr Solzhenitsyn summed them up in an address to the Academy of Science in Moscow titled "The Exhaustion of Culture," brought about by global "massification, materialism, mediocratization[2],"also referring to Pope John Paul II's declaration that the "absolutism of money" has became the third totalitarianism of the century following communism and fascism. To these I would add educational impoverishment, especially in liberal arts and design. All of these have greatly diminished architecture as a traditionally respected cultural value. Only show pieces by starchitects now seem to be identified as architecture while worthy modest work is largely unnoticed and unappreciated, lost in a developer dominated world.

In the face of all these negative external pressures as they have built up in the last thirty years, we as architectural educators and those of us in practice too can take heart that we, though an ever tinier minority, still remain trustees, along with others who care, of advancing the art and science of human and environmental well being.

We need reminding too that we as architectural educators still lie within the heart and soul of civilization's greatest invention—the university—sharing the same assaults from outside and the same internal sins like Balkanization, elitism, spin, politics and disproportionate use of meager resources. I need not spell this all out, we know the details well enough, but I must single out just one.

As Americans we have always rejected or played down criticism of our culture as a whole. Remember when in the seventies after Watergate President Jimmy Carter spoke up about how the nation was "suffering a cultural malaise," and how he was attacked—"You can't say that!" In our AIA/ACSA world we shy away from the fact that opportunity in both practice and education is not exactly a level playing field as it is dominated by power, money, privilege, elitism and networking. Those of us who have devoted our careers to architectural education in public universities have long hesitated in being frank with our students about how privilege works in this "land of equal opportunity" for fear of discouraging them.

Getting all this off my chest, I rejoice that we as educators in AIA, ACSA and all others dedicated to learning, after long years of going our separate ways have for some time now refocused our attention on our common cause, coming together again I would like to think for timeless reasons rather than in rebellion against the distresses of our time. Examples of this new awakening abound, like the Educator Practitioner Network (EPN) and at the grass roots level of "hands-on," "design build" programs at many schools, pioneered by Samuel Mockbee and others not yet well known across North America. ACSA's recognition of these small starts as they generate new themes like the Journal of Architectural Education's I:IJAE Theme Issue (2006) and other down to earth programs that include both craft and poetry, loom

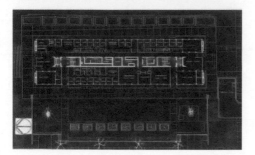

College of Education, University of Illinois, Champaign, Illinois, 1963
Lundeen + Hilfinger Architects
A. Richard Williams, FAIA, Architect for Design
Wade Abels, Associate for Design Development
(Drawings: Gerry Exline)

large for the future. I rejoice too that it is a return to the same spirit of the immediate post World War II years affirming that architecture is, after all, the timeless art of building, a full scale medium rising above the panoply of words, paper and digital simulation, important as all these tools are.

Maybe in "earning our spurs" all over again through excellence in the design of dwellings and other small scale structures as our heroes did of yore, we might, just might be again on the brink of a New Golden Age.

It so happened then at Illinois that the College of Education was in line for a new building on a site framed by older Neo Georgian structures conforming to the standard three storey block plus a dormered slate pitched roof with a cornice line at 50 feet above grade. The faculty of Education, in writing their program, strongly expressed their dismay that their forward looking curriculum had to be fitted into this standard block, pointing out how anachronistic it would be for their students to go out to positions in brand new contemporary schools that responded to new design break throughs in spatial organization, flexibility, use of light, air, furnishings and closely integrated landscape design.

On returning from San Francisco I had an urgent call from Dean Allen Weller of our College of Fine and Applied Arts: "Could I make a study of how Education's program could be accommodated in a contemporary

design in such a Neo-Georgian context?" He also reported that the university architect's office would use the same program to develop a Neo Georgian design—in other words we would do an in-house competition to be presented to the powers that be, including the Board of Trustees, for a decision. I thanked the Dean for the challenge, saying I'd be flattered and delighted to take it on, but wondered if we shouldn't keep the competition under wraps, what if it got out in this day and age that the University of Illinois was still engaging in a battle of styles? So it was decided. Now I had a special mission for a planned trip abroad that summer with my mother, to spend more time in England to become an "expert" on Georgian in order not to do it, and at the same time learn more about contextual harmonics of different styles as they existed side by side at Oxford, Cambridge and elsewhere.

Maybe it was a preconception, maybe not, that the key to solving this problem of style harmonics might be to respond to the College of Education's desire for a more open, flexible plan by working it out in lower level spaces, much as lower garden walls tie the higher block building masses together. The long, low orangerie pavilion enclosing Mantegna's huge painting of Caesar's Return to Rome, attached to the Georgian three-storied mass of Blenheim Palace embodied this idea as did Wrens' arcaded library addition to the Gothic quad of Trinity College in Cambridge. At Nancy, France the architect Emanuel Heré composed the Georgian style

Place Stanislaus with three storey blocks on three sides of the square with the fourth side a one storey pavilion with a gateway leading to a series of gardens. On return to Illinois I tried this scheme for the chosen site on a north–south axis connecting the two east/west parallel blocks of 50 foot high corniced buildings facing each other about 300 feet apart. The Education building thus became in appearance a one storey link with a deep overhanging roof fascia thick enough to act as a balcony for stateroom like offices around the building perimeter at a second level. This fascia of pre-cast concrete panels picked up the same height as horizontal limestone belt courses on the Georgian facades between their first and second floors. The ground floor became a transparent colonnade just high enough to enclose classrooms with mezzanine offices above but under the wide overhanging, inhabited roof. Labs, shops, and other flexible spaces were placed at a below grade level opening on a sunken court to the east. On the west side a wall enclosed courtyard at grade level gave some seclusion for classrooms opening on it as well as serving to make the whole building appear lower. It may sound like cheating to try to make four floors seem to be just one—in any case the scheme was enthusiastically supported by the faculty. It now remained to convince the higher authorities that this approach would gain their approval.

Meanwhile, the university architect's office was preparing a typical Georgian block scheme. At the first presentation of the two proposals, President David Henry and key university committee members were delighted with the contemporary pavilion design that I presented so it went forward to the Board of Trustees and was approved. Along with other new master planning proposals across the campus, most involving a much more positive role of landscape architecture, particularly in prairie grove character, the yoke of Neo Georgian conformity was broken. I like to think of this new enlightenment in campus planning as inseparable with new concepts in higher education, the breakthroughs in collaborative science, computers, electronics, agriculture and other areas of research, all stimulating a renaissance of interdisciplinary activity, for a while at least a reversal of creeping Balkanization of academia into fiefdoms of departments, schools, colleges, institutes and other minutia of special interests. All this was building in the sixties leading up to the university's centennial in 1967/68. Growing out of this building of collegiality and in many ways standing for it was the creation in the Graduate College of the Center for Advanced Study, fostering post-doctoral fellowships and interchange of cutting edge ideas among faculty and invited artists, scholars and researchers. Though modeled on Princeton's Center for Advanced Study, Illinois as a public land–grant university had an even wider scope of interaction with its heartland constituency. Under the brilliant leadership of Dan Alpert in physics, Dean of the Graduate College, then David Pines, one of the nation's top theoretical physicists, the

College of Education, University of Illinois, Champaign, Illinois, 1963
Lundeen + Hilfinger Architects
A. Richard Williams, FAIA, Architect for Design
Wade Abels, Associate for Design Development
(Drawings: A. Richard Williams, Photographs: Richard Koch)

Center flourished in these years. I was lucky to be a part of it working on policy and in designing the remodeling of a campus edge residence to accommodate offices, meeting rooms and a library as a setting for conferences but mostly for informal gatherings. We could experiment with integrating painting, sculpture and graphic design, contemporary furniture, gourmet vending and coffee machines as they enhanced collegiality. All this worked so well that plans were made to build a permanent headquarters, and I was asked to develop a design for this concept that would be adjacent to the new Krannert Center for Performing Arts. I have no doubt that if it were not for the debacle of the Vietnam War, all this promise would have been fulfilled, but it was not.

As alienation of the public against universities as settings for unrest and riots climaxed in 1969 and was reflected in the negative reaction of state legislatures as well as of our fellow citizens, the zest for innovative interdisciplinary activity melted away or was driven into hiding as it symbolized somehow a threatening, radical direction. Both faculty and students retreated into safe haven within traditional disciplinary boundaries. Would the exciting spirit of innovative collegiality ever return again as the nation swung back into another era of "me-tooism" in the seventies and on?

But let me return to 1960, the beginning of those too few "Belle Epoch" years that we now see nostalgically, much more than

we could imagine then, as a shining prime time, not only in the large dimension of our society as it was newly inspired, but in our personal lives as well. I think that summer in Europe with my mother as companion, embodying through her poetic literacy and compassionate regard for all people of whatever ethnicity and station in life, gave me a new sense of balance to offset my narrow absorption in architecture. It was another spur to strive for greater depth of meaning than before; to invest in each new project as it came along more respect for its physical context in the society of its neighbors as well as in the more subtle investment of poetic and analogic meaning that might be not only perceived visually but felt in other sensual dimensions, such as the harmonics of sound, smell, touch and most of all a satisfying sense of presence and fit in the flow of time, informed by knowledge of historical relevance and its rightness in the ageless, ever-present phenomenon of Nature and Man living together.

I must try to explain, as an example, how this new awakening inspired the design development of a new project: After designing the College of Education just described, the opportunity came to be design architect for the state's new 2nd Appellate Court building to be located in Elgin, Illinois, in the western suburban area of Chicago. This project was an interesting example of a public structure in which both the symbolic and real functional needs had not changed significantly over a hundred years. The program for the

new project was almost identical with the amount and relationship of space provided in the original 2nd Appellate Court in Ottawa, Illinois, built in 1879. The requirements included one courtroom supported by a ring of anterooms for judges, clerks, and attorneys. A generous public lobby and modest audience space in the courtroom were to be included as were a law library and clerks' working area. The three judges required a conference room, garages and apartments for in-residence sessions, with all of these spaces strictly controlled and separate from public and semi-public circulation.

The court building was sited in the new Civic Center of Elgin as one of several important new structures (a city hall, post office, library, and auditorium) to be built around a central plaza on the Fox River. In this respect, the project had its internal needs to meet as well as its role to play in the urban design of the city center. Through study of the program and observations of court in session, it became evident that the judicial function of an appellate court lies in a transition zone between civil law, which is directly related to the public and the most sacrosanct functions of the Supreme Court. This meant that the nature of the appellate function is more discreet than a civil court and more discreet than a supreme court in terms of symbolic function. The essential nature of discretion suggested restraint in site relationships to the other explicitly public buildings in the plaza.

The one courtroom and its top hierarchical position in relation to all other program components form a clear example of a major frontstage area supported by a set of backstage areas. This ensemble in turn is linked to the civic center by an exterior "lobby" or court which as an audience gathering area is more symbolic than real. The idea of discretion of the appellate court function led to partially closing the court to the plaza by extending the walls of the court building to form this transition space and also to form, through the long, unrelieved nature of the wall, a background spatial definition to the frontstage functions of the City Hall and Auditorium in the plaza.

All of these considerations of hierarchical relations, particularly that of the courtroom itself surrounded by its ring of ancillary service rooms, were powerfully analogous to very similar arrangements of space in Norman castles. Those of modest proportions and importance that were found in great numbers in Ireland in the 13th, 14th, and 15th centuries, had almost identical arrangements of a central frontstage space, formed by a very thick surrounding wall in which existed a labyrinth of minor service rooms.

This single important space, which served many functions of eating and drinking, worship, assembly and ruling, was the "keep" of the castle, its ultimate defensive position and symbolic expression of ever-present threats of conflict. The rooms, stairs and openings in the thick, strong walls of the keep served

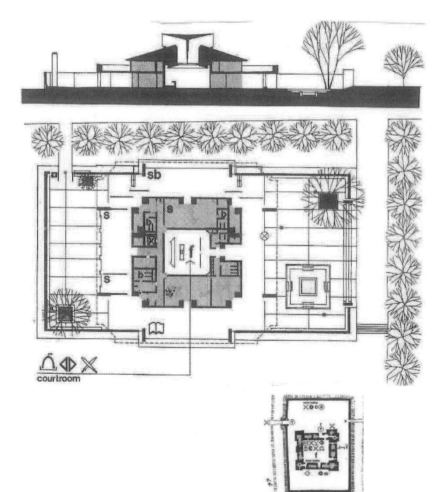

Second Appelate Court, Elgin, Illinois, 1967
Lundeen + Hilfinger Architects
A. Richard Williams, FAIA, Architect for Design

Shaughnessy Castle, Galway Ireland
Note frontstage/backstage relationship: Backstage spaces within
thick wall surrounding main frontstage space

Second Appelate Court, Elgin, Illinois, 1967
(Pencil on Board)

Entry Courtyard
Second Appelate Court, Elgin, Illinois, 1967
(Photographs: Gene Astbury)

the double purpose of defense and services support of activities in the central space, which was called the inner bailey. The external space surrounding the keep and its enclosing wall was called the outer bailey. It also served the double purpose of defense and support of domestic functions such as shelter and storage of supplies and other logistical support of the castle's sovereign territory.

The Irish or Norman castle became a spatial analogy for the appellate court in this way and was further reinforced by the literary and historical origin of the dominant symbol of English law (and therefore of significance to American law) which was Old Bailey in London. The link was now complete between the physical analogy of the castle as a prototype for the court and the historical tie between the name Old Bailey and a court of law in America.

This choice of analogy had more influence than that of spatial concept alone. Its influence persisted in attempts to achieve consistency in all subsequent design decisions of structure, materials, furnishings, light and sound configurations that intensify the basic idea of one major space supported (and defended) by its service and backstage functions. This follow-through idea resulted in a mono-material and monochrome control of all service and enclosing spaces, with rich contrast of light and color in the courtroom itself.

In retrospect, I now see this series of projects in the sixties as rising to a kind of peak of learning, especially in trying to clarify and refine design principles that respond to the prairie landscape. The two main charac- teristics that evolved were the use of wide overhangs in the Education Building, the Concordia College Library in Springfield, the Baby Fold in Normal and courtyard schemes as in residences like my own and that of the Werstler family in Champaign.

Sometimes these two characteristics were combined as in the Appellate Court, the Edu- cation Building and the Presbyterian Church in Urbana. Both the wide overhangs and the court idea seemed to be influenced by the horizontality of the flat prairie landscape as this quality could be intensified architectur- ally and that in an urban setting there was little chance for a distant view - a courtyard could make its own. Add to this, the majesty of tall, cathedral like prairie grove space and you can celebrate the seamlessness of architecture and landscape not only as aesthetic partners but also in the husbandry of energy as the seasons change.

I like to think as well, that the courtyard schemes offer, indeed require, closer at- tention to the details of up-close relation- ships of materials and sensory harmonics through finely tuned scaling and balancing, if the inner world of privacy defined by the courtyard is to find the most complimentary juxtaposition to the public outer world of community life.

The following excerpt from The Urban Stage attempts to discern a basic "organic" prin- ciple guiding these design decisions:

A fundamental spatial concept refers to what might be called the "living membrane" of human habitation. This is the horizontal zone of space around the surface of the earth in which human activity patterns take place. Although these patterns of activity vary according to their archetypal function, they nevertheless all display concentrations of intensity from ground or floor plane, to overhead enclosure and in an even narrower range, from low table height to just above arm's reach, which is a horizontal spatial layer only about six or seven feet deep. Within this membrane, there is an even more concentrated activity zone that is deter- mined by hand to hand, hand to eye and eye to eye movement.
This even denser activity membrane is perhaps no more than three feet deep with greatest emphasis of all at eye level height in either a seated or standing position. Of course, the cone of vision as it is directed up or down has much wider scope, but the focal plane of all such oscillations would still lie within a rather thin horizontal membrane.

Lighting for work tasks, reading, conversa- tion, and play tends to concentrate in this same membrane as does the provision of thermal comfort, air quality, sonic, olfac- tory, and tactile response. Furniture and hand operated equipment has to be molded in relation to this membrane, carefully re-

Concordia College Library, Springfield, Illinois, 1962
(AIA, ALA, National Merit Award, 1971)
Spangler, Beall, Salogga Architects
A. Richard Williams, FAIA, Architect for Design

lated to body metrics. Properties of a more portable or more decorative function such as dinner ware, coffee table artifacts, pictures and other useful or decorative objects reflect the nature of the activity pattern and/or the personality of the occupants. The closer one gets to the points in space that trace the most intimate patterns of movement, as between hand and eye, the more scale is reduced and the fineness of detail becomes important. Fine optical instruments and jewelry indicate this most intimate scale range of properties that equip a setting.

The roof, on the other hand, is a hovering, widely overhanging, sheltering plane, with as much transparency or delicacy as possible in the vertical structure that supports it above the ground-related lower walls and sills. The roof, too, is attenuated in the horizontal plane as much as possible, even to the point of exaggeration. Its edges, corners, and fascias are much more lightly and delicately formed than the ground elements but retain a clarity of silhouette against the sky and far horizon that is of the same simplicity and boldness as the ground-hugging foundation structure. The ground element expresses its nature as a supporting structure, while the roof as a sky element is expressed as a cover or as a supported element. The space separating these two elements is the space of the living membrane.

The progressive scale reduction that responds to the several different degrees of activity intensity in horizontal strata as they

vary between the floor and ceiling is directly expressed in the progressive fineness of detail of walls, openings, grilles, objects of furniture and other properties as the most intense level of activity is reached from about two to five feet above the floor plane.

Of course, this is my own subjective interpretation of design decision making that relates to this set of projects. For another perspective, I would like to refer to the February 1969 issue of Inland Architect in an article by Rob Cuscaden titled "The Suburban House—Dick Williams and his Courtyard Motif:" (See Appendix)

Baby Fold, Normal Illinois 1961
Lundeen + Hilfinger Architects
A. Richard Williams, FAIA, Architect for Design
(Photograph: Gene Asbury)

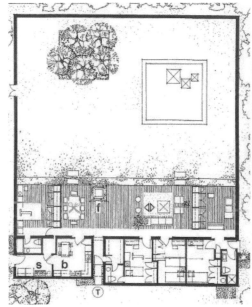

William J. Werstler Residence, Champaign, Illinois, 1967
A.Richard Williams, FAIA, Architect

This mix of practice and academic life during the exuberant sixties became more than ever one calling instead of two—a singularity of joyful intense involvement. But it still prompted the same old desire for a getaway during the summer for a brief month or two to those charismatic places abroad I already knew, rather than to venture to as yet unexplored regions, which could come later when longer stretches of time for a sabbatical leave would open up.

Despite the feeling of guilt that those of us brought up in the depression found hard to shake off, one's alter ego always wants to be liberated. I'd already related earlier on how a taste of this had built up in 1959: the sense of escapade beginning with oddly amusing incidents on the TWA flight over the Atlantic, revelry in Paris, northern Italy, Rome and in Greece, climaxing abroad the "Angelica" five day Aegean cruise–Lady Godiva basking by the sun deck pool, Helen of Troy appearing in the ruins of Delos and Captain Nick Paridis' surprised distress in having to send the girls who were aboard modeling native Greek costumes back to Athens because they really were "available."

The same irresistible urge for escape built up in 1962, as I have already touched on, describing the all black Karman Ghia delivered in Osnabruk, acquiring the chrome legged black leather Jacobsen chair in Copenhagen, the black leather Gucci suitcase in Florence, finally boarding the black hulled Leonardo da Vinci in Naples for the voyage home.

When I am one month in Philadelphia Pennsylvania University, and I walk past an exit-entrance of Drexel Institute of Technology and a man is leaving the buildings with books under his left arm, an umbrella under the other, and having kind of baseball shoes on his feet and for the rest a white shirt and gentleman black-tie-like pants: I don't know if he is studying baseball, rain or technics from Drexel books and then I walk on and the same street is ending in a dark space with trucks under a big gray stone granite post office but before coming under it it is still a street at one side a man clothed in fine gentleman suit is swinging a stick to catch a piece of rubberball which is thrown to him from the otherside by a gentleman-clothed man and I understand that they are playing baseball or hockey in an adminstrative-office-like surrounding and I know that you can study technics in baseball-fitting-shoes-shirt, can have an umbrella under the arm and not not a baseball or hockey stick and that you can be a post office adminis-trator playing in lunchtime that you are hockey or baseball man and that we all are still happily mixed up in spite of so called separation by specialization.

Quote by Jacob Bakema, 1967
Published as part of Bakema's Firm Portfolio

To fill out that tale a bit more, after acquir-ing the car in Osnabruk I picked up Chuck Gordon in Bremen, where he was visiting Ingrid, his bride to be, for a brief revisit to old friends in Sweden—Karen, Per, Hasse and their families in Stockholm and Boras, then returning Chuck to Bremen on the way to Rotterdam where I stayed with Jacob and Zia Bakema for a few days.

Jacob, already famous for his own work and as a key member of Team Ten, a second generation carry-through of CIAM, had been a Miller Professor at Illinois in the late fifties. It had been my good luck all through these years to act as host for eminent visiting architects, in many cases becoming their close friends.

Bakema was most memorable in his eager, joyful response to grass roots American cul-ture like football marching bands, cowboys, pop entertainment, especially Las Vegas—all with a great sense of humor and enjoyment. For example he told of his visit to Harvard— "They're like balloons filled with hot air, not knowing that their cables have been cut."

He was proud that he came from Groningen, a rough and tumble port in northern Holland and that his father had been a sea captain. His own personality reflected this same light hearted zest, I think partly as a cover for a deep sincerity in his work, particularly in the design of multi-family dwellings, a com-passionate concern that each family could find and express its own identity in the face of the usual anonymous monotony of high density housing.

On down through France to Albi, Carcassone, Aigue Mortes, the Riviera and to Florence for a reunion with Paolo and Grazia Sica, the Russonis at the Annalena, to Rome again, this time to the heart of the city staying at the Seguso in the Piazza Rotunda. Gabriel and Ninette Guverkian were there too, ar-riving in their antique Citroen—we could still park anywhere we wanted to.

That summer ended luxuriating in Ischia, Ravello and Capri. On board the Leonardo I managed to fit the Jacobsen chair and the Gucci suitcase in the cabin locker, with the Karman Ghia stored below in the ship's hold, to enjoy ten calm, salubrious early August days through Gibraltar and the Azores to New York. I shared a table in the dining room with three most attractive young American school teachers and lounging around the pool on the after deck—who could ask for more? The only sad note, heard over the ship's radio while on an errand back to the cabin, was to bring the news to the pool area of Marilyn Monroe's death by suicide.

Returning again to more serious travel as a new sabbatical began in January 1964, I headed west this time on a Pan American round the world ticket, Flight No. 1, first to San Francisco, then Hawaii, Tahiti, Samoa, Fiji, New Zealand, Australia, Indonesia, Thailand, Hong Kong, Japan, India, Iran, Greece, ending up in Italy for the major amount of time during the spring at the American Academy in Rome, as I have describe on pages 127-141.

San Francisco's charisma was well into its ascendancy as a Mecca expressing its own interpretation of what the sixties' threshold to a "Great Society" might be—its smiling street life by day or night, its new vernacular of easy-going but sharp fashion, food, wine, music, art and architecture. My own eagerness to soak all this up was naturally focused on fresh new work like Sea Ranch by local architects which still had the feel of its Maybeck and Green brothers roots but was now more casual, reaching for a more relaxed tie with graphic design, ceramics, fabrics and furnishings. Somehow this was all breaking down the long standing attitude that fine architecture and design of all properties in a setting was elitist and out of reach for everybody else. Another way to think of it is as a renaissance of youthfulness across the entire spectrum of society.

In a quite different way I felt this same spirit in Honolulu. Most of my contacts there were Asian American, like my old Illinois classmate Ken Onedera, my recent student Tom

Katsuyoshi's father and mutual friends of those at home. Much more than I expected, even from World War II time in the Pacific, the feeling of America being a part of the Pacific Rim community was expressed by my old and new Honolulu friends, not so much in terms of art and architecture but in the spirit of a relaxed, most welcoming life style so close to nature, so much in sync with the daily and seasonal rhythms of climate and community life. I guess the link to the new spirit in San Francisco as felt in Hawaii had a more timeless dimension, that of an archipelago achieving its sense of community over centuries, as measured by the time/distances of sailing canoes. There was an osmosis of communication somehow between all these friends who didn't know each other before that almost immediately filled my calendar with sight seeing ventures, parties and quiet visits. I was to experience this same enchanting mysteriously organized hospitality two months later in Bangkok and then again in Honolulu in the late nineties as a visitor to the School of Architecture of the University of Hawaii, Manoa, where I was a guest at the East West Center. All this quiet gentility and smiling, welcoming hospitality that I've enjoyed for so long has raised questions: Isn't there a link between this timeless friendliness across the Asian World and the design sensitivity, delicacy and harmony of dwellings, their furnishings and their seamlessness with nature, that constitutes a powerful lesson for the Western World? Don't we as Americans, living at the crossroads of cultures more

than any other nation or set of nations have a special obligation of learning and then building more sensitively designed models for the future, daunting political problems of today notwithstanding?

I was staying at the Royal Hawaiian Hotel on Waikiki Beach at what seems today an incredibly low rate of $16 a day. Soon after arrival I had an invitation including an air ticket from John and Robert Allerton to fly to the island of Kauai for a brief visit. On pages 41 and 42, as part of my chronicle of the Allerton Scholarship, I recalled details of this visit as it first prompted a deeper awareness of the Pan Pacific culture in the continuity of its art history as displayed at the Honolulu Academy of Art, notably by the Allerton collection, which together with the temporary exhibit there of Kionori Kikutake's architectural work in Japan stepped up my eagerness to be more alert for whatever other ties I could find in the weeks ahead through Polynesia and other parts of the Orient that would shed more light on the evolving timelessness of art and design throughout this vast region of the world.

Next: Tahiti! When making reservations on Pan Am for the flight between Honolulu and Papeete, Tahiti, I didn't know that this was the inaugural flight, and that there would be a magnificent bon voyage party at the airport. Somehow all my fifteen or twenty new Honolulu friends found out about it and showed up with traditional Hawaiian leis to join in the send off. So much champagne

Sketch (Pencil on Cameo Paper), 1943
A. Richard Williams

flowed both before the noon departure and during the flight that on landing at six p.m. we were all still in a festive mood ready to join with the Tahitian dancers greeting our arrival. In this blissful state we found our way to our various hotels, most of which were new pandanus thatched pavilions along the beach.

Even 1964 was long enough ago that there were still only a handful of tourists, both the town with bars along the waterfront and outlying villages still had much the same character made famous by Paul Gaugin and other adventurers when contact with the rest of the world was only by infrequent ship arrivals. By now all of this is so well known I need not try to add any more color except to record a few special insights of my own about the lightness, the almost basket-like quality of pole and mat membrane construction and its poised interface between the sea and tropical landscape. Time after time, all through the archipelago to Moorea, Bora Bora and other tiny island lagoons between, then extending to Samoa, the Fijis and Tongas, you would find the same stilted dwelling clusters responding not only to the threat of sea storm surges but also to the undisturbed flow of ground surface, even on higher land.

Pan Am had added many side trips to my air ticket without added charge, the first of these an all day round trip to Bora Bora aboard a large flying boat, flying at low altitude at slow speed from lagoon to lagoon along the way. Passengers in native dress would leave or board from outrigger canoes, many with produce and intriguing artifacts.

Another day, in a rented car with three others I drove about sixty miles all around the island of Tahiti, stopping to help villagers pull in fishing nets, gathering mangoes and exploring the low stone walls of an archaic structure, the temple of Mahiatea, that must have had some long forgotten ceremonial function. At Taravoa, a delightful village on the most remote side of the island we stopped for lunch, delighted to find it was the home village of the same troop of dancers that had entertained us one night at the hotel, joyfully welcoming us as if we were old family friends. By the way I should note that the dances were almost identical to the Hawaiian hula-hula but at a much faster tempo, the grass skirts whirling wildly. The few male dancers were doing what I though was the "Charleston," a step that I had learned long ago, so when it came time in their dance series for the "invitation to the dance," when the girls would split up to choose a partner from the audience, I knew exactly what to do, much to their amazement. So I had a special almost smothering, cheering greeting at their village.

You can imagine how all this easy life was persuasive to linger on indefinitely like beach bums of yore, but time came to move on—aboard a day's flight to Auckland stopping briefly in Samoa and Fiji. A close Urbana friend, Margaret Erlanger, head of the Illinois dance department, had been in New Zealand on sabbatical the year before and had alerted her friends in Auckland when I would be arriving so I was met at the airport at dusk and after checking in at my hotel taken right away to a welcoming party—it was is if I was still in Hawaii or Tahiti only a few miles away the "cloud nine" spirit was the same and was to continue, visiting Dick Toy and colleagues in the University of Auckland School of Architecture seeing their refreshing new work, and submerging myself at the museum and in the surrounding community trying to absorb the character of the Maori people, their dwellings, boats and other crafts all of which were variations of the far-reaching Polynesian culture, in many ways more vigorous, of bigger scale, more sharp-edged and colorful than in Tahiti.

Ever since Bill Alington, from Wellington, New Zealand had been a graduate student at Illinois in 1958/59, we had kept in touch so he and his wife Margaret met my plane at Wellington airport and we drove to their house in Karori, an urban village district as far up as you can go up the mountainside within the city limits. Their house, in its crisply ordered, beautifully detailed rectilinearity influenced by Mies, had its own unique character related to its sloping site, nestled at the edge of a dense, indigenous fern forest all the way up to the mountain top. One felt suddenly like a Lilliputian, so close to the ground in greenish light with giant out of familiar scale fern trees towering above. Staying with Bill and Margaret for a few days in such a magical setting on the opposite

side of the world, yet still feeling the same warmth of Pacific Rim hospitality, was an extraordinarily new and rich experience. In meeting Bill's partners and colleagues including another of my exceptional graduate students, Brian Bining, I was struck as I was later in Australia with their eagerness to develop an architecture abreast of the cutting edge elsewhere in the world but distinctly fitting in the unique ecology and sociology of their remote global region.

At that time you could sense how the great distance of "down under" from America and Europe in the old days of ship travel was still affecting travel planning despite the fairly recent advent of air connections. Bill, Brian, Ivan Glover, Graham Brawn and other students from New Zealand and Australia all made long range plans for two or more years ahead for study, travel and working abroad. What I noted too, possibly prompted from this same sense of remoteness was their stimulation to be in the vanguard of computer technology. Even back then at Illinois, in developing Illiac, the pioneer main frame computer, New Zealanders were among the most prominent members of the team.

The combination of all these new impressions of energy, talent and work in such a unique setting was a powerful incentive to return soon, especially insisted on by Bill and Margaret. But it took almost thirty years, in March 1993, to come back again for about three weeks in their summer, first to Auckland, then to Wellington and on to

Melbourne and Sydney. On this visit I was a guest of Isabel (Jinty Forrester's sister) and Norm McFarlane for several days at their villa in St. Heliers overlooking the Hauraki Gulf, sailing one day with them in their sloop in waters later made famous by New Zealand's triumphant victories in the America's Cup. Dick and Sally Toy were again gracious hosts too. This time I took the train to Wellington winding leisurely all day through mountainous terrain, scattering thousands of sheep from their peaceful grazing up close to the tracks. Bill and Margaret met me at the station as if it were just yesterday since my 1964 visit, and we were soon in their house in Karori, nothing seemed to have changed. Of course the cities had grown enormously but still they seemed remarkably faithful to their settings.

But what was so wonderful to see was the body of work accomplished by Dick Toy and his colleagues in Auckland and Bill in Wellington in those thirty years, each rising to the top in national esteem—exemplified by Dick's Auckland Cathedral and Bill's municipal projects in Wellington. Bill had become the Ministry of Construction's chief architect, of the New Zealand Embassy in New Delhi and the brand new School of Music at Victoria University in Wellington. Again on leaving Wellington for Melbourne I felt the same deep urging to come back soon. I was greeted by the same sense of deja-vu, meeting Graham and Trish Brawn again in Melbourne, where I was to spend about a week at the university as an exchange professor, representing Illinois, a relationship set up some years before honoring Walter Burley Griffin, an Illinois grad in 1899 who had designed Canberra, Australia's capital and Trinity College in Melbourne. Graham, after leaving Illinois had built his reputation as a facilities planner first in Vancouver then at Melbourne University, and had also been a classmate of Glenn Mercutt who more than any other Australian architect had by then and even more so since achieved such success in demonstrating architectural excellence responsive to its unique regional environment.

Returning to the 1964 summer (February) "down under," Pan Am Flight No. 1 carried me on to Sydney for a few days to prowl around the new Opera House under construction and explore the harbor, then over the vast outback to Jakarta, Indonesia all the way to Bangkok. The strength of the dollar in those days meant I could stay in splendor at the Erwan Hotel. Our recent Illinois graduate student Chalerm Soocharit was now back on the faculty at Chulalonghorn University and although I had never been in Thailand before Chalerm welcomed me as if my visit were a true homecoming. He had arranged that on the very first morning at the Erwan, Momchitra, the wife of Prince Varavarn, of the royal family and head of the architectural school, would come to call, to ask how she might help in making my two week visit most pleasant. At first I though this might mean a few suggestions of what would be interesting to do on my own, but it turned

out that she had arranged something for every day, visits to the palace, early morning markets, society weddings, receptions, parties, even arrangements for a three day trip to Angkor Wat, by way of Saigon, which would nave been difficult at the time to do without connections in high places. I quickly understood there would be no diplomatic way to decline her graciousness in planning this very full schedule, but as the days flew by I learned how artfully Momchitra had allowed for intervals of rest, usually long afternoons in the lushness of the Erwan.

Visiting Angkor Wat in those days was a strange mix of a borderline war atmosphere as tension built up in Vietnam and a kind of shopworn vestige of affluent French colonial empire days as they developed luxurious hotels for rich travelers. The Grand Hotel at Siem Riep, a small colonial village at the edge of the vast Angkor complex of ruins was a palatial, decaying edifice of high ceilinged rooms equipped with towering mosquito nets over enormous beds, otherwise sparsely furnished, attended by native servants. It reminded me of the Winter Palace in Luxor, Egypt, a remnant of former Victorian splendor, now almost deserted. There were only a few other guests who had somehow managed to arrive there as I did in spite of the uncertainties of travel. This added a special feeling of privilege to exploring the exotic, sculptural stone ruins totally free of the usual hordes of tourists. The long empty corridors, in elaborate symmetrical composition with intersections emphasized

by towers and courts between gave an air of the opulence of seven centuries ago suddenly interrupted and frozen in time—the only enemy the ravishment of wet, tropical vegetation.

I was enjoying the exploration of this almost endless system of courts, towers, levels and corridors with an Australian woman when we came out on an overlook at the northwest tower and were suddenly confronted by a loud speaker voice commanding "get that man and woman off of there!" As we looked down, spread out before us was a large troupe of movie production people and all their paraphernalia. I guess we had appeared in the midst of a "take." Once we climbed down we were invited to sit in director's chairs as the scene went on. It turned out to be the location set for "Lord Jim," starring Peter O'Toole and Akim Tamaroff, with a host of other actors, production people all camped at the other tourist hotel deep in the adjacent tropical forest. This sudden confrontation with the outside world portraying the past only added to the surreal aura of Angkor, making it all the more memorable. Apparently there was to be a break in the shooting, for the next morning as we boarded the DC-3 to fly back to Saigon, we were joined by Peter O'Toole and a few other actors still in a partying mood, carousing up and down the aisle. However, this conviviality did not diminish the drama of seeing Angkor Wat from the air as the pilot made several steep banked circles around the entire complex.

On return to Bangkok I found Momchitra had arranged that I should attend a high society wedding at a sumptuous residence in a lush garden setting along one of the city's network of canals. Many guests, up to at least two hundred arrived by boat and in Mercedes limousines. A Thai wedding traditionally takes place as a series of separate ceremonies, each in a separate space prepared as stages and audience areas, with both guests and wedding party moving from place to place in the residence and in courtyards. The major ceremony of the series took place in the largest reception hall with guests seated in rows as in a church, finding their places leisurely with much graceful bowing and smiling. Once everyone was seated attendants brought trays of identical tall glasses of what appeared to be chilled lemonade, most welcome since the temperature even in late February was hovering close to 100°. I took one of the glasses nearest to me off the tray. It was straight Scotch! Needless to say I was astonished, knowing that alcohol is forbidden in Thailand. How did our hosts know ahead of time where I, as the only Westerner present would be seated and would select this particular glass, which looked exactly like all the others? But I did note sly smiles all around—another one of those inscrutable happenings in the East that you intuitively know might be spoiled if you asked questions. There were many more delightful events that Momchitra and Chalerm had arranged including several visits to the university, spending time with students and faculty in their studios for slide presenta-

tions and seminar discussions. I was struck by their command of English and their eagerness and alertness to current trends in architecture, especially influences from abroad. At the center of this discussion, as it had been in New Zealand and Australia, was the question of how their own traditions could be fully respected and balanced with the allure of international modernism, most notably the influence of Le Corbusier. I was to encounter this same puzzlement, almost a preoccupation again in Japan and India.

Even by that time there were scattered examples of a delightful eclecticism, a mix of contemporary clarity of structure, lightness and material craftsmanship with traditional elements of spatial organization, roof overhangs and details, sensitivity to privacy and relationship to sky, gardens with subtle transitions to high density street scenes and neighboring dwellings. Chalerm and I were lucky to be invited to Jim Thompson's house, a delightful dwelling along a canal that exquisitely embodied this balance of East/West influences. Jim by then was well-known for his development and marketing the Thai silk industry both at home and abroad. It seemed strange to me both then and now that this sensitive eclecticism has not enjoyed critical applause as has strict modernism and the signature styles of well publicized architects. Saying goodbye to my many new Thai friends was far more difficult than I ever expected—their charm and the almost Narnia, fairyland-like quality of the whole country, including Cambodia too was

such a magnet for an early return, which sadly I never have done.

The magic of this brief encounter was carried aboard the Thai Air flight to Hong Kong for a few day's stay, then on to Japan and back to Bangkok three weeks later when I again was to pick up my Pan Am around the world ticket. It was uncanny how the atmosphere aboard the Thai Air flights was in such harmony with all the best I knew of my Thailand visit, graciousness, delicacy of décor, attention to detail, deliciousness of food, all transforming the interior of the standard Boeing aircraft into a flying microcosm of the country.

In Hong Kong I was met at the airport by the whole Ng family, so it seemed, numbering at least fifteen, to escort me to my hotel in a large Chevy van. Jack Ng, one of my graduate students still back in Illinois had sent word to his father about when I was to arrive, a total surprise to me—I never did learn how he knew the exact time—the mysterious East again! For the three days I was in Hong Kong I was totally in the care of the whole family in the van for sightseeing, visits to yacht building yards, the skyline overlooking the harbor and dinner aboard a floating restaurant at Aberdeen. Jack's father, mother, brothers and sisters, cousins, other relatives and I were seated at a large round table and an endless series of delicacies in tiny dishes was passed around for at least two hours, lubricated by tea and again by straight Scotch (duty free Johnny Walker

Red Label) which the brothers brought out from under the table. I had great difficulty overnight coping with all this nutrition and getting ready to fly out the next morning on another Thai Air flight to Tokyo. My enormous hangover was very much in need of the gentle ministrations of the stewardesses. I was chagrined too that I wasn't at my best since my seat mate was movie actress Gina Lolobrigida.

Tokyo then was far less crowded than it is today, still getting from the airport to the new International House in the Minato Ku embassy district seemed confusing and devious but still pleasant. The International House was newly built in Corbusian style on the site of the destroyed Mitsubishi family mansion but beautifully related to the mansion's gardens, still intact. In addition to elegant stateroom scale guest rooms, the new establishment included a series of lounges, a well stocked library, gallery, meeting rooms and dining room, all arranged around the garden. I was astounded that all these facilities so magnificently designed and comfortably appointed, equal to deluxe hotels, only cost $3.50 a day. Of course the yen at that time was a bargain in exchange for the dollar. By the time I arrived in early March 1964, the International House had become a most prestigious setting for weddings and receptions almost every day. I was amazed not only to be invited to join in by total strangers but to receive invitations elsewhere by Tokyo architects, who, as had happened in Honolulu, had found out by some kind

of grapevine network that I was in town. I think this had all started back in Hawaii, from the exhibition of Kionori Kikutake's work in the Honolulu Museum of Art. It turned out that Kikutake himself had somehow received word from the AIA Honolulu chapter, having given him the Pan Pacific Award, that I was coming and that he had taken the initiative in helping to welcome me to Tokyo and indeed elsewhere in Japan. In fact I was soon invited to his office and presented with an architectural itinerary in the Tokyo region as well as for a loop south to Kobe, Osaka, Kyoto, Hiroshima, Izmu Taisha and Takamatsu. It was a replay of what Momchitra had done in Bangkok. So after getting over a few days of "tropical trots" resulting from the culinary delights of Hong Kong, I was kept busy being shown work by Tange and other architects, all pretty much Corbu influenced, along with parties and other informal visits. It had even been arranged that on my return from the loop south I was to be guest lecturer for a Metabolist group meeting at Waseda University's Faculty Club about two weeks later.

The itinerary led first to Kyoto as a hub to experience both historic architectural highlights in the city and surrounding region including Nara, Ise shrines and recent contemporary work as well. I was first quartered in a ryokan traditional guest house in the Gion district close to temples on the elevated north rim of the city, then moved to the Kyoto Station Hotel, much more central for using the city's bus system. The girls in

the station's Japan Tourist Bureau, JTB, were most helpful in giving me notes in Japanese to show bus drivers so I would not get lost in trying to reach desired destinations. I would sometimes have five or six of these notes in a given day, worrying about getting them mixed up. Fortunately, this didn't happen but I had second thoughts—what if it did—it might turn out to be a truly delightful adventure.

Of these many excursions over a period of four or five days the most rewarding were to Zen temples, especially Ryoanji, the Katsura villa, the Imperial Palace grounds and the nearby village of Ohara in the northwest foothills. I had first visited the office in the Imperial Palace, showing my gold sealed letter of introduction from the president of the University of Illinois, requesting permission for an extended visit to study the Katsura villa, staying for several hours instead of the usual one hour visit. This caused consternation and frowns and I had to wait some time for a response, it apparently was an unexpectedly perplexing request for authorities behind the scenes. After patiently waiting at least a half hour, a clerk came out of the inner office broadly smiling, exclaiming and waving a paper: "We give you one more permission on another day. Highly unusual!" So I ended up with two separate visits to Katsura on different days, an hour each. Actually this worked out better—time between allowing for reflection and special focus on certain features of the villa such as its moon viewing and tea house area in the garden.

I was accompanied on the bus to Ohara village by a charming English girl studying Japanese and together we enjoyed a day having tea and sandwiches at the village inn and exploring the densely wooded village paths, several times invited into houses through their entrance gardens. Although most if not all the houses were very old, probably much more than one hundred years, they appeared timeless, like Katsura, still fresh and clear ancestors of modernism, seamlessly woven into the landscape.

Highlights of the loop, in addition to tra-ditional architectural gems of the past, just discussed, included Tange's work at Hiroshima and Takamatsu and most notably Kikotake's administration pavilion at the temple of Ismu Taisha.

This project, in reinforced concrete, had, through its exquisite range of scale from a rugged single long span beam at the ridge, with sloping vertical supports at each end framed by an infill of grillage of lattice like delicacy, picking up from the older shrine buildings the same balance of principle structural elements, overhanging roofs and modular vertical columns with panels between patterned interlocking strips vary-ing in scale from openness at the ground plane to ever finer spacing above lintels up to bracketing under the roof, allowing modulation of transparency/translucency of reflected light. Since Ismu Taisha is well off the beaten path between larger cities, this visit, staying in a typical ryokan (inn) was

an exquisitely primitive experience in sharp contrast to rapid Westernization of the rest of the country.

At Hiroshima I found myself alone among dozens of uniformed school children and their teachers as we visited the Peace Memorial Museum by Tange at the site of the atomic bomb dropped in 1945. It was suddenly clear that even this long after the war, here I was as a single person embody-ing the enemy responsible for all the terrible destruction so graphically portrayed on the walls and in free-standing exhibits. All I remember is this appalling feeling and the need to disappear quickly.

You approach Takamatsu, the capital of Kagawa Prefecture on the island of Shikoku by ferry from Kobe. My arrival was at dusk with the lights of the city already glowing and reflecting in the mirror- calm waters of the Inland Sea. It was an amazing and thrill-ing experience, so much so that it inspired a poem I wrote titled "The Signs of Taka-matsu," also to include a set of other most memorable city skylines across the world.

One of the first questions I was asked on return to Tokyo by my new friends in Kikutake's office, who had prepared the list of notable old and new architecture I had seen was "which ones pleased you most?" It obviously surprised them when I responded by asking for forgiveness in offering my own favorites, not on their list. I was enormously impressed by segments of the new Tokaido

Ryoanji Temple, Kyoto, Japan

Adminstrative Pavillion, Ismu Taisha Temple, Japan, 1963
Kionari Kikotake, Architect

176

As life forms a mosaic
of performances and settings
inseparably linked,
so villages and cities become
works of art
in the global gallery.
The signs of Takamatsu
trace a nocturnal signature in light,
a horizontal gossamer glow,
slashed by vertical neon stripes
in the mirror
of the Inland Sea.
The signs of Takamatsu
weave a necklace of marquees
that proclaim
the city is a theater,
the theater is a city.
The signs of Chicago,
the signs of the Great White Way
on a rainy night become
twice as tall,
double image
of the urban stage.
The signatures of cities
form in color as in light.
The saffron of Rome,
the sienna of Sienna,
the brick-red of Albi,

the bluing-white of Myconos,
set in Homer's winedark sea.

San Francisco,
painted lady in drag,
looms white as a bride
from the Marin side.
The great grey grain elevators
of Salina, Kansas
rise in majestic silhouette,
city of the prairie,
landmarking vast horizons.
London is black and white.
Centuries of carbon
blacken stone facades.
White highlights
etched by rain, fog and sun
distort architectural precision.
Streets are black,
curbstones white.
White gloves
of black-uniformed bobbies
make disembodied signals.
White pigeons fly
through black buttresses of Westminster.
Overhead, through black wire cobwebs,
the sky is white.

"Just you and your mind on
Lake Shore Drive"1
may be transfixed in reverie
by Chicago's towers
as they fuse together at twilight,
a prismatic promontory
afloat in the lake,
a crystalline structure that thrusts up
from the center of the world
at this chosen edge
where prairie, sky and water meet.
Beyond these galaxies
of light, color, form and silhouette,
what is the true signature of cities
if not the pulse of life becoming art,
tracing the living membrane
in ever more diverse patterns,
transfiguring a random, irregular
mosaic
into the order of a jewel,
each one as different
as a diamond
or a human face.

1. Allotta, Hanes, Jeremiah, "Lake
Shore Drive" Big Foot Records. 1975
(Title song, Lake Shore Drive")

The Signs of Takamatsu
Williams, A. Richard, The Urban Stage, San Francisco, 1980, p. 279.

Line, the new high speed railroad structures not yet completed as seen near and far from the train I took from Tokyo to Kyoto; the grace of long span elevated ribbons all in white as they laced through foothills and over industrial areas, appearing intermittently, along with new station construction seamlessly interwoven with the linear elegance of the whole system. My other favorite was the Signs of Takamatsu. As for architecture, my two candidates for top awards were the Zen temple of Ryoanji and Kikutake's new shrine building at Ismu Taisha. Of course the office crew was pleased by this and I assured them I was not just being politically correct.

Within a day or two the "Metabolists" gathered as planned at the Waseda University Faculty Club for their monthly meeting. By now this group, mainly architects and planners, had become well-known as they were advocating futuristic urban design at large scale in order to manage extremely high density chaotic growth trends in all of Japan's major cities. Kenzo Tange's imaginative grand scale design for Tokyo Bay expansion on bridge structures had already been widely published. The Metabolist's idea evolved from the analogy of human metabolism and its organic capacity for new cellular growth replacing the old, fueled by a constant supply of new energy. I remember how those of us in the English-speaking world would smile when we first heard this term as a title for the new movement. It had been fashionable in Japan for a long time to use English for titles without consulting native English speakers, with sometimes amusing results. For example, a new up-scale department store in Kyoto chose "High Taste" as its name, displayed prominently in a large sign over its entrance.

About thirty Metabolists showed up for the meeting, ranging widely in age from the twenties up to the seventies. It was explained to me that this represented six generations but it remained inscrutable how they determined what defined a genera-tion—it might have had something to do with the length of time for a university advanced degree, six or seven years, but I wasn't sure.

As we all arrived at the Waseda Faculty Club, I was asked which meeting room I would prefer, the Western style or Japanese style one. What could I say—but of course the Japanese, which meant sitting on cushions in a large U configuration fitting the pattern of a tatami mat floor. Along with Gunther Nietsche, a German scholar studying the Metabolist movement, and Mira Nakashima, daughter of George Nakashima, a renowned American furniture designer, I was guided to the center of the U base, with Gunther and Mira on each side. Then for at least three or four minutes, the members found their places by shifting in some sort of trial and error procedure, almost like a dance, bowing and smiling until they seemed to find a satis-fying hierarchical arrangement. My presen-tation was easy, simply using slides of our

Collaborate Design Studio projects at Illinois, especially visionary ones about Chicago, which they seemed already to know about from various journals.

After this rather brief presentation, less than an hour, we had a few questions and most pleasant refreshments of sake, tea and sushi. After the meeting Gunther, Mira, I and a few others were taken to a magnificent tiered residence on a steep slope, owned by Professor Martin, an esteemed member of the Waseda faculty, who happened to be away at the time. His architect was Tsuto Kimura, one of the youngest generation of Metabolists who had made arrangements for this delightful aftermath of the meet-ing, which lasted into the wee hours. I was reminded again of the unlimited flow of Johnny Walker Scotch and delicacies of food that I had experienced in Bangkok and Hong Kong. Anyway it was a most salubrious party. By coincidence I was to meet Profes-sor Martin later in the spring in Florence and to welcome Tsuto Kimura the next fall as one of my graduate students.

While staying at the International House, I had called at our embassy nearby in the Minato Ku district to visit the Cultural Affairs office, mainly to enquire if there were any events that might be of special architec-tural interest, beyond contacts I had already made. It turned out that the office could help me make arrangements once I arrived in New Delhi to visit Chandigarh, the new capital of Punjab province in India since I had

been told that without special assistance were difficult to do. So after again flying back to Bankok, again by Thai Air then on to Calcutta on Pan Am and another add-on trip aboard a DC-3 to Katmandu in Nepal for a few days I arrived at the elaborate Ashoka Hotel in New Delhi as my main base for India.

Katmandu was exotic beyond belief. Just opened up to tourists the year before, it was another sudden immersion in a strange almost out of this world experience, another Land of Oz, but this time in Asian, Shangri La dress. Adding to this immediate sense of intriguing strangeness, was the almost total absence of automobiles, people still moving on foot or in rickshaws and carts yet with the very obvious presence of many helicopters and their high tech mainte-nance facilities at the airport. I stayed in an elaborate vacated Maharaja's palace on the verge of decay that had a few small guest rooms in contrast to a luxurious main lounge and dining room. You had the impression of vastness and emptiness of other courts and terraces beyond being taken over by vegeta-tion, birds, butterflies and monkeys.

The food served was amazingly like conti-nental cuisine, but in appearance only and barely edible—I was to experience the same thing at the Ashoka Hotel in New Delhi a few days later. Anyway it was absolutely fas-cinating to wander around the city on foot, along narrow streets with their tiny market displays, fanciful fabrics, crafts, aromatic spices, oils, with smoking fires under the grilles of food 'vendors' kiosks. The city center with its crenellated, pagoda like sky silhouettes and open spaces full of Tibetan refugees in native costume was truly a tapestry of unfamiliar forms, colors, sounds and smells—or rather I should say fragrances. Again I had a strong urge to return soon, certainly before this remote alluring place would be spoiled by swarms of tourists and the onslaught of "civilization."

On arrival in New Delhi I found the American Embassy was within easy walking distance from the Ashoka Hotel. So soon after checking in, I went there to see if my message about getting help with introductions to officials in Chandigarh had come through. The new embassy building by architect Ed Stone was by now well-known for its wide overhanging flat roof supported by modularly spaced slender gold columns and recessed walls of delicate grillage, the whole impression being that of an airy pavilion most suitable to India's sub-tropical climate and at the same time most welcoming to visitors. Of course this sense of inviting openness was to change radically as security against terrorism was to change our embassies into just the opposite architectural expression, that of fortresses.

Our Cultural Affairs office had indeed received my request and had made contact with authorities in the Secretariat at Chandigarh to meet me at the airport and take me to a small hotel near the government building complex. They had also arranged that a car and driver would be at my disposal to visit various segments of the new city, first to Corbusier's office for guidance.

So a day or two after arriving in New Delhi I booked a flight on another DC-3 for a brief stay in Chandigarh. I remember vividly the beauty of Punjab from the air with the white Himalayan Mountains on the far north horizon and the sloping semi-arid agrarian landscape below with scattered brick red villages and towns, each one embracing a brilliant green reservoir. The view was truly magnificent in its organic harmony of man and nature even knowing that on the ground close up the reality would be of century-old poverty and almost primitive existence without sanitation and other modern infrastructure needs. How would Chandigarh as a new city embody the same outer beauty of form yet include all the advantages of education, health, diversity of employment and modern community facilities missing in the towns and villages I had seen from the air?

When I checked in at the hotel late in the day I seemed to be the only guest, but on coming down for breakfast the next morning there was another visitor already seated whom I immediately recognized to be Kenzo Tange, from the time of his visit to Illinois a year before, when I had been his host for a lecture and seminar. When I went up to greet him exclaiming what a coincidence it was to be in Chandigarh at the same time, he explained he was on his way back to Tokyo after several days in Skopje, Yugoslavia, for a meeting with officials there. He had won an international competition for redesigning the city after the disastrous earthquake of 1963. He had a sly look as he remarked that he had "sneaked" in this visit to Chandigarh unexpectedly, entirely on his own. So I told him a car was coming for me from the Secretariat for a day of architectural sightseeing—would he be free to come along, saying I was sure whoever was coming would be delighted if he could join us? He seemed very pleased to agree.

Soon a large, old, dusty American sedan, I think it was a Buick, arrived, and I introduced Tange to the driver and his assistant. They were astonished to meet him knowing of his celebrity and were delighted to have him come with us. Tange and I got in the spacious back seat. It was warm and the windows were wide open. We both had cameras at the ready, but I was amazed that Tange had several cartons of Fuji film and would take dozens of exposures with his arm out the window extending above the roof without looking through the view finder. "You'd be surprised how many good ones I get this way," he whispered.

We went first to Corbusier's on-site office, where his cousin M. Jenneret was his representative, a small meek-mannered man who seemed entirely intimidated by the Punjabi officials in charge, especially by a most energetic, vocal woman. She pronounced with sweeping gestures the long range goals of the new city as if it were already completed.

But our view of it was of a largely vacant grid of roads and streets with only an occasional rather forlorn beginning of a commercial and office center and a few dwellings here and there. The office's priority was obviously the grandeur of the government buildings, the Courts, Secretariat and other institutions at the "head" (the north end) of the city. Of course these structures, in concrete, were enormously sculptural and monumental in Corbu's signature manner, already world famous, but even after only a few years, showing signs of wear and tear, with mechanical systems failing and landscape neglected. The exception was the new university campus in typical Punjabi red brick, well-designed buildings by Indian architects in much the same character of the regional towns and villages, with already maturing landscape around ponds, ramadas, grilles and other sensitive shading and ventilation devices that seemed totally missing in Corbusier's grand complex.

We visited the new architectural school on this campus, much to the surprise and excitement of students and faculty that Tange was on this impromptu tour. Our driver/guides were even more impressed too, allowing us to skip other planned stops in order to spend more time with the students. Despite all the architectural images and memories that crowd in of that highly packed day, the one that lingers most is of a lone bicyclist pedaling far in the distance on the empty, dusty grid of the city.

Like the centuries-old culture of Japan as in Kyoto, the richness of India's past had to be found outside modern New Delhi in such nearby places as Fatipur Sikri and Agra. I was able to bargain with the cluster of self-promoting tour guides posted just outside the entrance to the Ashoka, choosing one enterprising looking young man who had an old dented but still reliable looking car to drive me on a day's excursion the twenty miles or so to Fatipur Sikri then on another short distance to Agra, where I could spend most of the day in the lush compound of the memorial temple enjoying not only the romanticism of its minarets, central dome in silhouette and filigreed decoration, but also the symmetries of its site plan and formal landscape extending for such distance, with its almost fortress-like engineering of retaining walls along the river. It was remarkably similar to Baroque site planning with long formal vistas at vast scale edged by dense groves and extending vistas of the countryside beyond the river. This was surprising since most of us know Agra by photographs of only the building itself framed by its minarets and reflecting pool.

Fatipur Sikri on its raised acropolis like platform, had an even more powerful sense of center focus, a small exquisite marble pavilion with its delicate pierced screen infill panels modulating the brilliant light in ever shifting shadow patterns. It was a timeless lesson, like Kikutake's new shrine building in Ismu Taisha, of the richness achievable in only one material of balancing opaque sur-

Sacred River, Varanasi, India
from *Roads Less Travelled*
James P. Warfield, ACSA Distinguished Professor in Architecture, Professor Emeritus, U. of Illinois

face planes of ceilings, walls with modulation of scale from larger smooth elements to intricacies of gradation of openings, edges, perforations from bold to almost jewel-like fineness, unbelievable in marble or concrete.

Carlo Scarpa had achieved this same poetic range of coarse to fine in the Brion family cemetery at S. Vito, Italy, in the use of concrete. I think this discovery of mono-material workability to the level of art, wherever and of whatever age it may be found all over the world, is one of the very most rewarding of all lessons in design learning, regardless of time or place, by celebrated artists or by unknown craftsmen.

Much as I would like to linger longer in India, my Pan Am schedule wouldn't allow it. On to Teheran, Isfahan, Shiraz and Athens. Too bad not to have more time in Isfahan and at the splendid site of Persepolis, near Shiraz, again a platform Acropolis, but at giant scale.

I have to confess that in spite of all the fascination of travel through the Far East, India and Iran, arrival in Athens, as the cradle of Western civilization was like returning home. No doubt this feeling was intensified in warmth and anticipation because it would be my third visit to the city (in 1954 and 1959). Adding to this sense of familiarity and confidence was the plain and simple fact of relief from all the spicy, curried, almost inedible (to me) food of India and Iran.

I felt somehow at fault personally since most of my fellow travelers didn't seem to have a problem. So after getting settled in a hotel near Syntagma Square, my first priority was to go to the Corfu restaurant nearby to enjoy artichokes a la polita, a delicious stew of veal, artichokes and other vegetables that strangely I've never been able to find in Greek restaurants in America. Also, along University street, two enormous café/soda fountain/restaurants, whose owners had returned home from Chicago after years of building up a nest egg, offered a great variety of delicacies at amazingly low cost, the dollar/drachma exchange being so favorable for foreign tourists.

Thanks to an introduction by Anna Cannavou, one of my early graduate students, who was from Athens, now married to Costa Midis, a civil engineer, I visited Doxiadis's home office, on top of one of Athen's hills. Costa and Anna were still in the U.S., in charge of Doxiadis's Washington D.C. office. This was a time when giant international conglomerates were gaining momentum and Greek entrepreneurs like shipping magnate Onassis were in full swing.

As one of these impresarios, Doxiadis had developed a global practice in architecture, urban design and regional planning, especially in developing countries of the world. His office occupied all floors of a high rise on top of the hill with reception and his own suite on the top floor, as if it were a pilot house in command of the world's future. On one of the walls of the reception area was a huge map of the world with projects tagged on every continent. Doxiadis's location at the moment was indicated by a pulsing light. I was told that his executive style was to be present at all these locations at key times for presentations, in consequence he was seldom in Athens. All this was a clear prophecy of coming globalization and big brotherness carrying with it an unmistakable feeling of shrinking special identity for each of us as individuals as well as the "genius loci" of each of our communities.

As if to compensate for this uneasy feeling I joined a small tour to Delphi and on north to the monasteries of Meteora, staying overnight at the new motel "Xenia" at Kalambaka, by architect Aris Konstantinidis, a beautifully designed small scale structure gracefully sited on a slope at the base of massive stone bluffs in this mountain region. I suddenly realized that this motel had been published in the same issue of the Swiss magazine Bauen + Wohnen, June 1963,[21] in which my house in Champaign had also been published. Visits to the monasteries and the overall experience of travel in friendly company to both historic and modern settings, all at human scale, restored my equilibrium once again from the depressing prospect of future giantism and one-worldness implied by the Doxiadis visit.

Soon after, by chance, I ran into Serge Chermayeff in Kolonaki Square, a totally unexpected coincidence that allowed us to catch up on both old times and new insights. This too was reassuring of the human dimension in the design of higher density growth and change, as Serge and his collaborator Christopher Alexander had emphasized in their new book Community and Privacy in 1963.[22]

Before leaving home I had hoped to rendezvous in Jugoslavia with my old friend Gee Gee Robinson from Urbana, who was working on her dissertation on the subject of media communication in Belgrade. While in Athens I found I could easily fly up to Belgrade for a weekend before going on to Rome on my Pan Am ticket. Gee Gee and her friends met me at the airport on a Friday night and installed me at the Hotel Majestic downtown, with fascinating plans already made for both Saturday and Sunday. These two days were an amazing mix of parties, meeting people and sightseeing both in the city and the nearby countryside. I was totally surprised that Gee Gee's friends were so open, engaging and intellectually exuberant, thinking that under Tito's dictatorship they would be guarded and reticent not only among themselves, but especially in the presence of new acquaintances.

A large public park adjacent to downtown was the scene for a party beginning at 10 am Saturday morning at the studio of a celebrated woman sculptor. It had happened that early in Tito's regime the government had built at least a dozen studio/residences for well known artists in the park, a fact hard to imagine anywhere else in the world. Soon the gathering had grown to twenty or more

guests, a cross section of mostly young artists, writers and other intellectuals.
By noon it was clear the level of inebriation was high and the party would go on for hours, so our small group of Gee Gee's friends quietly made our retreat for other destinations in the city, a siesta and then dinner at one of Belgrade's fashionable restaurants. Again I couldn't believe the free-spirited atmosphere and the cosmopolitan quality of food and drink, which I had anticipated would be grey, dull and tasteless, from what we thought was typical of Soviet dominated countries. It began to be clear that though Gee Gee's friends were no doubt among the young intellectual and artistic leadership of the country, their status didn't appear to be a matter of elitist privilege, others of all ages and lifestyles appeared to be enjoying the same absence of repression or else they were concealing it.

My visit was just too short to understand what was really happening. Sunday was an all day excursion out in the country to visit the two small, exquisite 13th century chapels at Ravanitsa and Manasia, both meticulously restored, each a gem in their tiny impoverished villages, surrounded by large farm collectives, with gangs of workers operating farm implements organized in rows like army platoons. It was astonishing to me to observe such tender loving care for historic preservation in the midst of poverty. I was to encounter this same contrast many years later, 1996, in Warsaw, observing the total rebuilding of the city center, destroyed dur-

ing the war, exactly as it had been before. After this very full weekend in and around Belgrade I boarded the flight back to Athens and then on to Rome with a sense of pleasantly saturated, unexpected events, almost like being in a capsule of time and place totally separate from the flow of travel so far. At this point I'll refer back to my chronicle of years at the American Academy in Rome, pages 127-141 for the remainder of this round the world adventure in 1964.

21 Bauen + Wohnen, June 1963, p 257, 259

22 Chermayeff, Serge, Community and Privacy, New York, 1963

In the rear view mirror of the sixties it's clear that our enthusiasm for addressing large scale issues of urban design and planning in response to newly perceived unmet social and environmental needs tended to take priority over normal architectural practice—the usual series of individual projects as they came along. In both education and practice this sense of the priority of what I began to think of as "multi-client" projects carried with it, more than we then realized, an expectation that the quality of design would almost automatically be at the same high level that we had always sought in each new individual building, working with individual clients. It didn't take long to see that brilliant, exciting master plans and urban design schemes if and when they reached implementation would usually be executed by firms of well placed political connection and unpredictable talent under various time and financial pressures. A laudable overall concept could easily result in mediocre architecture. This sense of loss of design control in the domain of multi-client practice was disillusioning for most of us who had been so turned on by new "golden age" opportunities that we soon tried to compensate by returning to small scale projects like furniture design, crafts, art or whatever other creative activity would allow us to have personal "hands on" design control. Of course this twist in direction to the micro scale did not imply any diminishing interest in normal architectural practice and education—it was rather a new dimension for a designer's creative energy that might not have been

stimulated without being prompted by the frustrations of mediocrity at the macro scale of environmental design. For me this yearning for intensely personal design control led to a new cycle of my youthful hobby in designing and building boats. At first I thought this return to an old hobby was just that, as any hobby existed in one's life, a thing apart from one's profession, purely for pleasure or in counterpoint to the imperatives of earning a living. Soon my memory returned of experience in the Navy, when I began to wake up to the fact that involvement in the design and performance of ships was not, after all, an imposed duty assignment away from my training in architecture. So this was another cycle of awakening, what new dimensions of connection and enrichment could I find from my old hobby?

Without going into laborious detail of each of these efforts beginning in the mid sixties, probably counting up to twenty different types of small craft of both sail and power over a period of almost forty years, I will single out one example that may illustrate particles and principles of design learning, the "ΚΑΙΜΟΣ" series of high speed, outboard powered sea skiffs. For the meaning of the Greek word "ΚΑΙΜΟΣ," I'll refer the reader back to the SENIOR ΚΑΙΜΟΣ 1936 heading in the text (p. 46) relating the sweet/sour emotions between undergraduate and graduate school. I had already finished and tested the first of this series of high speed craft in 1967, each about 17 feet long powered by a six cylinder in line 150 horse power

Mercury motor, of mahogany strips laid in epoxy resin over marine plywood. The performance was both thrilling and scary, over 60 miles an hour. I definitely had the feeling of being at the edge of no control, no doubt the same edge of danger in all high powered racing machines, flirting with the same edge of no control at highest speed, always pushing this edge. In fast boats resistance is almost entirely water friction, not air, so when you're headed into the wind that creates a slight chop, you're putting a lot more air under the boat reducing water friction with unpredictable effect on lateral stability, without diminishing, even enhancing speed over the bottom. In a 15 mile an hour head wind, your actual speed may be 60 but your apparent speed would be 75 which may be almost (depending on weight) at the point of taking off as an aircraft.

Since I had not yet selected a name for the boat, its scary, but irresistible performance prompted a flash back to my experience in Greece in the spring of 1968 when one of my Greek friends whispered the word ΚΑΙΜΟΣ as the fishing fleet left the harbor at dusk, expressing the emotion of sweet/sour dread. I have already described in the heading SENIOR ΚΑΙΜΟΣ (p. 46) the same feeling as one graduates from university facing an unknown future. I asked her if this name would be too strange for a high speed boat, as it seemed to me to fit so well to the feeling I had that first summer of testing. She replied "why not?"

So as soon as I returned the name ΚΑΙΜΟΣ was lettered on the stern as I was getting the boat ready with other architectural work to be in a joint exhibition with painter Billy Jackson in the Krannert Art Museum as part of the centennial celebration of the University of Illinois. I must add that the name had mixed reaction from Greek-American friends, from frowns to smiles. I never could get the same exact translation of the word in English—so it still retains its delightful ambiguity.

More than anything else in boat design and building that compliments architectural skill is the reinforcement it gives to fine tuning the whole orchestration of design decisions in a single project, especially in appreciating the importance of fine scaled, strong, elegant but simple hardware, lighting, appliances and other functioning gear as they all work together to provide a sense of ensemble rightness that in turn intensifies spatial openness and harmonics. The old term "ship shape" expresses this idea as well by focusing more attention on craftsmanship and the implicit beauty of high quality performance.

ΚαιμοΣ

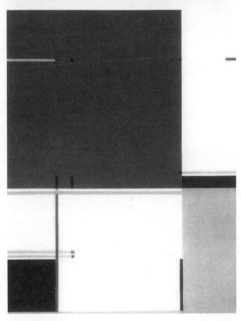

Residence, Stillwater, OK, 1959
Bob Wright, Architect

Collage, 2005
Bob Wright

It's hard to avoid bragging about people in your life. For most, of course, this sense of pride grows and glows from one's personal family, but for those of us who have missed this blessing, thinking of our closest friends in this same way, is a great gift that gains in wealth as time goes by. My mother, of strong Irish Catholic background, was the heart of compassion and understanding but still was always gently applying pressure on me to get married and start a family of my own, reminding me that after all, based on our Irish heritage of often postponing marriage because of economic necessity, it was never too late. I tried to explain that the depression, World War II and the sudden postwar immersion in exciting work extending without let up into the future all combined as an entirely new kind of situation, especially if you had somehow not fallen deeply in love. It was difficult too, to explain that by this time I was becoming envious, observing how much freer my married European friends were to lead separate lives than was then acceptable in America. I recalled the Aegean cruise of the "Angelica," when the group of American journalists aboard were comparing notes on how much flak each had taken for not bringing their wives along. At that time "togetherness" was the guiding light of married life at home.

I think that by then I had convinced myself that the fabulous family I mentioned earlier, of students and colleagues was growing by such leaps and bounds that a fulfilling life as a single person no longer seemed to require

making excuses. Indeed, my calling to architecture and education had now reached a level of devotion and dedication that became most fulfilling.

The phenomenon of cycles again loomed up as a time structure underlying the flow of events in the sixties. I now began to see more clearly how proportions in the fabulous family were changing—more and more the numbers of students increased in each new cycle, or generation, as our Japanese friends saw it, while one's colleagues tended to continue close ties over a much longer time span. But taken together, this distinction becomes blurred, as so often happens when so many former students, formal or informal, become close and lasting friends over a lifetime.

For example, a very special new cycle of graduate students began to come to Illinois from Oklahoma State, a new generation with the same extraordinary combination of talent, hard work and joyful spirit that I had experienced in Stillwater twenty years earlier.

Bob Wright, Jim Knight, Bob Heatley, Dick Cramer, Virgil Carter, Dale Durfee, John Bryant and John Kelly all came to Illinois in the early and mid sixties, joining in the thick of both individual and team projects with zest, hard work and enthusiasm that matched and even exceeded the somewhat more reserved pace of our own highly talented Illinois graduates, those from other parts of the country and abroad. I have already mentioned students from abroad who contributed so much to the graduate program in the late fifties and into the sixties.

This generation of Oklahoma State students, like the first ones I knew before World War II, has gone on to great careers in practice and education. Bob Wright, whose combination of extraordinary personal talent in design, collage painting, devotion and dedication to students, mainly to those in their first years, has been unmatched in advancing the cutting edge of basic design innovation at Illinois, Georgia Tech and Oklahoma State; his influence spreading across the country as an exemplar and pace-setter inspiring students right from the start and on through their later years in school and professional life. In most architectural schools, as in most universities the most talented and experienced faculty tends to be concentrated at the advanced undergraduate and graduate levels, leaving the great numbers of entering students in the hands of teaching assistants. Fortunately, there have been exceptions to this trend all along, like Kirby Lockard at Arizona, Tim McGinty at Wisconsin at Milwaukee and Arizona State, Olaf Fjelde, Claude Winklehake and Gerry Gast at Illinois and a few dedicated others.

Like Bob Wright, Bob Heatley combined amazing design and painting talent seamlessly, and in coaching more advanced students in national design competitions, establishing an as yet unexcelled record

of wins. He is now continuing a most successful painting career from his studio in southern France.

Jim Knight, while in graduate school at Illinois also set a record, winning both the Paris Prize and Le Brun competitions for travel and study abroad. He too, has had a most distinguished career in education and practice at Illinois, then back to Oklahoma State, becoming Head of the school, also active in practice. In recognition of his excellence of accomplishment he was elected to fellowship in AIA, and now continues his consultation from Colorado, as a visiting critic and collaborator in practice.

John Bryant who had already achieved top responsibility in a leading Oklahoma City office before coming to graduate school at Illinois, set the highest standard yet of professionalism and design quality in his thesis for a high tech experimental hospital. After returning to OSU, he too, along with Jim knight, broke new ground in studio criticism focusing on high rise and multiuse projects, also serving as Head of the school for several years. John also became well known for his expertise in short wave radio communication, particularly as it related to aerial research and exploration in the Artic.

Dick Cramer, after contributing so much to collaborative projects, especially in the creative organization of their presentations and publication, went on to a distinguished career in Washington, D.C.

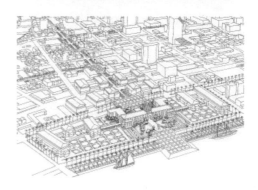

I-57 Rest-Stop, Will County, IL, 1975
Jim Knight, FAIA (Paris Prize, 1966), Architect

San Diego Government Center, Master Plan, San Diego, CA, 1990
Gast/Hillmer Urban Design Consultants
Gerry Gast (Professor of Architecture, U. of Oregon), Architect

Canale Venezia (Oil on Canvas)
Bob Heatley (ACSA Distinguished Professor)

Clinton Presidential Library Advisor, Bill Lacy, FAIA
with President Bill Clinton

Virgil Carter, completing his graduate study at Illinois, advanced rapidly in a major San Francisco Bay office, eventually returning to OSU as Head for a few years, then moving on to AIA headquarters in Washington, D.C. as director of education.

John Kelly also won the Paris Prize while at Illinois. Both he and Dale Durfee went on to Atlanta to join the faculty of Georgia Tech with distinction, both active in practice too, Dale joining with several other partners to form one of today's leading Atlanta firms.

Cheryl Morgan has perhaps exemplified even more this most salutary mix of talent, inspiration, and dedication involving the rapport of OSU, Illinois, the San Francisco Bay Area offices and in the Southeast at Auburn University where she has been a leader for many years. She personifies so beautifully the very best of mid-continental ethic, wholesomeness, rigor and spirit in contributing to architectural education, as distinct, for example, from East Coast sophistication and elitistism reflecting the latest European aesthetic trends and directions.

More than as yet has been fully recognized, the unique stature of the architectural school at Oklahoma State University as a leader representing the "genius loci" of mid America has been the achievement of these two generations. One must hope this extraordinary accomplishment, can survive and flourish still more.

Although I have been describing the alumni of OSU I knew best because they were my graduate students at Illinois and friends ever since, there have been other distinguished graduates of OSU or faculty members there who have made enormous contributions to architecture in America and abroad. First of all among these was Bill Caudill, who had just graduated the year I first came to Stillwater, 1937, and as I have already related, became one of my close friends, went on to MIT, and had a most innovative practice in Texas, founding the famous firm of CRS, and as a prominent educator too at Texas A. & M. and Rice University, finally awarded the AIA Gold Medal. Bill Lacy also rose to fame as an architect in Texas, as Dean of the new school in Tennessee, as President of the American Academy in Rome and most recently as Administrator of the Pritzger Prize. Bill Fash was a fabulous critic at OSU and Illinois, finally moving to deanship at Georgia Tech. Alex Notaras, recruited from the Ecole in Paris, brought his sly, crafty, superb skill as a critic to OSU first then to Illinois, and to the Illinois overseas program in Versailles as Director until his retirement. The charisma of bringing all this OSU, Illini, Versailles spirit so uniquely together belongs to Alex. I must include David Hanser too in this treasured cadre of talent. Even though he is not an OSU alumnus, he came from our Illinois program first, then to join the faculty in Stillwater and has been the spark along with Alex of giving the program in Versailles its special magnetism and breadth of cultural value beyond the usual educational program.

This fabulous family would not be complete without the inclusion of our French exchange students and key French faculty colleagues at Unite Pedagogique d'Architecture No. 3 (U.P.3) at Versailles. Ever since our overseas program was set up in the late sixties, first at La Napoule on the Riviera, the first American architectural overseas program in France I was one of its initators, but except for brief visits I was never in residence for longer periods of time. Nevertheless I was lucky to know some of the first French administrators from the Ministry of Culture, Jean Pierre Biron and Guy de Brebisson. When in 1968 the French students at the Ecole in Paris, along with labor trashed the system, the Ministry under André Malraux reorganized the old architectural atelier system into new units, one of them to be established in Versailles in the restored stables in the approach to the palace. The Ministry then invited the Illinois program to join U.P.3 at Versailles. About fifty Illinois students would go to Versailles for their third year while only five or six French students would come to Champaign/Urbana on the exchange program; this small number was mostly due to the fact that only about this proportion of French students had enough command of English at this point in their education. It was amazing, though, how quickly they adjusted to being in the U.S. Most of all they demonstrated an eagerness and capacity for hard work, not just in a competitive sense, but because of their genuine zest for learning. Since most of them were from the affluent suburbs of Paris close to Versailles,

this kind of joyful intellectual curiosity and discipline for work was in contrast to the rather laid back attitude of most American students from wealthy backgrounds that I had encountered as a visiting critic at Yale and Notre Dame. Over the years many of our French students would join my graduate seminar in theory and criticism, contributing sharp and incisive points of view, particularly those who would return to Illinois for their M. Arch degree. On studio projects too, I found they were especially alert, responsive and imaginative in critical dialogue. The thesis projects of Olivier Heudebourg, Jean Brice Viaud and Valerie Mancret were especially memorable for their insights, sophistication and all around architectural design quality. Valerie's design for an American Center in Paris, based on the same program of space actually built from Frank Gehry's bump and grind design, was acclaimed as catching the American spirit in much greater depth, free of clichés, almost Chicago School like in its integration of space, structure and high tech systems—open, welcoming and unpretentious.

These three remain among my closest friends ever since they were among the former French students at Illinois in the seventies and eighties. Maybe it's partly because Valerie married Greg Taylor from my home town and Olivier (Olu) married Beth Janowski from the north shore of Chicago. Their wedding in 1993 at Culan, a delightful small town of Olu's grandparents in the Limosin region south of Paris was unforget-

Plaza of Nations
University of the Nations, Kailua Kona, HI, 1998
H. James Miller, Architect

Global Outreach Center
University of the Nations, Kailua Kona, HI, 1998
H. James Miller, Architect

Cultural Center, Massy, France, 2008
Devaux Fassio Viaud Architectes
Jean-Brice Viaud (M. Arch, U. of Illinois, 1989), Architect

St. Thierry School, St. Thierry, France, 2006
Fassio Thomas Viaud Architectes
Jean-Brice Viaud (M. Arch, U. of Illinois, 1989), Architect

table for its joyful mix of families, friends, both American and French in abundance; for an emergency helicopter trip back to Paris to pick up the forgotten bridal dress; for the civil ceremony by the mayor in the town hall; for the long, long church service celebrated by an ancient priest; and finally for an exuberant dinner and dancing in the local château until the wee hours. Whenever I'm in Versailles, Olu, Beth and I repeat our traditional Sunday jaunt to Chartres for lunch at the Grand Monarch then to bask in the glory of the cathedral's great stained glass, delightfully made more glowing by Sincere, the region's vin blanc. Jean Brice Viaud did his design thesis of a monastic retreat on a site in St. Ignace called Rabbit's Back. He and his wife Elizabeth have been back to St. Ignace to visit since as my guests at Singassin; now they live in Versailles and I see them whenever I'm there. By now all three, Valerie, Olu and Jean Brice are thriving in practice, among the leading young firms; Jean Brice is also teaching part time at U.P.3.

The beat goes on at Versailles much as it always has although Alex is now retired. Over the years the twice a year sketch trips in France, Italy and Spain in the spring and fall, first under the guidance of Larry and Midge Perkins, then Larry and Joyce after Midge passed away, have carried on along with other Illini. More recently Michael and Gloria Plautz have imaginatively piloted these safaris, and it has been my good fortune to join them several times in Tuscany, southern Spain and France. All through these

times the Versailles program has benefited enormously by the administrative skills and tender loving care of Marie Annick, who is now enjoying her own retirement, and by other Illini visiting faculty as well as close association with the French faculty and students in U.P.3, especially with its President Jean Castex.

As I have already applauded the work and careers of our graduate students from abroad, from New Zealand, Australia, Thailand, India, China, Japan, Argentina, Poland, Greece, Egypt, Italy, France, Sweden, Canada and Great Britain, I want to honor especially those from other universities in our own country as I just have from Oklahoma State; Bob Ford from Washington, Bob Holmes from North Dakota, Gary Burk from Texas, Gayland Witherspoon from Clemson, Bruce Hutchings from Nebraska, Joe Shaughnessy from Notre Dame, Phil White from Ohio State, Jim Miller from Kansas and those from other universities whose names that I regret have escaped from memory.

All along our own Illinois graduates formed a solid base for the graduate program up to about half the total number of M. Arch candidates each year. At that time, in the late fifties until the seventies, I don't think we fully appreciated what an advantage it was to have this particular mix of students from abroad, across America and locally from Illinois, which at that time was still the largest of all mid-continent architectural schools. Most undergraduate degrees were five year

B. Arch programs that encouraged gain-ing practical experience before going on to graduate school. The competition was stiff for admission since the experience record for applicants weighed heavily in their selection both locally and from elsewhere. For this reason it became clear that the combina-tion of both talent and greater maturity was critical in achieving top quality work in both individual and team projects. It wasn't until later, after most schools changed to a four and two year program for the M. Arch degree that we realized there was far less mobility and change of schools from undergraduate to graduate study and far less gain of experi-ence between, since most schools wanted to hang on to their strongest students all the way through to the M. Arch degree without a break between. Although most of our Illini B. Arch graduates had gone out for experience before coming back for graduate work a few did not, going directly into the graduate pro-gram, often finding out, even though they were "hot shot designers," that the compe-tition was much stiffer than they expected, and they could no longer enjoy star status as before, sometimes resulting in shock that required TLC.

In these years of buoyant, energetic, superb-ly talented and motivated students working together, many of our Illini graduates stood out as leaders, namely Chuck Gordon, Bill Miller, Stroud Watson, Jim Miller, Phil Green, Michael Flynn, Tom Katsuyoshi, Lou Narcissi, Derwood Schrotberger, Ron Schmitt, Larry Cannon on the Chicago Corridor, Lakefront

and Columbus, Indiana projects; George Albers, Jim Gibson and Russ Keune on East Humboldt Park; Phil Hodge, Ken Schroeder, Dan Miskie on Jacksonville; Bob Ford, Bruce Hutchings and Allen Johnson on Hennepin; Chuck Albanese, Pat Leamy, Guido Franc-escato, Michael Plautz and John Powers on the Temenopolis series; Gerry Gast and John Smart on City Hall Square, Milwaukee; Jim Babcock on Bloomington Downtown.

Santorini, Greece, 1985 (Watercolor)
Michael Plautz, AIA (Paris Prize, 1965)

Wolf Ridge Environmental Learning Center, Finland, MN, 1989
RSP Architects
Michael Plautz, AIA (Paris Prize, 1965)

Strada Roma (Watercolor)
Charles A. Albanese, FAIA

Perhaps the best way to include students from Illinois and other universities in America is by associating them, along with foreign students, with the collaborative projects in which they participated, listed in the order these projects were undertaken in the Graduate Design Studio as listed in the Appendix.

So much of the success of projects developed in the Graduate Design Studio in the mid sixties depended on my three graduate administrative assistants one each year: Chuck Albanese, Allen Johnson and Gerry Gast, all Illini graduates, of great talent both in design and organizational ability, to do so much of the leg work in program preparation, follow through on contacts with community leaders, planning staffs, grant paper work and other budget management expenses, time scheduling and on completion of each project, the publication of illustrated summary reports whether they were to appear as brochures, monographs, posters, exhibition material or in magazines such as Architectural Forum (Columbus, Indiana), Arts and Architecture, (Chicago Lakefront), Life (Chicago West), Skylines (Temenopolis and Hennepin new town projects). This publicity turned out to be an enormously effective recruiting medium for top-flight new graduate students, along with other forms of networking. Like winning athletic teams, it doesn't take long for the word to get around.

Chuck Albanese not only demonstrated and fine tuned his great managerial skills in the thick of complex project organization, a foreshadow of his later success as both an educator and practitioner, but also expanded his superb individual talent as a designer and painter, winning the Ryerson Traveling Fellowship for study abroad. He and Jim Knight who had won both the Paris Prize and Le Brun in tandem, teamed up in Europe with their young families along to advance the state of the art of learning from travel and documenting the experience creatively in itinerary planning, making resourceful contacts, and in photography, sketching and summarizing their new insights, especially as they would lead to guiding other travelers in the future, as Chuck and Claire, his wife, have done for many years and still continue to do in Italy and Greece.

Chuck then, almost forty years ago, was recruited to the Arizona faculty in Tucson, building up a most successful practice there, too. After retiring from both teaching and practice a few years ago, he has been called back to be Dean of the College of Architecture and Landscape Architecture, to which he is now bringing his enormous ability as an administrator as well as reaching great parallel recognition as a painter in watercolor, acrylic and in drawing. Like Jim Knight, Chuck's exceptional ability as an architect, educator and team leader has led to his election to the College of Fellows in AIA.

As I reflect later on designs for learning in Arizona I'll have much to say about Chuck's unlimited contribution to architectural education and leadership in the daunting aspects of practice in this developer domineered area of America.

Allen Johnson, during his graduate year as my assistant, brought his quiet, friendly soft spoken, good humored gift of working with people of all ages and experience, including most of all his fellow students, carrying these same gentle qualities of personality, much like Bill Caudill (who was often called the Will Rogers of architecture) to practice, first with the leading southern Illinois firm of Fields, Goldman and McGee, also Illini, then to establishing his own firm in Greenville, Illinois, near St. Louis, innovative in its outreach to small communities in the Midwest, helping them with HUD grants to improve their downtowns, especially courthouses in small county seats. Allen is a most skillful, experienced pilot as well and would fly his own plane to these often remote locations to plan and assist in the implementation of these projects, one as far away as Sault Ste. Marie, Michigan on the Canadian border. He has for more than twenty years now continued his most diverse practice in Branson, Missouri along with his son Tait, one of my two godsons (along with Erich Scheeler, Jim Scheeler's son). Tait is a graduate of both Oklahoma State and Arizona and is right at the top of my list of closest young friends.

Gerry Gast not only stood out as a leader in both his undergraduate and graduate class, along with his work as my administrative assistant, but demonstrated his unique capacity for organizational innova-

tion whether in tackling complex multi-client projects in urban design or in creative teaching, first with beginning students, then advanced undergraduates at Illinois, Miami University in Ohio, Stanford in urban studies and at the University of Oregon where he was the first Director of the graduate U of O Portland Center program in architecture. Most innovative of all was his initiative in building, in the late seventies, a new off campus program in San Francisco, attracting students from schools across America, Canada and abroad for semester long breaks (for credit) from their home schools, working on real urban design projects in the Bay Area, mostly relating to unmet multi-dwelling and institutional needs. He first apprenticed with me in my urban design consulting practice in Illinois, where I was fortunate to be asked by Dick Forbes, a most able downtown redevelopment consultant from San Francisco, to help with design concept proposals for Kankakee, Chicago Heights, Downers Grove, Champaign and Bloomington, Illinois, this consultation concentrating in the late sixties and early seventies.

When Gerry began his new off campus program in San Francisco in 1975 he joined with Dick Forbes there, working on Bay area projects, later independently with Dan Hilmer, another Illini grad, on multi-client projects up and down the west coast and in Scottsdale, Arizona, a consulting activity which he continues today. I often was asked by Gerry to be a visiting critic in the San Francisco program and more recently in Portland, and

Residence, Hollister, MO, 1990
General Design Inc., Architects | Planners
Allen Johnson, CEO

Miller Park Plaza, Chattanooga, TN, 1989
Stroud Watson (ACSA Distinguished Professor, U. Tennesse, 1997)

Proposed Convention Center, Tiannin, China
Lee Harris Pomeroy Architects
Barry Berg (B.Arch, U. of Illinois, 1966), Senior Associate

Key Colony, Biscayne Bay, FL, 1984
Sandy & Babcock International
James A. Babcock (President), Architect

Eugene, Oregon, so I can applaud directly with great admiration his gift of inspiring students and colleagues.

All through these years there was a rich variety of events, opportunities and involvements mostly arising from the surge of prosperity, deep concern for civil rights and the environment all at the same time. I'll try to sort out this kaleidoscopic mix as it relates to how my own life and tasks at hand relied on my students and young associates for help, for which I continue to be deeply grateful. Indeed, in some cases the inspiration came from them.

For instance, when the news came leading up to the protest march in Selma, Alabama, Bob Ford who had come from the state of Washington was the first to go and on his return brought back an aura of greater depth to all our projects, especially those involving new town design—what could we do in both programming and design response that would hope to avoid poverty ghettos and foster a mutually reinforcing mix of ages, life styles, income, ethnicities with truly inviting and open access to jobs, educational opportunities, health care, recreation and cultural amenities, at least as far as excellence of planning, landscape and architectural design could influence these goals.

Probably, the Temenoplis II project came closest to this goal as it programmed the idea of building a university city of the future, assuming that education would be the

prime catalyst for intelligence and compassion to rule and inspire a higher quality of life for everybody. In design terms this meant much more overlapping of learning spaces with marketing, office and service activities and with small scale enclaves for relaxation, casual meeting and dialogue in all season garden courtyards major and minor.

Bob Ford volunteered too, to help me with definitive alternate schemes for the 2nd Appellate court as these studies were prepared for exhibition. His inexhaustible skill, spirit and dedication were carried on with great career success at Mississippi State—he too, is now FAIA.

Jim Babcock, one of our graduate class leaders who captained the Bloomington Downtown project, had been an Illini undergraduate as was his partner Don Sandy. Together they formed one of the most talented and prosperous San Francisco firms with an international practice.

It was inevitable that the excitement of what was going on in the graduate studio would attract the most talented, turned on younger students to join in the fray—Andy von Foerster, Lebbeus Woods and Barry Berg were most memorable. They too, have had imaginatively innovative careers, Andy in California and Oregon, Lebbeus was my collaborator on the Kankakee project, along with Gerry Gast, Phil Hodge and Barry Berg, later Leb worked with me on design development of the new McLean County Court

House, a scheme that we were extremely proud of but that met with a fate that was shockingly revealing of how much the client cultural environment had changed, negatively I regret to say, since the intelligent, caring client responsiveness of immediate post World War II years.

Leb also was a most stimulating contributor to my book (The Urban Stage) and has for years now become internationally famous as an artist/architect, based in New York and at Cooper Union. Barry Berg who was also one of my most talented apprentices and closest young friends has for years now been based in New York too, doing exciting work with Lee Pomeroy whose practice has become international and Barry is deeply involved with projects in China.

It's very hard to applaud one of the graduate teams more than any other but I must single out the special exuberance and dynamics of the Chicago series of projects both hypothetical and down to earth. The studio became almost a madhouse of giant drawings, study models, with final presentation graphics and modeling of amazing professional quality. In addition to the OSU gang that contributed so much, our own Illini, including landscape architects were leading the pack: Michael Plautz, Chuck Albanese, John Rishling, Guido Francescato, Pat Leamy, John Powers, and on Hennepin II Allen Johnson, Frank Clements and I must mention Tony Goddard from Britain and Tsuto Kimura from Japan, Christopher Chan from China, and

Gary Hack from Canada—Gary now Fine Arts and Architecture Dean at Penn. Generating this excitement most of all was the combination of young faculty critics, Gerry Exline with his Pied Piper, fluent, captivating design and graphic crits and demonstrations, Norm Day's orchestration leadership and Bob Katz planning, urban design professionalism.

Chicago Heights, Proposed Galleria
Gerry Exline

194

Seven times in my long lifetime wars have interrupted the flow of our enormous American resources in advancing the quality of life for all not only at home but for disadvantaged people around the world as well. I was born as World War I began, served in World War II and have lived on, as so many of us have, through wars in Korea, Vietnam, Serbia-Bosnia and now in Afghanistan and Iraq. The trillions of surplus that could have been invested in higher quality education, employment, health care, institutional and cultural enrichment of all kinds including habitat and environmental infrastructure has been lavished instead on making war intermittently every generation, causing disruptions in the lives of millions with tragic loss of life, leftover disabilities, waste of physical substance and scars of destruction mostly abroad but also scars of emptiness on our conscience because we have been largely left untouched in our own cities and countryside.

This worrisome contradiction poignantly climaxed even more as the Vietnam war killed the surge of enlightenment and sense of being on the brink of a new Golden Age that was building up in the late sixties. This point in time like Pearl Harbor Day could be as precise as one night in May, 1969. As curfew was ordered in Champaign/Urbana, riots had broken out on the campus and the National Guard was called in. My good friend Jack Baker and I were working on a project in my studio when sirens sounded on the street and curfew was announced on the radio.

Jack couldn't go home and silence came down on the city. Fortunately, this time there were no casualties as there had been at Kent State when four students were killed.

After this moment nothing was the same. The visions we had of new model towns and cities and rebuilding our whole urban fabric vanished as if in a dream. The elation of new collegiality, joy in collaborative work, trying to make new images of the built environment in harmony with nature was suddenly gone. The idea of the university as an urban metaphor in which education was manifestly understood as the highest social, political, economic and cultural goal shared by all reverted again to the seemingly safer haven of inwardly turning, Balkanized colleges, departments, centers and institutes, a mirror of the even more intense segregation and ghettoization of our towns and cities as time wore on to the end of the twentieth century. Wasn't this caused, at least in large measure, by the folly of the Vietnam war? And by wars since then?

Quoting from the Prologue of this book:

Architecture is one of the noblest endeavors earning its eminence over the centuries through its infusion of grace, beauty, dignity and invested meaning in response to human needs, both spiritual and functional.

It's easy to understand that we, as architects and educators, feel and live with frustration and dismay time and again as war intervenes over the ages. The slow process of respond-ing most beneficially to the human condition flourishes in peace then is destroyed again by war. Peace gave us the grace and beauty of the most modest Truli house in Albero Bello or a tiny garden dwelling in Ohara Japan, all the way up in scale to the glory of Chartres cathedral and the great era in America of the Chicago and Prairie schools.

Of course we as architects share this distress equally with landscape architects and sensi-tive designers, engineers, inventors along with our most caring clients, community leaders, philosophers, artists, craftsmen and fellow citizens.

But we are now, and I repeat again, in an age called by Pope John Paul II another totalitari-anism, the "Absolutism of Money," a culture that may in fact be just as much a client for war as the lust for power has been histori-cally in the past.

This depth of frustration, having cycled up and down through several generations in my own experience is nevertheless, I fear, on a longer lasting downward slope as archi-tecture itself, along with all other realms of sensitive design, declines as a cultural value. In these recent years of increasing celeb-rity worship and media inflation, you can of course ride along comfortably with the spendthrift society, enjoy fast track luxuries and glitter, be persuaded that architecture is now only to be regarded as big time, exu-berant gestures by stars, and that worthy,

unpretentious work is now something taken for granted, given little notice and is hardly thought of at all as architecture. Or you can wistfully still be hopeful, patient and dream of a new day.

Along with this drift in the state of archi-tecture in America and increasingly all over the world, nostalgia grows and grows for those wondrous pre-Vietnam war years, of glowing, exciting all-nighters in the stu-dio making images of what might be in the future, of enthralling exhibitions, perfor-mances, of inspiring dialogues in the Center for Advanced Study, of world class artists, poets, scholars, critics, scientists coming, going, sharing their thoughts, of Bucky Fuller strolling up the Quad in cadence to chimes in the university's bell tower on the way to his almost interminable, spellbinding talk of imaginative future technologies of inhabita-tion, with hints here and there that all this could really happen, even that it had to for survival.

The message comes at certain times in one's life that it's time for change, whether from the flow of events or from the juxtaposition of stars, the reading of palms or the magic of numbers. All these converged as the new decade of the seventies began, and the alignment of certain numbers made the year 1970 the clear signal for change, in no way diminishing but reinforcing the significance of sudden end to the "Belle Epoch" decade just passed.

It so happened I was twenty-two when my academic career began on the faculty at OSU and that thirty three years later, the war years counting as time credit, I had reached the age of fifty five, the earliest age one could retire from the University of Illinois. Add it up—22 + 33 = 55 all double digits, carried an undeniable, if mystical, message that the time had come, as a milestone in life. Whether or not this made absolute sense and justification to take action, a decision for change was timely, not in any way a sign that I must enter the conventional domain of freedom from work and no responsibil-ity, on the contrary all sorts of opportunities for new action opened up—all enticing, not clearly defined in detail, yet all celebrating the freedom to design time, to balance all new callings that might come along. So we come, in a certain sense to an end to the formal rites of passage in life, to a point of turning, of trying to add up what it all has meant, perhaps even to attempt distilling one's learning, past and present, from wine into cognac.

Archipelago

Passage

Islands in the Academic Grove VII
University of Illinois: Champaign/Urbana, Chicago, Versailles
University of Wisconsin: Milwaukee
California State Polytechnic Univeristy, San Luis Obispo

Freedom to design time, or rather freedom from formal time contracts of employment, whether in academic, professional or business life, opens up new avenues of choice making. Depending on the wheels of fortune this can be an enticing mix of taking new initiatives on one's own or responding to a variety of invitations from near or far away. For an architect or anyone whose calling is design, the balancing of new choices of time commitment seems to fit right in as another facet of the way a designer's mind works now suddenly liberated in a new dimension. Even total leisure can be creative—as day dreaming no longer becomes an indulgence carrying with it a feeling of guilt; indeed it is now a new luxury enriching the process of design thinking no matter what kind of task opportunity is offered ahead. The wide variety of new client projects and inviting university engagements all require the design of short or long time spans overlapping, mixing with chances to travel, to indulge in old and new hobbies and the pursuit of leisure. But most of all the momentum to never stop learning can now accelerate more than ever before.

This momentum quite naturally lent priority to invitations from Illinois and other universities to continue in the academic world as a part time visiting critic for short or longer time periods, also to work in urban design consultation and individual architectural commissions as thy came along. Later I'll describe one of the latter that in retrospect became a milestone in reflecting all of a

sudden a sea change in architecture as a cultural value, a change that was building up all along especially triggered by the shock of the Vietnam War and the advent of the "all about me" era of the seventies, then to carry on to this day. This one commission as an architect was so singular that it merits its own place in the archipelago as an ISLAND IN PRACTICE, all alone, more truly an iceberg than verdant or inspring as a part of "our purple mountains majesty."

For those of us who have spent most of our life in one place long enough to call it home, it's very natural after "retirement" to linger on and stay involved in some way, even as a more nomadic existence beckons. With the disastrous effect of the Vietnam War on the essence of architectural learning in studio, we suffered a severe if not mortal heart attack on the joyful yet rigorous spirit of learning together, like jazz, the very embodiment of our mid-American character.

We could try to recover in some way, first by talking it over in bull sessions, for once free of bullshit, if you can imagine such a contradiction. So these discussions took form under the old umbrella of a theory and criticism seminar that I had always tried to integrate with studio; that is theory defined as the distillation of learning from immediate experience, rather than as a separate academic specialty (which has for so long been formalized as the history of theory). Criticism too, was exercised as an action process to develop skill in critical judgment

and ability in self—criticism as distinct from journalistic and scholarly criticism.

Thus, after I was asked to continue part time on the Illinois faculty as much as I could, the best choice seemed to be to focus on the graduate seminar which turned out to be a magnet for some of our most talented and dedicated undergraduates including the French exchange students from Versailles as well as the normal cadre of graduate students. This involvement was to continue for many years along with frequent visits to the university's architectural school on the Chicago campus and to the overseas program in Versailles. Soon, this beginning of a pluralistic life as a visiting critic expanded to the University of Wisconsin, Milwaukee's new program and once a year for a week to Cal Poly in San Luis Obispo. Each of these contacts was so unique in its own way despite the common dilemma we all faced in those post Vietnam years that I would like to reflect on each one in turn as indeed this body of experience expanded still more in the remaining decades of the century.

The seminar I have just described above did follow the traditional structure of reviewing the panorama of critical problems arising in individual and team projects, especially those that were most commonly encountered at a given time in the design process but also included an ongoing series of student reports on basic design principles like building to ground, building to sky, or other aspects of context, to critiques of exemplary

Passage

Islands in the Academic Grove VII
University of Illinois: Champaign/Urbana, Chicago, Versailles
University of Wisconsin: Milwaukee
California State Polytechnic Univeristy, San Luis Obispo

Studio, Seattle, WA, 2008
Graham Baba Architects
James Graham, Architect

Meditation Hut II "Le Cadeau", Urbana, Illinois, 2006
(AIA Central Illinois Honor Award 2006, AIA Small Project Award 2007)
Jeffrey S. Poss, Architect

individual work chosen by each student; more precisely, examples that they had personally visited, rather than had found in magazines, books or other media. However, the new ingredient of post war trauma added a new common denominator to each presentation and each discussion—what do we do about all this now? The "so whats?" had always been intrinsic in every critique, but now the "so what?" dominated almost to the point of disillusion and despair, soon even to retreat into the already wide spreading "all about me" preoccupation and deflation of enthusiasm for common cause values that had flourished the decade before.

Nevertheless it was probably this trauma and change that more clearly than ever separated the very small percentage of most talented and dedicated students from all the rest. This difference had of course always existed as all of us knew who had been in the thick of architectural education for years. And all through that time it became an essential part of our mission to increase this tiny percentage if even only a little more, knowing that this could happen mainly in studio through an atmosphere of something special going on among the best students, even if they were very few in number, that was contagious and very likely to capture a few more into their ring of inspiration and learning together. This gap, always difficult to overcome, now seemed almost unbridgeable as the studio itself appeared to be more and more obsolete. The growing affluence of most students for at least a generation also

played against work ethic in both individual and team endeavor.

All of this is why certain of our students in the post war era are more memorable than ever before as they enter and belong in the "fabulous family" pantheon. I've already reflected on the exceptionality of several of our French exchange students (p. 188) and it's interesting to note that some of our own American students I first met in Versailles in 1971 and 1972 are very much in this same pantheon, beginning to earn their place not only because of a most unusual set of circumstances there but by everything that's happened in our lives since then. Perhaps the simple fact that just being away from America at that time, away from shadows of doubt at home and being in France, which always seemed able restore its "joie de vivre," our students in Versailles could for a time, shake off their feelings of an uncertain future. But what turned out to be even more special was an invitation to our students and faculty in Versailles, a few at a time, to spend two week periods of work and study in the south of France at the Ecole Nationale d'Art Decoratif in Nice, a brand new art school built in Corbusian style around the Villa Arson in its grounds on the slope of the Alps Maritime above the city. Our students, ten or twelve, were quartered along with the French students in monastic like accommodations and could choose to join any studio, painting, sculpture, ceramics, print making, or a special study group called Cadre de Vie.

Archipelago

Passage

Islands in the Academic Grove VII
University of Illinois: Champaign/Urbana, Chicago, Versailles
University of Wisconsin: Milwaukee
California State Polytechnic Univeristy, San Luis Obispo

Cadre De Vie – an expression meaning the frame or setting of life—was an educational program under the direction of Professor M. F. Cali. Its intention, as I understood it while a part-time participant there in 1971 and 1972, was to present art students with a comprehensive sense of the cultural and physical aspects of the setting in which they might be working, so that they might be more sensitive and responsive to the influences of such environments on the forms, or media of art in which they were engaged. The scale of Cadre de Vie settings could range from an entire rural region, village, or a section of the city, such as the Promenade des Anglais at Nice, to the more intimate settings of street corners or individual rooms. The idea was that the student might develop a more than casual sensitivity to the ensemble of the setting—to understand and respect its essential character as a basis for possible conservation, enhancement, or whatever other form of change might be appropriate. This special sensitivity of the whole would then become a source of depening perception in which all relevant works of art take on greater meaning. As it was demonstrated in Nice, the idea of Cadre de Vie was related to environments already rich in cultural accumulation, in some cases of a very modest vernacular nature. But the principle of intensified perception of the setting as a whole could apply just as effectively to new ensembles as well as to those already existing at a high level of equilibrium and refinement.

In 1971, I joined this group along with Tom Paxton, Tom Kubala, Allen Washatko, Louis Wasserman, Paul Rushing, and Mickey Collins for the two weeks we were there, exploring all kinds of settings from Vence in the mountains to the edge of the Mediterranean, taking notes, sketching and endlessly debating the uniqueness of each place, especially what it meant to us as architects, which excited Professor Cali, as so different from the perception of art students who always seemed to him to reflect much more highly subjective, personal interpretations.

Although this difference may be true in a general sense, I had a hunch then and later became much more fully aware that the two Toms, Allen, Louis, Paul and Mickey were far ahead of their peers in their eagerness to absorb the nature of settings as inseparably linked to the act of design and any other intervention that may negatively affect or positively enhance the spirit of a given place that has earned its special identity over time.

Tom, Tom, Allen, Louis, Paul and Mickey were members of the class of 1973 and on return to Champaign/Urbana for their final year, were in the last class of the old five year B. Arch degree curriculum. The new four and two program had been initiated in 1970. This class that I was especially close to honored me by asking if I would be their commencement speaker. I believe this was the first time that the various colleges and departments in the university began to have their own celebrations in addition to the all-

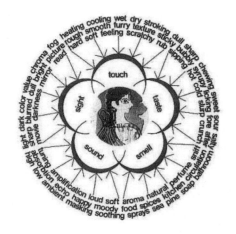

Diagram for *The Urban Stage*, 1975
Allen Washatko

First Source Center, South Bend, IN, 1980
Mickey Collins, V.P. HOK, Chicago with Murphy/Jahn Architects

university ceremony, a new tradition which has continued everywhere since then.

I have had the advantage and privilege ever since that time to watch in admiration as each of these former students has carried on the high expectations they set for themselves back then, building up to today. Tom Kubala and Allen Washatko formed their partnership early on in Wisconsin, centered in Cedarburg, north of Milwaukee and after combining teaching at University of Wisconsin, Milwaukee with their practice for a while inviting Paul Rushing to join them. Since then they have built up an amazingly diverse body of work and just recently celebrated their 25th anniversary in practice. The excellence in diversity of their work has just earned them the AIA's State of Wisconsin Firm Award. Louis Wasserman went on to Harvard's Graduate School of Design, where he met Caren Connolly, a landscape architect and they too returned to the Milwaukee area; teaching at UWM and gaining an outstanding reputation in practice; Caren becoming associate dean of the School of Architecture at UWM, then returning to practice and for some years now joining with Louis as authors of several successful books with Taunton Press on ranch houses, bungalows and cottages. Both Tom Paxton and Allen were enormous help to me with graphics for The Urban Stage, as was Mark Romack. Tom and Mark also worked with me on developing architectural and other projects then in process, Tom on drawings for Osimo, my 40 foot motor sailer launched in 1977. Mark worked with me as well on drawings for the

Carrousel Shops on Mackinac Island in the early eighties, and several times was crew on Osimo, as were Tom, Scott Morris and Jeff Tock. Sad to say both Tom and Mark have both passed away, Tom of a brain tumor and Mark of hepatitis. As I have already related in my chronicle of the American Academy in Rome, P. 133, another of my finest students, Paolo Sica, from Florence, died of liver cancer in 1988. This kind of tragedy can only be assuaged by memories of how much love we shared and how much we learned together, a treasure that is certainly immortal. Mickey Collins, like so many of our Illini, along with her boyfriend Aki Knezivic, also of extraordinary talent chose to make it in Chicago; both soon became a part of the vanguard there in innovative design, mixing interior, furniture design and painting with architecture. I was their guest several times in those years, enjoying their hospitality in their loft, so memorable for its imaginative use of space, light, color and found objects.

Another Illini, Mark Keane, although never directly one of my own students became close through our contact at Versailles and because he and his wife Linda also chose the Milwaukee area for their careers, Mark at UWM and Linda commuting to the Art Institute in Chicago. They too, have become well known for their individual achievements and together through publication in advancing the cutting edge of learning from travel, and Mark through fresh insights about the Prairie School's heritage. This is especially apropos and interesting since they and their family live in one of the Prairie School's most fascinating houses, on the shore of Lake Michigan. I'll have more to relate later on about my own luck in experiencing sometimes distant sometimes close connection to this great heritage of mid–America and its echoes around the world.

On return from Versailles and the Cadre De Vie seminar with Professor Cali in 1971, I was invited to participate in a new experimental UIUC residential college program called Unit 1, in which a small number of beginning students, mainly in liberal arts, would join in informal seminars of interest to faculty undertaking special studies. In my case I had just received a grant from the Graham Foundation in Chicago in response to my proposal to gather inferences together from our collaborative projects as a monograph or book under the title of The Urban Stage.

The idea of the experimental seminar was to see what effect the design of settings as in Cadre de Vie might have for non–architectural students involving better choice making in the microenvironment (aside from those more formally a part of the professional urban design program and regularly a part of the graduate program in architecture) clarified by intensive discussions and experiments with an enthusiastic group of Unit 1 students: Martha Spatz, Jude Stephens, Sarah Bayer, Pam Gross, Michael Franklin-White, Linda Harbert, Beth Barnhill. Garry Leonard and Allen Washatko were advanced architectural students who volunteered to

help—Allen, as I related earlier had been a participant in Professor Cali's seminar in France.

Each time we met in a different setting of more than usual interest, such as an artist's studio, the stage of a drama theater, a board of trustees conference room, a small chapel, a client's house, etc. Several times, the occupant of the particular setting was the guest in the seminar. Since our subject for the series was this very question—the influence of the setting on performance, and vice versa, perhaps the participants were overly self-conscious. Nevertheless, the response was significant and memorable.

Each of the students has commented long since that their awareness of the setting/performance relationship was greatly increased and that they are now more interested than ever that the character of their individual environment truly fits their personality. We tried to pin this down to something more specific than personal taste, which in spite of efforts toward individuality, might display a common fashion or conformity. We were most sure that a setting that contains cues related to the special skills and interests of the occupant was closest to projecting this character even if some of these are overt status symbols, such as trophies, diplomas, medals, etc. This kind of display of special interests and skills is of course very commonplace, but it is far from commonplace to do this "stage setting" well. Above and beyond the obvious need to

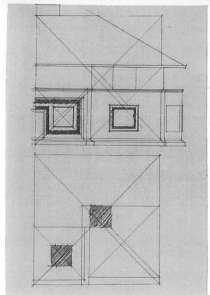

Illustration of the Winslow Residence from
The Geometry of Wright (Book), 2001
Mark and Linda Keane

Passage

Islands in the Academic Grove VII
University of Illinois: Champaign/Urbana, Chicago, Versailles
University of Wisconsin: Milwaukee
California State Polytechnic Univeristy, San Luis Obispo

The Roman Court, Metropolitan Museum of Art, New York, NY, 2005
Kevin Roche John Dinkeloo and Associates LLC, Architects
Garry Leaonard, Senior Design Associate

identify this as one of the essential freedoms of choice of each individual, is the long range implication of better consumer education in choice-making.

In writing about these years nostalgia is bound to creep in, I guess largely because of the ΚΑΙΜΟΣ feeling of the time, in such contrast to the charisma of the 1960's. The very idea of what the Chicago area has meant for so long in our mid continent culture lies at the heart of it. So when the invitation came to commute part time to the Chicago campus I was eager to see what difference this close participation might make in the perspective I had had of Chicago's "genius loci" up to now.

Asked to be a critic at large, rather than assigned directly to one studio or another I had a new kind of responsibility to become a kind of low key referee, in juries, seminars, meetings and in what counts most, I truly believe, as an informal participant in many other ways. It was strange and new to me in a way, since UIC, like so many commuter campuses elsewhere, hit its communication peak at high noon. I, like other students and faculty, had difficulty arriving before 9 or 10 AM, and then having to leave again by 4 PM to avoid the evening rush hour. All this added an extra compaction of time and urgency to communicate directly, a situation that soon sharpened one's skill in pruning away excess rhetoric, dare I say bullshit? Maybe this was a truer preparation for rapidly developing, jam-packed professional

and business life than the more relaxed extra urban atmosphere of Champaign/Urbana. Thanks to Dean Len Currie, Tom Jaeger, Ed Deam and Bruno Ast (Tom, Ed and Bruno had all been my former students and colleagues downstate). I still had the feeling of being right at home. We would escape from time to time for lunch at one of the fabulous Greek restaurants nearby or in the evening for dinner at Cliff Dwellers downtown or on the North Shore with Ed and Doris Deam and later in Evanston when Dick Whittaker became dean. Aside from this life in close contact with UIC I could see other Chicago friends more often on their own turf, Larry and Midge Perkins, Walter and Dawn Netsch, Harry and Kitty Weese, others at the annual FAIA dinners at the Tavern Club, as well as to visit with so many former students. This stroke of luck went a long way in countering the depression we all felt as the Vietnam War came to its anguishing end, along with Watergate and other scandals.

It was refreshing too, to work with the students in Chicago as they reflected the same no nonsense work ethic on their projects that we had experienced in the immediate post World War II years, when Chicago students of many different ethnic backgrounds would come to Champaign/Urbana after their first two years in the Navy Pier program. Even though our time for critiques was so limited and so much energy had to be spent in travel every day, the atmosphere of eagerness to learn pervaded the studios, resulting in a quality of directness and straightforwardness in the work, even though it might lack the added measure of sophistication and finely tuned design refinement that a more round the clock presence might have afforded. It was also clear that the absence of a graduate program at that time meant that the emulation potential of more mature students was missing. Over the following years this gap was closed as well as when more nearby student housing was provided.

One of the most memorable times in the five years I would commute to the Chicago campus was a brief period when Louis Kahn was also there as a visiting critic. Since we were together often I had a chance to ask questions updating his most recent thoughts of finding the "existence will" within the design process, most particularly wondering if by now there seemed to be a more direct path to eke out the essence of each project. I had remarked that each time in my own experience, the earnestness and depth of the search seemed to demand so much more time, often wearing out my own patience and certainly that of our clients. I remember him shaking his head, saying that especially now in our era of faster and faster tracking and shorter attention spans, along with the inflation of egos on all sides, it seemed ever more difficult, and especially that in his view there were no new short cuts looming up in the quest—it still required that extra measure of recognition and will. Many years later I was to discover through the inspiration of membership in Arts Religion and

Contemporary Culture, of which Kahn was one of the leaders, a deeper understanding of existential philosophy most notably in the writings of Martin Buber and Paul Tillich as they explored "the in-between realm" and "intrinsic authority" of what any action process wants to be on its own—of course this includes architectural design. In other words if we can convince both ourselves as designers and our clients of the truth and integrity of what potentially lies within each project at a deeper level between our two egos and purely subjective notions, our joint effort can reach a both timeless and timely level of invested meaning, enduring quality and excellence in diversity. After all this time of testing I truly believe this principle is ageless and immune from the whims of style, vanity and superficiality.

The new campus of UIC had been built a decade earlier as a permanent solution to the temporary use of Navy Pier in responding the ever increasing demand for higher education in the metropolitan area. It was innovative in both planning and design, to be an entirely new homogenous structure built in a short time span in contrast to the traditional building by building growth of colleges and universities in America and everywhere else. Its immediate predecessors were military institutions such as the Air Force Academy in Colorado Springs and the Navy's new post graduate school in Monterey. Skidmore Owings and Merrill (SOM) had been the architects for both of these projects and were chosen for the new UIC.

Since I had been close to the firm and an old friend of Walter Netsch, partner in charge of the new project I had over a period of years a chance to observe its design development at close hand. This was also in part a result of being involved with campus planning in Champaign/Urbana offering an opportunity to have some idea of the academic programming and decisions that led to a "megastructure" approach, especially knowing there would be little encumbrance and adaptation to a newly cleared site at the southwest edge of Chicago's downtown. By now, of course, the design is well known for its upper deck pedestrian circulation system feeding class room, laboratory and library blocks, with faculty offices mostly gathered in a single tower, a decision that has generated considerable feedback over time, especially from the architectural faculty who always want to be close to studios. For the time I was there as a visitor I hardly ever used the office assigned to me, nor did others; we simply gathered in lounges, review spaces all close to studios.

The architectural school itself occupied space at the north east corner of the site, as close as you could get but still in view of Chicago's concentration of skyscrapers, where they almost seem to be one. But except for some open glazing of circulation connecting links and in a few other locations, the studios and classrooms all had little external view, leading to students joking that they inhabited "a five story basement." I often thought if Harvard's new GSD building, with

Passage

Islands in the Academic Grove VII
University of Illinois: Champaign/Urbana, Chicago, Versailles
University of Wisconsin: Milwaukee
California State Polytechnic Univeristy, San Luis Obispo

its all glazed, north facing tiered studios like a grandstand, could magically be transported to this commanding site, the essence of Chicago's dramatic loop skyline to the north east would always be in dramatic view; a constant reminder to the students of Chicago's "genius loci."

It's funny how some small memory may stick that looms much larger in the maturity of time. At one of the project reviews with a group of Ed Deam's students I guess I got a bit emotional. One of the students spoke up: "I think you're in love." I think I said something like this: "Yes, with all of you and with architecture!"

As a Great Lakes sailor I had known for a long time that the entire west shore of Lake Michigan, starting from the far north in Door County, Wisconsin, all the way south to Chicago is in low profile, with almost all settlements inhabiting places where rivers small or large empty into the lake providing harbors. As you come south along the shore, small villages become towns, then cities, each becoming progressively larger. In almost every case industrial, commercial uses and workers dwellings occupied the south side of the river mouth, with more up scale retail, office and residential uses on the river's north side and up the north shore of the lake. So when I accepted the invitation to be a visiting critic at UWM in Milwaukee and that the campus was only three miles up the lake shore north of the Milwaukee River, I immediately felt I was in a smaller Chicago,

but with a certain more relaxed feeling arising from a lower pace of activity, less urban noise, more humanely scaled street spaces and the lakefront itself more walkable and verdant. It all seemed a welcoming balance of urbanity and the more leisurely pace of smaller town and city living that I had grown up with,

Like UIC, UWM had been established after World War II and its new school of architecture the first in Wisconsin was formed in the early sixties, adding one year at a time until a full five year program was in being. Along with a few other faculty from architectural schools nearby, Michigan, Notre Dame, IIT, Illinois and Minnesota, I had tried to help as the new program took from. The new faculty quickly took hold. The UWM campus was much different from UIC in that it was adapted to and grew within its older well established neighborhood near the lake. The school of architecture moved into a vacated high school with little remodeling needed, where it remained until a new building was built in the eighties. As I remarked about Milwaukee as a more relaxed Chicago, so was the atmosphere of the school as I grew to know it then. I haven't yet been able to pin down just why there seemed to be an aura of almost naïve enthusiasm among the students in spite of the dampening effect of the Vietnam War that I have already alluded to at Illinois. Over the several years I was a visitor there, again mostly as critic at large, I always felt, even with advanced students, this same spirit of excitement about

architecture very much like that of client enthusiasts and laymen buffs that you may have known (I resist using the label "dilettante!"). In retrospect I think this quality of excitement a bit lightweight and resistant to really working out details might have arisen anywhere you have a very bright faculty who may be stronger in purely academic specialties than in professional experience, as I have pondered earlier in reflecting on the history of architectural education as it shifted from apprenticeship to academia. Gradually over time, thanks to Tim McGinty, Harvey Rabinovitch, Bob Beckley and a few other faculty as well as local architects like Bill Wenzler, the school reached a more balanced roster of experienced practitioners on the faculty including more recently my former students Tom, Allen, Louis as I have already related.

In spite of the dramatic and abrupt change in the nation's political and cultural climate brought on by the Vietnam War some federal programs had enough momentum to carry on into the seventies. The two that I happened to participate in were a National Academy of Science committee on national land use planning studying the interface of prime agriculture land and urban sprawl—the other was as a consultant on new subway station design in Chicago, a part of the city's transit system expansion that had planning funds appropriated by Congress during the Johnson administration. The NAS initiative was carried by Professor "Gunny" Gonzales a most eminent member

Archipelago

Passage

Islands in the Academic Grove VII
University of Illinois: Champaign/Urbana, Chicago, Versailles
University of Wisconsin: Milwaukee
California State Polytechnic Univeristy, San Luis Obispo

of our Illinois faculty who had earlier been elevated to the NAS. Gunny, a close friend of mine, asked me to chair a subcommittee on environmental design and I in turn asked Phil Lewis, leading landscape architect in Wisconsin, Ralph Knowles, architect, and pioneering environmentalist from USC and our own Bob Riley, architect, landscape architect and regional planner from UIUC to join me on the committee. This was a fascinating and timely challenge, still hopeful even though effective national land use planning now seemed almost a lost cause. Over a period of two years, we met in Washington and at the Graham Foundation in Chicago doing work on innovative urban/agriculture edge condition policy that sadly remains as another long forgotten report buried somewhere in the NAS archives. Anyway this experience lingers in my memory for the rich contacts I was fortunate to have not only with colleagues on the committee but also for a series of interviews I was able to arrange with leaders in think tanks at Cal Tech, Santa Barbara, in Portland with Willamette regional planners, and in Washington. It was on this safari up the west coast that I stopped at San Luis Obispo to visit Paul Neel, head of the school at Cal Poly. Soon after Paul invited me to become one of the school's adjunct critics, a program that had been initiated using a full salary budget line to bring in visiting critics from around the country and abroad for one week sessions with the students. Like my UIC and UWM experience this annual contact was to continue for about five years, but at Cal Poly I was only there each year

for the first week in April, rather than for extended periods of time.
Cal Poly had the same joyful spirit I had felt in Milwaukee but quite different in other ways. I had already begun to sense that I should carry my passport every time I entered California like entering another country, as if the whole state was "Hotel California," an enchanting combo of beach life, Haight Asbury, Sea Ranch, Hollywood, vanguard youth culture and Nob Hill all rolled into one. Cal Poly was very much all this yet had its own character too, something like the ethnic mix of students from blue collar families I knew in Chicago, already knowing their careers would be mainly on the production, technical and construction side of the aisle in architectural offices in contrast to Berkeley's graduates, who were high on theory and more focused on the esoterics of design, the dynamics of name identity and California's unique laid-back elitism. I had many fascinating conversations about this later as I got to know Charles Moore, Bill Turnbull, Joe Esherick and Dick Whittaker, all becoming well known for their work in the San Francisco Bay area.

Cal Poly already had a solid reputation for its graduates' preparation for practice and being able to become quickly productive in architectural offices up and down the state, especially in the Los Angeles area. George Hasselein as dean and Paul Neel as head had worked for years with practitioners to develop the kind of curriculum that would concentrate on technology and design develop-

ment pointing to the special needs of the California environment such as earthquake resistance and integration with landscape. This highly professional orientation had a lot to do with the school's recruitment of Illini for the faculty. While I was there I felt right at home to be with Don Sweringen, Brian Kesner, Steve Hahn and Louis Wasserman. Louis and Caren had come to San Luis Obispo right after finishing their graduate study at Harvard GSD. There were other visiting critics as I was who were repeaters adding to a sense of reunion, like Betty Hill from England and Marion Tournon-Branly from France. Bill Fash was also a visitor from Illinois.

Travels of an academic nomad unfold a wide diversity of educational philosophies, directions, settings and personalities in different schools, yet sooner or later many similarities emerge, another version of the old aphorism "the more things change, the more they stay the same." For example, as I traveled up the west coast in 1971 interviewing authorities for the NAS Agriculture/Urban Edge Committee, it was possible to visit six architectural schools along the way: UCLA, Cal Poly, UC Berkeley, U. of Oregon, Eugene, U. of Washington, Seattle and Washington State U. Pullman. UCLA was just initiating its new school in the Ivy League mode as a graduate program still small, but much like Berkeley in its intellectually dynamic aura, in contrast to Cal Poly's practice orientation that I've already described. This same contrast seemed to exist in Washington between the sophistication of Seattle and Pullman's

Passage

Islands in the Academic Grove VII
University of Illinois: Champaign/Urbana, Chicago, Versailles
University of Wisconsin: Milwaukee
California State Polytechnic Univeristy, San Luis Obispo

programs, although both the Seattle and U. of Oregon curriculum seemed to balance design, theory, technology and practice very much like the Midwest schools I was most familiar with.

What was most alike in many of these I visited was that one or more of the faculty would eventually whisper; "This school's in a mess," no doubt an exaggeration, but still a reflection of a tendency for opposing factions to form, usually based on differences in design philosophies. In general terms these polarities as I've observed them anywhere, over a much longer time span, boil down to opposition between those who stand fast for finding and maintaining long term criteria of excellence and those who are swept up by current fashions and clichés or the work of certain stars who were at their peak of influence at a given time. In Pullman for instance, there was then one studio that exactly replicated one of Mies at IIT, under Peter Pran from Chicago. There's no doubt by now that Peter is the champion example of all those who over the years have followed one star or movement after another, from Wright to Mies, to Post Modern, to Deconstrucivism and now to Structural/Sculptural Exhibitionism.

Later in the seventies I was to visit several other schools one or more times as a lecturer or studio critic: Miami University in Oxford Ohio, Louisiana State in Baton Rouge, Texas Tech in Lubbock, Cal Poly, Pomona, Cranbrook in Bloomfield Hills, Michigan and the San Francisco Center for Architecture and Urban Studies and for longer periods like UWM and UIC at Ohio State and Notre Dame.

The San Francisco Center, initiated by Gerry Gast, was most innovative as an off campus, one semester program for advanced students from America and abroad to be involved in multi-family, affordable housing and other needed infill studies identified by the San Francisco Plan Commission. Attracting between twenty and thirty students each half year, the studio was located in the heart of the city. Frequent visiting critics were Charles Moore, Nat Owings, and other leading architects, planners and members of SPUR, the city's most active body advocating optimum policies of urban planning. I would usually participate for two week periods, in the fall and spring. After continuing successfully well into the eighties, the program terminated as Gerry developed his own urban design consulting practice and then in the nineties was appointed the first director of the U. of Oregon's Portland Center for graduate study in architecture concentrating on similar project types and has continued also as an adjunct professor in Stanford's urban studies program.

In about 1975 Am Richardson who had been the first director of the graduate program at Illinois after World War II, after being engaged in practice for a number of years, moved on to become head of the school of architecture at Notre Dame bringing with him on the faculty several Illini, Brian Crum- lish, Don Sporleder and Ken Featherstone, who had been a graduate student at Illinois from England. So when Am invited me in 1978 to commute for a semester as a visiting critic it was again a case of experiencing the same warm sense of familiarity I had known in Champaign/Urbana, Chicago and Cal Poly. Soon though I began to feel a difference among the students. As you can imagine in a Catholic university their ethnic backgrounds were mostly Irish, Italian, Hispanic or Polish but I was surprised to discover they were mostly from affluent families from all over the country since of course Notre Dame is a university of national appeal and support rather than of local state or city identity. Although most friendly, intelligent and engaging, the students were not nearly as excited about architecture as they and the whole community were about football and the mystique of Notre Dame.

I didn't fully realize this at first until later in the semester I was asked by a small number of more serious students if I would meet with them privately. It turned out they were being harassed by their fellow students for "placing architecture above Notre Dame" and thought that as an outsider I might have some insights about how to cope with the problem more than their own faculty might want to. I tried to point out that I had encountered this same laid back attitude among well off students at Yale (p. 52, 111) but without the rationale of allegiance to a higher loyalty (Notre Dame in this case) as an excuse. This wasn't much consolation reminding them that life after graduation in the real world would be much the same especially in these post Vietnam War days as architecture continues to decline as a cultural value in our society. On the encouraging side, as I have attempted to do ever since, the silver lining was always potentially present in at least a few projects opening up in their careers ahead when for whatever combination of reasons they will share with their clients and even the public at large the gratification and exhilaration that enduringly radiates from work well done, even if it happens only once in a while.

About 1990, Notre Dame's architectural program made an abrupt change in direction from the open ended quest for excellence in contemporary terms that characterized most American schools with a return to Neo Classism under the new headship of Thomas Gordon Smith who came from practice in a largely revivalist "traditional architectural" style. This change, championed on an international scale by Prince Charles in England of course had already taken hold long before in affluent suburbs everywhere, and had by now reached such a magnitude that it now carried with it a greatly expanded market for architects. However, from my own experience many times later as a visiting critic in Notre Dame's overseas program in Rome, the brightest students tended to take this shift in stride (or I should say "tongue in cheek"). In project design and development usually based on sites in the city with strong context constraint both students and critics

found ways to keep focusing on universal design principles such as scale, composition and material harmonies rather than explicit style references and details. I discussed this situation in my review of visits to the American Academy in Rome over the years. (p. 127)

All these islands in the archipelago of learning, though multiplying in number and perhaps not allowing as much depth of understanding with each new experience, still seemed to be adding up to an overall positive view of architectural education as it moved to the end of the century. While the culture at large became more and more materialistic, hedonistic, and money oriented you could always find a few truly dedicated faculty and students in every school who stood fast as trustees for the timeless values of architecture in spite of all the negative pressures around them. It was reassuring that these few, like the few sincere, perplexed students at Notre Dame, could continue to be found anywhere, joining with others of high integrity in whatever calling—as the university itself became more and more under siege, the bulwark of human intelligence, compassion and cultural advance. I'll now try to find the same trusteeship of cultural value in the outside world of everyday life.

Downtown Champaign, IL, 1969
Champaign Development Corporation

Champaign Circle
(Drawing: Gerry Exline)
Collaborative Team:
Richard Forbes, Gerry Exline, Burce Hutchings, Richard Cramer,
John Neils, Jr., Jorn Thorpe, Robert Armon, A. Richard Williams

No doubt as a consequence of all the years working in Chicago and with various neighboring communities on problems of urban growth and change as director of the Collaborative Design Studio at Illinois, contacts developed leading to serving as a consultant along with others who were specialists in downtown redevelopment of Chicago suburbs as well as downstate cities.

Chicago had initiated a new program of planning for subway expansion during the Johnson administration, as I related earlier, with leftover funding that continued after Nixon became president. I was asked to be a consultant on subway station design. This was an exciting period of two years as a rebirth of Chicago School energy and spirit took hold again in the collaboration of engineers, architects and transit specialists despite the fact that everybody knew the whole project was redundant.

It was in the air that Chicago could advance the state of the art well beyond the San Francisco Bay area's splendid achievement with BART. Cars, tracks, system and station design were all cutting edge; particularly station design that I was most in touch with would set a new high in image consistency of architectural design, with iconic graphics both fixed and electronic celebrating the special character of each district. Sad to say it was not to be. I had a similar relationship to Mayor Daley's effort to redevelop the edges of the Chicago River from Lake Michigan all through the downtown loop. It too, could

not be carried out as matching federal funds were cut off in the Nixon administration.

There seemed more chance for real accomplishment in smaller scale downtown redevelopment. Along with Dick Forbes, an urban renovation consultant from San Francisco, I served as a design and master planning consultant in Kankakee, Chicago Heights and Downer's Grove all in the Chicago metropolitan area and downstate in Champaign, Bloomington and Marion.

All these projects consisted in consolidating a mosaic of property fragments into a temporary not-for-profit development corporation in order to carry out a master plan of improved traffic flow, urban landscape, parking, consolidated pedestrian spaces, preservation and new mixed use building all carrying out an appealing local identity theme. The main motivation of course was to counter the burgeoning threat of edge city shopping malls. Among these Kankakee turned out to be most successful in the long run in carrying through its plan. Others accomplished a start, like Downer's Grove, with its slogan "bring the Grove back to Downers," but most others suffered the same fate as across the country the automobile and urban sprawl sapped away the energy of saving downtowns. I believe the main lesson learned was that as complicated "multi-client" projects they took years to fulfill, beyond the patience and attention spans of our citizens in the late century's drift away from valuing its local pride of place in the face of media inflation, entertainment and increasing preoccupation with private quality of life rather than that of the overall public environment.

Exemplifying this trend in our culture as it affects individual civic architectural projects was my experience as designer of the new McLean county courthouse in Bloomington, Illinois. The city had already cleared a decaying area at the south edge of downtown as the site for the new building, an entire city block, so the prospect looked good that we could set a new high standard of design and construction most appropriate to the heritage of the community, long known as "the heart of the corn belt," a wealthy, healthy center of agriculture and cultural institutions in the Midwest. The old courthouse in the city's central square was to be restored and preserved as the county's historical museum.

After working on the design for several months with the firm in Bloomington: Ed Lundeen, Dean Hilfinger, Gene Asbury and Wade Abels and with Leb Woods in Champaign who had made a magnificent perspective rendering, I presented the design to the county board of supervisors building committee. The concept was based on an open ground floor plan for general public contact surrounded by a terraced urban park with courts on the "piano nobile" above, their solid limestone walls projecting and forming an overhang on all sides. Although very contemporary in design, the use of

limestone, carefully studied proportion, scale and details echoed and continued the same palette of materials in other important civic structures in the city: the old courthouse, the city auditorium, the city hall and the post office were all limestone. The committee's almost unanimous reaction "Too much money! Make it straight up and down and cut out the limestone!"

I went into a state of shock. Where were the good people I had known before on school, church and other committees who understood and supported architecture as an essential civic value? Gone, retired or passed away. Instead, the frowning faces were all new, much younger, and seemingly only interested in bottom line, "no nonsense" building. Ed Lundeen, at my side, was in shock too but quickly recovered informing the committee that the added cost for quality was only five to ten percent, but to no avail. What had happened? This change to pragmatism and insensitivity to quality architecture had been developing all along but to me it seemed to have occurred overnight. On further reflection I now think that this cultural change was the result of higher education evolving from mostly liberal arts in the first half of the century to a heavy majority of specialties in business, engineering, applied science, athletics and creature comforts, now the background of most building committees. I was so distressed that I couldn't see my way to compromise the project; Gene pitched in and carried on splendidly as the building was completed.

Robeson Crossing Shopping Plaza, Champaign, IL, 2007
Bruce Hutchings, Architect

Entry in Winter
Shakespeare Theatre, Ewing Manor, Bloomington, IL, 1990

Entry in Summer
Shakespeare Theatre, Ewing Manor, Bloomington, IL, 1990
Lundeen, Hilfinger, Asbury, Architects
Gene Asbury, Architect
(Photographs: Gene Astbury)

Interwoven with practice and education all along was participation in AIA and ACSA, the two organizations now separated even more as the spirit of interdisciplinary collaboration that was flourishing in the sixties faded away. AIA became more and more concerned with marketing and political activity at state and national levels and ACSA with specialization and tenure track pressures. As president of the Central Illinois Chapter AIA and the Illinois Council in the early seventies, I was definitely out of my element in all the intricacies of legal and organizational problems, relying on my staunch friends Fred Salogga and Jack Hartray who were so skillful in adroit political maneuvering and at AIA board meetings in Washington. But we did indulge in trying to dispel total preoccupation with dull business affairs by calling meetings in unusual settings and trying to address these new issues. I guess I was still on a Cadre de Vie high in sending out post cards for a special Central Illinois Chapter meeting in Lincoln's historic court room in Springfield (the post cards were of this room) and later for the Illinois Council state convention on the sixtieth floor of the as yet unfinished Sears tower in Chicago, with Father Andrew Greeley as our speaker. In both cases attendance broke records, no doubt partly because the setting was an abrupt change from the usual gathering in some hotel just like so many other organizations. Also the nature of the time was up front with its sense of what might now happen in the profession in the aftermath of Vietnam. I think many other architects had had recent experience similar to my own in facing a new kind of purely business oriented client who no longer appreciated (or understood) the historic legacy of architecture as a cultural value. In one way or another this basic change in practice took form in both formal and informal discussions, meeting agendas and conference themes, leading, I think, to an even greater separation between practice and academia which had had its beginnings earlier when the two organizations AIA and ACSA in the late sixties no longer met jointly for both local and national meetings.

This divergence in interest and direction was most evident when as Illinois Council president, I made frequent trips to AIA headquarters in Washington. Even though ACSA offices were also in the Octagon—educators were becoming more and more focused on specialization and individual advancement, while practitioners increasingly turned toward developing marketing skills in response to the public's drift away from Vitruvius' timeless regard of architecture as "firmness, commodity and delight" to "commodity, commodity, commodity."

Maybe prompted by the Martini lunches in the Octagon and at the risk of exaggeration, I also began to see how in other ways, despite so many changes in our professional lives, Washington bureaucracy remained much the same as I knew it, déjà vu, back in the Navy's Bureau of Ships at the end of World War II: it took some time to realize that if you really wanted to get something done, in wading through all the intricacies of office hierarchies, you might finally reach somebody who could and would take some action. It appeared, sad to say, that the ratio always turned out to be one in ten, unchanging over all those years.

Lest all this may seem too cynical, I must relate that these were also times of personal reward and rejoicing in making many new friends across the spectrum of university, social and professional life. In 1971 AIA colleagues nominated me for fellowship with the investiture taking place during the AIA convention in Detroit at the Art Museum. I was so pleased that my mother along with other close friends from home could be there. It so happened she was seated on the bus from the hotel with Louis Kahn and enjoyed her visit with him very much. Later when we met again at UIC in Chicago, Kahn remembered her clearly, astounded by her graciousness and fabulous memory, just as so many others had at home and across the country. We also had vivid recollections of other events at the convention, one a reception at Cranbrook, hosted by Glen Paulsen, then president of the Academy of Art. Glen was another old Illini friend and one of Eero Saarinen's key associates. Another memorable occasion was getting to know Jacques Barge from Paris, a new honorary FAIA. I had been assigned as one of his hosts at the convention and the next fall when I was in Versailles, was his guest for a dinner party in Paris that surely broke a record for endurance, reminding me of an earlier one at

Robert Le Ricolais' apartment and another long delightful evening at Jean Pierre Biron's house in the Place des Invalides. Jean Pierre was then president of U.P.3 in Versailles. The next morning he drove me to the airport for return home aboard an Air France flight. I had what the French call a monumental "cris de foie" (liver crisis or hangover). The stewardesses aboard the plane put me in the front seat just behind the first class section, offering tender loving care, along with choice morsels from first class all the way to Montreal.

A year or so later my dear friends in Chicago, Larry Perkins and Phil Will much to my surprise nominated me for the AIA/ACSA Topaz Medallion, the highest national honor for an educator/practitioner. I tried to persuade them that there were many others more deserving and that this honor seemed so far to be in recognition for leadership as deans just as FAIA had been for executive success over the years. They went ahead anyway as did a host of former students and colleagues but it was not to be. Still, just being nominated was enormously encouraging.

Book Cover for *Memos from Egypt* (Watercolor), 1975
Bill Caudill, FAIA

Sketch of *Mashrabiya* Wood Latice (Ink on Paper), Egypt, 1975
Bill Caudill, FAIA

These years of nomadic life, including many lucky encounters long before were now adding up to a realization that my treasury of friendships now embraced winners of five AIA Gold Medals: Bill Caudill, Fay Jones, Cesar Pelli, Charles Moore and Joe Esherick. This is the order in which I had the good fortune to meet each of them and to keep in touch ever since. No doubt this has happened to many others, too, but I like to think that it's unique in certain ways. The first is a simple matter of geography. As a Midwesterner one tends to reach out in all directions, perhaps more eager to learn than most others from the coasts, open to all influences, less opinionated and locked into elitist establishment thought. Another quest was to seek validation of what is truly American architecture, emerging as a new identity from our mix of multi-ethnic cultures, epitomized by the Chicago and Prairie Schools, free of sophisticated, imported ideologies. In reflecting on my luck in terms of time and place I've tried to sort out what this advantage has meant in singling out what each of these five Gold Medalists has contributed to our American architectural culture as distinct from influences from abroad.

Soon after I arrived to be on the faculty at Oklahoma State in 1937, I met Bill Caudill, who, as related earlier, had just graduated the year before and was working in Phil Wilber's supervising architect's office across the hall from the studio. Bill's design talent and most engaging personality was not only remarkably unique in his class but it was clear even then he would have a great future. At the time I must have been playing up the value of MIT's graduate program, especially for those of us from the hinterland, since I had just been there. Bill decided that's where he wanted to go too for graduate study and after completing his M.Arch degree moved on to the faculty at Texas A & M in Bryan Texas, beginning his now well known innovative studies and experimentation in school design, which were soon to attract national attention, leading him along with his partners into an enormously successful career in education, research and practice, forming the now famous firm of CRS (Caudill, Rowlett and Scott) also as a leader of Rice University's architectural program. All this is familiar history, so I want to try to point out perhaps lesser known qualities that contribute to what I believe lie near the heart of an ideal architectural practice in America.

When I first knew Bill he had just mastered control of a slight speech impediment of stuttering, which over the years, as I had known with Sam Chamberlin at MIT and Lin Brightbill at Illinois, tended to develop along with it an ever-smiling, self-deprecating modesty that was immediately heartwarming and memorable. It struck me as a quality that was also somehow implicitly respectful to others, carrying with it a marvelous and disarming sense of humor. In fact, some years later Bill became known as "the Will Rogers of architecture." Many times later when I happened to run into Bill in so many different places, for meetings, panels, once by chance when we were both in the Navy in Sasebo, Japan. I could tell it was this rare combination of extraordinary but ego free architectural talent and an honest, genuinely charming manner that had gained for him his personal fame and fame for American architecture on its own as it reflected the element of human compassion possible and most evident in a true democracy: in schools, hospitals and other civic institutions. Now, we have to ask, can these qualities survive in the face of rampant materialism? Bill's Gold Medal now is in a special glass display case in the reception area of Oklahoma State's architectural school, as a quiet reminder and mentor to the students and faculty that has no doubt been a major inspiration for them as they have gained a national reputation for mixing exceptional design talent with hard work, quiet responsibility, easy-going openness and friendliness.

It was only a few years after World War II that I met Fay Jones. As with Bill Caudill it was the Oklahoma State connection that did it. In my first studio at OSU, also in 1937, one of my students was John "Gibby" Williams. As I related earlier "Gibby" was the founder of the School of Architecture at the University of Arkansas at Fayetteville soon after World War II sixty years ago. Fay was one of his first students who after graduating spent some time with Frank Lloyd Wright at Taliesin before returning to Fayetteville to join the faculty and begin his own practice

on the side, often with Gibby. But usually they were on their own designing houses in that rocky, forested Ozark Mountain landscape, a most fortuitous circumstance for their Prairie School influence to flourish. Sometime in the fifties "Gibby" (by then he had asked everybody to call him John) invited me to come down for three days as a visiting critic. It was so good to see him again and to meet Faye, his wife, and Fay and his wife Gus, along with their faculty, students and friends. It was very much the same spirit of laid back friendliness I had felt in Stillwater; everything informal with no sense of rush and exacting time schedules.

The first day John and Fay wanted to show me their work around town and in the nearby countryside. I was struck with both the amount and quality of their work, all highly integrated with each site, nestled into rock outcroppings, pines, using natural materials almost exclusively, respecting views, sun shading and exquisite detailing of stone work, beam structure, cabinetry and outdoor/indoor garden landscape. Nowhere else I had ever traveled in America revealed a more harmonious organic response to indigenous settings in enough quantity to be so impressive as a whole except the summer community I've already spoken of at Desbarats Ontario that grew around Wright's Pitkin house on Sapper Island. (p.12) What contributed even more to this impression was the number of other houses of the same character by independent builders, whose carpenters and masons had worked on

Thorncrown Chapel, Eureka Springs, Arkansas
Fay Jones, FAIA, Architect
(Drawing by John Womack during design process)

214

Pacific Design Center: Final Phase (Rendering), Los Angeles, 2007

Pacific Design Center: Final Phase (Watercolor), Los Angeles, 2007
Pelli, Clarke, Pelli Architects
Cesar Pelli, FAIA, Architect

houses by Fay and John. I thought this was a story worth national attention since it was so rare with few other communities like it across the country. But as far as I know this unusual extent of an architect's influence has never received the publicity it deserves.

From then on Fay's practice flourished as is now so well known, carrying the Wright and Prairie School influence to even richer levels of refinement in the use of light, detailing and seamlessness with landscape, with the Thorncrown Chapel now recognized as a masterpiece, on everybody's list of the ten best examples of modern architecture in the world.

Ever since that first experience in Fayetteville I would meet Fay and Gus when our paths crossed at Illinois and on other campuses, at FAIA convocations at AIA conventions, at the American Academy in Rome and in Tucson as one of Fay's hosts. With the same spirit of joyful modesty, like Bill Caudill, Fay has enriched the smaller scales of residential and spiritual architecture as Bill brought these qualities of humaneness and grace to the larger dimensions of American educational and health care settings across the country.

My friendship with Cesar Pelli goes back to 1951 when he came from Argentina to graduate school at Illinois when Am Richardson was in charge of the program and I was often involved for crits, reviews and informal gatherings. As I remarked earlier Cesar spent the summer of 1952 working with me

in Bloomington on a rural electric cooperative headquarters, revealing to all of us his superb design talent in sensitivity to scale, proportion and refinement of ensemble harmonics that was later to be the extraordinary, and singular character of his work, like that of Eero Saarinen, responding to each new project in terms of its potential to be uniquely excellent on its own terms.

Of all the many foreign students I've known, who have made their careers in America, Cesar has embraced the true nature of our culture more than anyone else, in fully valuing and respecting every other team player in a given project including fellow professionals, clients and the wellbeing of the public at large. I was reminded again of Asplund's charge long ago in Stockholm and Aalto's in Helsinki that extra effort in refinement of detail should honor the anonymous public as if they were family.

I think too often architects come to this country as prima donnas from Europe or elsewhere, whether to become citizens or on commissions for individual projects, even more so in recent years, either not fully understanding the dynamic of American team playing or ignoring it to do their own thing, make their gesture and leave it up to local associates to make it into architecture. In a complete opposite way Cesar's gentle nature and superb talent as did Saarinen's set the pace of excellence for all others to follow, demonstrating that the essence and mission of a new world culture like America is to advance the quality of the multi-ethnic human condition through architecture that mirrors and brings together the best we know of each component of all separate systems involved in the design process.

In a very different way Charles Moore brought a new dimension to this quest. He had perhaps a drier, more ironic sense of humor than that of Bill Caudill's, but in its own way was just as compassionate. I had always had the impression that Ivy League wit and literacy tended to serve itself, like art for art's sake, rather than larger social consequence and benefit. Charles and his partner Bill Turnbull, as graduates of Princeton somehow managed to bring the quality of literacy more positively into their work with less irony, perhaps leavened by California's "love in there" mix of exuberance and caring. I first knew Charles in 1960 at the AIA/ACSA convention in San Francisco/Berkeley, through my Illinois friend Harold Young's connection to Princeton which led us to be guests for a party at Charles' house in Orinda and also at other informal gatherings in Berkeley, including the now famous one at Bill Wurster and Katherine Bauer's house. (p. 183)

Charles was from Benton Harbor Michigan and graduate of the architectural school in Ann Arbor before going to Princeton and on to San Francisco. I guess the fact that we both had the Great Lakes in our blood and were bachelors free to enjoy a semi-nomadic life mixing education and practice

was the main basis of our rapport as friends, often meeting in various places for lectures and seminars, at Gerry Gast's off-campus program in San Francisco, at Cranbrook and AIA/ACSA gatherings like AIA Wisconsin's annual design conference where we, along with Jean Paul Carliahn from Boston, were jurors and performers in a symposium titled "Form, Function and Delight." Being the straight man in the trio I was assigned to Function, Jean Paul did Form and Charles Delight. Another time Charles and I were guest lecturers at Washington University in St. Louis inventing and presenting our versions of what it means in society for an architect to be among those few in our culture who think and act subjunctively, that is to have both the privilege and responsibility always to deal with the future, in terms of what could, might or should be. (p. 19, 158) Though we were in earnest, it was clear that this kind of literary metaphor was fragile or borderline in being taken seriously. Indeed this borderline between whimsy vs. seriousness seemed to underline the whole Post Modern movement, the Piazza d' Italia in New Orleans becoming the focus of this architectural ambiguity. This is the one issue that in my view diminishes Charles' great contribution to the intelligence, gentleness and humaneness of American architecture, that for a time seemed to be taking hold.

When one thinks again of the Californianess of America, either California as the foreshadow of and major influence of what the whole country may be or vice versa, architecture

FOREWORD

One of the basic human requirements is the need to dwell, and one of the central human acts is the act of inhabiting, of connecting ourselves, however temporarily, with a place on the planet which belongs to us, and to which we belong. This is not, especially in the tumultuous present, an easy act (as is attested by the uninhabited and uninhabitable no-places in cities everywhere), and it requires help: we need allies in inhabitation.

Fortunately, we have at hand many allies, if only we call on them; other upright objects, from towers to chimneys to columns, stand in for us in sympathetic imitation of our own upright stance. Flowers and gardens serve as testimonials to our own care, and breezes loosely captured can connect us with the very edge of the infinite. But in the West our most powerful ally is light. "The sun never knew how wonderful it was," the architect Louis Kahn said, "until it fell on the wall of a building." And for us the act of inhabitation is mostly performed in cahoots with the sun, our staunchest ally, bathing our world or flickering through it, helping give it light.

It comes with the thrill of a slap for us then to hear praise of shadows and darkness; so it is when there comes to us the excitement of realizing that musicians everywhere make their sounds to capture silence or that architects develop complex shapes just to envelop empty space. Thus darkness illuminates for us a culture very different from our own; but at the same time it helps us to look deep into ourselves to our own inhabitation of our world, as it describes with spine-tingling insights the traditional Japanese inhabitation of theirs. It could change our lives.

Charles Moore
School of Architecture, UCLA

Book Cover for In Praise of Shadows by Jun'ichiro Tanizaki
Foreword by Charles Moore, FAIA

Interior, Romano House, 1970
Jospeh Esherick, FAIA, Architect
(Photograph: Henry Plummer)

has been its mirror, with two reflecting faces: L.A. and the San Francisco Bay area. We have already considered at some length the post World War II surge of innovative modern dwellings around L.A., the Case Study House initiative and the fresh new development of more various building types in the Bay area. This has included the influence of schools, mainly USC, Cal Poly at San Louis Obispo and Berkeley locked almost inseparably with practice. As this whole movement gained momentum into the later part of the century we came to know more and more about the architects who were leaders in the smooth flow from early pioneers like the Green brothers, Maybeck, Neutra, and Schindler, then Wurster, De Mars and their counterparts in landscape architecture, like Garrett Eckbo, then the Sea Ranch team of Moore Turnbull, Lyndon and Joe Esherick who in many ways personified the excitement and broadening influence of the whole team not only in California but across the country and abroad. My friendship with Joe Esherick began when we both were on a jury in St. Paul, Minnesota in 1986, to select an architect for the new Appellate Court building adjoining the State Capitol. It was a large jury with other Californians, who along with Joe enlivened our breaks between sessions as wine experts. Everybody turned to Joe for final choices as we did when it came time for selecting the competition winner among the five finalists, which was the firm of Leonard Parker. This whole event turned out to be even more memorable a few years later as the building when completed was an exact

fulfillment of the presentation drawings and model, an almost unheard of outcome in the whole history of architectural competitions.

While we were together in St. Paul, Joe and I realized that our work had been published in the June 1964 issue of Progressive Architecture, two of his houses in the Bay area and mine in Champaign, Illinois, the one of his in Oakland featured on the cover of the magazine. In the next few years after our meeting on the jury, I visited Joes's office in San Francisco several times, once after the 1989 earthquake when their building, which had escaped major damage was undergoing dramatic interior steel X bracing. In this interim of time Joe had agreed to come to Illinois as a Plym Professor, visiting for several weeks at different intervals during a semester, as had Gunner Birkerts and Paul Rudolph in preceding years. Since I was already emeritus, Henry Plummer served most ably as his host and as long as I was in town I could join in on the side for critiques and most stimulating informal gatherings in a variety of unusual settings, much as we had enjoyed in our earlier Cadre de Vie experiments. Henry's depth and sensitivity in the study of light through exquisite photography in Japan and elsewhere, including some of Joe's work gave us a central theme to speculate about as unmet opportunities in design, especially as it could be demonstrated in our mid-continent culture learning from the far east and the Pacific Rim, as was already exemplified by the best work on our west coast, Joe's firm among the leaders.

Very much like Fay Jones, whenever Joe would discuss his own work, his answers to questions and comments were always modest, direct, unassuming, finding the easiest understandable phrases linked as much as possible with drawing. Again, like Cesar, Saarinen and Louis Kahn you felt at once a deep respect for a client's needs and the underlying often unspoken special ingredients to be encountered within each new intervention in respect to its natural setting as well as its larger context.

I think this quest for an ever deeper understanding of guidelines and inherent qualitative potential, along with consciousness of what it means in America is the common denominator, along with superb talent that has merited the Gold Medal Award to each of these five I had the privilege to know. I want to emphasize too, that they all have been leaders in architectural education as well, a legacy I fear may no longer exist in these days when international stardom and signature styles seem to be overwhelming the timeless ethic of architecture as an expression of human learning, ne plus ultra.

Much as these five AIA Gold Medalists have merited this recognition, there are, have been and will be others who in their own way have and may enrich the world of architecture over their lifetimes in their own regions or in terms of some breakthrough detail, in the use of light, energy, structural technology or in the larger context of orchestrating new harmonies of ensemble design.

I would nominate my old friend Larry Perkins as an exemplary candidate for this particular as yet unnamed honor. Although Larry was both an inheritor and leader in advancing the heritage of the Chicago and Prairie Schools, he has added so much more through his deep warmth and caring in each dimension of his life, as a partner of one of the largest firms in Chicago, as an artist architect and as an interpreter whether between professional associates, public officials, contractors, clients or Illinois students in Versailles on sketch trips that he and his wife Midge led for so many years. Perhaps more than anyone else he personified the human, compassionate dimension of Chicago's great contribution to modern architecture in America and to the world. It was clear, for example, that Perkins and Will of all the large Chicago firms was most unique in its organization as a collection of small firms instead of and in contrast to the singularity and uniform hierarchies of SOM, Holabird and Root, C. F. Murphy, Mies Van der Rohe and with few exceptions everywhere else in the U. S. and abroad. It was really a model for

the very small number of others that later became known like Bill Caudill's firm, CRS in Houston. In fact, in a way Larry and Bill were friendly enemies and keen competitors which in the end only intensified still more their joint achievement in advancing the design of many different building types, especially educational and health facilities, to new heights of quality. The idea of small offices under one umbrella implicitly reflected the extra measure of attention given to each project through closer personal client contact, with contractors and workmen on the job, becoming another iteration, as with the work of Saarinen, of excellence in diversity— no cookie cutter stamp-outs of the kind now so prevalent by both large and small firms specializing in schools or whatever else, using fast-track computer technology and bottom line money-making priorities that overwhelm timeless architectural values.

But on a personal level, I have other reasons to consider Larry a hero. He was an avid sailor with the Great Lakes his domain, as captain of Allegro, a magnificent 43-foot Alden designed schooner out of Belmont Harbor Chicago and Charlevoix, Michigan. For many years he, Midge and crew would sail much of the upper Great Lakes, becoming widely known as a veteran of Lake Superior, the most challenging of all. In the mid seventies he was Commodore of the Great Lakes Cruising Club, the most eminent of all associations embracing the entire lake system. It was then I had the luck to be one of his crew several times, in Lake Superior

and the North Channel archipelago, all waters I already knew well from childhood. Of all the many sea stories I could tell of these voyages, ports and rendezvous, the most memorable is the quiet morning ritual, after getting underway, of Midge appearing in the companionway, notebook in hand, addressing us in the cockpit, "now, please give me your thoughts," Before long all of us in the crew, usually no more than three or four, learned to be prepared, not too seriously with anything heavy but in a certain mix that was both light-hearted and as deep as you cared to make of it. This usually resulted in something poetic or an apt quote that fit some recent happening, like on a calm hot day, a line from Coleridge's Ancient Mariner:

As idle as a painted ship
Upon a painted ocean
Water, water, everywhere,
And all the boards did shrink;
Water, water, everywhere,
Nor any drop to drink.

This brought a laugh since there's no more drinkable water anywhere than that of Lake Superior. In fact when as a child on arrival in Sault Ste Marie for the summer, the first thing my grandfather would say was, "Here! Have a glass of Lake Superior water, the purest in the world!"

I think Midge's idea was really to make a segue or metaphor from something routine or commonplace into a larger or deeper meaning, just as she was always asking the

Versailles students for historic reference or for signification beyond the immediate impression of a sketch or painting. I recalled Professor Cali's quest for more profound learning in Cadre de Vie settings. I'm sure this kind of blue water experience awakened again more vividly yet the desire of getting to the root of causes and perceptions from even a trivial source or circumstance, that might trigger and inspire the recurring question, so what might it signify or portend in the larger realm of philosophy? Naturally for us the focus evoked would be something within the broad scope of architecture or in wider dimension, the entire world of design as it might now imply more enlightened benefit to the human condition and environmental ethic.

From this lofty perch I found myself saying to myself, "Get off your high horse and be more specific!" Right at hand was the same notion I had had before but in another new form. I now have to get beyond the joy and experience of designing and building small boats like the KAIMOΣ series into larger craft, not at the scale of Larry's "Allegro" but at least as seaworthy, in order to enjoy and learn more about the Great Lakes archipelago and at the same time keep on with the quest of learning more about architecture by designing and building in another medium, an endeavor that I had tried to clarify earlier on. (p. 13, 55, 81, 184.)

This inspiration led to building "Osimo" (meaning "escape" in Ojibway) a 40' motor sailer, a steel hull modified from the lines of a commercial fishing trawler. The best builder of this type vessel in the upper lakes was Dale Vinette in Escanaba, Michigan at the north end of Green Bay. For two years I worked with Dale and his crew along with my own helpers Tom Paxton, Paul Rushing and Scott Morris for a launching in August 1977 and a shakedown cruise to Neebish Island. Thereafter for seventeen summers aboard cruising the archipelago was first based from Neebish Island then from the eighties on at St. Ignace, "the center of the freshwater world" (a rather flippant answer to those who have no idea of St. Ignace's location or of the Straits of Mackinac, for that matter). St. Ignace is an ideal harbor, a quiet, central, convenient base for "gunkholing" in the exquisite but sometimes threatening waters of the archipelago stretching from northern Lake Michigan, the entire north shores of Lake Huron, mostly in Canadian water. Each of the seventeen summers was different, not only in finding new courses, channels, ports and anchorages but most of all with changing crews, mainly former students and close friends like Tom Paxton, Jeff Tock, Mark Romack, Jim Grey, Bob De Haven, Tait Johnson or local friends like Charlie and Mike Lillequist, Tim Collins, Annette Theut, the Vining family and Kel Keller from Neebish. I really have to think of these voyages as informal, delightful seminars as much as simply pleasure cruises. The fact that most of my longer time crew members were related to architecture in some way tended to be another version of studio and

I'm absolutely sure I learned more from each of them than vice versa. In retrospect it was the human dimension of learning more about architecture—ensemble design and performance interlocked.

The design of "Osimo" was innovative in certain ways. You quickly learn, at some risk, how much you can or should not deviate from the tested principles of hull design and powering systems (both sail and motor). Some ideas worked, others did not. For example while cruising with Larry aboard "Allegro" I asked why couldn't something be done about trying to steer from the aft cockpit with all the masts, rigging and deck appurtenances blocking a straight ahead view (with all due respect for classical schooner design)? So this desire for greater visibility led to rigging an A frame mast pinned aft of the cockpit so the view was entirely open ahead and on each side. With a large single Genoa type sail it was also very easy to come about on a tack. The original idea to rig a mizzen sail as well proved cumbersome. A few other details such as teak strips epoxied to the steel deck that would tend to come loose required more maintenance than anticipated but on the whole most of the design decisions worked out well. Probably the most enduring lesson learned was that before making any final set of choices, either in architecture or boat design, its' wise to take a closer look at time-tested assemblies and systems in terms of their balance with innovative ideas. Of course this should not imply retreat to superficial stylistic traditions—the

OSIMO is a composite of several objectives, with highest priority on ruggedness of construction, sea keeping ability, high visibility and control from the helm, spaciousness and livability below decks and economy of operation and maintenance. A 360 gallon diesel fuel capacity with a Perkins 4-236 85 h.p. diesel provide a 1440 statute mile cruising range.

The double-headed sail plan with its "A Frame" mast augments the diesel propulsion for motorsailing when sea and wind conditions permit reaching, broad reaching and down wind sailing. The "A Frame" mast improves visibility forward and latterally from the cockpit, permits single sheeting of the main headsail and facilitates lowering the mast for low bridge clearances, so that the cockpit and helm are unemcumbered. The mast when lowered becomes the structure for a large canopy protecting the entire deck when in tropical harbors for longer periods.

The advantages of a steel hull and flush deck are obvious in providing great strength, an uncluttered deck and great spaciousness with full headroom below. The main transverse frames on 3 foot centers of "Bulb Bar" construction are exposed the full length of the interior. The weather deck is teak, laid in one inch wide strips with a 3/8 inch gap, adhered to the steel deck with a special black epoxy adhesive. Cockpit coaming, deck lockers and toe rails are also teak; as are the overhead, engine compartment panelling, navigation and galley counters below.

The cabin sole is black rubber disc "Norament", made in West Germany, laid on removable steel plating. Mast, lifeline, stanchions and bow pulpit are aluminum. Steel rod rigging is used instead of wire.

The interior arrangement consists of a combination forward cabin and companionway, a great cabin aft with walk-through passages containing the galley and navigation area on each side of the engine compartment. The head is recessed into the starboard side of the engine space. Hanging lockers are under the forward cabin bunk platform where the depth of the forefoot permits it. Storage is continuous under benches and counters on each side and in the lazarette under the great cabin bunk platform. Three hatch-skylights and a large transom portlight daylight the interior. Glazing of these openings is of ½" solar gray plexiglass.

OSIMO

port of
neebish island, michigan

The name "OSIMO" means escape in the Ojibway (Chippewa) language. Using Ojibway names is an old tradition of the Uppe Lakes.

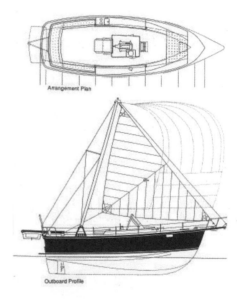

Arrangement Plan

Outboard Profile

Statistics:

Length Overall	39' - 8
Waterline Length	35' - 3
Beam	14' - 6
Draft	4' - 0
Displacement	31,000 Lbs.
Ballast	8,000 Lbs.
Sail Area:	
Main Headsail	500 S.F.
Mizzen Staysail	150 S.F.
Power: Perkins 4-236 Diesel	85 H.P.
Reduction Gear	2.54
Propeller: Bronze	26 Dia. - 17" Pitch
Cruising Speed @1800 RPM	8 M.P.H.
Radio	Horizon - 25
Depth Finder	Aqua Probe
Compass	Ritchie B-60
Anchor Winch	Selectric 519
Fresh Water	90 Gallons
Fuel	360 Gallons
Sails	Murphy & Nye, Chicago
Builder	T. O. Vinette Co., Marine Division 2201 6th Ave., N. Escanaba, MI 49829
Owner-Designer	A. Richard Williams, FAIA Architect

lesson should, I believe, direct more critical attention to how largely invisible sets of systems work well together and will ultimately become outwardly perceivable, even beautiful, especially as these qualities of superior design are revealed through performance.

Blue water horizons, aside from provoking new inward-looking synergies of design, more obviously open up wider vision and interpretation of the world around us, signified by landmarks and seamarks ahead. Navigating either in the archipelago or in wider seas is a constant reminder of one's time passage through life. In certain light conditions mirages will appear, islands way beyond earth curvature sight lines will show themselves in profile in exact bearing as on charts, passing ships miles away on the horizon may have giant bows and miniature sterns, low buildings on shore will suddenly become high rise structures and in open water ahead the earth's curvature will be vividly revealed. During all these years and ever after driving on highways too, took on this same sense of navigation, whether across prairies or in mountainous terrain; a game of recognition, estimating distances and heights, direction by the sun or stars, reflecting on what lies beyond and imagining such prospects as historic events and as once perceived by travelers in covered wagons or centuries before by migrating Native Americans. The game could as well take flight spotting rivers, lakes, mountain peaks, cities and towns by both day and night, aided by the same time, speed distance

measures gained by the experience of sailing by dead reckoning.

This return to life in the Great Lakes archipelago as experienced in childhood but now, in the much wider dimension of space, glorious as it was could not slow down the passage of time. Legend has it that all sailors should go ashore by the age of eighty, at least retire from being captains of larger vessels. Rather than selling Osimo, I donated her to Lake Superior State University at Sault Ste Marie for their underwater research program, feeling this future respected the existence will of a vessel of her character, much as a work of architecture might face a new life of adapted reuse. But of course my addiction to smaller craft design, building and summer life on the water could go on.

Having been based in St. Ignace for so long, the blessings of new friendships there and familiarity with the realities of life on shore, greatly enhanced knowing more about the lore of history and magic of the Straits of Mackinac area, and made the transition of moving ashore easier, even welcoming. My good friend Charlie Lilliquist, many times my crew aboard Osimo, offered to let me build a studio on his property on the Lake Michigan southwest facing shore just two miles west of the Mackinac bridge, at Point La Barbe in a magnificent stretch of northern white cedar grove so typical of the dolomite limestone geologic underlayment of that part of Michigan's Upper Peninsula. This offer of Charlie's led to building Singassin in 1993

View from Lake Michigan Side
Singassin (Ojibwa: *song born on the wind)*, St. Ignace, MI,
A. Richard Williams, FAIA, Architect

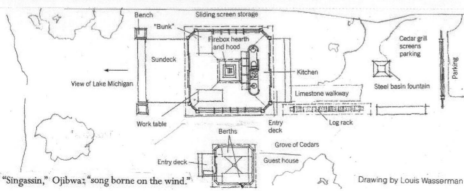

"Singassin," Ojibwa: "song borne on the wind."

Singassin, St. Ignace, MI,
A. Richard Williams, FAIA, Architect
(Photograph: Rob Karossi, Drawing: Louis Wasserman)

overlapping with the last summer of living aboard Osimo.

This began a new kind of existence yet reminiscent of years before at Neebish—the passing ships offshore were the same but further out in the seaway, now at vaster scale, the open lake stretching out to the west—you could easily imagine that 330 miles southwest over the horizon lay Chicago, the home port of the great fleet of sailboats that would annually sail by flying colorful spinnakers on their last leg to Mackinac Island seven miles east. We had our own fleet of small craft and could go out to greet them if it wasn't too rough. However, very different from Neebish in its sheltered archipelago setting, ours was an open weather shore, in the prevailing westerly winds the breakers would come crashing in, at times intimidating and threatening, especially in high water cycles.

Without fully realizing it, life in St. Ignace gradually began to take on a new dimension beyond that of a pure vacation. Among my closest early friends there the Maurer family, Wes senior and Margaret, Wes junior and Mary were the first to ask me to help in their building projects. Wes senior who had had a great career as head of the journalism school at Ann Arbor had early on initiated a summer internship on Mackinac Island to publish the weekly Town Crier newspaper for the summer season. After spending summers on the island for a number of years, Wes and Margaret decided to retire in St. Ignace, buying a house there and the St. Ignace News which included a general printing business as well. At the end of my very first summer season aboard Osimo, I met Wes when he had the newspaper and printing office in a storefront close to the St. Ignace marina. Just before leaving for winter storage of Osimo in Escanaba, Wes came aboard asking if I could design the remodeling of a larger building he had acquired. So after returning to Champaign I worked on this project which turned out to be a simple and straightforward plan of offices and ample workspace. We decided to use native rough-sawn cedar inside and out which not only simplified the work but seemed to please everybody with its feeling of belonging to the region and with its surprisingly pleasing aroma which even to this day retains its fragrance. Little did I realize then that this small task done, as all of us do from time to time, might later lead to other work as it did years after, not only for Wes and Margaret on Mackinac Island but for Wes junior and Mary as well, then the Wellman family on La Salle Island in the Les Chenneaux archipelago and eventually to the new St. Ignace Public Library. It took quite a while to think of all this more relaxing architectural engagement in the same way as it had been in Illinois mixed with life in academia. It was a very different feeling to be both a sailor and architect at the same time in such a salubrious water world, at such a small scale level of "hands on," working directly with local builders, all of whom were such a delight to be with because they were so skillful and dedicated

to their craft, being survivors in a long term impoverished economy except for tourism. Even tourism was unpredictable in the ups and downs of the economy everywhere else. I've often reminded students after this kind of experience that you don't really, truly feel like an architect until your own effort is understood in direct proportion of the appreciation you feel for the skill, I would even say the art of experienced carpenters, masons and all those other sincere capable people at work on each project.

Cruising the upper Great Lakes brought back memories of travel with my parents in our Hudson Super Six with the Lippman trailer in 1924 and 1925 following the same north shore of Lake Huron to Lake Nippising, North Bay then connecting with the Ottawa River all the way to Ottawa and Montreal; visiting our Canadian relatives along the way. Remembering the enchanting feeling of wilderness as endless forests, lakes and islands as they stretched all the way to the North Pole, I was tempted to recapture again this magnetism by driving the same road as before, this time as if to complete the total impression of landscape and waterscape together as one. Canada, like Alaska, Siberia, northern Russia, Finland, Sweden and Norway possesses this wonder of edgeness with the North, somehow most poignantly felt from the bluff of Canada's parliament complex in Ottawa overlooking the river below and vast unspoiled space beyond. The urban centers of Ottawa, Montreal, Quebec, Winnipeg, Calgary, Edmonton and Vancouver east and

Interior View with "Fire Lantern"

*Niji (*Ojibwa: *Small Companion)* Guest Cabin

View from waterfront
Singassin, St. Ignace, MI,
A. Richard Williams, FAIA, Architect
(Photographs: Rob Karossi)

west across the country all have this aura, each in their own way, maybe because Ottawa is the capital with its elevated prospect I feel this elation strongest there.

I'm sure my own special feeling for Canada comes from my father's side of the family. His forbearers came from Wales to Canada in the early eighteen hundreds; Richard Williams, after selling his commission as a captain in the British merchant marine immigrated to Peterborough and the family spread out from there, to Montreal, Toronto, Owen Sound, Orilla, and other cities out west. As I related earlier, I have over the years been closest to the Edmisons. My grand aunt Jennifer married Ralph Edmison and their son Ralph became a dentist settling in Montreal. It was his daughter and son Ruth and Sandy and their families who I've had the pleasure of knowing ever since my first trip to Europe in 1938. Ruth married John Lewis, who became head of a most successful accounting firm based in Montreal—their son John Jr. and daughters Betsie, Barry and Claire all remained in the Montreal area, too. I think Ruth was a true Anglophile and it took some time for her to adjust to her three girls all marrying French-Canadians. But all three of them have had remarkable careers. Betsie's husband Pierre Boudreau became a justice in the Quebec Supreme Court, Barry's a renowned aeronautic engineer and Claire's, Pierre LaLonde, a famous Quebec pop star. I became closest to Betsie and Pierre because Betsie as a librarian was so instrumental in building up the library of

the Canadian Center for Architecture (CCA) under the sponsoring leadership of Phyllis Lambert.

Much as I would visit the Notre Dame architecture program and the American Academy in Rome on irregular but repeating intervals of time in the remaining years of the century, I would take a break from sailing and summer living in Michigan's "water wonderland" to cross into Canada for reunions with my dear cousins Ruth and Ed Hook at Llewellyn Beach who together with their son Paul, and daughter Ruth junior, Richard and their family would be vacationing from their homes in New Jersey. Occasionally, too, I would stay with them in New Jersey while on trips to New York for ARC meetings or events in New York of the American Academy in Rome. Their wonderful family, like the Lewises in Montreal reflect, epitomize and foster the joy of combining in another way one's desire to mix friendship with intellectual and professional stimulation in unique networks, each one of singular character.

This networking through Canada and Montreal would also often include most pleasant visits with Gee Gee Robinson, my old friend from Champaign/Urbana who has had a fascinating career as head of the communications department at McGill University. We would reminisce about old days in Urbana when Jack Baker and I had designed her house, of our meetings in Belgrade, Rome and once in Frankfurt. It just happened that these Montreal visits would also interlock

with flying on to Paris, to Versailles or to Beth and Olu Heudebourg's unforgettable wedding in Culan and of my recuperation from "cris de foie" aboard a returning Air France flight following Jean Pierre Biron's farewell dinner in Paris.

The blue water link to Montreal in summer would usually happen when John and Ruth Lewis would be in residence at Hudson Heights on the Ottawa river about 20 miles west of Montreal and with Sandy and Ingrid Edmison next door. It was just my luck that twice I would arrive on the very day of the annual lobster fest at the Yacht Club, with John junior and Phyllis there too aboard their cabin cruiser "Tumblehome" from Kingston. Sadly, though, in the next year or two Ruth passed away and Sandy and Ingrid's daughter lost her life in an auto accident. Tragedy for the family deepened still more when Betsie died of an aneurysm soon after that.

My memory of Betsie remains so vivid not only of her gracious and charming personality, and of her family; her husband Pierre, Charles and Julie, their son and daughter now both successful lawyers, but for her special contribution to the CCA library which I was to visit several times later. Once when I happened to be there in the elevator at the same time by chance with Phyllis Lambert, I introduced myself as Betsie's cousin, relating how much I missed her. Phyllis insisted I linger long enough so she too could express how deeply she had valued and loved Betsie, with a warmth that I might not have expected since Phyllis was so well known for her strong, disciplined character as chief executive and benefactor of the CCA.

The CCA is a really most remarkable institution not only for its library, which I understand is the most complete architectural library in the world but also for its resources of study space for scholars and its world class exhibitions and publications. It is in the same league with both Sweden and Finland's architectural museums and libraries as they reflect peaks in the world of architecture as a national cultural value.

The last time I saw Betsie before her death was at the CCA in the summer of 1994 when I was on my way to Nantucket Island to take part in a symposium there at the National Preservation Institute on issues of coastal conservation, covering the broad scope of ecology, history, literature, human encroachment, threatening forces of nature and possible avenues of effective local, regional and national planning. I happened to be the first presenter, having the assignment of discussing the Great Lakes coastlines, their lore, present state and future destiny. At no other time in my life up to then and since have I ever experienced a more moving, diverse, eloquent, knowledgeable set of presentations by the some thirty of us there from all walks of life, the whole revealing how fragile our best know-how, experience and ingenuity is in the face of both nature's wrath and man's exploitation. As we sometimes think of certain brief episodes

in our lives as most poignant in distilling the essence of many meaningful events over much longer time spans, this one stands out for me, linking the glowing memory of Betsie as she personifies the treasure and fragility of both architecture and human life, with the glories and fragility of the Great Lakes and their blue water horizons.

From now on in this narrative, I find that recollections and the musings they generate will overlap and intertwine more and more. Two very different paths and spaces for living were evolving in parallel, causing one to move with the seasons like other forms of wild life. In response to the new freedom to design time, the annual signals of migration took command. Within the borders of the United States I don't think you can find two more contrasting regions than the Straits of Mackinac, the "center of the fresh water world," in the lush, forested green/blue expanse of the Great Lakes and the bone-dry brown/red/purple/grey green high deserts of Arizona, with Tucson at the heart of the Sonoran islands in the sky. This tale will now flow back and forth between these archipelagos, skip-stop, fast-forward, flash-back as the networks of learning take new form.

Celebrating the new freedom of retirement in the winter of 1970-71, I set out for Mexico in a new Camaro with my good friend Jack Baker. Starting out from Santa Fe we headed to Acapulco down Mexico's center spine through San Miguel Allende, Mexico City and Cuernavaca. After a few days relaxing at the Boca Chica in Acapulco, enjoying its sheltered cove for swimming and snorkeling, Jack had to fly home because of his father's illness. I soon began a leisurely drive back north through Taxco, Morelia, Guadalajara, Puerta Vallarta, Mazatlan and Guymas on the west coast re-entering the U. S. at Nogales, Arizona. This long stretch along the Pacific shore, alternating sweeping vistas of beaches and vast emptiness with sudden, intense city congestion sharply reminded me of Navy days in the South Pacific archipelago during World War II, in the way it prompted thoughts and memories of tranquility, silence and solitude for days on end, in high contrast to the vivid compaction, climaxing and chaos of war making or with blinding storms and treacherous seas.

These thoughts could easily switch to sailing on the Great Lakes too and the extreme range of emotional contrasts from sheer bliss to utter terror. Times like these weave and warp between reality and as they live again in dreams. I'm sure the slow, languid days of returning north up the coast of Mexico, enthralling and provoking as they were in turn, prompted or at least hinted for the first time at the idea of planning life ahead in two very different landscapes and seascapes moving

in harmony with the rhythm of the seasons, and as the great mythologist Joseph Campbell advised, to "follow your bliss," dismissing all worries from one's thoughts.

This hint, or premonition, came more sharply in focus as I was warmly greeted in Tucson by Chuck and Claire Albanese, Chuck now on the faculty of the University of Arizona who then began to suggest that I might become a "snowbird," (local slang for spending winters in the glorious desert climate of the Sonora). What had before been a vague notion of some other charismatic place as a winter destination in complement to summers in the "center of the fresh water world," now became precise. Each vision of other magnetic places like Hawaii, the Caribbean, the Mediterranean, or even far away Tahiti was of course already clear from travel over the years, but taken together they were kaleidoscopic and indecisive as to which might be most appealing as a personal choice. But now I realized, thanks to Chuck and Claire, that ties like friendship and cultural continuity in one's life count just as much if not more in choosing where to dwell in winter, beyond the attraction of salubrious weather and scenography.

But this first visit to Tucson, occurring as it did at the beginning of my mission of gathering information and seeking interviews with authorities on the west coast while on the National Academy of Science committee, (that I described on P. 205) postponed any choice of a winter residence well into

Il Duomo, Firenze, Italy (Watercolor), 2005
Charles A. Albanese, FAIA (Dean CALA, U. of Arizona)

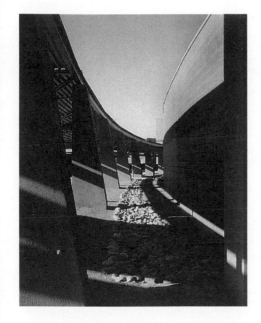

School, Vail, AZ, 1992
Albanese Brooks Associates, Architecture and Planning
Charles A. Albanese, FAIA, Architect

the future. But as the chain of events and involvements cohere, forming a complete cycle on their own, as they did all through the seventies, an awareness grew that the time had now come for the ramblings of an academic nomad to change back to a less vagrant life.

So in the winter of 1979–80 I towed my 22 foot sailing dory, Ojimo along the southern route through Texas and Arizona stopping again in Tucson for two weeks to visit Chuck and Claire on the way to Sausalito in San Francisco Bay where the boat would remain for sailing twice a year while I was a guest critic at the San Francisco Center for Architecture and Urban Studies. This time I was definitely on the track of finding a place to settle for the winter, with the added thought of being able to sail off and on either inland or somewhere on the southern California coast. No doubt this new appetite for sailing year round had been greatly stimulated by summer cruising aboard Osimo in the upper Great Lakes then at the peak of its cycle of enjoyment. After two seasons, though, I found the waters of San Francisco Bay too rough for Ojimo and decided since the boat was easily trailerable, a variety of destinations in the south, out of San Diego, the Sea of Cortes, or on one of the lakes would offer opportunities for calmer, warmer sailing. By this time too I was thinking more and more about Tucson as an ideal winter base, remembering all the other enticements that spoke for themselves but were given especially convincing allure through Chuck's

persuasiveness. Since he had been my administrative assistant during the mid sixties when we were in the thick of collaborative projects in the graduate program at Illinois and had demonstrated such extraordinary all around talent and judgment it was no surprise to find that these skills had been sharpened even more, including persuasiveness. It was his and Claire's idea that I consider building a small studio attached like a guest house to one of the two rental houses they had acquired in the heart of the Sam Hughes neighborhood near the University of Arizona campus. We decided to do this on a life lease basis which entailed agreement that I would finance the building of the studio and that this investment would be in lieu of rent for the rest of my life and that title would go to them in my will. I was to make this same arrangement later with Charlie Lilliquist to build my summer studio, Singassin, on his Lake Michigan shore property at St. Ignace.

Again following the naming tradition of the Ojibway tribes, I chose to name the new studio Camaralta which means pilot house and/or captain's quarters in Spanish. As the illustrations show, the two storey octagonal plan is a recall on the upper level of a pilot house, with windows on all sides with unobstructed views to the mountains. Since most of Tucson is one storey and the native tree canopy is low, screening close up views of other dwellings, the prospect opens up a sense of the horizon in all directions, like aboard a ship at sea.

No less persuasive in the choice of Tucson as a winter residence, as Chuck pointed out, is that there were then and had been other Illini on the U of A architecture faculty, Kirby Lockard, Ken Clark, Bob Giebner, Stroud Watson, Bill Miller, Bob Wright, David Saile and Jim Larson, most of whom had been my graduate students. Not only would this add to the sense of welcome, reunion and homecoming but would also offer a chance for participation in the school as an informal visiting critic much as I had served at Illinois after retirement and at other universities, but on a more permanent basis. As I am now writing, this rewarding relationship is in its twenty fifth year so I can now testify how gratifying this experience has been, especially in its pro bono role liberated from academic politics, as a confidant, adviser and mentor to so many new students and colleagues. As this expereince unfolds there will be many more insights like these to share.

The charisma of the Sonoran desert reveals itself slowly, overcoming the stereotyped notion most of us have had of a hostile, parched, featureless landscape of sand dunes and great distances between places of refuge and survival. Gradually, though, through a kind of osmosis its special richness of flora, fauna, land, sky and cultural diversity comes into focus. Of course this sensitivity of perception grows mostly from one's personal contacts with friends who in low key serve as guides and as gentle reminders that it's up to you to let your own curiosity

unfold a deeper understanding, through local travel, reading and whatever other sources of stimulating information turn up. Of these, the university's innovative local public TV programs have been a continuous inspiration in appreciating the host of fascinating detail that builds a more comprehensive perspective.

The first of these, appealing to my archipelago concept of life was a program called "Islands in the Sky." Its idea was to assume that the desert is a sea with its surface at 4500 feet above sea level thereby leaving mountain ridges, mesas and peaks as islands each with its own evolving specialties within species of both living matter and inorganic systems of erosion, sun, shade, wind and water forces over millennia of time. To these would be the added their influence on human inhabitation and survival through hunting, gathering and agriculture. This was an enchanting, imaginative and continuing educational revelation about the Sonoran desert itself and the wider understanding of arid lands elsewhere in the world. Another program, "The Desert Speaks," took much the same approach to the entire continuity of the desert surface, to unfold the phenomenon of migration, history and "genius loci" of a host of places radiating in all directions from Tucson at the center.

There was no sense that in a certain number of years, say twenty, all will be known that one needs to know—the impression instead was that the search and revelations there-

from were limitless and would continue to enrich one's sphere of sensibility. Coming in the sequence of a long life in which all relevant nuances of perception relate to architecture, this Sonoran desert domain became for me the ideal opposite polarity to the same depth of emotional and intellectual inspiration as the Great Lakes archipelago, in establishing both timeless and timely principles to follow.

DESIGN DRAWING WILLIAM KIRBY LOCKARD

Cover of *Design Drawing*
Kirby Lockard, FAIA

Ramada House, Tucson, AZ, 1977
Judith Chafee, FAIA, Architect
(Photograph: Glenn Allison)

The College of Architecture of the UA was founded in 1958 with Sid Little as dean. Like most newly established disciplines, it first occupied temporary quarters, a vacated Safeway store on Park Avenue at the west edge of the campus. Some years later in 1965 the college moved into a new building as a part of a fine arts center including art, music and photography and is now undergoing expansion to relieve overcrowding and to provide space for the School of Landscape Architecture as well. Completion of this construction will now bring the two schools physically together, following the university's earlier reorganization of the college to include architecture, planning and landscape architecture as one.

As had happened in the formation of several other new architectural schools across the country as well as some older ones, many of the faculty brought with them Illinois' long-standing reputation for rigorous design and architectural engineering orientation along with strong emphasis on graphic communication which was smoothly directed to desert architecture as a particular focus, a clear mission of the curriculum from the beginning.

By the time I began to join in as a pro bono critic in the early eighties, this sense of direction had already built up great momentum, closely in rapport with the underlying spirit of the school's Sonoran desert setting free of superficial stereotypes like pseudo-Spanish, Mission Style and other revivalist trends. Kirby had by then established a uniquely high standard of design communication skills in drawing and composition, especially for beginning students which not only had lasting impact on the quality of student work on through advanced years but also had strong influence in many schools across the country as seminal and pace setting for foundation studios. Chuck brought his own personal talent in design presentation and organizational skills to upper level studios especially focusing on final fifth year comprehensive projects. For the relatively short time they were on the faculty before moving on, Bob Wright, Bill Miller, Jim Larson and Stroud Watson all reinforced this dynamism of compositional, drawing and presentation skills while Ken Clark, who like Kirby and Chuck had stayed on, moved in the direction of planning at the larger scale of urban growth. Bob Giebner, who had concentrated on architectural history at Illinois added this dimension to the depth of understanding the past as its cultural heritage is so significant in the Southwest.

I don't mean to imply that Arizona's strength in design relied on Illini graduates alone; Gordon Heck, Harry Boghosian, Doug McNeil, Bill Stamm, Harris Sobin and Ellery Green were all just as influential. Ron Gourley became dean shortly before I began having contact with the school, bringing his feeling for directness, simplicity and integrity springing from his special talent and experience first in Minnesota then at Harvard and MIT and as a partner in the firm Sert, Jackson and

Gourley. Unlike some (if not most) from the Ivy League and abroad who come to the hinterland and remote provinces with the Word and the Way, Ron well understood the intrinsic qualities and potential of desert architecture as did Bob Nevins, coming from Yale. It was at that time too, that Judith Chafee, of the vintage at Yale when there were virtually no other women in architecture brought her salty, astringent, hardy, survivor character and design talent to practice in Tucson and to be a part time critic in the school. She soon demonstrated new and powerful interpretations of what architecture in the desert can be, both timeless and timely in contemporary terms. She had the same no holds barred impact on her students, of sometimes brutal honesty and strictness but leaving no doubt that the search for rightness in the use of materials, light and shade, closeness with indigenous landscape would end up as most lasting and fulfilling, as her clients and students bear witness perhaps more strongly than for any other architect of her time.

Arizona and Tucson especially, like California, had its early architectural heroes, Joseler, Frost, Wilde and Arthur Brown making the link to the post World War II years. It has been daunting for others since to withstand the onslaught of rapacious sunbelt growth in the hands of developers motivated only by profit, with politicians and civic officials at their beck and call, overwhelming an educationally impoverished public and the small minority who still yearn for architecture that responds beautifully to its time and place.

Examples of quality architecture, sensitive to the fragility and beauty of the Sonora do indeed exist but are rare, isolated and almost lost in a sea of mediocrity or worse. But even these few fine pieces of work in the past and more recently by Judith Chafee, Les Wallach, Rick Joy and a few others are somehow enough to keep this spirit of inspiration alive in the school, however tenuous, as a kind of trusteeship in the face of big time, trendy internationalism led by celebrity taste makers.

Now that more than a quarter century has passed during which I have been privileged to live in two very different worlds, the winter season in Tucson with summers in the upper Great Lakes, I see another opportunity to contemplate cultural and physical change over this time span as it has affected architecture as a value in our lives. This has been perhaps the most important theme carrying through my chronicle from the beginning and now in later years to seek a way to bring these many insights gained over the years into clearer focus.

Living in these two worlds reveals both contrasts and similarities influenced by about as wide a variety of historic, social, economic and natural landscape differences as may be found in America. Since my look at this panorama of diversity is that of an architect, it is perhaps more limited in its focus than that of a cultural historian, but with the advantage of being closely involved in such a range of activity in each place as a hands

Poetry Center, University of Arizona, Tucson, AZ, 2007
Line and Space, LLC
Les Wallach, FAIA, Architect

Poetry Center, University of Arizona, Tucson, AZ, 2007
Line and Space, LLC
Les Wallach, FAIA, Architect
(Drawing: Lei Jin)

Residence, Tubac, AZ, 2000
Rick Joy Architects
(Photograph: Jeff Goldberg)

on builder, citizen, client and educator all on parallel tracks, this composite experience may speak out in the larger dimension of criticism in our society. Still it seems wise to limit my frame of reference to certain observations of events, and facets of change in the vernacular fabric, design-build, as well as in exemplary architecture for dwelling, spiritual spaces, urban design and architectural education each as they stand on their own reflected in the composite mirror of life today.

Coming back to Tucson, the flow of such changes over this past quarter century may first be seen in the trend to globalization and all the influences that come with it: priorities of bigness, rampant commercial sameness, money, power, "success" and "look at me" ostentation as they have negatively impacted regional loyalties and identities such as inherent respect for land ethic (its fragility and beauty), cultural heritage, and the integrity of building what is most fitting to its time and place. Of course these external forces are not new; they have always been present to some degree. What seems most critical to discern is the extent to which this influence has accelerated. If we were to single out highest quality work in Tucson both vernacular and architect designed at any given time in proportion to everything else in the built environment, it would be increasingly small, say ten percent or less. Even though there may be debate as to what exactly is highest quality, this should not be a question in the light of our accumu-

lated intelligence, experiential knowledge and ability today to establish criteria of excellence that are not subject to cycles of fashion, vanity and arrogance. On this basis of judgment it certainly is clear by now, that the highest quality of work, however its proportion of the total is defined, is steadily diminishing and unappreciated in the face of the growing mediocrity of building across the nation, most sadly seen in those regions of extraordinary natural beauty and cultural heritage like the Sonoran desert and the Great Lakes "water wonderland."

For the most part this decline has been slow enough that it took some time before it stimulated some concerted community effort to face the issue. On the initiative of architects Les Wallach, Phil Dinsmore, Dean Dick Eribes, including planners, landscape architects, U of A faculty and civil officials, a group called Civitas Sonoran was founded to promote action in bringing public awareness to community design quality through exhibitions, programs and media influence. This effort coincided with the city's establishment of the Rio Nuevo project to renovate its downtown to include beneficial connection to the older barrio districts now separated across the I-10 freeway and the Santa Cruz river flood plain. For a while this joint action seemed hopeful and optimistic aided by the inspiration of a new millennium, but like so many other new civic enterprises in the past soon suffered from public insensitivity, implementation problems and the enormous amount of patience required on the part of everybody concerned. Finally, so it seems, this initiative has lapsed to the old status quo of developer rule.

It isn't as if superior work doesn't exist or come on line anymore, indeed there is probably more of it now than ever before, but in proportion to the great increase of all other building it is not only harder to find but sadly of less interest to the public even those of means who now have returned with more pack instinct than ever to copy-cat revivalist styles. I repeat once again what the public now thinks of as architecture is now even more polarized in the form of high visibility signature work of international stars, as much in Tucson as anywhere else.

Within the College of Architecture and schools almost everywhere, the allure of avant garde work by celebrity architects is now made more compelling than ever through elegant photography, graphics and rhetorical spin in all media forms. Of course a good part of this influence is of the highest order and is beneficial as long as students have the maturity to understand how the basic principles of excellent design are in synthesis with the task in hand. As one can witness time after time, this abundance of powerful external influences is hard for students to get in balance with intrinsic, equally powerful local site forces and design requirements, a difficult challenge of trying to get the best of both. Of course there is nothing new about this struggle but now in the new millennium it has taken on new

pressures, intensified by hypnotic persuasiveness of high technology and its esoteria of both hardware and software.

However, certain new architecture in Tucson and its surrounding Sonoran desert, like the work of Judith Chafee mentioned earlier has been gathering its own momentum as a counter force. Out of the variety of this new work I would single out for clarity that which employs the simplest form and material vocabulary. Some time ago a most talented young woman on the U of A faculty, Dominique Lloyd distilled the essence of historic vernacular building in the Sonora as it has significance today, titling her study "Walls and Wickerwork"—thick walls of plentiful adobe, stone or other earth material demanding simplest geometry of spatial form, square, rectangular or circular with few simple openings, offering high insulating and heat sink qualities, this material and form in complementary contrast to "wickerwork" light weight shading devices, ramadas of ocotillo or other lineal pole material with infill. Dominique's clarifying study paralleled built examples of rammed earth and strawbale pioneered by local builders and within the university's design build projects led by Mary Hardin and Rocky Brittain. These projects focused too on shading devices of both wood and synthetic materials. Les Wallach and Rick Joy[23] have brought this clear cut juxtaposition of heavy walls, openings and shading elements into their architecture with such sensitivity to the landscape that their work has merited international acclaim.

Healing Garden, St. Lukes Medical Center, Milwaukee WI, 2007
David Brubaker, Architect

Mariposa Residence, Phoenix AZ, 2004
DeBartolo Architects
Jack DeBartolo III, Architect

Foundry Square Office Building, San Francisco CA, 2002
STUDIOS Architecture
David Johnson, Architect

Sho U Restaurant, Singapore, 2007
Ministry of Design
Colin Seah, CEO

Residence, Green Valley, AZ, 2008
Bruce Hutchings, Archtitect

Following this path of design excellence established by the likes of Wallach, Joy and Rob Paulus, more recent graduates of the U of A are similarly achieving national and international recognition: David Brubaker in Chicago, Scott Sargent in Vermont, David Johnson in San Francisco, Jack DeBartolo III in Phoenix, Lei Jin in Tucson and Colin Seah in Singapore.

It is most encouraging despite the forces of "big brother" globalization to observe a surge of new interest and participation in learning from hands-on work in design/build with its focus on the art of architecture at small scale that is of such direct, intimate significance in enhancing the quality of life, recalling for me the advice of Asplund so many years ago in Stockholm (p. 67) of how important it was to give extra attention to detail at intimate scale in honor to everyone as if they're members of one's own family. So now in both domains—the public sector and within the academic world the battle goes on to win hearts and minds, fought on the extremes of scale, the big-time and the intimate.

In the world of both practice and public perception there is no doubt we are now witnessing further dissection of the whole into a miscellany of each-on-their-own pieces of exhibitionistic display: structural, technical, sculptural or whatever "look at me" form of ostentation, sapping away our traditional focus on excellence based on highest comprehensive criteria of judgment, which surely still includes as well humanism and all the grace notes of sensitivity working together, as learned over the ages.

I must repeat again that choosing sides between internationalism or regionalism, for example, is a superficial choice that ignores the depth of understanding architecture as a distinct holistic endeavor judged excellent or not by evermore inclusive criteria informed by the best we know from the wealth of cumulative experience, rising above ego, fashion and shallow indifference. So, for instance, such criteria of excellence if applied to vastly different physical and cultural landscapes like the northern Great Lakes and Arizona, should result in work that is distinctly different and beautifully regional, without the fuss of requiring purely visual stereotypes of forms, materials and gingerbread ornamentation.

All through the years of architectural education since its first inclusion as a respected university discipline, virtually all schools have placed a comprehensive design project—a thesis (now called capstone) as the center focus of validation for the professional degree. Thus the quality of a harmonious, balanced, orchestrated synergy of many parts around a singular creative concept reflects mastery of the discipline rather than mastery of one of its parts alone. So as long as the capstone maintains its historic focal place in the curriculum honoring the full criteria of excellence it remains the measure of trust a school accords to architecture's

timeless, unique identity reflecting mature civilizations. I fear we are now seeing a widespread relaxation of this measure in favor of rewarding disproportionally subjective interests in some enticing specialty, assuming its mastery somehow justifies and authenticates awarding the time-honored basic architectural degree or honor awards in practice. Is this most noticeable trend toward specialist dilution of the whole a true and basic sign of change in direction or another popular cliché?

I'm inspired to respond to this apparent change in both academia and professional life based on my own experience as a critic and mentor for many years on both individual theses and team projects at both the undergraduate and graduate levels. I certainly applaud the sincere effort to strengthen the research (hypothesis/proof) aspects of capstone projects but would like to look more closely at the meaning of proof in architecture as its special nature is elicited and compared to the generally understood interrelationship of hypothesis/proof in the wide pursuit of knowledge.

23 Joy, Rick, *Rick Joy: Desert Works*, Princeton, 2002

Webster's most succinct definition of proof: "...Anything serving or tending to establish the truth of something or to convince one of its truth; conclusive evidence..."

It has been my good fortune over the years to have close friends who are leading mathematicians, physicists and other scientists. Time and again we discussed the nature of proof as it is established in different disciplines, agreeing that certain of its characteristics are in common: evermore rigor in light of accumulating knowledge and its distillation and accessibility through communication technology; the persistent, enduring process of trial/error testing in ever refining cycles; the emergence of hard-won truth as a kind of inevitable rightness finally achieved and widely recognized. Einstein's relativity theory, the "big-bang" theory plus many more breakthroughs in science and technology all seem to have evolved proof in this way.

Rightness in architecture, true to its time and place, has of course had many interpretations across the spectrum of history, technology, theory and criticism; all special considerations within the discipline, but the nature of architecture as a whole, as a unique, noble calling in human existence requires a broad yet singular critical regard, still relying and depending on the consensus of comprehensive intelligence (e.g. juries); a synergy in which "the whole is more than the sum of its parts." Proof, then, for a capstone project in architecture is demonstrated by excellence of wholeness, an orchestration above and beyond (but including) excellence of any of its components alone.

The flow of this thought recalls again how the quest for holistic excellence mandates cycle after cycle refinement to elicit what a project wants to be on its own terms. Louis Kahn's spiritually inspiring way of seeing the process of "trial/error testing in ever refining cycles" was a poetic extension of the opportunity I had earlier for close observation of work in the Saarinen office in the late fifties. Each project went through a relentless but joyful study after study of concept/detail refinement possibilities. For example, Glen Paulsen made at least a dozen elevation studies including detailed profile and material choices of the U.S. Embassy in London. More recently Fay Jones took me through an amazing sheaf of study drawings and models of Thorncrown Chapel, as did Erik Bryggman years before in Turku, Finland for the Resurrection Chapel there. This intensity and dedication to excellence through cycles of concept/detail refinement, today as in the past, reconfirms its timeless essence as proof in architecture.

Now it seems the computer is able to work miracles; reiterations and refinement appear to be automatic or so regarded. Students, especially, are so charmed by colorful computer print outs and line quality they don't understand and resist the need for restudy. Also observe that professionals as well don't take or are not given the time to restudy and refine projects, under more and more pressure" to get it out fast at the bottom line." This current fast track state of the art in both practice and the schools mirrors again how the absence of refining cycles of the full synergy is diminishing overall quality and that in schools the capstone project needs more than ever many earlier rehearsals in the course of the curriculum, not just once at the end.

Thank God the university is still the guardian for advancing the search for truth and that we as architects within its domain continue to be steadfast in our interpretation of this mission, especially as it is exemplified in capstone projects, in the extent to which they demonstrate comprehensiveness at manageable scale and proof of excellence achieved through over and over testing and refining.

So it seems to me that as much as we delight in and continue to encourage capstone projects that focus on a single element or phenomenological component of a larger whole, the inclusive, composite dimension of architecture responding to the human condition and environmental ethic remains our encompassing challenge, especially as it obliges sensitivity to the "genius loci" of whatever region in which we live and work.

In the grand archipelago of life, as one's enchantment with living alternatively in two contrasting, charismatic places like the Sonoran desert and the Straits of Mackinac, the spaces between are also loaded with islands that in their own appeal serve as fresh interpreters of learning. Imagine the opposite—how dull it would be always to follow the same path back and forth between two stars. The freedom to design time is inseparable from the freedom to design new connections in space, either deliberately or by chance, responding to some unforeseen invitation or premonition. Long ago the magnetism of new destinations and travel between had established its power as a precedent in the quest for learning new insights for design and for the larger dimension of penniless wealth in living. Now much later in life the same quest has taken on new meaning—not so much to add new experience in widening one's spectrum of knowledge as before but to concentrate on a distillation process in pursuit of greater wisdom, pretentious as this may sound.

Justification for such pretension may no longer be needed. Since I wrote the prologue to this memoir of learning, expressing hesitation in adding *"one more barely audible voice in the great chorus celebrating art and life,"* we have entered the new world of nanotechnology in which almost infinitely small measurements (one nanometer is one billionth of a meter) soon may describe the power of tiny forces harnessed for beneficial change, like successfully attacking the micro

cells of cancer. Maybe it isn't so pretentious after all to eke out insights of wisdom in architecture no matter how small, as in everything else—who knows? So distilling wisdom for architecture in nanosized bits has new inspiration for hope—an embrace not only including the stars of the North and their blue water horizons, the Sonoran stars with their desert seas and their islands in the sky, but all the spaces and islands between wherever they may beckon.

I have to admit that nostalgia plays a major part in the urge to revisit many old familiar places rather than venturing to new destinations. It takes many years to see this pattern as it has evolved, as it now reveals deeper insights that seem to have been there all along but now have energy as if on their own to come to the surface, like having a glass of Campari once again on the Piazzale Michelangelo overlooking Florence as it suddenly tells you for the first time the meaning of Dolce Vita all the way from Dante's Vita Nuova to Fellini's great film. Perhaps what turns out to be most indicative and magnetic for return is obvious—the number of times you keep coming back. Rome, the Eternal City heads the list, not only because its existence for twenty five centuries is truly an inexhaustible source of inspiration, measured by the depth of emotional and of intellectual meaning combining time after time in different ways but always building in wealth as a totality, a kind of museum or library of all Western civilization—each revisit adds some new discovery or more importantly

a revision of lessons learned before into a new ranking order. As an example I would refer the reader back to my chronicle of the American Academy, in particular my effort to sum up what it all seemed to mean under the heading, INSIDE THE MIRROR-AAR (p. 127-141): "Certainly unchanging is the idea of presence in Rome, the Eternal City, as the western world's center of creative study and work—now revealing still deeper and timeless dimensions of canonicity in architecture, art and landscape that transcend neo-classicism and other stylistic limitations." More than anything else, the reaffirmation of canons of design excellence strengthened over centuries now looms up as the most powerful antidote to today's architectural uncertainties of direction, vanities, aberrations and most of all public indifference to high quality work of restraint and integrity that now seems lost in a widening sea of mediocrity.

Although Rome remains the timeless mecca for the study and appreciation of urban design over the full spectrum of scale, large or small, the same may be said for Florence, Verona, Lecce and Urbino, my other favorite Italian cities, each progressively smaller in size but each seeming no less powerful in its influence on new contemporary work in achieving highest levels of quality, fitting so harmoniously in its historic urban context. More precisely, this is a skill in using traditional materials, like local stone, wood, brick, tile, non ferrous metals, with sensitivity of composition, scale, seamless ties to older

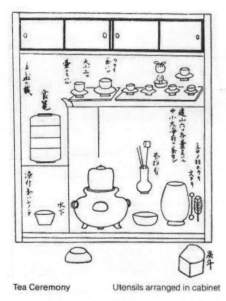

Tea Ceremony   Utensils arranged in cabinet

structures, paving connections and urban landscape. The work of Carlo Scarpa in Verona, S. Vito and Venice, Massimo Carmassi in Pisa, Giancarlo di Carlo in Urbino, Arco Progetti in Florence exemplify the work of many other gifted architects too who are lesser known. This particular quality of contextual harmony is in high contrast to the lack of it in so many other parts of the world, like Ando's work in Japan and the U. S. and most of the current crop of work by starchitects wherever they are doing their ego-loaded interventions, regardless of surroundings. One could add to this consideration of seamlessness of old and new in architecture, landscape and urban design, the consistency of good design in Italy throughout the spectrum of graphic, industrial, interior and fashion design as well. At the extremes of wealth from the very rich to those of modest means, from high style Prada and the world's leading yacht designers of Viareggio, to customers of Standa and Upim, the lower cost supermarkets of Italy, you can spot good design, although it's a game to find it in the abundance of everyday utensils, table ware items or other gadgets. But if you visit countless stores like this in most of the world today the search for superior design of commonplace objects would be frustrating.

However there is one conspicuous exception that coincides with my addiction to return again and again to another charismatic corner of the world like the Nordic countries, especially Sweden and Finland. My first encounter there in 1939 had been mainly motivated by the appeal of a more humanistic direction in modern architecture than that of the Bauhaus and Le Corbusier. So it was a discovery to find that the term "Swedish Modern" really referred in a more limited way to the simplicity and freshness in the design of furniture, ceramics, fabrics, lighting and a host of other small scale objects which had evolved from hand craft skills refined over centuries in households and cottage industry. It was an awakening strikingly similar to my first encounter with Shaker design in Kentucky a few years before. This new inspiration carried over to Finland too, as I recalled earlier, now identified with the name of individual designers like Aalto, who were known for their work over a full range of objects and furnishings as well as architecture.

This heritage has gained momentum ever since not only through new generations of architects in Finland I have been privileged to know like Aalto and Bryggman long ago; Markku Komonen, Jan Sunderland and Juhani Pallasmaa, all of whom carry on the same breadth of talent, skill and range of interests applied to not only a wide range of architectural scales–intimate settings to urban design, but to education, museum curatorships and critical writing. I don't think it's just a happenstance that as individuals they have chosen this diversity of professional life but rather as a reflection of a culture that for many, many generations has recognized the enormous significance of design not only as an imperative for survival but a necessary key in achieving a higher quality of life that does not depend only on richness of material resources but fully appreciates the joy of making and refining all the accouterments of living as works of art from a highly limited vocabulary of materials and technologies. For almost seventy years now in my own experience I think of the Finland station as much more than just one stop in a journey of architectural exploration but as a destination exemplifying the best we have yet achieved in the modern world of good design covering the full range of scale, not only as environmental art but as built wisdom as well.

Inferences of direction for the rest of the world may clearly be drawn from Finland's example and heritage, as most eloquently expressed by Pallasmaa himself as keynote speaker in April 2006 at the 50th anniversary celebration of the Museum of Finnish Architecture in Helsinki. His title was "The Human Mission of Architecture." From his entire text, which I most highly recommend for all to read, I choose a few quotes as he first does from Walt Whitman, "great poetry is possible only if there are great readers then his own follow-up: "great architecture is possible only when there are great clients." Later: "A core condition for architecture to evolve is artistic autonomy. By this I mean that the mission of architecture does not stem from rationalism, utility or economy but from the autonomous and existential poetry of building. It provides our existence in the world with lived metaphors, or more precisely, the instruments of a

poetic life." To bring us down to earth from our own ego, quoting Milan Kundera's plea for the "wisdom of literature," and that "all great novels are wiser than their authors," Pallasmaa urges us toward humility "that significant buildings also stem from the wisdom of architecture and are thus always wiser than their individual designers."

The quote "great architecture is possible only when there are great clients" is another reminder of the wane of architecture as a cultural value in America and elsewhere as it so clearly relates to the impoverishment of public education of future clients from preschool all the way to university, especially in the drift away from liberal and fine arts.

In Finland Maire Gullichsen (p. 70) as a client of Aalto along with others less well known in Denmark, Sweden and Finland, whether patrons or advocates in other ways, became leaders through exhibitions and marketing in firms like Artec, Den Permanente, and now in the world-scope Ikea outlets, bring consistently high quality design of all sorts of furnishings at surprising low cost to customers everywhere. This, at least, is one ray of hope in educating the public about good design, along with the influence of more upscale Crate and Barrel, Williams Sonoma and others—but one wishes there could also be a renaissance of design education in the schools as an intrinsic component as important as competence in language.

Lake Arrowhead Golf Pavillions
Bill Yudchitz, Architect

Schlitz Audubon Nature Center, Entry Shelter, Bayside, Wisconsin
Kubala/Washatko Architects
(AIA Wisconsin Firm Award 2006)

240

Cathedral Place Rooftop Terrace, Miwaukee, Wisconsin
Louis Wasserman, Architect
(AIA Wisconsin Honor Award 2006)
(Photograph: Mark Hefton)

1936 Bugatti + 5756 Atlantic (Best in Show, Pebble Beach, CA), 2003
Peter Williamson, Owner (Photographs: Schlegelmilch)
Scott Sargent, (B. Arts, U. Arizona), Car Restoration

Now to swing all the way across the globe to the Pacific Rim on the same mission of finding enlightenment through impressions or interpretations of timeless design principles. As observed earlier (p. 170), they have yet to be filtered through a fine screen in search of balance and complementary relation to the best we have tried to learn in the West.

Perhaps more important than anything else to consider is how much the compacting pressures of high density living in Japan, China and the Indonesian archipelago have evolved an extra measure of attention to the refinement of detail in intimate settings and their ensemble harmony. For example, the exquisite balance of all the senses and objects in the Japanese tea ceremony symbolizes patterns in the wider scope of activities of everyday life. Sight, sound, aromatic, thermal and tactile senses flow together as one with all the properties in the setting, from the whisks, heat source, tea cups, low tables, tatami mats, shoji screens and the enclosing shelter itself as it is sensitively poised in the surrounding landscape. Sensitive relationship of inhabitation to both the close up and distant landscape is likewise a desired harmony throughout the Pacific archipelago, especially as man made adaptations of natural materials like bamboo, reed and pandanus, etc. are woven into structure, roof and wall membranes and all sorts of utensils. At more sophisticated levels we see from the panorama of mountains, rivers and seas their miniaturization in gardens like those of Zen temples, even in residen-

tial gardens woven seamlessly with interior space. Many of these thoughts surfaced again years later in 2000 as our IFRAA group visited temples, churches, museums and other noteworthy contemporary structures, this time in quest of both the tangible and intangible qualities of spiritual space.

On my own in 1993 I revisited New Zealand and Australia finding again the same awareness of opportunity and desire to develop their own direction in architecture in spite of powerful influences toward internationalism. This spirit had been so strong among my graduate students from "down under" in the fifties and sixties. They kept pointing out that they felt a parallel existed between the Prairie and Chicago schools as examples of freedom in America from European stylistic influences and that the same objective for special architectural identity existed for them at home, even in the face of even stronger colonial pressures from Great Britain. Even though Bill Alington was influenced by Mies, his own work over the years in Wellington reveals a freshness of innovation in response to typical sloping site conditions and local material use, notably his new music school on the Victoria University Campus. After winning the competition in 1915 for the design of Canberra, the new capital of Australia, Walter and Marion Griffin brought the Prairie School influence of openness to Australia through their work in Melbourne and Sydney as well. The most vocal and demonstrative through his own work has of course been Glenn Murcutt in his steadfast quest for finding solutions most appropriate to their time and place, whether or not it may achieve a character of national identity.

Back on our own West Coast, especially in the Pacific Northwest, site forces such as the abundance of prime timber like redwood and Douglas fir have inspired the development of its own regional feeling, a splendid affinity to the landscape through the work of Paul Kirk and many of his contemporaries, more recently the work of James Cutler in Seattle and the Patkau firm in Vancouver. Of course we find similar sensitivity to the landscape in the San Francisco Bay area, with more cosmopolitan flair, but from my own recent experience it seems to me that the Portland area has most successfully achieved the highest level of urban planning, urban design, architectural and landscape architectural consistency of quality of any other large metropolitan area in America.

As our students, colleagues, clients and friends spread out both near and far across the world, other islands in between take form as all—too—brief reunions and celebrations. Usually cycling with the seasons, they seem always to grow on an intimate personal level out of the broad pilgrimages in search of timeless/timely canons of design excellence that I have just related. Though informal as treasured time together, each visit so often becomes a spontaneous miniature seminar, probing and seeking to uncover new quality of life insights, no mat-

ter how small or episodic in scope, that may turn out to have much wider significance. Let me reflect on a few of these star-like moments as they reappear in memory:

A bonfire on the beach at Neebish long ago, with Chief Howard telling of Ojibway legends, when a lunar rainbow cut across the sky, through the Aurora Borealis, suddenly revealing a new dimension of the universe; how poverty in the depths of the depression sometimes reminded us of beauty in austerity, as when Tom Danahy and I on the Allerton Fellowship in 1935 (p. 48) were so warmly welcomed by the almost destitute owners of the 1763 Sparhawk Mansion in Kittery Point Maine as they strove to protect spotless, stripped down ancient carpentry in trust of eventual recovery; or later on that summer as we found our way to Sakertown, Kentucky, discovering the same austere beauty this time as unaffected minimalism in the design of buildings, furnishings, tools and landscape all deriving from the humility and simplicity of their religious faith; years later to rendezvous every summer or so with Bill Yudchitz, his family and crew in Central Wisconsin working so steadfastly and with joy on superbly crafted design/build projects, by now so deeply appreciated by their hard-working, multi-ethnic community; or on a more urban level in the Milwaukee area, the amazingly diverse and excellent body of modest-scaled work of Tom Kubala and Allen Washatko, now marking their twenty sixth year in which the teachings of Bahai have guided them in respectful ego-free

interpretation of clients needs, especially in reverence to all landscapes as gardens— these influences absorbed and enhanced through their personal talent and dedication; also in Milwaukee, the work of Louis and Caren Wasserman seamlessly bringing together their architect/landscape architect design sensitivity and skill authoring books for Taunton Press, and in projects for both disadvantaged neighborhoods and higher end commissions, with great wit and caring, mixing time to time in academia at U. of Wisconsin, Milwaukee; across decades visiting Gerry Gast, his students and co-workers in the San Francisco Bay area, Stanford and later at the U. of Oregon, Eugene and Portland, mostly concentrating their special skills and dedication to unmet needs in housing, education and urban design; also in Portland, as mentioned earlier, returning at irregular beats of time to visit Ingrid and Chuck Gordon, whose firm, GDS, has now become highly recognized for successfully taking on the time-consuming, patient, political, technical complexities of rebuilding the central city Brewery Blocks; or skipping across the country again for brief drop-ins on Scott Sargent and his family in Fairlee Vermont, first in the eighties as he was building the woodland house I had designed for him-at a time when he was building his career in car restoration, finding such rapport in design refinement—cars, boats, houses—Scott now just having won "best of show" for one of his Bugatti restorations at Pebble Beach, California, now the world's top venue for car shows; or in Boston visiting with Don

Cervo, Italy (Ink on Paper), 1984
Chuck Gordon, Architect

4000 Market St., Portland, OR, 1990
GBD Architects
Chuck Gordon, Architect

Brown, chairing the work/study program at the Boston Architectural College, or on stops in New York on my way to and from Rome to catch up on state-of-the-art matters with Barry Berg, former student assistant and close friend who all through his career, whether in Saudi Arabia, Marblehead, Rome or recently in China has kept his singular skill and devotion focused on ensemble design harmonies over a great scale range of work both at home and abroad; while in Rome at the Notre Dame program to have enjoyed mixing near and far out ideas with directors Frank Montana long ago, more recently with John and Erika Stamper, Don Sporleder, Jason Montgomery and Jeff Burden—all of us excited by the special challenge of learning more through the seeming contradictions of classicism and modernity; of course at the American Academy too as I have chronicled in some detail (p. 127-141); now in the new millennium to relish a few days in Santa Fe every January with Michael and Gloria Plautz in their winter house facing the Sangre de Christo range, often with old friend David Hanser, a most eminent architectural historian, theorist and bon vivant coming in from Oklahoma State, or with David and Suzy Pines, David, one of the world's leading theoretical physicists now living in nearby Tesuque, always reaching in our exuberant conversations some (to us) new pinnacle of revelation, each time on vastly different subjects; Michael, one of my most talented graduate students, Paris Prize winner now CEO of RSP, a 260 person firm in Minneapolis, Gloria, a superb catalyst, master of language and arbiter of thought, together host and hostess par excellence giving us the setting for exchanging visions—imagine a silent movie of just the gestures exploding from such flows of ideas—; across the board in time, place, planned or by chance, whether illusory or not, whether or not enhanced by a single malt, margaritas or a sauvignon blanc with cracked Dungeness crab and sourdough, a certain bliss of consciousness is aroused in knowing a few nanometers more of life, wisdom and love. Many more of these tiny constellations are yet to form, as I shall now relate.

In reflecting on these cycles of global wandering in search of timeless/timely qualities of design excellence, the series of IFRAA trips every two years has been most helpful and revealing, as it has focused on the best we can find in contemporary religious architecture across the world.

My first experience with these tours began in 1996 in East Germany and Poland, then in 1998 to Finland, Japan in 2000 and Portugal and Spain in 2002. The series had originated long before, initiated under the joint sponsorship of IFRAA and AIA, with Professor Don Bruggink, from Hope College in Holland, Michigan as director, organizer and leader of each tour. The time scheduling seemed to work out best for a two week period in September or October attracting a most dedicated, congenial group of about thirty architects, artists, theologians, scholars, critics and their wives, with few exceptions, the same participants each time. Don always did a masterful job of researching the most notable work to visit, often arranging for the architects, artists and clergy of each destination to be present as guides and to engage in discussion of their work.

As a result of the special collegiality and rapport between us, I feel so blessed to have made many new and lasting friendships, especially with Betty Meyer who has made such an extraordinary contribution to both IFRAA and ARC for many years as a leader, editor of Faith and Form magazine and historian of ARC. Also it has been most rewarding

to visit Paul and Joanne Kelly of Berkeley once in a while and other San Francisco Bay area fellow-travelers who make up the core group of repeaters including others from scattered locations across the country like Don and Joanna Sunshine from Virginia and Phil Van Eyl, my roommate, also from Holland, Michigan. It's this continuing depth of friendship and shared curiosity to find linkages of design excellence and inferences for the future that has constituted an on-going seminar of enormous value in enriching my own understanding of spiritual space that I am now trying to distill.

Over the years Betty, as editor of Faith & Form, has asked me to write articles for the magazine; from which I would like to include excerpts that attempt to summarize my thoughts about spiritual space, thoughts that owe so much to my fellow travelers, eked out from our any many hours of dialogue. One of the critiques I wrote at Betty's request may serve as an example of how this exchange of ideas develops. Its title is "In the Presence of Greatness," appearing in Faith & Form November 1997:

A true measure of greatness in art and architecture is its power to be deeply felt by all who come in its presence. Of all the churches visited by our IFRAA Tour Group to East Germany and Poland in October '96 the Swietego Ducha Church in Tychy, Poland, by architect Stanislaw Niemczyk, was by acclamation our choice for top honors. An awareness dawned that beyond the limited

Book Cover for *The Arc Story*
Betty Meyer

244

scope of comparison, it found its place at global scale in the company of such masterpieces as Corbusier's Notre Dame de Ronchamp and Fay Jone's Thorncrown Chapel—another milestone of excellence in this pantheon of modern architecture. One realized again that crossing this threshold is so rare that when it happens it is hard to explain, made more difficult because there is such diversity in the best we know.

At the IFRAA Biennial Conference in New York, architect William Conklin lamented the "ill-at-ease" relationship of the religious mind and the artistic mind, the narrowness of definition of sacred spaces as blocks to an exalting spiritual experience in so many contemporary churches. He said we were more likely to find a religious experience elsewhere; for example, in the best of art museums. But at Tychy, an extraordinary level of spiritual experience was unmistakable. What might account for its success while others fail?

One observation is that Tychy achieves its inspiring sense of presence because it is both timeless and timely. Timeless in its reflection of regional character—its sky silhouette of a low-pitched pyramidal roof topped by slender Byzantine-like spires and in the ambiance of its mystical dark interior. We responded as well to the timeless sense of welcoming approach under the eaves from all sides. The external ambulatory gathers the flock from the fields still open on the east and south and from the city on the north.

The convent on the west is a further symbol of hospitality and welcome.

This invitation of gathering around the focus of worship is fulfilled by the spatial organization of the interior, almost as a theater in the round, by its pyramidal form made asymmetrical enough so that the sanctuary is not an island in the center but the altar area remains as a focus under the pyramid peak.

The low profile of the roof edges and details of openings maintains a consistent human scale, avoiding monumentality. No doubt a large part of Tychy's humanistic appeal is enhanced by an almost Venetian romanticism of textural richness in concentrated areas: for instance, where the roof silhouettes against the sky, the freestanding bell tower and the interior focusing of colorful iconography on a natural wood background. There is a certain added attraction, an aura of strangeness of the kind found in far corners of the world like Katmandu. Tychy's low-keyed exuberance of art and architectural collaboration, together with its harmony of limited materials, is in contrast to so many modern churches in which the egocentric personalities of artists and architects clash. In Poland as well as all over the world, it is rare to find a work so free of fashionable clichés and signature styling.

Time itself is a key design force and dimension. It allows for deeper study, refinement and investment of meaning. Tychy reflects the advantage of a long time span process.

Again and Again, we were told by clergy and participants of the long frustrating delays in obtaining building permits from communist authorities and of difficulty in finding materials and construction equipment once permits were acquired. Not in short supply, however, was the eagerness of volunteer labor and dedication of the clergy, architects, artists and craftsmen over long time spans, reminiscent of the Middle Ages. Construction finally began at Tychy in 1979 with substantial completion in 1983. In the face of Poland's historic, social, political and economic hardship particularly in this century, such wealth of response seems paradoxical.

The Tychy church is a timely success, too, as judged by our evermore exacting modern criteria of excellence—functional, aesthetic, social, economic, technical, environmental and contextual qualities in the total equation of critical judgment. But still today in many elitist quarters, as in the past, preoccupation with style and other superficial attributes of looks over substance still persists.

The design of time lies at the heart of human performances and rituals just as it does for the settings that accommodate them. The quality of each is inseparable from the other, becoming a single work of art with time as a dimension. Stars are awarded by the Guide Michelin for ensemble excellence, not for either performance or setting separately. For instance, full enjoyment of the Semper Oper in Dresden depends on superb architecture and musical performances as a single interwoven experience. One might contemplate that the quality of the spiritual experience in sacred spaces depends not only on the harmony of the art and architecture but on the ritual performance and the individual worshipper.

Even deeper in the design process is the search for the "existence will" of a project. Martin Buber speaks of the idea of an "in between realm" in the I and Thou relation-ship that gains its own strength and identify through mutuality.

Louis Kahn spoke of what a project wants to be on its own terms. Such a theory demands a new order of humility and a greater invest-ment of time and patience. All are neces-sary to evoke the desired essence, identity and beauty of "what wants to be in its own right."

Musing further on Conklin's projection of the museum as spiritual space:

If I were asked to give examples of museums that have achieved "existence will," Kahn's Kimbell Museum in Fort Worth; Richard Meier's Kunsthandwerk Museum in Frankfurt and James Sterling's Statsgallerie in Stuttgart would be strong contenders. The top quality of the collections, the curatorial expertise, and the precision craftsmanship match the talent of the architects, resulting not only in ensemble excellence but a moving spiritual experience as well. Tychy's achievement is of the same high standard, an example of

sacred space in today's world of fast-track superficiality.

Tychy and other great works of modern ar-chitecture, rare as they are, redefine by their very existence a true canon of excellence in diversity, both timeless and timely. What-ever depth of analysis one might attempt— to shed light on the separate ingredients of canonicity that bridge past to present pinnacles in art and architecture—the quest remains elusive, just as the notion that "beauty is more than skin deep is hard to pin down. But when it's all there, as at Tychy you know it and rejoice.

Now that several years have passed since each of these visits prompted immediate im-pressions that tended to be of equal interest and importance, it may now be possible to offer a few thoughts as to which of the many sites now loom up as most timeless/timely in significance. Above all it seems clear that the best of the old must be compared with the best of the new in the perception of spiritual space as it informs and enriches our culture, especially in intensifying the exis-tential link between old and new, between preservation and new building, most impor-tantly between the man-made environment and nature—trying to find how much the essence of spirituality in both these domains of life depends on their harmonious exis-tence as one.

Combining what I recall from our exchange of observations and my own insights over

Cathedral Place Center, Krakow, Poland

Swietego Ducha Church, Tychy, Poland, 1983
Stanislaw Niemczyk, Architect

this span of time I would like to consider sets of pairs from each of the visits that may hopefully shed some new light in the quest for understanding spirituality as it may become embedded in the design process for the entire spectrum of architectural endeavors as well as for new places of worship.

In Poland I think that the old palace ensemble in Krakow that locks together both the religious and secular centers of the city in an embrace of romanticism, refuge and architectural uniqueness through its harmonics of materials and scale over several hundred years can be compared with the Swietego Ducha Church in nearby Tychy (see above critique) in terms of its embodiment of the same characteristics of romanticism and charisma, now brought together in a singular religious structure that is both contemporary and highly respectful of its heritage. In the old city center I felt this richness and depth most in the courtyard that though open to the sky still seemed to be an interior room of great variety on all sides of punched openings, arcades and galleries on five or six levels forming the enclosure, with roof edges and finials that miniaturizes the larger city skyline, these same qualities embodied in the layering of the church's roof planes, textures and skyline accents. These thoughts lead me to the question of how much these characteristics of miniaturization of the larger uniquely urban and national contexts become components of spirituality, like the miniaturizations of nature in the garden courts of Zen temples in Japan.

At a greater distance of a mile or more the old palace ensemble of Krakow as seen in silhouette looking east from a main street bridge reveals a unity of pinnacled skyline that appears again as miniaturized in the skyline of the new church as one beholds it across the sweep of grain fields.

Finland, like Poland has been a fertile ground for exceptional church architecture from the time of rustic wood and stone structures to the present. In the global scene of modern design, perhaps nowhere else has the heritage of design sensitivity developed from traditional arts and crafts made a more seamless transition to modernism, with the exception of Italy as I have observed earlier. Of the older heritage, the meticulously preserved wooden church at Petäjävesi, circa 1765, now on the United Nations' highly selective list of historic world architecture expresses the length of time in which this distinctive art and craft of building has evolved and been refined.

Among the dozen or so highest quality modern religious buildings in Finland one of the smallest examples stands out, the university chapel at Otaniemi by Heikka and Kana Siren of the mid fifties, to be paired with the Petäjävesi church as they share the very Finnish character of two principal materials, brick and wood, in antiphonal relationship, like Aalto's Säynätsalo Town Hall built in the same period as the Otaniemi Chapel.

I must include as well the Resurrection Chapel by Erik Bryggman already referred to in describing my visit to Bryggman's office in 1939 (p. 71) but now to consider it in more detail as it reflects spirituality. Its approach is a carefully arranged sequence through mature pines along a path modulated by glacier-smoothed granite outcroppings partially covered by lichen and moss, edged with wild flowers. Entering the chapel one immediately experiences a mood of quiet reverence achieved by a smooth, white, unbroken north wall rising to a barrel vaulted ceiling, lighted by a low, continuous, horizontal glass wall along the south side facing a pine-wooded terrace that then drops off to a semi-clearing. Natural light is intensified in the altar area as the glazed south wall becomes vertical. The sanctuary space is subtly enriched by a tracery of interior planting and shadows from tree foliage outside. Symbolism, iconography and furnishings are all low key, allowing the quiet majesty of space, light and landscape to be the main instruments of spiritual space; again, landscape and architecture as one. More recently two churches by Juha Levitska manipulate light through spaces between vertical wall planes of brick and interior smooth white surfacing of varying heights and space with glazing between, both transparent and translucent. This play of light is balanced with finely scaled interior wood and organ pipe textures and graceful suspended light fixtures. Here again the quality of light as a precious commodity in the far North, combines with sonic, olfactory and thermal senses all becoming instruments of spirituality.

Although not included in our 1998 Finland itinerary, the Villa Mairea as I visited it in 1939 and again in 1954, also described earlier (p. 70), is a prime example of spiritual space as it may infuse grace in intimate residential life, leading me to place it along with the Katsura Villa in Kyoto, Japan (1620) in the pantheon of pairs of design excellence separated by centuries of time. Again, sensitivity to timeless principles of the man-nature relationship, to landscape, to night and day, dark and light, sun, moon and stars, and to all the senses in balance seem to combine the same attributes of spirituality.

In Japan from our IFRAA tour of 2000 the Katsura Villa, the Ryoanji Zen Temple also in Kyoto and the shrines of Ise, all of ageless beauty, can be matched by only a few modern icons, the small, exquisite new museum for the Horyuji bronzes by architect Taniguchi in the Tokyo Art Museum complex heading the list. In Japan, perhaps more than anywhere else, the diversity of spaces, old and new that evoke the essences of spirituality abound; I wonder if this quality of excellence in diversity as it achieves spirituality might at root come from the interlocking at intimate scale of human inhabitation so close to nature far back in the past, epitomized by the delicacy of membranes and transitions between the two zones. A characteristic we observed time and again was the effort to partially

Church, Petanjausi, Finland, 1765
(UN List of Historic World Architecture)

Chapel, Otaniemi, Finland, 1970
Heika and Kana Siren, Architects
(Photograph: Henry Plummer)

Garden and Pavillion, Katsura Villa, Kyoto, Japan, 1620

Sauna and Pool, Villa Mairea, Noormarkku, Finland, 1938
Alvar Aalto, Architect

conceal dwellings, temples and all sorts of other structures in wooded landscapes. Almost everywhere the older traditional fabric, where it could, seemed to peer out of the forest, a corner here, a roof there, but always sensitive to viewing out rather than in. This inherent respect and honor of nature at both macro and micro scale, especially the latter, is perhaps the most basic expression of how much meditation, contemplation as religious experience is enhanced in settings that include both real, natural environments (gardens) and miniaturizations of them as in the art of bonsai and flower arrangement. A most notable indication of this esteem of nature is the ritual of entering a dwelling or temple through a garden. The entrance to the private domain is thus the garden gate rather than the front door as in the West. Here perhaps is the prime lesson of insepa-rability of architecture and landscape. These thoughts will appear again later in epilogue as they try to find their place in balance with all other facets in the pantheon of design learning.

The 2002 IFRAA visit to Japan brought back to mind an earlier invitation from Tsuto Kim-uru, one of our Illinois graduate students in the mid sixties, to come to a special celebra-tion in 1991 at the Kobe Museum of Art of the work of Togo Murano, one of the most honored Japanese architects who had lived and worked well into his nineties. Tsuto and Kionori Kikutake (p. 170–177) had both won the Murano Prize at Waseda University, endowed by Murano, and had been active

as organizers of the exhibition. Both too, had had most successful careers in practice, Tsuto taking us to visit his work and that of others in and around Tokyo and the Kobe Osaka area. My close friends Jack Baker and Bruce Hutchings were also guest of honor for this special journey, always enjoying luxuri-ous accommodations on a magnificently organized itinerary for the several days we were in Japan.

Most strikingly revealed in the exhibition was the diversity of Murano's work over a sixty year time span, as it reflected such a strong and successful effort to respond to each new project as a fresh new start, reminding us of the excellence in diversity of the work of Eero Saarinen, yet always unmistak-ably Japanese, not explicitly traditional in visual terms but in principles of sensitivity to landscape, use of light and delicacy of detail. It was immediately clear that Murano was far better known in Japan than in the rest of the world, leading us to realize that recog-nition of leading work in Japan during the past century has been focused by western critics on Tange, Ando and others who have been so strongly influenced by Corbusier, the Bauhaus and other variations on the International Style. It seemed strange that much delightfully sensitive new architec-ture mostly modest in scale that we visited, particularly in the Nagano area, has been overlooked despite its fresh contemporary feeling, possibly because it stills seems to be too "traditional." Years before I had felt that architects in Thailand and Indonesia as well as in Japan were themselves often reluctant to interpret their own traditions in new work, thinking that it might be considered too eclectic and not in the main stream of modernism as acclaimed in international, elitist circles. Doesn't this persistence of elitist taste-making at world scale still exist as a dampening force on full recognition of architectural excellence of great diversity in so many charismatic regions, in nations large and small, in resisting the bleak monotony and giantism of globalization? Can spirituality of space as a special grace note in life ever survive these relentless pressures?

Coming back to Europe for the 2002 IFRAA seminar, to Portugal and Spain in September, the itinerary of visits to the work of Siza and Calatrava, especially, brought these questions even more prominently to the fore, in two main categories of concern. In visiting the several projects of Siza in Oporto and Santiago de Compostella, including new museums and the new architectural school in Oporto, any sense of regional character was elusive or entirely missing in favor of a continuation of International Style attributes that could be anywhere in Europe or the world. Interviewing the students at the school revealed their disappointment that they didn't feel a real identity of place and that the classic "master class" system of old had been built in the form of repeating blocks of separate studios limiting flexibility for the future. The other concern was that in spite of the great architectural traditions of the Iberian peninsula including the

Alhambra, the Great Mosque of Cordoba, the Escorial, Burgos Cathedral, the mosaic sidewalks, streets and plazas of Lisbon, starchitects like Gehry, Meier and Calitrava now come in to do their signature thing largely indifferent to context just as they do anywhere else in the world. Given that situation, it was interesting that in Bilbao we all agreed that Calitrava's new airport equaled or outshone Gehry's Guggenheim Museum in today's world of competing egos and icons. In Valencia, Calatrava's home town, the grand scaled new cultural complex in the vacated river bed, (a great planning idea of re-routing the river so that its former curving course through the city could become a continuous linear park) is a campus including a science center, elaborate park parking, planetarium, opera house, reflecting pools and other civic structures yet to be built, all by Calatrava. Our consensus: too much Calatrava all in one place. Much as we all admired Calatrava's virtuosity in all white structural elegance as single artifacts where they do fit as bridges or promontories, so many of them all together in one place as in Valencia becomes an overloaded buffet of rich whipped cream desserts.

You can now see how the spreading fan of our search for spiritual space now includes many more building types than places of worship alone—museums, schools, civic structures, even residences, implying that design excellence wherever it may be found, especially if it is poetically interlocked in an inspiring landscape is the ultimate instru-

Resurection Chapel, Turku, Finland, 1939
Erik Bryggman, Architect

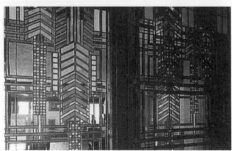

ment in the creation of spiritual space. In this bracket of years entering the new millennium, probing new directions in art and architecture, as our participation in IFRAA and ARC has helped us to understand the nature of spiritual space, I would like to include my report to Faith & Form, November 2000, as the magazine's correspondent to the Vatican's Fifth International Liturgical Congress hosted by the Pontifical Institute of Liturgy in Rome and then conclude with a personal, widely diverse collection of spaces that are awe inspiring to me in their spirituality:

The Fifth International Liturgical Congress hosted by the Pontifical Institute of Liturgy met recently to focus on the subject of Architecture and the Arts at the Service of the Liturgy. Close to 300 people gathered from around the world in high expectation that the provocative agenda would not only distill historic insights and critical judgment but also open up new visions at this turn of the millennium. An impressive selection of prelates and liturgical scholars examined questions of liturgical space, architecture, sacred art and iconography with responses from architects, artists, critics and educators.

Cardinal Virgilio Noe, Vicar General of Vatican City, welcomed participants to the Congress underscoring its timeliness in bringing all involved with renovation and new construction still closer in the understanding and interpretation of liturgical doctrine as the church faces the future. Yet, in looking

Kimbell Art Museum, Fort Worth, TX, 1969
Louis Kahn, FAIA, Architect
(Photograph: Henry Plummer)

Fountain Doors, Dana House, Springfield, IL, 1902
Frank Lloyd Wright, Architect
(Photograph: Henry Plummer)

Kasuien Annex, Miyako Hotel, Kyoto, 1959
Togo Murano, Architect

ahead, he and other authoritative clergy and well-established Italian scholars, architects and critics continued to reflect a preference for conservative/traditional spatial forms, styles and rich iconographic symbolism.

A similar traditional outlook was taken by American Mons. Francis Mannion, president of the Society of Catholic Liturgy, and Prof. Duncan Stroik of Notre Dame University, who affirmed this advocacy in terms of even more specific guidelines of form and detail. This seeming consensus was surprising in view of the choice of Richard Meier's contemporary design for the Church of the Jubilee Year 2000, now under construction in Rome (featured in Faith & Form No. 2, 1998).

The most forward-looking presentations were made by two priests: fr. Frederick Debuyst, OSB, from Belgium, whose poetic interpretation of the work of Calfeldt and Guardini (and other less known architects of small churches and chapels) revealed qualities of refreshing simplicity—open and prophetic; and Fr. Gabriel Chavez de la Mora, OSB, from Mexico, an architect who conveyed the same spirit.

While there was some debate, in the view of the majority of participants in the Congress, it became clear that further mutations in liturgical form foreshadowed by Vatican II would face increasing opposition. It would appear that "traditionalism" in church art and architecture would prevail over an ongoing quest for a new freshness, a new rich-

ness and beauty of spiritual space through humility, simplicity and a new respectfully sensitive orchestration of all the arts in celebration of the liturgy.

In the broadest view, the essence of spiritual space may exist anywhere across the world, in or out of formal religious settings: a path through virgin California redwoods, Cape Sounion in Greece with its spectacular panorama of the Aegean Sea framed by fragments of vertical columns of Poseidon's temple, the sand garden of Ryoanji Temple in Kyoto, the endless forest of columns and arches in the Great Mosque of Cordova, Thoreau's Walden Pond, the south transept of Chartres Cathedral with the blazing reds of Blanche of Castille's rose window made more intense by the afternoon sun, the galleries of the Kimbell Art Museum in Fort Worth by Louis Kahn, a gray December dawn in the deserted Piazza San Marco, Venice, with echoes in mind's ear of the Modern Jazz Quartet's "Golden Striker" theme from the film No Sun in Venice.

When Walter Gropius was in his eighties, long after he had retired from Harvard, a group of his former students in the Boston/Cambridge area gathered to honor him. It was at about the same time in 1968 that we at Illinois presented him with an honorary doctorate. Because of his advanced age we were cautioned not to expect him to deliver a speech. But after President Henry read the citation and the doctoral hood was in place Gropius proceeded to speak for twenty minutes about mid-American's leadership in the cause of team work for the future and how important it was for the design professions. At the Harvard tribute his advice was more personal: "Assume you'll live forever and cast your plans far ahead."

Of course the realities of aging and time marching on relentlessly make clear limitations on maintaining one's active life of engagement as before. But maybe the same idea of miniaturization as a factor in enhancing the spirituality of both natural and man-made space can now be directed to the quality and art of life too: do less at much smaller scale and take more time to do it.

Think of this time of life as an endless summer. How can the essence of learning design now reach a deeper level of understanding in a Sonoran dwelling in a Sonoran garden? How can the essence of making things up north using the same simple tools as before now reach new perceptions of design refinement?

These questions present a challenge even late in life beyond thoughts and words alone. Again the old adage, practice what you preach comes back with the same force it always did. I had thought that simply returning to my old hobby of designing and building boats would satisfy these pangs of conscience and that taking on new architectural projects was no longer something that one was expected to engage in at advanced age. After all, wasn't continuing to be active in academia as a critic and pro bono consultant in public projects enough?

From time to time while enjoying summers sailing OSIMO with St. Ignace as a home port, I got involved in proposing ideas for harbor improvements including designs for a new board walk and marina expansion which eventually led to working on design concept development for a new library, hardly imagining that this would eventually lead to becoming architect for the project once it appeared that funds could be raised to make it a reality. The long time initiative and leadership of Larry Rubin, who had been the executive director in building the Mackinac Bridge, along with a few other steadfast supporters of the library was the signal to go ahead. A number of sites were considered, each one requiring study of appropriate design concepts. First one location then another proved unfeasible until finally the Della Moretta family offered an ideal, sloping wooded site on the main highway approach to downtown St. Ignace of high visibility and views across the lake to Mackinac Island.

Five years had passed for all these steps in the process of design study, site selection and fund raising to take place. We were most fortunate to secure the firm of U. P. Engineers and Architects to develop construction documents, with J. P. Bodeman as project architect in charge. J. P. was also an Illini, of great skill, patience in carrying through the many trials and tribulations of so many site changes as were other members of his firm. We were also lucky that the low bidder was the Gerace Company from Midland, of high reputation for concrete work, a major construction material in the final design. Their foreman on the job was Gary Shepard who embodied an amazing versatility of personal hands-on skills himself as well as being a fine manager and a joy to work with. In my own long experience I can't remember any other project that combined such a rapport of team players—architects, builders, board and building committee members. Perhaps the best way for me to convey the hoped for significance of the library project is to include my own remarks at the dedication on June 18, 2005. I would ask the readers' indulgence for my inclusion of certain design principles and expressions that have been introduced earlier in this chronicle. At the suggestion of Wes Maurer, editor and publisher of the St. Ignace News, my remarks were published in the June 30, 2005 issue:

I have always been inspired by a wonderful Latin phrase, "genius loci," which means "spirit of place." Perhaps more than anything else, the spirit of place has guided all of us working to bring the new St. Ignace Public Library into reality after many years of planning and fund raising. The dedication ceremony on June 18 is at once a symbol marking this community achievement and an opportunity to reflect on the many influences affecting its design, influences as they come together that may in turn serve as guidelines for community development in the future.

The spirit of place of St. Ignace, and indeed the whole Straits area, is, I believe, an extraordinarily unique and rich combination of natural setting—"The center of the freshwater world"—and human history. In the heartland of North America, it is a place at the center of the Great Lakes of water bodies, rocky crags, sandy beaches, dunes, forests, marshes and evolving water, land, and airborne life. The waterscape also mirrors history over millennia: The migrations of human inhabitation—tentative, fragile, surviving over centuries, then meeting the accelerating pace of foreign discovery and settlement. By now we know how this natural sense of center became a place of meeting of Native Americans; Ojibways, Ottawas, and Hurons, Mackinac Island a legendary spiritual place as well as a kind of Switzerland, a neutral zone for peacemaking. Also for explorers, for traders and Jesuit missionaries it was a central place or base for further exploration, trading and spreading the faith. But for General Wolfe's defeat of Montcalm on the plains of Abraham in 1765, St. Ignace might be Montreal today, or whatever other set of circumstances history might have brought to the destiny of the Straits area.

The uniqueness of place in history has of course deep significance for the library in terms of its special collections beyond the timeless value of a community library anywhere as both a treasury of knowledge and a symbol of learning. In architectural terms this meant we had to search for ways to express this special significance, such as the circular "kiva" space honoring Native American lore and the tendency of the tribes across the continent to form circles for religious worship, powwows, and simply gathering around a fire. The centering of computer space in the main reading area honors the advance of communication technology as a unifying global force in education, as does the pyramid form of the building itself attempt to express the unifying power of all traditional forms of stored experience, learning and literature in books, journals, and all other types of recorded information.

Traditional in libraries, too, is the need for retreat or quiet space for special individual study like genealogy. The library itself as a community resource and symbol makes it an ideal place for community gatherings of all kinds, available in the evenings as well as during the day by its placement off the entrance foyer so that it may be used when the library is closed. The foyer also includes a "Wall of Honor" panel recording the names of donors, reminding visitors that the major

254

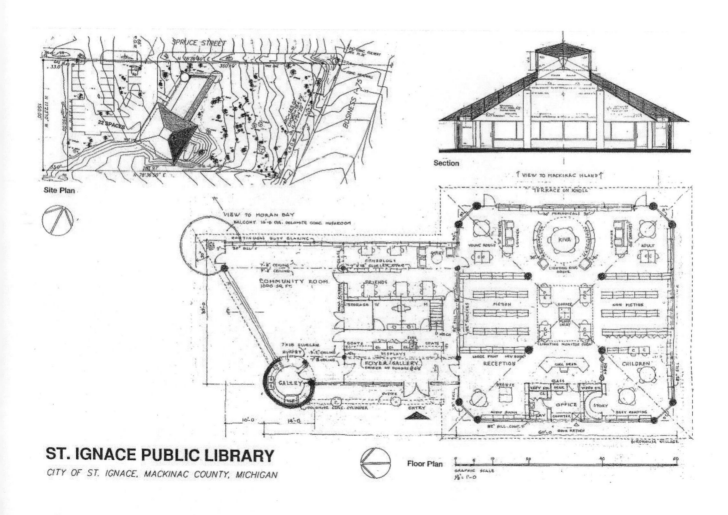

Site Plan

Section

Floor Plan

ST. IGNACE PUBLIC LIBRARY

CITY OF ST. IGNACE, MACKINAC COUNTY, MICHIGAN

Drawings for St. Ignace Public Library, St. Ignace, MI, 2005
A. Richard Williams, FAIA, Architect

financial support for building the new library came from private sources. Likewise, major spaces such as the reading rooms, information center, community room, and foyer/gallery have been named for individual donors.

The natural setting played a key role in the architectural design of the library as well. After several other sites had been studied and for one reason or another had not been workable, the present one became available, admirably meeting the criteria of convenient location, high visibility, relation to views to the "center of the fresh water world," yet in a wooded setting typical of our region. All this was an inspiration to use local materials in a clear-cut, honest way, avoiding imported style influences like Victorian or Disney World imagery. The natural geologic underlayment of the St. Ignace peninsula and Straits area is dolomite limestone, thus the main structural columns of dolomite aggregate concrete "grow" up from the bedrock, as do a few of the other walls, such as the kitchen cylinder and mushroom column terrace off the community room. Other infill walls of split face block pick up the bark color of the cedars and other evergreens. The dark bronze color of the standing seam steel roof and glass trim also repeats this same earth color, carried inside as well for some ceilings that extend from the underside of the wide overhanging roof form. The wide roof overhang is intended as well as a strong expression of shelter in all seasons. The choice of steel as a roof material recalls

Entry Facade
Lecturn
Columns (Photograph: Al Feliksa)

St. Ignace Public Library, St. Ignace, MI, 2005
A. Richard Williams, FAIA, Architect

the "Iron and Copper Country" identity of
Northern Michigan, as do the copper insets
on the vertical centerline of the pyramid
form of the building, both in the floor and
ceiling of the clerestory, which brings in
natural light by day and is illuminated as a
kind of beacon at night.

The bright colors of the clerestory ceiling
are taken from the Ojibway spectrum of
favorite colors. Since the dominant evergreen species of our limestone base geologic
region is northern white cedar, this material
was selected for the main pyramid ceiling,
in narrow rough-sawn horizontal strips to
express a reposed feeling as well as to take
advantage of acoustical absorption. Natural
oak finishes of the stacks and other furniture
carries the same feeling of repose and timelessness. The idea was that there is enough
bright color in the books themselves and in
the clothes of the library users, so why not
keep the color range of all surfaces of the
interior on a neutral level?

The hope is that all the above design decisions will be both timeless and timely,
reflecting the endurance and key importance
of learning in the community, perhaps ours
more than most because of its uniqueness
of setting. In a way, this is an added opportunity and responsibility to set a tone of
architectural character that may influence
others in our great northland region to rise
above the temptations of current fashion
and shallow surface veneer.

I have a vision that all the patient effort and
enduring motivation of all those involved

Interior (Photograph: Wes Maurer)
Drawing of Proposed Interior (A. Richard Williams)

Birdhouse Village
Children's Room with view to Birdhouse Village

257

with building the new library will carry on in inspiring future growth of St. Ignace, not only in the building of new and renovated civic structures but in the private sector as well, truly reflecting St. Ignace's "genius loci." Although this is a personal vision and hope, perhaps it may be shared by many others in the community, including most of all its young people who, along with the much needed existence of new economic incentives, may be persuaded to stay and take pride in being part of making a new charismatic spirit of place.

I have a vision, too, that although these thoughts may seem like dreaming, they may not be so complicated and unrealistic after all if we just try to know more about our own history and natural setting to resolve to bring the forest back into town, to clean up the waterfront, to rebuild and build new in a low key structures of durable natural materials without pretense, and to intensify the embrace of the harbor by watermarking its entry at the Chief's pier and Millslip point with lighthouses. I truly have a vision that if these goals could be achieved, St. Ignace would then rank with some of North America's finest historic nature/man settings like the Black Hills, Lake Louise, Provincetown, Cape Cod, Key West, and Santa Fe, New Mexico. Thereby, along with fulfilling its own sprit of place expectations, St. Ignace might become a similar top ranking tourist destination with all the economic benefits of prosperity without having to resort to exploitive popular images and entertainment attractions.

Such visions of the future for St. Ignace may be wishful thinking in the face of trends everywhere today, chasing the quick buck and the pursuit of entertainment, even in regions of great scenic beauty and historic heritage like the Straits of Mackinac. We more and more avoid frankness in calling attention to this darker side of our culture. Not to diminish all the blessings we have had and still enjoy, the local mirror reflects the gradual decline of respect for history on both sides of the Straits.

The Upper Peninsula since the prosperous logging and mining days, has suffered economic deprivation with only a brief summer season to attract tourists to its main destinations of Mackinac Island, Sault Ste. Marie, the splendors of the lake shores, islands and other natural features like the Taquamenon Falls, the Porcupine Mountains, state and national forests. Despite their own historic significance, St. Ignace and Mackinaw City have mainly become the two points of ferry access to Mackinac Island making every effort to attract tourist dollars in whatever exploitive way possible. In St. Ignace, highest priority as been given to car shows, casinos, trinket shops and the usual cheap commercial glitter of resort areas, while Mackinaw City has become another imitation of Disney World, with both communities marketing and hawking their genuine historic attractions in much the same way as entertainment attractions, appealing to the ever shorter attention spans of visitors.

Years before, Wes Maurer Sr., as publisher of the St. Ignace News had asked me to write articles pointing out ways that the great historic heritage and natural setting of the Straits as a whole might be recognized with new planning and architectural guidelines, especially emphasizing the potential of entry to the Upper Peninsula as the "Gateway to the North" by reforestation, restraint in the use of other than local materials, toning down commercialism, all of which I tried to summarize again in my piece about the library. Since Wes Sr. passed away, Wes Jr. and Mary have kept up this editorial effort and with Mary's sustained leadership of the library board we have tried to make the building and its setting a clear demonstration of how these visionary aspirations may be exemplified.

In spite of this effort St. Ignace is like so many communities in America, large and small, in resisting the extra measure of initiative and manual work in completion of civic projects. For whatever reason, laziness, indifference, lack of pride and will, probably at root all are symptoms of a spoiled, educationally impoverished society; city payrollers, like others in our inflated bureaucracies seem to be "carried" on the backs of ever fewer stalwarts who still can be counted on to get the job done.

On a more personal level, building my own studio "Singassin" in 1993 was an attempt to embody design canons at a modest scale, using the simple, strong geometry of the

Wellman Guest House (Photograph: Chas Kerschner)
North Facade at Twilight (Photograph: Wes Maurer)
Dining Area at Twilight (Photograph: Wes Maurer)

Wellman Guest House, St. Ignace, MI, 2001
A. Richard Williams, FAIA, Architect

pyramid form influenced by a small square clearing in a cedar grove on the lakeshore, building the structure of this same local cedar in antiphonal relation to a black steel "fire lantern" at the geometric center, with copper accents on centerlines, these metals both being indigenous to Michigan, all rising from a dolomite limestone bedrock base just thirty inches below the humus soil accumulated from the growth of cedars over the centuries. The next year in 1994, I built "Niji," a guest cabin, an eight foot by eight foot miniature of "Singassin" in the same form and materials.

Little did I imagine that a few years later in 2001 I would be asked by Cy and Sue Wellman, long summer residents of Coryell Island of the nearby Les Chenneau archipelago to be their architect for proposed new dwellings on their newly acquired property of over one hundred acres on La Salle Island, a magnificent wooded site on Government Bay, long a favorite anchorage for sailors seeking shelter from the open waters of Lake Huron.

One could not ask for a more fortuitous combination of client, program of needs and site. In all this acreage including a wide variety of native evergreens and hardwoods there was just one existing cabin in good enough condition to be enlarged and remodeled in harmony with the new structures which were to include a guest house, shorefront pavilion and Cy and Sue's own lodge. Right away I could tell this was going to be a most exceptional opportunity to carry on the same spirit of discovery of what architecture of the North might be with the library and Singassin as attempts to reach this goal, and perhaps a direction that might interest the Wellmans. As indeed it did.

We made a pact right at the beginning that we would not use the word "style," in our effort to be guided by what the projects wanted to be in terms of space and materials as described earlier in the design of the library-limestone, cedar, steel and copper. Once Cy and Sue came over to Singassin to discuss the sense of direction and how it might meet their own desires, they became most enthusiastic, so over a time span of four years for the sequence of dwellings to be built, we have reached an enormous sense of pleasure and confidence that our initial visions have not only now become real but in many ways enriched and molded by the process itself. In fact we have coined a new "tongue in cheek" term, "Darwinian architecture," to describe the many mutations of site determinants, going with the flow of builder preferences, our own on the spot changes and other apparent improvements, all evolving fortuitously. We made a rule never to use the word "mistake," preferring "adjustment," "enhancement"—our own version of spin.

Endless summer days of the North had for years been bridged to the summery days of winters in Tucson by October in Rome, basking in its world-unique aura of timelessness. What is it about Rome if not this quality

of endurance and survival that time after time inspires visions of the future? Student design projects at Notre Dame's architecture program, with their Roman sites always seemed to evoke the question of what can you do that meets today's needs and on into the future that in intimate relationship still fully respects such a powerful presence of the past, in seamless continuity? Copying the past is always up front as an easy cop out, placing greater challenges on finding what is really timely. At the American Academy too, I had found that the excitement of such a high concentration of talented artists and scholars, drawing inferences from the glories of the past seemed so often to provoke questions of so what does it all mean—a host of if-then clauses as I had remarked earlier (p. 138) in the subjunctive mood—leading to my own conjecture of what the Academy might ideally mean for architects not only in terms of critical study, design and dialogue but in a visionary architectural setting instead of its magnificent copy of a renaissance Roman palazzo (p. 138).

As these October visits flew by year after year I began to have more clearly focused ideas of what the Rome inspiration might mean for contributing to the future of the College of Architecture and Landscape Architecture in Tucson and visionary concepts for the Sonoran genius loci. My mind flashed back in vivid memory to that afternoon in 1957 in the hill town of Fiesole beholding the city of Florence below just after receiving

Wellman Lodge South Wing
Wellmand Lodge Entry Patio
(Photographs: Wes Maurer)

Lodge, Wellman Residence, St. Ignace, MI, 2001
A. Richard Williams, FAIA, Architect

news of my new responsibility of directing graduate architectural studies at Illinois
(p. 147). Florence in the distant view was
a glowing singularity expressing its world
preeminence as a work of art in itself,
symbolizing the highest standard of human
achievement—an extraordinary challenge to
those of us entrusted as leaders in education
for both the present and future. How can
this link between the timelessness, of design
learning in Rome and Florence now be made
to the wisest and most timely environmental
design decisions in the Sonora?

At that earlier time, of course the challenge
was in the thick of team action that being on
a faculty and in practice involves, with all its
here and now galaxy of problems, opportunities and academic politics. Now in the new
millennium and for some time before I knew
how vastly different one's relationship is as
an emeritus professor apart and away from
the direct responsibilities of decision making.

After retiring, I made several proposals at
Illinois in regard to campus planning, curriculum change and for programming and
direction for the new architecture building
built in the mid-nineties—all received with
smiles, thanks, but to no effect whatso-
ever. It's so easy to kid yourself that your
influence, built up over years, has enduring
respect long after you're "liberated" as an
emeritus. I can't resist including here a verse
I wrote when I woke up to the fact that this
kind of self esteem can be an illusion.

Agaming Shore Pavillion from Beach
Agaming Entry Deck
(Photographs: Wes Maurer)

Agaming , Wellman Residence, St. Ignace, MI, 2001
A. Richard Williams, FAIA, Architect

EMERITI *
I MORTI

"Do not go gentle into that good night
Rage, rage against the dying of the light" [1]

       Twenty years to know the meaning of Emeritus.
Freedom in the design of creative time.
       The blessing of best associations.
       A fabulous family.
       A dreamline.
       A metastream of hopes, poetry, highest expectations.
Immortality foreshadowed?
       But in paradox flows an undercurrent.
Realities, black and white
       Ebb in and out of focus.
Mortality, unmasked,
       Reveals a threshold crossed long ago
       Into a hall of mirrors, periscopes and cameras.

Mirrors reflect self-images,
       Cloudy in a collage
       Of rituals, honors.
       Scepters, crowns.
Periscopes scan Sacred Mountains
       Above an Illuminated Plain.
       Scan below roughcalm seas
       Opaque depths of lost friendships,
       Hidden reefs of betrayal.

Cameras take flashback images
       In a reversal of time to find
       Linkages where the dreamline drove reality
       And reality changed the dream.

       These fragile threads of connection
       Appear, tangle, break, then reappear.
       Do they really exist?
       What is their substance?
       More than a gossamer web of illusion?
       Choose one thread to trace the
Quest for transcendence:
       The university as an urban metaphor,
       As a unity of diversities,
       A synergy of separate realities and dreams
       Coexisting on highest known summits of learning,
       Searching, yearning for still higher summits yet unknown.

Transcendence:
       A crystallisis of performance and setting inseparably linked.
       Life and art as one.

Performance:
       A plurality of starseparate games, plays, actors
       Seeking constellation, seeking community.

Setting:
       A singularity of architecture and landscape as a single medium.
       "The set is a fellow actor," [2]
       Its brilliance cannot exist
       Without eloquence of script and action.

       The singularity of setting is spectacular
       In scrolls of Chinese painting:
       Sacred Mountain settings for immortals
       Residing in exquisite pavilions and terraces
       Interlocked delicately with dramatic landscape.

       The quest for transcendence becomes personal,
       Lucky in a lifetime to feel, but too rarely, the
Exhilaration of extraordinary encounters:
       Queens of Hearts, Kings of Diamonds,
       "Fanfares to the Common Man" [3]
       In peaks and valleys of time.
Encounter:
       A university centennial, once upon a time
       Touched by the edge of greatness.
       A fluorescence of intellectual, artistic crossover;
       Collaboration, teach in, teach across, show, tell.
       A luminous foreshadow of Sacred Mountains.

       Then came unrest, riots and curfew.
       "Where have all the flowers gone?" [4]

Begin Emeritus, enter the hall of mirrors
       Cross a River Styx, a figurative death?
       Become an icon beckoned to lead and join in ritual?
       Apart from realworld strategies and directions
Wisdom, volunteered in the realworld realm
       Of benign smiles and nodding heads
       Seems cut off behind a heavy wall of glass.

       The role of gadfly Emeritus is hard to play.
       Lines of script are barely heard – fade into silence.
       The icon turns to scan again, in sunset red
       The Sacred Mountains
       Across the Illuminated Plain.

1. Dylan Thomas Collected Poems   2. Brecht on Theatre
3. Aaron Copeland Composition   4. Song by Peter, Paul and Mary

Still in spite of these misgivings, there was hope that in Arizona the dreamline and pondering the future might be more rewarding as indeed it has. The theme again took its inspiration from our classical heritage, this time from the Golden Age of Greece, choosing the word Archon (leader, which together with "Tecton," meaning building technology combine as the root of the word architect) as the name for future-oriented projects, prizes and spaces that could involve what resources of mind and substance remained for me in support. It had been so clear that the forces and pressures of the present in both education and practice had been so consuming—money, competition, materialism—that little time or concern was left for visionary concept development, surely one of the uppermost missions of both universities and an enlightened public.

With these thoughts in mind I found that there already existed a tiny core of like-minded enthusiasts in the community joining together in Civitas Sonoran (p. 233) and in the museum of Contemporary Art, MOCA, all seeming to spring to new life with the new millennium. The spirit of collaboration in looking ahead had new energy and momentum—so it seemed. In this mood I offered a new incentive called the Archon Prize to foster collaboration of teams of two students—one architect and one landscape architect, each year on a small scale visionary project. Coinciding with the programming and construction of a new addition to the university's existing architecture build-

Piano Location, Stage 2B
Bench, Stage 3
Piano Location, Stage 3

Camaralta, Tucson, AZ, 1982, 1992, 2004
A. Richard Williams, FAIA, Architect

ing, I made a donation to include the Archon Seminar room, as a penthouse on the new structure, as a think tank space, for planning and executing collaborative projects within the college that prioritizes visions of the future. It would also invite and encourage visionary discourses among leaders in the university as a whole, as a countermeasure, you might even say refuge, from the "slings and arrows" of today's overwhelming pressures. It remains to be seen how all this works.

This kind of day dreaming becoming reality is of course most exciting personally. Too, saying to myself "I've got to do something at small scale, even at this ancient age, that tries to be part of the new millennial "seit geist"—namely, greatly to enlarge the upper level of Camaralta, as described by the following text, drawings and photographs, so that its prospect is visually and dramatically in touch with the magic of the Sonoran Mountains and cityscape—a personal reciprocal to the Archon Seminar.

The name "CAMARATLA" means "pilot house" and or "Captain's quarters" in Spanish, so named because the owner is an "ancient mariner" as well as an architect, with experience in boat building and design, service in the Navy in World War II, and as captain of "OSIMO" a forty-foot steel hull motor sailer on the upper Great Lakes for many years.

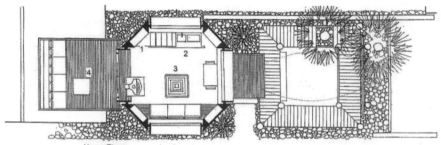

Upper Floor
1. Stair Down
2. Galley
3. Living/Dining/Sleeping
4. Deck

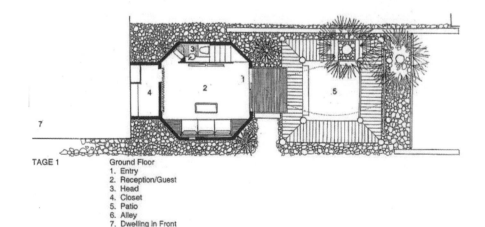

TAGE 1   Ground Floor
1. Entry
2. Reception/Guest
3. Head
4. Closet
5. Patio
6. Alley
7. Dwelling in Front

Ground and Upper Floor Plan
Camaralta, Stage 1, Tucson, AZ, 1982
A. Richard Williams, FAIA, Architect
Kurtin Residence (Ground Floor), Charles A. Albanese, FAIA

Camaralta is an example of "mutant architecture" built in three stages. The first was in 1982, followed by additions in 1992 and completion in 2004. Its location is in the Sam Hughes Neighborhood in Tucson, a 1920's and 1930's subdivision of small bungalow dwellings bordering the east edge of the University of Arizona campus. Since that time many of the houses have been expanded with "guest houses" in back; Camaralta is one of these.

Stage 1 (1982) was designed as a two story addition embodying the efficiency of marine design: compactness of kitchen (galley) and bathroom (head) through careful planning and detail, to allow for more spaciousness of living, dining, studio and sleeping areas, all necessitated by a small lot. The basic form is an octagon with eight foot sides and four foot corners, taking advantage of modular sizes to avoid waste. Most houses in the Sam Hughes neighborhood are one story, even though a second story is permissible. Enabled by this possibility, the upper level of Camaralta has a view to all four cardinal points of the compass, although the views north to the Catalina Mountains and south to the Santa Ritas dominate, with a deck to the south over the roof of the house in front. Entry was from a patio on the north side through a sliding door to a reception area with closets and a "head" under the stairs. This first floor space served as a camp style guest room as well as an entry. The upper level "captain's quarters" served as a living, dining, cooking and sleeping space. Above

waistcoat height the interior was black as in Navy ship' pilot houses to emphasize looking out as well as to provide a contrasting background for instruments – clocks, barometer, radio and other devices. Corner cupboards serve adjacent functions, for cooking, sleeping, etc. The main color and material theme is white stucco and black painted wood, with natural finish Douglas Fir as trim.

Stage 2 (1992) added a "music room" in place of the patio on the north side, with the entry changed to the east side of the octagon. In addition to providing space for a seven foot Baldwin grand piano brought down from Illinois, this new room included a social area with bar, work space with north light, also serving as a guest room. Two years later the piano was moved to the east side of the room with its long side supported by the sill of the long, low bay window. At this time as well, the entry area became an inner octagon for book shelves. The music room's ceiling joists were salvaged from the old Safeway store on Park Avenue, which was the first location for the College of Architecture. The forty-five degree angle derived from the octagon form is echoed at various scales and in details of furniture. Color accents come from southwestern and Mexican influences.

Stage 3 (2003-2004) expanded the upper floor as much as possible within zoning setback and height limitations. By coincidence, the resulting floor plan rectangle turned out to be almost exactly the Gold Section

Camaralta, Stage 1, Upper Level
Camaralta, Stage 1, View from East

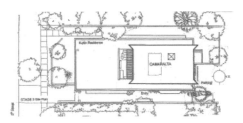

Camaralta, Stage 3 Site Plan

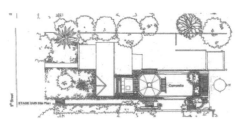

Camaralta, Stage 2B Site Plan

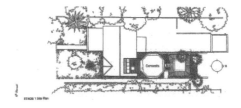

Camaralta, Stage 1 Site Plan

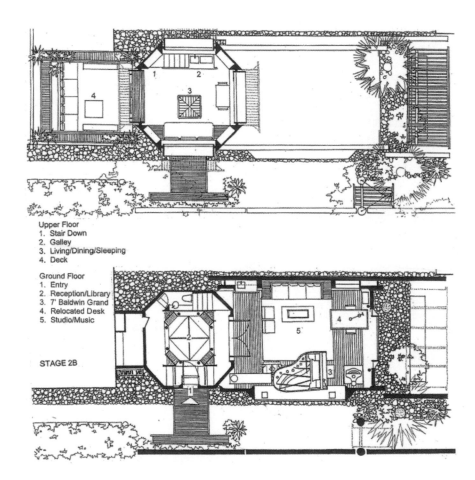

Upper Floor
1. Stair Down
2. Galley
3. Living/Dining/Sleeping
4. Deck

Ground Floor
1. Entry
2. Reception/Library
3. 7' Baldwin Grand
4. Relocated Desk
5. Studio/Music

STAGE 2B

Ground and Upper Floor Plan
Camaralta, Stage 2B, Tucson, AZ, 1982
A. Richard Williams, FAIA, Architect

Camaralta, Stage 2B, North Facade from Across Alley
Camaralta, Stage 2B, North Facade from Alley
Camaralta, Stage 2A, Interior of Ground Floor looking North

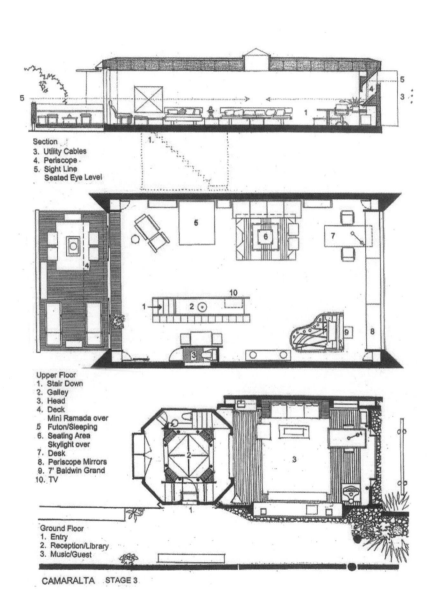

Section
3. Utility Cables
4. Periscope
5. Sight Line
    Seated Eye Level

Upper Floor
1. Stair Down
2. Galley
3. Head
4. Deck
    Mini Ramada over
5. Futon/Sleeping
6. Seating Area
    Skylight over
7. Desk
8. Periscope Mirrors
9. 7' Baldwin Grand
10. TV

Ground Floor
1. Entry
2. Reception/Library
3. Music/Guest

CAMARALTA   STAGE 3

Camaralta, Stage 3, Mirror Reflectors of West Sunsets
Camaralta, Stage 3, View to the Southwest

Ground and Upper Floor Plans and Section
Camaralta, Stage 3, Tucson, AZ, 2004
A. Richard Williams, FAIA, Architect

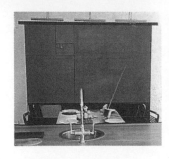

Camaralta, Stage 3, Periscope Mirrors and Desk looking North to the
Santa Catalina Mountain Skyline

Camaralta, Stage 3, Sleeping Area/Futon
Camaralta, Stage 3, Interior Looking South
Camaralta, Stage 3, Galley looking towards *head*

proportion ratio of 1.618. In order to achieve this new space, the upper level octagon was removed except for the stair access and galley sink plumbing, allowing new frame construction of heavily insulated east/west side walls and roof, with glass walls to principal mountain views north and south.

A characteristic of the Sonoran Desert landscape is that most trees such as palo verde and mesquite have a low canopy so that a seated eye level at about 5 meters above the ground allows distant vistas of the mountains above these trees framed by widely spaced palms, cypress and pine. This horizontal eye level visual plane also presents the maximum density of green vegetation obscuring most other dwellings except for a few desert colored roof parapets here and there. You are hardly aware you are in the city. In Illinois or other verdant areas you would have to be on a fourth or fifth floor above the trees for a similar view to the horizon.

To enhance the horizontality of this prospect the two glazed areas north and south are as wide as possible, 6.5 meters with every effort made to entice you psychologically to sit down to enjoy these dramatic eye level views, especially north to the Santa Catalina mountain skyline.

This was done by placing this wide window head just 1.7 meters above the floor. In order to achieve this wide but low proportion at seated eye level it was necessary to use a

periscope arrangement of two 45° mirrors to avoid a cluster of horizontal utility cables that otherwise would have obstructed a clear view if the normal window glazing had been at that eye level. As the building section shows, the actual glazing strip is at ceiling level so the mirrors can reflect the mountain skyline above the objectionable cables.

As before, the galley and head are small in size for maximum ergonometric efficiency and to create strong scale contrast with the large open space for living, working and entertaining. Navajo white walls, ceiling and carpeted floor are intended to intensify the lightness and airiness of the space, and also serve as a background for strong widely separated color accents such as the red screen wall on the head which repeats the Golden Section proportion of the floor plan.

On the opposite wall a Navy signal flag (the letter Z) from World War II is composed with the main social and sleeping area, with the center of this grouping accented by a skylight above on vertical axis with the coffee table. The overall intention of the interior space is to respond to "genius loci" of the Sonoran Desert environment, its quality of light, distant vistas, landscape and cultural heritage of Pre-Columbian and Hispanic settlement, seeking both timeless and timely expression.

This intention is carried to the exterior as well. The small bungalow house in front was

removed and replaced by an entirely new dwelling, including living/dining, and three bedrooms for the young family, Lia and Jeff Kurtin and their two small daughters. This white stuccoed concrete block structure thus forms a unified whole, a ground floor base for the rusted steel clad walls of Camaralta studio on the floor above.

270

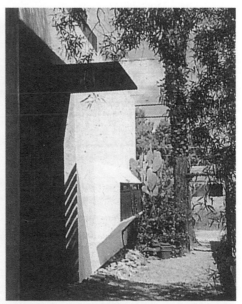

Camaralta, Stage 3, South Facade from 5th Street with Kurtin
Residence on street side and *Camaralta* to the rear

Camaralta, Stage 3, Entry Area
Camaralta, Stage 3, North Facade from Alley

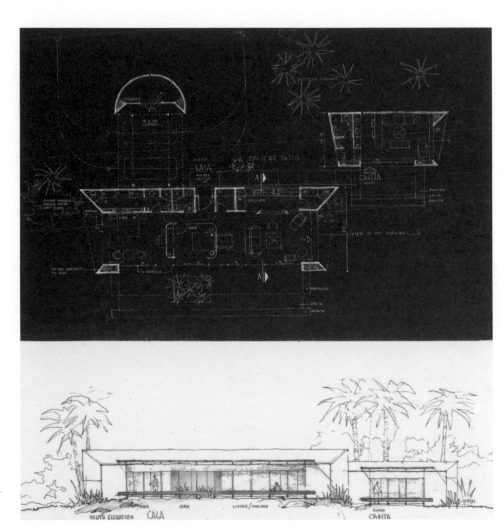

Casa Imaginativa (Imaginary House)
Proposed desert dwelling, Green Valley, AZ

Views east to Santa Rita Mountains and south to arroyos and distant peaks. East/west linear plan at 82 degrees and solar collector panels on the roof maximize solar energy efficiency and water harvesting for nearby desert planting. Inspiration for the study: property owners Bruce and Ingrid Hutchings

A. Richard Williams, FAIA, Architect

As still-living members of Tom Brokaw's Greatest Generation[24], those of us in architecture and education are now bound to contemplate the future of America with special nostalgia and concern. Having first experienced the dark days of depression and war when it seemed doubtful that both architecture and the university as timeless cultural values could survive (p. 27), even to the point of threatening the very existence of higher learning and the grace of a sensitively designed environment, we had somehow through adversity acquired an extra measure of determination and inspiration to be turned on team players in the time of recovery.

Little did we imagine then that the post-war years would be regarded as anything more than a return to normal times or that by the end of the century our generation would be called "greatest." Naturally taken by surprise, how can we understand this new acclaim? Although having been actors in the thick of unprecedented growth and change over all this time, I truly believe we have been more like Tolstoi's character Pierre in War and Peace, tuned all along to be involved and enchanted observers too, now in awe to be thought of as heroes.

So in retrospect as both an actor and observer I want to return again to the idea of the university and architecture interlocked in the same mirror, trying to trace their well-being, rise and fall as an analogue of modern culture.

Recovery from the depression and war brought a new surge of unquestioning support for public universities, states bearing the major costs of growth both in quantity and quality. Too, university leaders, trustees and legislators well understood the value of architectural excellence as imperative for higher education and as an exemplary model for all new built environments in our society as well as preservation of the best from the past.

Then gradually, sometimes suddenly in the aftermath of the war in Korea and the debacle of Vietnam the drift away from this trust began. More and more, states have pared down their budget support of total costs to ever lower levels, down to the twenty per cent range or less, forcing families to pay ever higher tuition rates and administrators and faculties to spend more and more of their time and energy raising money instead of advancing academic quality. In parallel, campus architecture has become watered down to mediocrity through fast track, bottom line pressures, with fewer and fewer exceptions. Meantime private universities have flourished, widening still more the gap that has always existed between the privileged class and the vast majority of young people seeking a quality college or university education. Likewise quality architecture has been increasingly confined within gated precincts, but even there we are seeing a shift to pretentious show pieces and expressions of shoddy affluence.

I must also observe that as our generation was deeply engaged in the crescendo of recovery building up to the sixties—the decade now called by our great Native American poet Scott Momaday as the star time of the twentieth century—that this was also a time when our architectural heroes were mostly American—Kahn, Saarinen, Rudolph, Jones, Kirk, Caudill, SOM, Perkins & Will, Harris, Eames, Wurster and others. They became known for the quality of their work not only on campuses but at modest scales of dwellings and other smaller structures. Most were also engaged in architectural education as well. This was a sea change from earlier in the century when we were still a colony bringing in European stars to head our schools and dominate directions in modern architecture. We were also still innocently unaware in this post-war time when fame was truly earned from quality of performance, that games of politics and networking were already being played and that stardom could be manufactured by PR—games that in the later decades of the century were to become so pervasive.

Our generation can now see clearly how much the spirit of collegiality and collaboration in our universities that we took for granted during our golden age has changed to today's preoccupation with individual career advancement above everything else, especially the very essence of mutual learning. This is a severe blow to architectural education in particular as fewer and fewer talented architects are deeply involved in studio criticism, the ageless heart of comprehensive design learning. Somehow we have now been persuaded that bringing in starchitects, again the more foreign the better for a brief time meets this need, kidding ourselves in much the same way that our whole society thinks it is moving ahead in the aura of big names, mistaking the allure of osmosis, (in reality entertainment) tending to rise above honest learning through our own hard work in the midst of our peers. Does our increasing "all about me" attitude, vanity as a nation, global power and empire, plus our casual regard (or indeed ignorance) of history now make us blind to learning from the affluence of decadent empires in the past, notably fourth century AD Rome before its fall?

Isn't this same syndrome of world-wide big time how invading our cities as well? Our compulsion to build icons designed by even bigger names, again mostly foreign, now appears to be polarizing the public's idea of architecture only as ostentatious monuments, obscuring its timeless heritage as the art of building through much more modest scales of human environment. Even critics and some scholars seem to be swept up in this era of high fashion and celebrity—seldom do we find any critical attention given to less spectacular, unassuming work of true excellence, which though increasingly overwhelmed in a sea of mediocrity, does indeed still exist. May it be the seed for new enlightenment—a new Golden Age!
This is the glimmer of hope that our genera-

tion, greatest or not, may be most able to truly understand and value, retaining our perhaps naïve optimism and trust in communicating to our students and younger peers, while we still have time, that architecture entwined with landscape and with highest aspirations of learning/living may reach as yet unimagined pinnacles of excellence and compassion, despite the present storm of vanities, waste and self indulgence.

From this nostalgia and concern for the future I feel the need to reaffirm again hard-won, timeless canons for American architecture and education that may in turn be universally understood and valued:

A basic compassion for the human condition, with determination to bring excellence of design, in harmony with nature, within the reach of all.

An understanding that heroes, greater or lesser, work together, or in respectful succession, over the full scale of environment— microscale settings, architecture, landscape, urban design, and region planning.

That the design response to well-being begins at the intimate scale of each individual, in both public and private life, as an extra effort to make ensembles of detail into works of art. Recognition, too, that architecture as building art is only possible through knowledge, experience and respect for the construction process, as well as for cultural intelligence .

To bring all scales of environment into harmony with themselves and with nature through higher team and/or individual compositional and orchestrational skill-architecture and landscape as one.

To bring spiritual and poetic qualities into every design ensemble—art and architecture as one.

To ensure that the principle of excellence in diversity is understood and respected as a most fundamental readable common quality, transcending superficial differences in fashion and style, possessing qualities that are both timeless and timely.

24 Brokaw, Tom, The Greatest Generation, New York, 1998

Rather than attempt to sift once again through the kaleidoscope of designs for learning as they have revealed themselves to me over such a long span of time, I implore the reader to find his or her own perceptions and priorities. But I would reaffirm how important it is to seek and find the dynamic equilibrium that lies between old and new wisdom, always in a new synthesis pointing ahead. This becomes a singular bliss on its own with power to overcome vainglory and indifference to past learning.

In my own archipelago of appealing afterthoughts I would choose but one out of many—the idea of how the whole realm of enlightened design, especially architecture, is a beneficial mediator between Nature and Man. This in essence is an antiphonal relationship, as in music, "the responsive singing by a choir in two divisions."

ARCHIPELAGO has tried to see and celebrate the joy of learning through architecture. It sees the life of the mind as a repository of penniless wealth, accumulating, sifting, fine tuning over a lifetime. It sees architecture as a treasury of built thought. Along this lifetime path the joy of learning builds as well, perhaps because architecture more than any other art is so closely interwoven with the human condition. After countless cycles of mixing an insatiable desire to learn with experience in action the idea of an antiphony gains strength and holds one's thoughts.

At the heart of this process lies the interface and interaction between complex animate and inanimate forces that ebb and flow, shifting, seeking survival, truth and beauty of meaning. These forces seem always to form themselves in two synchronic sets, balancing in opposition or in harmony: Nature in dialogue with Man.

Of Nature | Of Man

Land	Sea	Individual	Society
Surface	Sky	Mono-ethnic	Multi-ethnic
Mountain	Plains	Privileged	Under Privileged
Verdant	Desert	Past	Present
Flora	Fauna	Timeless	Timely
Life	Death	Theism	Atheism
Light	Dark	War	Peace
Sun	Shadow	Urban	Rural
Macro	Micro	I	Thou
Stable	Evolving	Frontstage	Backstage

In architecture, antiphonies may be composed between space and structure, between two principal materials or sets, between light and shadow, between overall form and detail, between frontstage and backstage—most important, between the setting and human performance. Antiphonies extend, of course, in the larger context of inside and outside, building and site, ground and sky and in many more cultural and environmental couplets, sets and mediations.

Architecture is a composer and mediator of all these pairs, at root a song of Nature and Man, of their materials and processes.

As this vast panoply of forces and events unfolds in one's own richness of time, the quest to behold, to learn and to act, gains power and attraction in inverse proportion to scale. Design as a creative human act becomes most demanding, insightful and thereby most fulfilling in the smallest contexts of Nature Man interaction. All the networks of larger forces are still present, but in microcosm, distilled and balanced as the acts of life are intertwined with their settings, becoming single works of art. The grace of performance belongs to the inhabitant and the harmony of the setting to the architect but in space and time they become one creative interaction.

So I now take leave of this archipelago of experience, thoughts and dreams, no longer with hesitation as to why it should exist at all, and knowing that my fabulous family may be inspired to dream many of the same dreams and many, many more of their own.

Archipelago

The phenomenon of life can be extraordinarily rich in its detail at any point in one's existence but becomes overwhelming as a gift with the flow of time, spaces and events as they form a composite single blessing. This gift is also a debt—mounting more and more with reflection on how incomplete each effort to offer thanks at a given moment is in proportion to the need to express a deep collective gratitude to what I've called a fabulous family. Beginning with my parents and expanding in ever wider circles of teachers, mentors, students, colleagues, clients and friends, this compass must also include our finest institutions and cultural heritage, wishing that all anonymity would disappear, replaced by names we would like to know, revere and love as family, too. Let this moment now reflect my profound appreciation for this totality of the gift that in turn may be dedicated to all those yet to come.

This celebration embraces the entire archipelago of realities and dreams I have been blessed to have experienced over a long life span, but a separate reality exists in the making of this chronicle, building up a special need to thank those most patient and devoted few who have been such a help in advice, encouragement and transcription of writing, drawings and photographs, all of which have come together tentatively, then contemplated and revised countless times over the past ten years. It has been a design process exactly like the flow of ideas and decisions involved in making architecture—concept, trying alternative schemes and their detail resolutions, then cycling and refining as a whole. The body of thought and writing has taken place in three living/working settings over this decade of time; St. Ignace in summers north, Tucson in winters south with Rome in Octobers between. Up north I am much indebted to Wes and Mary Maurer, owners, editors and publishers of the St. Ignace News, not only for their generosity in printing and copying drafts, drawings and photography but also for their inspirational suggestions and counsel. In Tucson I'm kept on a steady keel by the encouragement of Chuck Albanese, Dean, Mary Kay Dinsmore, Kathy Hancox, Michael Kothke, faculty and students of CALA, the University of Arizona, most of all by Linda Craig, who has been a champion of patience and skill in word processing. In between in Rome the ambience of the American Academy has set a quiet, timeless tone of quality expectation for thinking, dialogue and writing. Beyond these three main bases for working I hear voices and echoes from so many other all-too-brief encounters in Wisconsin, Illinois, San Francisco Bay, Oregon, Santa Fe, Florence and in other parts of the world. To all these, including all whose names have inadvertently escaped memory, my lasting thanks.

Contents

A.1
Epilogue from the Urban Stage
A Reflection of Architecture and Urban Design, San Francisco, 1981
Theme: Learning from the dramatic metaphor

The path toward humane architecture and urban design stretches ahead. Will the way be clear for a gentle, compassionate response to human needs, or will this hope be entirely crushed in the avalanche of global exploitation, conflict, greed, energy depletion and narcissism? Though the reality of this millennial crisis is upon us and cynicism and pessimism abounds, must we despair and every voice of hope be stilled? In trust that hope does spring eternal and with the persistent vision of a new Golden Age ahead, I would like to summarize the most important inferences for design as they have evolved in the foregoing chapters.

Space for human activity should be consciously composed in major and minor juxtapositions, as frontstage performing areas supported by backstage areas. This reciprocal relationship seems to exist or want to exist in all types of archetypal settings. The performance needs that arrange these basic major and minor spaces are played out in a choreography of movement pulses: entrances to performing areas followed by a performance sequence and exit to a backstage area. This basic movement pulse, in its complexity and diversity, has great opportunity for reinforcement by design, involving choices of spatial dimension, manipulation of levels, sense of scale gradient in the living membrane, which is responsively equipped with properties of a functional nature as well as rich with cues for the environment of the mind.

The composition of frontstage spaces includes sensory reinforcement in the use of light, sound, touch, taste and smell in a subtle but positive balance beyond commonly held norms of environmental control. Thus the fine tuning of a setting requires a balancing act of design decisions over the full sensory realm, well beyond the static, fixed sets of present and past high fashion architecture, interior and urban design. Study and practice of

this balancing act must be related to the simplest and most commonplace private and public settings for dialogue, dining, drinking, learning and working tasks, rather than interpreted as a call for new displays of high technology. But, where appropriate, the resources of sophisticated knowledge, materials, and high technology must not be neglected or disdained. The development of restraint and critical judgment in the choices of possible design responses over the full spectrum from low to high tech is a most crucial educational and experience goal for both users and designers.

In the design of frontstage areas, a most significant principles is that of the inseparability of human performances and settings. This concept of inseparability inevitably entwines the user (performer) and designer in a close relationship with a strong focus on skill development and responsibility in ensemble choice making. The most skillful performers generate the most skillful settings, a fact which should alert designers to the quality of a client's performance that may not be evident in a written design program. The Guide Michelin principle of perceiving gradients of quality in performance/ setting interaction is applicable to all scales of settings and should be a practice mechanism for all choice makers in the design of frontstage spaces.

Backstage areas in service and support are equally critical for reform and design improvement. Even though our materialist, self-indulgent culture seems to understand and handle backstage space with assurance and mechanical competence, this confidence in designing and equipping kitchens, bathrooms and all other kinds of appliance shrines becomes irresponsible in lavishness of space, gadgetry and energy consumption, while much of the world is still without minimum life support systems. As a part of this moral question,

A.1
Epilogue from the Urban Stage
A Reflection of Architecture and Urban Design, San Francisco, 1981
Theme: Learning from the dramatic metaphor

a sensible proportioning of backstage systems is vital because they are in aggregate such ravenous consumers of material and energy resources and enormously wasteful in the use of space and extension of utility networks. These trends extended at global scale could be ruinous to the world community. Seen conversely, a reasonable shrinkage in the material and energy demands of these millions of service spaces would constitute a great breakthrough in conservation, analogous to but of far greater significance than the global trend toward more fuel-efficient cars.

In a new Golden Age, the husbandry of material, energy and land would be well understood and respected. The medium of good design would be directed to intelligent miniaturization of space and equipment needed in backstage areas and in the connection systems that service them. Miniaturization of service systems is already well developed in marine and air installations as it is in many parts of Europe and Japan, where design response to high density living patterns has been evolving for centuries. Careful three-dimensional planning of space derived from a full understanding of body metrics, plus the availability of trim, slim, strong and elegant devices and hardware can transcend the rationale of dire necessity to a level of desirability in its own right. Good design has no sterner discipline and greater reward than in the successful orchestration of small spaces.

Much of the skill exerted in the creative miniaturization of backstage service spaces and systems can move out again into frontstage space so that principal acting areas can be more finely turned and become more compact in physical dimension without sacrifice of livability. I have noted at some length in THE MOLD OF FORM chapter the benefits of sensitive manipulation of scale, for example, finely scaled ensembles tend by contrast to make

the open space of living areas seem even more spacious. Actors, in moving from miniaturized backstage areas to frontstage carry with them the memory of this finely scaled environment; thus experiencing scale and spatial contrast and a pleasant intensification of "making an entrance" to frontstage space.

All through this study I have described many types of thresholds or transition zones between backstage and frontstage spaces, noting their potential for design response. Of all the combinations of choices that are involved in the design of entrances and exists or any other form of transition from offstage to onstage, the most important choices are those that enhance adjustment and fine tuning of this valving function in the flow of human performances. "Waiting in the wings" is so often a negative, nowhere experience and depressingly pervasive as a force of alienation. But such thresholds in the asphalt jungles of modern cities are ripe targets and opportunities for design. They are a vital component of the frontstage/backstage movement pulse. They form what Martin Buber calls, "the in-between realm," zones of dawn and twilight that have spatial and time dimensions as yet little explored. Threshold zones are intensely personal places in which the pause before action is solitary—terrifying or exhilarating. Therefore, the design of these "valve spaces" is most crucial in affecting the environment of the mind, as well as in modulating the physical process of entrance and exit. Thresholds in depth are on the frontier of design exploration and speculation, stimulating a search for prototypes. To allow room for this speculation and imaginative design response, the growth and change of human environment must include many more "valve spaces," not only in the familiar guise of vestibules, foyers, anterooms, entrance and exit attenuations, but also in a variety of "unassigned" semi-private and private

alcoves, side aisles, bypasses and other intimately scaled spaces that exit between or at the side of major performing stages. They might be rooms within the "thick wall" or the "thick roof" as suggested in THE MOLD OF FORM discussion of the use of analogy and metaphor. They are in effect extensions of backstage space but of a more special function: to support the very personal experience of entrance (waiting for cue) or exit (a decompression chamber?).

If the husbandry of the finite resources of spaceship Earth is to avoid oppressive regimentation, intelligent and compassionate design is increasingly imperative as a countermeasure to crisis. As global urbanization continues within whatever limitations to growth may be required, all design tasks become urban design over the full scale spectrum. THE URBAN STAGE becomes real in aid of privacies of great diversity and in aid of a new sense of world community.

The concluding inference for design is that the ethics of architecture and all realms of environmental design must acknowledge responsibility in the same global context, but with increasing strength through education in support of the environment of each individual. This is the idea of CADRE DE VIE and the hope of learning from THE DRAMATIC METAPHOR. Most of all, the making of truly meaningful real life settings infers a much wider spread of literary and cultural awareness of the part of all participants, both users and designers. There is a great need for new dimensions of invested meaning: a penniless wealth that springs from literature, art, compassionate human experience and love of nature. The extent to which these qualities may be invested in modest, everyday settings is the greatest challenge for design, perhaps foreshadowed most poignantly in the make believe recesses of the dramatic metaphor.

Archipelago   Appendix

A.2
Projects in the Graduate Design Studio
University of Illinois, 1961–1970 Roster of Students and Critics

1961/62

A Sector of Metropolis
A Study of Radial Corridor Development for the Chicago Metropolitan Region, including Chicago West, A proposed new settlement for 100,000.

Students:
Bal Baswant, Brian Binning, Michael Flynn, Alan Forrester, Paulo Sica, Robert McKenzie

Critics:
Norman Day, Robert Katz, A. Richard Williams

Chicago Lakefront Plan
A study of Redevelopment of Chicago's Lakefront for Causeway Dwelling and Recreation Expansion

Students:
Walter Buss, David Brors, Wichit Charenbhak, Paul Davis, Paul Magierek, Bir Bal Malik, Carl Mark, Ernest Porps, Ron Schmitt, Lakshmi Sharma, Ed Womak

Critics:
Robert Katz, A. Richard Williams

1963/64

Columbus, Indiana
A Downtown Redevelopment Study

Students:
Lon Frye, Ivan Glover, Tom Hartley, David Kahl, Tom Katsuyoshi, Louis Narcissi, Jack Ng, Adib Wahby, Larry Cannon, Derwood Schrotberger

Critics:
Stow Chapman, A. Richard Williams

Drawing,
Gerry Exline

1965

East Humboldt Park
A Study of a Grey Area Neighborhood in North Central Chicago

Students:
George Albers, Zofia Borkowska, Lida Budko, Larry Cannon, Tom Elliott, Jim Gibson, Alan Glass, Jogindar Gupta, Gary Hack, Criag Johnson, Russell Keune, Richard Pollak, Max Ruppeck, Derwood Schrotberger, Jean Wasmann, Julian White

Critics:
Stow Chapman, Robert Katz, Norman Day,
A. Richard Williams

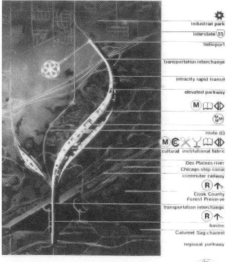

Temenopolis I, Urban Mosaic

A.2
Projects in the Graduate Design Studio
University of Illinois, 1961–1970 Roster of Students and Critics

1966/67

Jacksonville, Illinois
A Study of Downtown Redevelopment and
Peripheral Growth Potential

Students:
Vern Budge, David Davis, Phil Hodge, Taka Ishi, John Kaip, Derwood
Schroteberger

Critics:
Norman Day, Robert Katz, Don Walker,
A. Richard Williams

Hennepin I + II
Studies of New Town Development on the Illinois River,
100 Miles West of Chicago

Students:
Richard Cramer, Christopher Chan, Frak Clements, Tony Goddard,
Bruce Hutchings, Allen Johnson, Tsuto Kimura, Robert Ford

Critics:
Gerry Exline, Don Walker, A. Richard Williams

Temenopolis I + II
Studies of New Town Development of the South West Chicago
Metropolitan Region

Students:
Charles Albanese, Dewayne Anderson, Tony Barnes, Gordon Burns,
George Curry, Guido Francescato, Marty Gilchrist, Ken Gritter,
Richard Jensen, Jim Knight, Ed Moery, John Rishling, Lou Roberts,
Jim Urbonas, Ed Verkler, Bill Cloe, Gerry Fuhriman, Pat Leamy, John
Powers, Nick Scarlatis, Bernie Wideroe, Phil White

Programming: Gary Hack, Guido Fancescato

Critics:
Robert Katz, Norman Day, Jack Baker, Don Walker, Tom Hazlett,
A. Richard Williams

1968

Indianapolis Centrum
A Study of Downtown Redevelopment

Students:
Malcolm Barksdale, John Baxter, Lynn Bender, Dale Durfee, Ken
Griitter, Bruce Kriviskey, Steve Nitekman, James Toya.

Critics:
Gerry Exline, Guido Francescato, Ed Womak, Alex Notaras, Don
Walker, A. Richard Williams

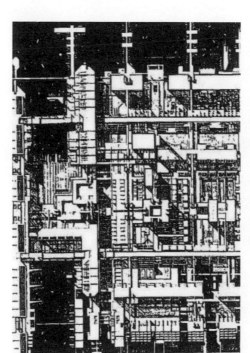

Hennepin II, Drawing, 1967
Tony Goddard

1969

City Hall Square, Milwaukee, WI
A Study of a Central Square facing Milwaukee's City Hall

Students:
Virgil Carter, S. T. Chen, Jerry Clement, Bob Dyson,
Tom Findley, Larry McChesney, Dan Miskie, Bill Robbins,
John Smart, Richard Rosine

Critics:
Guido Francescato, A. Richard Williams

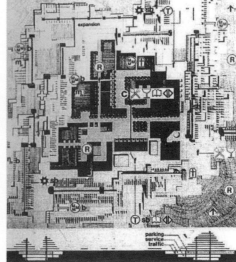

Temenopolis II, Plan of Center
Drawing
John Powers

A.3
The Suburban House:
Dick Williams and his Courtyard Motif
Article by Rob Cuscaden in Inland Architect, February 1969

"A COURTYARD CONCEPT runs like a leitmotif through the work of A. Richard Williams, AIA, of Champaign, Ill……

…He has a special bent for residential design, although he cannot be pigeonholed as his work ranges from church to campus to courthouse, from an 18-foot skiff to large-scale urban projects. And he has been fortunate in finding "intelligent, sympathetic clients." Clients, it must be said, with a love for the courtyard concept.

Certainly one such client was A. Richard Williams. His own home, built 1958–60 in Champaign, has become a central Illinois showplace. Almost too much of a showplace. "I'm somewhat amazed," he notes, "at the continued interest a large number of people have in seeing the house—perhaps it's the insatiable curiosity generated by all the blank walls!"

His own requirements were strict. "I wanted separate areas for living, dining, kitchen, sleeping and studio. And at the same time I wanted all areas combined into one continuous space with a direct relationship to the enclosed, outside court. Bathroom, wardrobe, dressing and storage units had to relate to the sleeping area. And maximum privacy was essential."

As can be seen in the photos (p. 96–99) privacy is definitely the word. The home is set well back on its lot from the fronting street in its own grove of trees. The wall facing the street is vine-covered, and the entrance door is a tall slit in the leaves. The residence is completely walled, and there are no windows facing out. The house dodges the question of compatibility with its colonial style, suburbia type neighbors by becoming virtually invisible.

But there is no shut-in, closed-off feeling in the home itself. If maximum privacy is achieved on the outside, the inside creates a self-contained environment, and a tremendous sense of spatial freedom. The effect is calculated indeed: one walks through a wooded landscape, through the narrow entrance door, and then, suddenly, into space. As the floor plan indicates, only one-third of the walled space is the living area, per se, and this opens out immediately into the courtyard. But "opens out" does not quite describe it, for the glass wall actually seems to continue the inside environment on out to the courtyard; there is really no sense of "inside" or "outside"—it's all continuous. Moreover, the trees in the courtyard become one with the trees on the other side of the walls and one feels there are, in reality, no walls at all, and one's spirit simply flows on through the trees, which stretch out, in the mind, forever.

The furnishings carry on the idea of inner security by simple lines and natural materials—leather, wool, wood and so forth. The predominant inner color is white, laced with dull black. Chairs and tables are set low, lending a Japanese, or at least Oriental, feeling.

But Williams objects to this interpretation strenuously. "No, it's not a Japanese house, although practically everyone says it is. It is a Mediterranean concept. I think of the earliest court houses of Delos, or Pompeii."

In his 1964 project, the William J. Werstler residence in Champaign, Williams further developed and refined his courtyard theory. The architect considers this home to be his most successful effort in residential design.

The plan is essentially the same as its prototype. The living room, dining room, master bedroom and children's room are virtually part of the courtyard, a visually unified space seventy-two feet square. To dramatize the spaciousness of the courtyard; the only objects in it are a reflecting pool-fountain and a copse of golden raintrees. Surrounding the exterior walls is a dense grove of trees, although somewhat less dense in front, so that this residence, too, is not seen as an object on a site, but as a space internally perceived. Pyramids in black metal for the fireplace, fountain and garden lights are intended as solid form reciprocals of the square plan of the courtyard and reflecting pool. (P. 166, 167)

"The Werstlers are marvelous people, and long time friends," Williams notes. "I suppose it's an obvious statement, but a generally unrecognized one anyway, that the quality of co-operation between an architect and his clients ideally goes both ways. A sort of social interaction, resulting in a thoroughly successful design solution. I'm not interested in simply enforcing my own personality and likes and dislikes on a client. I suppose this is an ego-satisfaction for many, but to me it's a failure of the architect-client relationship. The Werstlers gave me carte blanche on their home—all the way from the landscaping to silverware and china. But this was only because they have a level of discernment which enabled me, because I know them so well, to truly give them what they wanted."

Williams has not confined his courtyard solution to residences only. The College of Education Building for the University of Illinois (1964) continues his thinking in this area. In the handling of the east and west courtyards, he attempted to create some intermediate spaces as a foil to the great malls on the campus, and to use the walls of the west court as a transitional element to the lower masses of

A.3
The Suburban House:
Dick Williams and his Courtyard Motif
Article by Rob Cuscaden in Inland Architect, February 1969

the college of Law and the Krannert Museum to the west. (P. 159, 160)

This building, too, solved some of the complex problems of compatibility that a modern work of architecture faces in a neo-Georgian setting. The college wished to avoid the implicit contradiction of housing vanguard educational programs in a building of anachronistic architectural style. But Williams adds in a self-critical mood:

"Though a great deal of effort was expended to develop all the spaces in the building without compromise, the final design is perhaps over-respectful of its neighbors in its symmetry, with some hints of eclecticism and mannerism.

...For the past ten years Williams has been heavily involved in teaching, new concept and prototype design research, large-scale urban or multiple-client projects (both theoretical and real), regular architectural practice, and "built essays" at the smaller and more personal scales of environment which are directly controllable.

It is a kind of composite design activity which is becoming rare in a profession becoming ever more specialized. If there is a degree of specialization to Dick Williams it is in the area of design excellence, a tenacious commitment to quality and taste in all aspects of a project.

A summing-up of much of this past decade of activity has recently been on view in two separate exhibitions in the Krannert Museum of Art at the university.

A year ago, a massive exhibition was held entitled "Century for Design: Countermeasure to the Urban Crisis," held on the occasion of the university's centennial celebration. Williams was chair-

man of the exhibition, which was jointly sponsored by the Graham Foundation for Advanced Study in the Fine Arts and the Krannert Museum. Through photographs, models and drawings by faculty and students, the particular tone, style and character of Mid-America and the vigor of the regional design heritage centered in Chicago were reflected in a series of urban design studies for new and existing cities in Illinois.

Last month he and Billy Morrow Jackson, professor of art at the university, were the subject of a two-man show. Much of Williams's work was on display, in black and white and color photographs and slides, renderings and plans. But there is also a summing-up going on in his own mind, as to where he has been and where he goes from here.

What might be termed the first phase of his activity reached a peak in the late 1950's and early 1960-s—design work and consultation for the firm of Lundeen, Hilfinger & Asbury of Bloomington, Ill. Projects in collaboration with this firm produced the College of Education Building for the university and the Second Appellate Court, Elgin, Ill. (See Inland Architect, January, 1969, pages 26-27, for photos of these buildings); the Baby Fold, a child welfare agency of the Methodist Church in Normal, Ill., and others. His involvement with the firm has leveled off, although it does continue.

The second phase climaxed last year with the "Century for Design" exhibit. In this multiple project exhibit, he was most intimately involved in the Lake Michigan Regional Planning Council project design study for the Little Calumet River/Illinois-Indiana; and as director of the Graduate Design Studio in the Hennepin and the Temenopolis One and Temenopolis Two projects (temenos: Greek for platform, and polis: Greek for city). Necessarily, much of his outside work had to be diminished

to accommodate these enormous projects. Also, he has redoubled his efforts in recent years to strengthen the university's graduate department, especially to affect a fusion of planning and urban design to aid in the solving of complex, re-growth problems.......

"Yes, it is a time of re-thinking for me," Williams concludes. "I've been teaching, designing and building for a long time. I want to continue working on buildings, and maintain a strong relationship to teaching and research. But what I want to do most of all is to increase my communication with a wide spectrum of people as a sort of sociologist-dramatist-architect. I believe, along with Burke and Duncan and other social scientists, in the dramatic model of society as a hierarchy in which all levels of social structure define their roles by symbolic communication, and that the architect should be a central actor in both the design of social drama and its setting."

A.4
Aries Ascending: Campus Architecture
Article in The Laputa Gazette & Faculty News (Excerpt),
February 1969

Apollo 8

The millennial event of Apollo-8 has changed forever man's perspective of himself and his habitat. Now we see the earth as it really is in space—small, beautiful and blue, "an oasis in an endless black void." The vast, complex and problem-ridden world is suddenly compressed to the size of a pearl.

To each of us this revelation evokes new meaning, new curiosity, new speculation. To Apollo-8's crew it was a cascade of reflections from the opening verses of Genesis to a question: "Is it inhabited?" To all the world, a paradox of unity: "We few-we happy few-we band of brothers!"(From William Shakespears's Henry V.

To me it is a sign of ARIES ASCENDING (ARIES, in the Zodiac, represents the face and mind of man.) It is a foreshadow, a prophecy of the day when the collective mind of man will become so powerful that his face and presence on earth will become a shining opalescence in the pearl from enormous distances in space.

Biosphere
Nousphere
Omega Point

Theilhard De Chardin's view of the world as a series of spherical layers is now dramatically vivid: it is a progression from the highly visible terrasphere and atmosphere to the more subtle BIOSPHERE or gossamer layer of living organisms to the invisible, imaginary NOUSPHERE, or sphere of the mind of man. His concept of the nousphere embraces the evolution of consciousness or reflective thought from Paleolithic times to an ultimate future level of total consciousness called OMEGA POINT. As a super-consciousness, Omega Point is the transcendent sum of knowledge and individual consciousness of such intensity that it becomes a totally new collective identity of man. What will this new identity look like, from the microscale of an individual's habitat through the ascending scales of community, city, regional and global configuration? What is the face of man at Omega Point? Of course this face cannot be imagined except in abstractions of brilliance. One could speculate about lace-like surface and earth-orbital networks, cities, signs and symbols as tall as the atmosphere, glowing in solar light or some unknown incandescence. But they must remain as fascinating abstractions because even our computer aided intellect can only project form in high focus a short distance into the future; our projection beyond becomes increasingly arbitrary. However, decisions for the near future are terribly important; sure steps toward Omega Point will be taken if neither capacity to change nor quality of environment is compromised.

The effort of this essay is to develop some of these insights, particularly in respect to the university as an urban metaphor and foreshadow of change in human society.

Urbis et Orbis
Urbino I

Urbino is a marvelous university hill town east of Florence. It is the birthplace of Raphael and on a clear day the Adriatic is visible. It has slowly refined itself over the several centuries since the time of its chief patron, Duke Ferderico. Perhaps it is just a prophetic accident that one of Francesco de Giorgios's best "Ideal City" paintings is hung in the Duke's study and that the palace itself, fusing with the university, cathedral and the entire fabric of the town is an exquisite work of architecture and urban art. Urbino, as much as any city in the world, is an ideal namesake for some new university-city of utopian aspiration.

Urbis et Orbis
Urbino II

URBINO II is a myth. But as a set of idealized yet changeable university-city components, URBINO II could become very real, but of such quality and charisma that its existence might still seem mythical, like Mecca, Kyoto or eleventh century Cordova. URBINO II can be anywhere—it can be small yet loom enormously large as seen through the eyes of a learning child or it can be at fantastic world-city scale, yet seem fragile and jewel-like from the Moon.

URBINO II need not be considered only as a new free-standing utopia but its spirit and imprint may also be found in many past, present, and future cities of man.

A.4
Aries Ascending: Campus Architecture
Article in The Laputa Gazette & Faculty News (Excerpt),
February 1969

Ideal City
School of Francesco di Giorgio

Urbis et Orbis
Universitas

The power of physical environment to attract greatness and to build greater universities cannot be denied. I do not know of any great university that exists in the midst of regional or urban mediocrity. The glamour of San Francisco Bay or the cultural richness of Cambridge-Boston are powerful reasons why Berkeley and Harvard are great universities. The special challenge to Mid-America and especially to the Chicago region is to recognize that at some point in the future a scintillating man-made environment may rise that does not depend so heavily on a naturally dramatic site or a more ideal climate.

It can then be imagined that the quality of the action and interaction in both people and think spaces would match the quality of the setting in such a magnificent YANG/YIN relationship that the line between is no longer visible. It would earn the mythical name URBINO II and the ascent of ARIES would begin.

A.5
The Future University as an Urban Metaphor
Article in The Journal of Aesthetic Education (Excerpt), October 1970
A. Richard Williams

In a political climate that currently seems hostile to an imaginative, liberal, and ambitious university, it is probably not timely to issue mainifestos demanding a brave new future, particularly if they describe an environment of untold intellectual and spatial richness. But this future is certainly imaginable in centers of agricultural and industrial productivity. With these unprecedented resources as an economic base, the opportunity exists to build for the first time in history a scintillating man-made environment on a vast scale that does not have to rely on a naturally dramatic site, scenery, or a more ideal climate. Leadership in achieving such a breakthrough in environmental quality must be accepted by the university not only as a center of environmental learning but as a model, an exemplar, an urban analogue and pilot demonstration of change in the wider process of urbanization. Because of its broad and heterogeneous social structure, its complex physical organization resembling a small city and its avowed search for truth, it is reasonable to expect that a fabulous, uniquely man-made environment could appear first in the university setting. It is indeed the most conspicuous institution in society in which the richness of interaction, drama, and symbolic communication centers most on concerns of the mind and its implicit influence on the wider circles of society. If this model of social interaction and allegiance to intellect is truly a foreshadow of an enlightened and education-oriented urban civilization, then the configuration, quality of function, and style of its physical container will express and communicate it.

A.6
Dedicato a Paolo Sica
Speech at Memorial Service for Paolo Sica, Florence, October 1989
Studi Sulla Citta e sul Paesagio –– Attiirtu 89/90 Alinea Editrice
A. Richard Williams

Mercoledi   11   ottobre   ore   16.30
Salone dei Cinqueeto, Palazzo Vecchio

Paola Sica
Immagine, cultura
e storia della città

parleranno;
Leonardo BENEVOLO
André Corboz
Gianfranco di Pietro
Lucio Gambo
A. Richard Williams

Colleghi, Signore e Signori, Amici di Paolo!

Siamo tutti amici di Paolo-in Italia, in Svizzera, in
Francia, in Inghilterrra, in America. Come uno dei
suoi professori in America, sono particolarmente
onorato de incontrarmi qui con voi per rendere
omaggio a Paolo. Grazie tanto per avermi invitato.

Dirò poche, brevi parole, perché il moi italiano é
cosi arrugginito, benché il mio cuore sia pieno de
pensieri e memorie di lui. Quindi, vorrei offrirvi
solo un pensiero o due. Ma questi pensieri forse
vogliono dire molto di più.

Paolo era il mio migliore "graduate student" nei
quindici anni in cui sono stato direttore del "Graduate Design Studio at the University of Illinois".

Ora vedo che non era unicamente un architetto e
costruttore di ponti:
Tra storia e vita contemporanea
Tra ieri, oggi e domani
Tra architettura e urbanistica
Tra accademia e pratica
Tra tecnica e letteratura
Tra mente e cuore
Soprattutto Paolo era innamorato di tutta
l'umanità !

Credo che possiamo vedere questo carattere
meraviglioso—diffuso nei suoi lavori e nei suoi
insegnamenti—ma specialmente nella sua immagine della città-dalla scala più intima all'intero
complesso.

Su questo tema vorrei leggere una piccola poesia
che ho scritto dieci anni fa nel libro "The Urban
Stage ". Si chiama "The Signs of Takamatsu." E il
mio tribute a Paolo.

As life forms a mosaic
of performances and settings

A.6
Dedicato a Paolo Sica
Speech at Memorial Service for Paolo Sica, Florence, October 1989
Studi Sulla Citta e sul Paesagio -- Attiirtu 89/90 Alinea Editrice
A. Richard Williams

inseparably linked,
so villages and cities become
works of art
in the global gallery.

The signs of Takamatsu
trace a nocturnal signature in light,
a horizontal gossamer glow,
slashed by vertical neon stripes
in the mirror
of the Inland Sea.

The signs of Takamatsu
weave a necklace of marquees
that proclaim
the city is a theater,
the theater is a city.

The signs of Chicago,
the signs of the Great White Way
on a rainy night become
twice as tall,
double image
of the urban stage.
The signatures of cities

form in color as in light.

The saffron of Rome,
the sienna of Sienna,
the brick-red of Albi,
the bluing-white of Myconos,
set in Homer's winedark sea.

San Francisco,
painted lady in drag,
looms white as a bride
from the Marin side.
The great grey grain elevators
of Salina, Kansas
rise in majestic silhouette,

city of the prairie,
landmarking vast horizons.

London is black and white.
centuries of carbon
blacken stone facades.
White highlights
etched by rain, fog and sun
distort architectural precision.
Streets are black,
curbstones white.
White gloves
of black-uniformed bobbies
make disembodied signals.
White pigeons fly
through black buttresses of Westminster.
Overhead, through black wire cobwebs,
the sky is white.

"Just you and your mind on
Lake Shore Drive"
may be transfixed in reverie
by Chicago's towers
as they fuse together at twilight,
a prismatic promontory
afloat in the lake,
a crystalline structure that thrusts up
from the center of the world
at this chosen edge
where prairie, sky and water meet.

Beyond these galaxies
of light, color, form and silhouette,
what is the true signature of cities
if not the pulse of life becoming art,
tracing the living membrane
in ever more diverse patterns,
transfiguring a random, irregular mosaic
into the order of a jewel,
each one as different
as a diamond

or a human face.
Translation of Italian:

Colleagues, ladies and gentlemen, friends of Paolo!
We are all friends of Paolo, in Italy, Switzerland,
France, England and America. As one of his
professors in America, I am particularly honored to meet here with you to join in homage to
Paolo. Thanks so much for inviting me. I will say
only a few words because my Italian is so rusty,
even though my heart is so full of thoughts and
memories of him. So I would like to offer only one
or two. But perhaps these thoughts wish to say
much more. Paolo was one of my finest graduate
students in the fifteen years in which I was Director of the Graduate Design Studio at the University
of Illinois. Now I see he was uniquely an architect and builder of bridges: between history and
contemporary life, between yesterday, today and
tomorrow, between architecture and urban planning, between academia and practice, between
technology and literature, between mind and
heart. Most of all, Paolo was loved by all human-
ity! I believe we can see this marvelous character
diffused in his work and teaching, but especially
in his images of the city from the most intimate
scale to the most complex. On this theme I would
like to read a small poem I wrote ten years ago in
the book "The Urban Stage," called "The Signs of

Takamatsu." It's my tribute to Paolo.
A sailor's interpretation of the Great Lakes
shoreline: reflecting the depth of primeval time,
ice age after ice age, shaping water bodies, rocky
crags, sandy beaches, dunes, forests, marshes and
evolving water, land and airborne life; reflecting
migrations of human inhabitation, tentative, fragile, surviving over millennia to meet the accelerating pace of foreign discovery, exploitation and
settlement; reflecting, now, our American culture,
maturing in its heartland.

*Can a brief candle in the wind of time light some
path of conscience, some way to greater harmony*

of nature's setting and the existence will of man?
I. Heritage of Primeval Time

North to south traces of ice-age glaciation: Laurentian shield granite, scraped, smoothed along
Lake Huron's shore, forming archipelagos, crags,
harbors, today a yachtsman's paradise; limestone, sandstone strata worked into polychrome
cliffs—alternating with great sable dunes and
beaches along Lake Superior's shores, emerging
again to form Lake Michigan's northern bays, islands and harbors; glacial layering, time after time,
depositing Goliath loads of rubble, sand and silt to
form low unfeatured southern shores, edged with
grassland prairies along the lower lakes. Likewise,
forests of evergreens north mix with hardwoods
in gradations south to open prairie shore space,
softening skylines, land and sea marks. A profile
of the mid-continent ecosystem, shaped in eons
of time, topography, climate and fertility, rugged
north to temperate south inviting the inhabitation
of life.

II. Inhabitation of Humanity

Legends of the Ojibway and other Algonkian tribes
trace in myth and oral histories the struggle of
survival over unmeasured spans of time. Transla-
tions in the written records of explorers, Jesuits,
traders, trappers, voyageurs, in the prose and poetry of Schoolcraft, Jameson and Longfellow, and
now in the chronicles of Native American scholars
like Basil Johnston, all portray human existence
around the Great Lakes before, during and after
foreign immigration. Three centuries of accelerating settlement at first largely waterborne, by
perilous canoe and schooner sailing, giving way to
steam vessels and overland rail, transporting and
mixing millions of Irish, Welsh, Swedish, Finnish,
Germans, Polish, and Italians to destinations at the
lake extremities and beyond.

III. Terminus Chicago

Thus, the chain of settlements, of river mouth
harbor origin, grew as a progression of ever-
larger links from village and town scale north to
city scale west and south, exemplified by passage
south down the Wisconsin shore, still small villages like Algoma to metropolitan Milwaukee and
Chicago. By chance or design, the upper lake
shores retain their great, unspoiled diversity while
the low southern shores bear the skyline imprint
of man-made America. This tale of land and
cityscape is told in song and story by Whitman
and Sandburg and in the built visions of Jensen,

Olmsted, Sullivan and Wright.

Ojibway Heritage
Basil Johnston

Kitche Manitou (The Great Spirit) beheld a vision. In this dream he saw a vast sky filled with stars, sun, moon, and earth. He saw an earth made of mountains and valleys, islands and lakes, plains and forests. He saw trees and flowers, grasses and vegetables. He saw walking, flying, swimming, and crawling beings. He witnessed the birth, growth, and the end of things. At the same time he saw other things live on. Amidst change there was constancy. Kitche Manitou heard songs, wailings, stories. He touched wind and rain. He felt love and hate, fear and courage, joy and sadness. Kitche Manitou meditated to understand his vision. In his wisdom Kitche Manitou understood that his vision had to be fulfilled. Kitche Manitou was to bring into being and existence what he had seen, heard, and felt.

Out of nothing he made rock, water, fire, and wind. Into each one he breathed the breath of life. On each he bestowed with his breath a different essence and nature. Each substance had its own power which became its soul-spirit.

From these four substances Kitche Manitou created the physical world of sun, stars, moon, and earth.

Song of Hiwatha
Henry Wadsworth Longfellow

By the shores of Gitchie Gumee,
By the shining Big-Sea-Water,
Stood the wigwam of Nokomis,
Daughter of the Moon, Nokomis.
Dark behind it rose the forest,
Rose the black and gloomy pine trees,
Rose the firs with cones upon them;
Bright before it beat the water,
Beat the clear and sunny water,
Beat the shining Big-Sea-Water

O Captain, My Captain
Walt Whitman

O Captain! My Captain! Our fearful trip is done.
The ship has weathered every rack, the prize we sought is won.
The port is near, the bells I hear, the people all exulting.
While follow eyes the steady keel, the vessel grim and daring.

Chicago
Carl Sandburg

Laughing the stormy, husky, brawling laughter of youth;
Half-naked, sweating, proud to be Hog-butcher,
Tool-
Maker, Stacker of Wheat, Player with Railroads, and
Freight-handler to the Nation.

Signs of Takamatsu
A. Richard Williams

"Just you and your mind on
Lake Shore Drive"
May be transfixed in reverie
By Chicago's towers
As they fuse together at twilight,
A prismatic promontory
Afloat in the lake.
A crystalline structure that thrusts up
from the center of the world
at this chosen edge
where prairie, sky and water meet.

Dear Professor Bloom:

As an architect with a passion for literature, I join in applause of your new book The Western Canon, The Books and School of the Ages. Your courage, energy and creative skill in distilling such an enormous body of great writing in quest of a central canon is a superlative act of design. Like an act of love, it is a "many splendored thing." I write in celebration of such a big idea, inspired to take on a similar act of design—a synthesis of canonical qualities that link literature and architecture. Risky business, but I'm dead sure that at the highest level of excellence there are striking commonalities.

Eking out the best we know in architecture through the School of Ages in a synthesis with the rigors of today requires intense devotion, inspiration and skill, if what we do is to be both timely and timeless. A world canon of excellence implicitly exists, within the finest vernacular building as well as in the work of known architectural heroes, past to present. But in our sophisticated present it is hardly acknowledged, much less accepted as an enlightenment and common responsibility in the thick of everyday life, except in the work of a dedicated few. To encourage recognition and widespread acceptance is an uphill struggle demanding the same arduous and sustained process you have employed in finding common qualities of excellence in widely dissimilar work as well as through juxtapositions of likes that jump across time and place. It will be as difficult as the persistent close reading and rereading, as you say, of Shakespeare and Whitman to perceive fully their timeless place in the canon.

In architectural terms this tough but thrilling assignment means, for instance, finding Palladio to be Shakespearean in his genius to embrace intellect and emotion—he is the hero of both intellectual Vicenza and the emotional fire of Venice.

Or, both Le Corbusier and Wright are canonically original like Whitman in their passion for learning firsthand from the art of the commonplace and of nature. Tougher still, and perhaps from the studies of heroes and heroines in literature, is finding canonicity in the great architecture of anonymous authorship: Pueblo Bonito, Myconos, Albero Bello, Ryoanji Temple, Shakertown, Ky, to name a few.

I myself have always been inspired by the best in literature, whether in the exhilaration and aesthetic pleasure one feels in the presence of all great works of art or in the identification and direct transfer of creative principles to one's own work. For example, in each rereading of Hamlet I find new evidence of a great designer overhearing himself, refining his self-critical capacity, so important for an architect. Or from Dante's Vita Nuova: Beatrice could not be such a sublime work of art without Dante's perception of Florence itself as a work of art, a central canon that is at least partially architectural. In modern literature I get a kick out of finding the designer's mind at work in Updike, Cheever and Vonnegut, in particular Vonnegut's Cat's Cradle.

Even more pointed is Hemingway's awakening in Death in the Afternoon, overhearing himself passing and changing from irreverent playboy to serious writer, employing the metaphor of ordinary building becoming architecture, to represent his own aspiration of passage. Maybe he gets from Montaigne's Of Experience his insight:

"There are some things which cannot be learned quickly and time, which is all we have, must be paid heavily for their acquiring. They are the simplest things and because it takes a man's life to know them, the little new that each man gets from life is very costly and the only heritage he has to leave."

This, too, makes great sense in the quest for a central architectural canon.

But finding inspiration in literature and philosophy for architecture in this "Chaotic Age" has its dark side. Along with media inflation has come a flood of architectural rhetoric in so much of our architectural press and in academia. "Talkitecture" has boomed, an east wind from across the Atlantic that gathers force along the east coast as it blows on westward. Self-promotion and star-making have flourished as never before from sources titillated by outrageous or obscure ideas that are somehow made to seem brilliant through PR manipulation. The cult of celebrity worship, so inflated in entertainment, athletics and politics has polluted architecture too with disastrous effect. Most serious is the growing public image of architecture as nothing more than cosmetics and skin-deep styling, packaging a product that is money-profit and creature-comfort oriented above all else. This relentless pursuit of the trendy and timely overwhelms the quest for timeless value and fuels the passing parade of superficial styles, from "Post Modernism" to "Deconstructionism" to "Neo-Neo-Classicism."

It may worry you at Yale that the great literary tradition of the university can sometimes go astray in its cultivation of wit. Some talented Yale architectural graduates I know seem to want to be clever above everything else in their presentations of themselves as well as in their professional performance. Architectural ironies and jokes die quickly but remain as unburied corpses. In Chicago, especially, this is a betrayal of Adler-Sullivan, Burnham-Root, Wright and others of the Chicago and Prairie Schools. Mies Van Der Rohe, who came on the scene much later, was faithful to the Chicago canon. He said, "I don't want to be interesting—I want to be good." The compulsion

to be witty and dualistic in oppositional dialogue is of course a trait throughout the elitist establishment, adding, hot air to the east wind.

Even more serious betrayals of the ennobling inspiration of literature in architecture are the attempts to translate recent vogues in philosophy. The influence of Jacques Derrida and other deconstructivists in generating architectural bumps, grinds, distortions, skews, large radius curves, ruins, collisions, separations and other geometric profanities is a travesty of architectural integrity. Fortunately this aberration is technically difficult and wastefully expensive to build, which explains why it exists in slick media, glossy publications and exhibitions—but hardly at all in everyday reality. Common sense could have predicted its early death as another shallow cliché through simple recognition that it is an antonym of architecture as the epitome of constructivist art.

I commiserate with you as we now find ourselves in the killing fields of academic bureaucracy. The Balkanization of literary studies has its parallel in architectural education. On the theoretical side of this cleavage, many younger scholars don't seem aware that they too follow bandwagons of intellectual clichés and star worship just as their designer colleagues continue to be enraptured with the latest visual fashions. In this age of instant fax there is remarkable sameness across the world at any one moment, of catchy titles and trendy content. The one pillar of strength remaining is the architectural jury, which despite many abuses such as rigging and dualistic cynicism, among others, is still an implicit affirmation of canonicity above vainglorious ego.

I take heart in knowing that there still are architects and critics of Updikean talent who stand fast for timeless principles yet seek originality in mold-

ing influences, old and new, that bear on each new creative act. Overshadowed by galaxies of highly publicized stars, they are mostly unknown and unheralded, with a few exceptions like the Saarinens, all of whom may be identified by their excellence in diversity rather than by a self-conscious signature style. Their work is steadfast, yet often lively and romantic, humanist, respectful of user needs, deeply involved with details of materials, poetic relationships, technological integration and environmental context. In a composite sense, both timely and timeless aesthetic value is invested.

There is a ray of hope as well in the realm of criticism. With precursors like Lewis Mumford and the best of our architectural historians and theorists going back to Alberti, editors and critics like Donald Canty, former editor of City magazine and the Journal of the American Institute of Architects have carried the torch. Recently a new wave of concern and depth of search is embodied in the journal Progressive Architecture under the editorship of John Dixon and Thomas Fisher. This new revival of critical insight may not yet be spelling out directly a central canon but it unmistakably implies and reinforces its existence. Like Pirandello's six characters we should search for an author (Shakespearean) of your eloquence and depth to champion this great unmet need at world scale.

Thank you for your astringent stimulation in the face of all our frustrations.

Sincerely Yours,

A. Richard Williams, FAIA
Distinguished Visiting Critic,
College of Architecture, University of Arizona
Professor of Architecture Emeritus, University of Illinois at Urbana-Champaign

Light

And then there was light. Light in the universe. Light from the stars. Light over the sea, over the land, over the Sonoran Desert. Light is the substance of design. Louis Kahn said, "All material is spent light." It is the essence of vision, of life itself; of flora, fauna, of human existence. In the desert it is at once sublime and severe, compelling modulation as nowhere else on earth: narrow openings in thick walls seeking ideal form and direction for sun, air and view, in partnership with shade.

Shade

Its consequence and reciprocal. Inviting the companionship of roofs in lightweight counterpoint to the supporting heaviness of walls: In ranges of solid surfaces to trellised ramadas. Inviting a marriage with nature's living marvels; Palo Verde, palm, pine and mesquite: architecture and landscape as one. Inviting by chance or design the magic of shadows and gradations of reflected light. (Read Junichiro Tanizaki's In Praise of Shadows.) Shade the cool refuge from heat of day.

Color

Light refracts into spectra of color; ephemeral in rainbows, beams, projections and areas, or "spent" as material surfaces of pigment applied or inherent in solids. Through design, color seeks balance and harmony in its manmade surroundings and with nature. In the Sonora, the living greens, the blooming color, the brown, tan, buff fantasies of caliche, sand and rock invite the white of San Xavier, the neutral ochres, umbers of stucco, weathered wood and metal, with primary color accents in areas or lines of red, purple, yellow, sharp green or blue. The spent light of day dies in glowing scarlet fading to the starlit black of night, its last embers mirrored in windows of the city.

Water

Water is the mother of life in the universe, most poignant and precious in the Sonora as an element of design. As it is a key to nature's husbandry in hidden aquifers, springs and the micro reservoirs of cactus, so it is a key to human sustenance and survival. The discipline of its conservation is the mentor of all other design choices in the manmade environment, as the heritage and wisdom of the old informs the new. There is enormous virtue not only in the exacting stewardship of water as a scarce commodity, but in quenching the thirst of delight in sheltered brooks, pools and fountains. In the embrace of nature's green, sunshade sparkle, and shadow, it is the heart and soul, the essence of oasis.

Patterns

The play of light, sun and shadow goes hand in hand with filtering screens and receiving surfaces, reflecting and mixing its projections with the texture, geometry and color of the surfaces themselves. The message for design with nature is clear and spectacular; involving orders of modularity, regularity and mathematical progression in contrast to random growth and change, a rich palette in a fragile desert ecosystem requiring extra measures of restraint and sensitivity to scale, balance and timeless fitness. Patterns, indeed, form in the orchestration of LIGHT, SHADE, COLOR and in waves, ripples and shimmering undulations, reveal WATER as the giver of life.

Lighting Study, M. Arch Thesis, MIT, 1996
Rich Stump

Scene

Arivaca is an unspoiled village in the Sonora desert southwest of Tucson. Its destiny twenty years into the new millennium will reflect either the present pace of unplanned growth and change or the enlightenment of a new golden age. The Arivaca region is one of many fragile landscapes in Arizona, little known but already in the direct path of exploitive development. Its rather typical mix of terrain and cultural heritage factors, especially its proximity to Mexico, make it an exemplary choice for intensive study in the hope that an innovative guidance strategy may be designed to counter impending environmental crisis and to communicate convincing alternative visions for the future.

The lessons of Arivaca could then become a pilot for other threatened regions of the American southwest, Mexico and arid lands around the world.

Actors

As an influence on public policy, the university is the one institution in our society that has traditionally enjoyed respect for truth, objectivity and unbiased judgment. It is the classic place in human culture where diversities in knowledge unite. But this time-honored respect is diminishing as Balkanization of its colleges, departments and other divisions intensifies, so that its authority in the synthesis of ideas, research and experience that addresses the larger purpose of public good is likewise fragmented.

Foreshadows of a reversal of this trend are tentatively appearing in collaborative science, technology and the design professions, on the frontier of awakening to both global and local environmental crisis. But these encouraging signs are largely self-propelled, pro bono, with little support or interest from the body politic. However the alluring prospect of a new millennium as a catalytic force might just be the spark that ignites a massive turnaround, not only to spur collaboration to overcome global malaise but to herald the day of a new golden age.

Assumptions

Looking ahead twenty or more years poses two basic assumptions of growth and change in Arizona and its Sonora desert region: one is a simple extrapolation of existing conditions and trends—the no-plan plan. The other supposes such advances in technology and the economy that coordinated planning becomes imperative to avoid chaos—or more optimistically put, that coordinated planning may mark the threshold of a new golden age. Again referring to the dominance of the no-plan plan and its characteristic short range vision (if any), attention span and preoccupation with selfish gain,, there are few models of long range planning sophistication, like military contingency planning, to serve as guides, ironic as it is that human culture knows more about future planning for war than it does for peace. Air and space technology, government equity futures and global science research may also be the sources in the search for new vision planning strategies.

It does not seem necessary to go into detail regarding the first assumption—the consequences of continuing the status quo—its threat is so well known, even if not acknowledged by authorities in the centers of power. From the other set of assumptions, wistful though their optimism may be, take just one possibility to illustrate the potential vastness of technological and economic change: if electrical energy becomes cheap through solar conversion, nuclear fusion or whatever other source of technological breakthrough, the impact on settlement patterns in the landscape will be dramatic. Movement systems, habitat, work, institutional environments and natural ecological systems will all be enormously affected. Abundant water through desalinization, for one thing, will be most profound as an influence in the desert region. Many consequences may be foreseen, many more not. The extent to which these forces are predictable, leading to optimal solutions, is a direct challenge to the design professions.

These thoughts are just a beginning. To repeat the large question to the university itself—if not we, who? If so, what part or parts with what earnestness, dedication and long term commitment? The destiny of best thinking for the future surely must not go by default to others like the Disney Corporation to make another Orlando in Arizona, as if they are the only images of a new golden age.

A.11
Poetry and Humility
Commencement Address to CALA Graduates, May 2006
A. Richard Williams

Thank you Chuck from the bottom of my heart for your kind introduction, and to all for the honor of addressing you on this salubrious day. In so many ways we are celebrating the countless hours we have spent learning together—now to distill these hours into minutes in search of what they mean for the future. So I plead to myself for clarity and brevity, like the prologue in Shakespeare's play Henry the Fifth:

"Piece out our imperfections with your thoughts... for tis your thoughts that now must deck our kings, carry them here and there, jumping o'er times, turning the accomplishment of many years into an hour glass, ...now prologue like your humble patience pray gently to hear, kindly to judge our play."

Seven thoughts to share—but one thought brings them all together—poetry and humility as one. As we look to the future in landscape architecture and architecture informed by the past, may we turn to poetry and humility in timeless bond?

Numbers are sometimes spooky, especially double digits. Exactly 33 years ago, I was asked by the students of the class of 1973 at the University of Illinois to be their commencement speaker. I was especially close to that class, having been with seven of them at Versailles, France, in Professor Cali's Cadre de Vie (Frame of Life) seminar. Two Toms, Allen, Paul, Louis, Mickey and Aki. 33 years later, just three days ago in Madison, Tom, Alan and Paul celebrated winning the 2006 AIA Wisconsin Firm Award. Louis is doing fabulously as well in Milwaukee. This leads me to imagine 33 years from now the honors that will be yours! I assure you I will be there in spirit to salute you as I do now in person.

For the seven thoughts I turn to seven authors,

Lawrence of Arabia, Henry David Thoreau, Lewis Carroll, Mies Van der Rohe, Juhani Pallasmaa, Edmond Rostand and William Shakespeare. Seven thoughts in seven minutes? The magic number seven may even become eleven!

First: Let me quote from Lawrence in his "Seven Pillars of Wisdom." He begins with a verse: "I loved you so I drew these tides of men into my hands and wrote my will across the sky in stars to earn you Freedom, the seven pillared worthy house..."

Love. Freedom. Surely the seven pillared worthy house may be Architecture! And our great calling cannot exist without the grace of landscape.

Second thought: Thoreau in "Walden" reminds us: "There is some of the same fitness in a man building his own house that there is in a bird's building its own nest. Who knows but if men constructed their dwellings with their own hands...simply and honestly enough, the poetic faculty would be universally developed as birds universally sing when they are so engaged...shall we forever resign the pleasure of construction to the carpenter? What does architecture amount to in the experience of the mass of men?"

Should not this mean homage to our hands-on design/builders today? In Alabama, to the late Sam Mockbee, in Wisconsin to Bill Yudchitz, to unknown others elsewhere and here at home to Mary Hardin, Rocky Brittain, Les Wallach, Rick Joy and the students who have worked with them. This is good news, full of hope!

Carroll gives us a puzzle from "Alice in Wonderland":
"The time has come, the walrus said
To speak of many things

Of ships and shoes and sealing wax
And cabbages and kings"

Let me try to interpret, working backwards; Kings, Cabbages, Sealing Wax, Shoes and Ships.

Kings: Not such good news! The rule of global-ization, internationalism, flat worldism is more powerful than ever, spreading giantism, same-ness and mediocrity, satisfied by the punctua-tion here and there of trendy, grandiose icons by starchitect kings: King Koolhaus, King Libeskind, Kings Herzog and de Meuron, King Calantrava, King Vinoly, and now we have a queen too, Queen Hadid—with only one of homegrown fame, King Frank Gehry, the king of bump and grind. Are we again a colony, worshiping royalty from abroad? What has happened to the recent memory of our own more modest heroes, Lou Kahn, Fay Jones, Eero Saarinen, Charles Moore, Bill Caudill, Judith Chafee, Paul Kirk, Paul Rudolph and many others left unsung? Can we renew again our own great heritage?

Cabbages: What to say about cabbages? Perhaps the opposite of kings. The honest virtue of our farming landscape and vegetable gardens, our plain simple coleslaw and sauerkraut buildings—the round barns of Illinois, the silos of Wisconsin and the great, grey grain elevators of Kansas?

Sealing wax: The seal of promises to be kept.

Shoes: Tread lightly on this earth, and, like J. B. Jackson, see once again our purple mountain majesty across our fruited plains.

Ships: To venture with courage into unknown seas.

Fourth: Imagine a scene forty six years ago, in 1960: The courtyard of Berkeley's rambling architecture building at high noon. A crowded AIA/ACSA student gathering surrounding Mies Van der Rohe, their guest of honor. It was a time when many exciting directions in new American architecture and landscape architecture were in full bloom. Quieting everybody down, the student chairman asked, "Mies, where do we go from here?" After puffing thoughtfully on his cigar, Mies replied, "Ve stay here, do good job!" Later, he went on, "I don't vant to be interesting, I vant to be good! If I'm good enough I can be a poet."

Fifth: Juhani Pallasmaa very recently, on April 6, was the keynote speaker at the 50th anniversary celebration of the Museum of Finnish Architecture in Helsinki. His title was "The Human Mission of Architecture." From his entire text, which I most highly recommend for all to read, I choose a few quotes as he first does from Walt Whitman, "great poetry is possible only if there are great readers," then his own follow-up: "great architecture is possible only when there are great clients." Later: "A core condition for architecture to evolve is artistic autonomy. By this I mean that the mission of architecture does not stem from rationalism, utility or economy but from the autonomous and existential poetry of building. It provides our existence in the world with lived metaphors, or more precisely, the instruments of a poetic life." To bring us down to earth from our own ego, quoting the poet Kundera's plea for the "wisdom of literature," and that "all great novels are wiser than their authors," Pallasmaa urges us toward humility "that significant buildings also stem from the wisdom of architecture and are thus always wiser than their individual designers."

Sixth: Lest we fear our egos might be wounded by this plea for humility, the playwright Rostand in

"Cyrano de Bergerac" has Cyrano proclaim in the face of frustration, "yet with all modesty to say, my soul be satisfied with flowers, with fruit, with weeds even; but gather them in the one garden you may call your own."

We gather here as architects and landscape architects celebrating our partnership in making gardens both inwardly and outwardly that will be wiser than we, yet without losing our own joy in the process of their creation.

Finally, I look out to you with love and hope that our mutual thirst for learning never stops. As your ancient mariner I quote from Shakespeare once again; from "Hamlet"; Polonius advice to his son Laertes as Laertes is about to leave Denmark for the outer world:

"The wind sits in the shoulder of your sail...keep these few precepts in thy memory:
Look thou character. Give thy thoughts no tongue.
Nor any unproportioned thought his act
Be thou familiar, but by no means vulgar:
Those friends thou hast, and their adoption tried
Grapple them unto thy soul with hoops of steel...
Give every man thine ear but few thy voice
Take each man's censure, but reserve thy judg-ment...
Neither a borrower or lender be;
For loan oft loses both itself and friend
And borrowing dulls the edge of husbandry.
This above all—to thine own self be true
And it must follow as night the day
Thou cans't not then be false to any man."

Thank you very much and God speed you on your voyage!

Born:
Evanston, IL, 1914

Education:

Bachelor of Architecture
University of Illinois, 1936
Highest Honors, AIA Medal

Master of Architecture
Massachusetts Institute of Technology, 1939
MIT School Medal

Appointments and Awards:

1957–1970
Director, Graduate Architecture Program
University of Illinois

AIA Honor Awards:
College of Education, University of Illinois
Concordia Library, Springfield, IL
Williams Residence, Champaign, IL
2nd Appellate Court, Elgin, IL

1971
Nominated to Fellow, AIA

1973–1974
President, Illinois Council, AIA

1981
Author of book *The Urban Stage*

1986
ACSA Distinguished Professor

1986
AIA Illinois Education Medal

1986 – Present
Distinguished Visiting Professor,
CALA, University of Arizona

2001
Invested as Fellow, Society for the Arts, Religion
and Contemporary Culture (ARC)

1964, 1991, 1999, 2002
Visiting Architect
The American Academy in Rome

2007
Illinois Medal
School of Architecture, University of Illinois

1976, 2006, 2007
AIA/ACSA Topaz Medallion Nominee

Photograph: Charles A. Albanese, FAIA